T0381554

A Religious Curse
—Judeo-Christian
History

A RELIGIOUS CURSE
—JUDEO-CHRISTIAN
HISTORY

BOYD GUTBROD

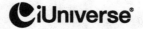

A RELIGIOUS CURSE —JUDEO-CHRISTIAN HISTORY

Copyright © 2017 Boyd Gutbrod.

All rights reserved. No part of this book may be used or reproduced by any means, graphic, electronic, or mechanical, including photocopying, recording, taping or by any information storage retrieval system without the written permission of the author except in the case of brief quotations embodied in critical articles and reviews. Website.

Scripture quotations marked NASB are taken from the New American Standard Bible®, Copyright © 1960, 1962, 1963, 1968, 1971, 1972, 1973, 1975, 1977, 1995 by The Lockman Foundation. Used by permission.

Scripture quotations marked NIV are taken from the Holy Bible, New International Version®. NIV®. Copyright © 1973, 1978, 1984 by International Bible Society. Used by permission of Zondervan. All rights reserved. [Biblica]

Scripture quotations marked NJB are from The New Jerusalem Bible, copyright © 1985 by Darton, Longman & Todd, Ltd. and Doubleday, a division of Random House, Inc. Reprinted by Permission.

Scripture quotations marked NKJV are taken from the New King James Version. Copyright © 1982 by Thomas Nelson, Inc. Used by permission. All rights reserved.

Scripture quotations marked KJV are from the Holy Bible, King James Version (Authorized Version). First published in 1611. Quoted from the KJV Classic Reference Bible, Copyright © 1983 by The Zondervan Corporation.

Scripture quotations marked NRSV are taken from the New Revised Standard Version of the Bible, Copyright © 1989, by the Division of Christian Education of the National Council of the Churches of Christ in the United States of America. Used by permission. All rights reserved. Website

Scriptures quotations marked NWT are taken from New World Translation of the Holy Scriptures, Copyright 1961, 1970, 1981, 1984, 2013 Watch Tower Bible and Tract Society of Pennsylvania

iUniverse books may be ordered through booksellers or by contacting:

iUniverse
1663 Liberty Drive
Bloomington, IN 47403
www.iuniverse.com
1-800-Authors (1-800-288-4677)

Because of the dynamic nature of the Internet, any web addresses or links contained in this book may have changed since publication and may no longer be valid. The views expressed in this work are solely those of the author and do not necessarily reflect the views of the publisher, and the publisher hereby disclaims any responsibility for them.

Any people depicted in stock imagery provided by Thinkstock are models, and such images are being used for illustrative purposes only. Certain stock imagery © Thinkstock.

ISBN: 978-1-5320-0354-7 (sc)
ISBN: 978-1-5320-0317-2 (e)

Library of Congress Control Number: 2016913610

Print information available on the last page.

iUniverse rev. date: 01/04/2017

To my friend Stan Holland for all his help
and knowledge of Judaism and history.

CONTENTS

Introduction ix

Chapter 1 — Judaism, Monotheism, Sin, Idol Worship, the Devil, Angels,
Hell, the Soul, Reincarnation, the First Written Bible 1

Chapter 2 — Apocrypha, Hebrew and Christian Bibles, Judith, Maccabees,
Bible Development, Esther and Ruth 40

Chapter 3 — Myth, David, the Witch of Endor, Daniel, Ezekiel, Job, Prayer 67

Chapter 4 — Lost Books of the Bible, Book of Mormon, Samaritans 90

Chapter 5 — Masoretic Text, Council of Jamnia, Climate Conditions,
Biblical Inspiration, Biblical Criticism 107

Chapter 6 — Pre-Christian Chronology 122

Chapter 7 — Early Christianity, James, John, Mary Magdalene, Peter Gnostics 138

Chapter 8 — Gnostics Christians, the Twelve Apostles, Judas Iscariot, Paul, the Woman Apostle, Mystery of Paul, Sethian Christians.................................. 163

Chapter 9 — Rome and Jesus, Was Jesus a Rebel? Judean Geography, John the Baptist, Herod the Great, the Death of Jesus, Who Killed Jesus?............... 187

Chapter 10 — Mary the Mother of Jesus, Was Jesus the Only Child of Mary? the Crucifixion, Parables of Jesus, the Trinity.. 214

Chapter 11 — Confusion in Early Christianity, the Second Coming, Jude, the Earliest Gospel, Mark and John Compared, Mark and the Romans................ 234

Chapter 12 — Historical Progress of the Bible and Christianity, the New Testament, 2 Peter Epistle, Who Were Paula and Eustochium, Women in Christianity, the Woman Caught in Adultery, Barabbas................ 257

Chapter 13 — Pontius Pilate, Caiaphus, History of Baptism, Faith, Death and the Afterlife, Heresy and the History of Arius, The Gospel of Thomas........... 279

Chapter 14 — Consequences of Jewish-Christian History, the Crusades.............................. 296

Epilogue.. 315

About the Author 317

INTRODUCTION

Sacred scripture originated from a number of written documents and combined with many oral traditions, which created the need to record these words of God into a written document. The Hebrew and Christian Bibles are a literary masterpiece that has survived for several thousand years. As is the case with any literary composition, the texts can be interpreted in different ways when applied to various situations. For centuries they were understood to be spiritual treatises to instruct proper behavior for all humankind as it relates to God.

This is still the case today, but as more people examined the sacred texts, they developed different ways to understand the Bible. Now arguments began, and denominations became abundant. And in several cases they produced strong hostilities. Downright hatred also took form in the areas where competition for new members was occurring, and polemical disputes led to acrimony.

My purpose in writing is to share my experiences in life, religion, and history. This book is aimed toward people who have a rudimentary knowledge of the Bible and Judeo-Christian history. I use many misconstrued biblical passages by offering theses supported by evidence obtained from various sources. I was unable to follow a strict chronological order (although I do make that attempt) because some historical events require flashbacks to provide a basis. My goal was to show how human nature and needs shaped our history and our religions with my utmost respect for all faiths and their sacred documents.

On a more personal level, I was born more than eighty years ago into a family that was as loving and caring as anyone could have. My parents and grandparents were wonderful people who surely loved me and gave me all that was necessary to become a good and responsible adult. They were certainly not perfect and had many faults. I came to know they were participants of the moral attitudes and standards of their time and generation, some of which have been passed on to my generation and to that of today.

History was my best teacher. I learned from the lessons of history coupled with the desire to find the truth in respect to religion, which in turn opened my mind. What I discovered through years of study was a remarkably different way to interpret the Bible by challenging my personal prejudices, which I indeed did and perhaps still do.

Just as in the Bible, it begins with my genealogy. My grandparents were all born in America. On my mother's side, her father was third-generation whose family came from Scotland and England. Her mother's parents were of the second generation of German descendants. On my father's side, his dad, or my grandpa, was Lutheran, and my grandma was Catholic. When they decided to get married, according to the customs of their day, neither church would perform the wedding ceremony, so one of them had to convert. Of course, a civil ceremony was possible, but religion was too important, creating a strong deterrent. So my grandpa converted, and they were married in the Catholic Church. His family was devastated by this and refused to attend their wedding. This was in 1909, and it took more than two years for most of Granddad's family to forgive him. Grandma, though, never forgave Grandpa's family. She only grudgingly tolerated them to the day she died.

Mom's dad was a reformed Christian who disliked Catholics while Grandma was only a so-so Lutheran. When my dad and mom decided to marry, the customs had changed a bit. The Catholic Church would do a mixed-marriage service but not at the altar. So Mom chose to convert and took instruction to become a Catholic. Of course, her parents were very disappointed, but they acquiesced. The wedding was set for May 1933. During her instructions to become Catholic, Mom and the priest fell in love. When Mom's mother found out, she promptly informed the pastor, who responded quickly and shipped the priest to another parish more than three hundred miles away. My parents then reconciled and were married in late October 1933. Needless to say, this scandal quietly simmered till my mother died in 1964, although I didn't find out about it until after her death.

I was born in September 1935 during the Great Depression and just before World War II began. I remember many family get-togethers where both sides attended. As a young child, I would play with my cousins while the old folks talked; however, I still retain clear recollections of some of the conversations they had. Politics was often a topic on which there was some strain, but at least the arguments were cordial. Of course, religion was strictly a taboo. The exception was the topic concerning the Jews. Conversations were unanimously anti-Jewish, and I heard and learned every depreciatory term. It didn't take long for me to understand that Jews were responsible for every foul act in the world. They committed the ultimate crime by killing Jesus, and because of that, they were cursed forever by God for doing so.

As the years went by, I heard the same anti-Jewish ranting over and over from friends and even in church from the pulpit and in religion classes. Mom now was Catholic, but she subliminally retained some of her Lutheran instincts. She still read from her Lutheran Bible. As a young boy, every Good Friday Mom and I would color Easter eggs while we listened on the radio to the Lutheran service on the crucifixion. She made me stay in the house and listen with her from noon to three in the afternoon. Her commentaries were generally about how terribly Jesus had suffered for us and how cruel and horrible the Jews who crucified him were.

From kindergarten to fifth grade, I attended public school and took Catholic religious instructions on Saturdays. My clearest memory from public school was concerning one of my classmates. His name was David Stern. He was one of the smartest kids, and he sat right next to me in class. One Christmas season I noticed he didn't seem to be singing most of the Christmas carols with our class. Although I never spoke of this, later on another classmate informed me David was a kike. He then explained to me that a kike was a dirty Jew. Of course, I already knew that, but David didn't look any different from other students, which was contrary to what I thought a Jew should look like. Obviously, my attitude toward David then changed.

Afterward I talked with Dad about this. He told me that the Jews didn't believe in Christmas and that we despised them because they were the cause for all the problems in the world and they killed Christ. He went on to tell me they would live with this curse until Jesus returned at the end of the world. He proceeded to inform me about the horrible things Jews did and had done in the past and how God continuously punished them. From that time on, whenever I heard the word *Jew*, I generally envisaged a caricature of an ugly, hook-nosed monster.

On Easter Sunday, we always would attend Catholic Mass. I also would hear the preachers on the radio and at the Mass talk about the Jews and how they were responsible for the murder of Christ. When I was nine, we moved to a neighborhood that bordered a Jewish community. Our neighborhood was mixed religiously, mostly Catholic and Lutheran. As kids we would occasionally fight with the Lutherans but would sometimes unite with them against the Jews. I am too ashamed to tell you of the cruel deeds we did to the Jews. My only excuse is I truly believed they were a cursed race condemned by God. I believed God would certainly have approved of my actions. My hatred toward Jews would last well into adulthood.

My interest in girls advanced as I grew older, and at fourteen I met a very nice Lutheran girl. We were a couple for about six months, and we soon began to discuss religion. She attended a Lutheran school and I attended a Catholic school. Her superior knowledge of the Bible flabbergasted me. This was 1949, and Catholics were just beginning to actually study the Bible. In fact, I had to buy a Catholic Bible for religion class that year. She was well educated on the biblical passages that argued against Catholic teachings, and she sharpened her skills by using them on me.

I turned to my priest for help. He dazzled me with church history and a few biblical passages, which gave me some ammunition, but for the most part, I simply could not compete with her. However, I was determined to find proof to support the idea that my church was the one true church. When I discussed this situation with my mother, she was of little help. In fact, she hesitatingly demonstrated some agreement with my girlfriend while Dad avoided the issue and brushed it off.

My priest had offered me some biblical proof for purgatory, which was recorded in the book of Maccabees, but much to my surprise, this book was not in my friend's or in my mother's Bible. My girlfriend confidently stated that the Catholic Church added this apocryphal book along with many others to the original Bible. My priest explained to me that Protestants dropped this book because Martin Luther didn't like it. Nobody I talked with could give me any solid evidence in this regard, even though I did talk to several people and teachers about it without gaining any satisfaction.

Over the next several years, I read the entire Bible along with several other relative writings, trying to find support for my faith. While reading the New Testament over and over, I developed a mildly skeptical suspicion over the passage in Matthew 27:25. This is the so-called curse of the Jews, where Pontius Pilate wanted to free Jesus but the Jews demanded him to be crucified and they swore that the blood of Jesus would be on them and their progeny. For some reason it seemed so implausible to me that anyone would even consider saying such a thing. But I continued on searching for my answers while slowly gaining a better understanding of the Bible.

Years went by, and I got married and had two sons. In my spare time, I studied history, leaning heavily toward Christian history. By the midsixties, the Dead Sea Scrolls discovery was in the news. Prior to this, my interest in Bible history was limited to a few books and the Bible itself. Now I finally discovered the difference between Catholic and Protestant Bibles and the answer to why the Catholic Bible had more books in their Old Testament. My main interest then focused almost exclusively on history and the Bible. The year was now around 1967, and more magazines would print articles on Christian history, which I would intently read. Within a few more years, I would discover that the Jews did not kill Jesus, even though I strongly resisted the facts because I didn't really want to accept the truth.

Around 1974, I subscribed to the magazine *Biblical Archeology Review*, which I received bimonthly. Numerous books also came out around this time, and I purchased several of them that were relative to the subject. Along the way, the law of unintended consequences seized me, and I began to grapple with historical facts that were diametrically opposed to what I had believed in all my life. At first, I denied the accuracy and tried to prove it wrong, but the more I researched, the more I had to admit that my past training was, at the very least, distorted—if not entirely wrong.

Most alarming was my past anti-Jewish stance, which was based on out-and-out lies and distortions of history. The religious information I received from my parents, teachers, priests, and ministers combined with the media was quite misleading. Next I needed to know how and why the actual historical events were tilted against the Jews. In very rudimentary terms, my findings revealed that Christianity was founded by Jews and originally was accepted within Judaism as a branch of the Jewish faith. Saint Paul revised the early Christian branch of Judaism, which soon led to the apotheosis of Jesus. Fundamentally mainstream Judaism could not accept this, as it seemed to be a contradiction of monotheism and the very foundation for their faith. Thus, a competitive battle for new members began.

From then on I was obsessed with the need to learn more. More and more books came out on the subject, and I read everything I could lay my hands on. In fact, it became the only reading I did for many years. In 1991, I took a course on Christian history at the University of Wisconsin–Milwaukee, and I continued to take related subjects nearly every semester over the course of the next twenty-four years, right up to the present.

The lessons I learned were difficult for me to accept, but the facts spoke out so loudly that I could not ignore them. I studied Jewish history only to find out that the Jews were victims of history and were falsely condemned from the birth of Christianity until this very day. Most remarkable is that few people realize this. A poll recently released by the Anti-Defamation League (ADL) reports that 26 percent of the American public continues to believe that "Jews were responsible for the death of Jesus, although the number has dropped from 31% in 2011."

As for me, I have reflected on my past with shame, especially when I came to the clear and shameful understanding that if I had been born in Nazi Germany instead of America, I would have been a Nazi without any doubt. When World War II ended and I saw the films of the Holocaust, seeing the emaciated human bodies and carnage caused me to feel deep pity for the Jews, but I was able to appease my conscience by accepting the Bible's message in Matthew

27:25, which suggested that God would continue to punish the Jews for killing Christ. So my hatred toward the Jews basically remained intact.

Learning to apply the disciplines of historical criticism to the Bible really opened my eyes. It is my sincerest desire to demonstrate exactly how these methods affect the way we interpret the Bible through the use of verifiable historical events and applying them within the contexts of events that existed at that time and place.

First of all, I want to convey the role the Bible played in the condemnation of the Jews, not to demean the Bible or Christianity but to show how the human elements of this book developed the false understanding that the Jews killed Christ. Human decency demands that justice should prevail and all people should recognize past errors and begin correcting the causes for these tragedies, which were thrusted upon Jews nearly two thousand years ago and for which they are still paying.

My approach to writing this book was to offer a succinct history of the Judeo-Christian relationship, emphasizing first on the Jewish portion followed by the Christian developments and reactions. My goal is to address historical events and related subject materials that occurred during the developments in the Jewish-Christian relationship up to the modern era. In so doing, I felt the need to show the role the Bible played, both Christian and Hebrew versions, in the proceedings, which led to some very tragic circumstances.

My sincere hope is that someone will read this book and be inspired to carry on the cause for religious justice and reform the methods in which we understand the New Testament and how divine inspiration interacts without interjecting or promoting theology.

CHAPTER 1

Judeo-Christian history is the study of the people who have come to embrace Judaism and Christianity. We have to start first with the history of the Jews. To begin with our study, we need to look into historical Judaism and how the terms *Israelites* and *Hebrews* and *Jews* had their origins and how it became a religion. At a specific time in history, it split or gave birth to Christianity. We must also examine how the relationship between the two religions progressed. Our earliest understanding of these people indicates they were originally called Hebrews, a tribal branch of the Semitic family as spoken of in the Bible or Tanakh as the decedents of Shem, one of Noah's sons.

The Jewish identification stems from the time shortly after the split of the Solomon kingdom (before the split, all the Hebrew people became known as the Israelites) into separate states creating Israel (Northern Kingdom) and Judah (Southern Kingdom) around 925 BCE. About 722 BCE, the state of Israel fell to the Assyrians and later the inhabitants came to be known as Samaritans. People of the Southern Kingdom soon came to be called Judeans or Jews. So these are people who will from this time on be identified as Jews. Judah was conquered by the Babylonians about 586 BCE, and the people making up the aristocratic class, which included the priestly class, were taken into captivity and exported to Babylon.

It is commonly understood that Abraham found God and is originator of the three major faiths that identify with monotheism. I will delve into the details of this later. For now we will explore the histories of some of the belief components that comprise the structure of Judaism and that also became a part of Christian faith.

THE HISTORY OF MONOTHEISM

As newborns we know absolutely nothing except how to eat and respond to a few physical discomforts. As toddlers we begin to learn speech and communication skills. Basically, we know nothing about God, but from then forward, depending upon our parent(s), we receive this information. We also begin to learn about our mortality, which further enhances our penchant toward God.

Most people believe in God. Those who do not are called atheists, and they will strongly argue that the belief in God simply cannot be proven. We can offer arguments to their claims, but in all honesty, the burden of proof makes this unattainable. Empirically, information would suggest that God (or gods) exists because most of our very basic knowledge points in that direction. How the universe and everything in it simply had to have been created by someone or something. Science proves everything had a beginning, even our planet Earth. The atheist merely asks the question, "Then who made God?" This profound statement then reverts into a circular argument with no clear conclusion.

I believe a God or supreme being is responsible for creating the universe and everything in it, but I acknowledge that I can't prove it. I will merely offer a very laconic history combined with a few of my philosophical views, all of which stem from limited provable conclusions.

Looking at the history going back to the dawn of civilization, humankind ultimately discovered that life would end someday. The next question was about the time after death. *Does anything happen then?* A struggle to understand the reasons for death, the environment, weather, relationships, and growing old perplexed humankind so that they started looking for answers. At some point somebody stepped forward and offered answers. Over time many answers were proposed, and some of them became acceptable and compatible with their reasoning process for their time.

Polytheism appears to be the first universal concept used to satisfy most of humankind's questions. This would lead to the belief that a creator god or gods was/are/were inherent in the human psyche. But actually, this was only the most reasonable and acceptable reaction for the time. Was the desire to find an explanation for the purpose or circumstances of life the reason for inaugurating the gods? I believe it had to be!

The Bible suggests that Judah was polytheistic until King Hezekiah tried to impose monotheism during his reign in the seventh century BCE. If any form of Judaism existed before this time, it was only a small sect that would have existed contrary to the wishes of the kings of

Judah. Manasseh, the son of Hezekiah, encouraged polytheism to return, clearly showing that monotheism was not as yet common among the general population.

It is important to note that monotheism unites people through a unified common faith in a single god. Clearly, a pantheon of gods divides them. With only one god, a ruler need only invoke that god to instill a form of divine nationalism for all of his people. National identity is then congealed under a single god. This was apparent in ancient city-states that had their special deities of local importance, such as Marduk for Babylon, Apollo for Athens, Diana for Ephesus, etc.

Many scholars believe that the Hebrew Bible describes a theistic arrangement called henotheism and not monotheism. The Hebrew God was not the only god but rather the special god whom Abraham knew (Genesis 15:7). Here we see that the god of Israel is not god alone but the God who was worshipped by Abraham's people. In this milieu the God of Israel is seen as a tribal god who is worshipped without rejecting the existence of other gods. (Henotheism is defined as worshipping a single god while accepting the existence of other gods.)

In the time of Moses, it was clear that other gods existed, although during this period the Bible claims that the Hebrew God is greater (Exodus 18:11) This acknowledgment is repeated in 2 Chronicles 2:5, clearly showing that Israel understood that their god was God alone. Though other gods existed, those were subordinate. This defines henotheism in the proper sense of the word. When Deutero-Isaiah was written (sixth to fifth century BCE), monotheism was now explicitly accepted. "Thus says the Lord, the King of Israel and his Redeemer, the Lord of hosts: 'I am the first and I am the last; besides me there is NO god'" (Isaiah 44:6). By this we can see the development of the people of Israel evolving into a true monotheism through a continuing process. An exception to this can be found in Genesis 1:1. This suggests that Genesis 1:1 was redacted later than the other examples I have given. Therefore, the development of monotheism had to originate first on a tribal level, gradually advancing into the recognition that the god of Israel is the only God. Later this was adopted by Christianity (John 1:1), which then laid claim to this form of monotheism and was consolidated later by Islam, a true monotheism in the strictest sense.

We can see by literally interpreting Deuteronomy 4:39, monotheism is explicit. The verse states, "Know this day, and take it to heart, that the Lord is God in heaven above and on earth below; there is none else." However, many scholars believe that this verse is a late addition to the Pentateuch (Torah) and that the later adaptation of monotheism was the work of Hilkiah or perhaps Ezra.

The calamity of the exile challenged the claim that God was the supreme god. Belief that their God could be substantiated by acts of power was dashed when the people of this God lost their independence and their land to a foreign power. The shock of the success the Babylonians had against Judah gave further credence to the Babylonian claim that Marduk, their god, was the supreme and most powerful god. In order to make sense of this disaster, the prophet's response was that the heartbreak of the exile was not the result of the power of Marduk rivaling the power of God but the results only show proof of God's control over all nations. Exile was the outcome instigated by the God of Israel using the Babylonians as His instrument to punish His own people because they had violated the terms of the covenant that bound them together. This apology for the exile (Amos 2:4–8) offered a theological and philosophical explanation that hereby established the entity of only one God who is *the God* not only of Israel but also of the entire world. From this point onward, these Hebrew people would be called Jews, and their religion was now a true monotheism. Christianity followed suit but developed a Trinitarian variation of monotheism.

The afterlife was basically only an implied consideration by Pharisaic Judaism, but the apostle Paul expanded this by claiming his form of Christianity through the sacrifice of Jesus provided for everlasting life or life after death. This was paramount! By having Christ's sacrifice on the cross providing redemption for all the past and future sins of humankind, he could claim that the most encumbering Jewish laws were no longer required for Christians.

This propelled Christianity, making it attractive to the pagan world, and within a few hundred years, it expanded throughout most of the known world. Starting in the seventh century, Islam would spread monotheism across the Middle East, Africa, and deep into Asia.

We can see how monotheism united many different peoples to a common cause, making governing much easier. The way I see it, ancient man discovered polytheism to explain reasons for existence and a way to understand the phenomena's of nature. The next step was henotheism, which gave way to monotheism, therefore making it possible to unite many people, even those of different cultures.

The world's great monotheist religions are called "revealed religions"; meaning God actively suspended the natural laws, through a divine revelation, to give humankind His statutes. Each of these great religions claim these laws were given to a single person (Moses, Jesus, and Muhammad) who then established their religion and confirmed this with a written holy book claiming it to be the Word of God. In each case these holy books would be decided by the consensus of a group of holy men. Their followers were then motivated through faith.

THE HISTORY OF SIN

Plotting a historical chronology to the source of sin is next to impossible because most ancient cultures adopted pantheons of gods that they believed controlled nearly every aspect of their physical world. If you displeased anyone of them, they could—or probably would—bring about an unpleasant situation. This act of displeasing the gods could be construed as *sin*. In a modern sense, we find that there is no precise biblical definition of sin. The Bible is concerned more with the remedy or avoidance for sin than with a definition of sin. Some believe sin originated before creation in heaven when Satan rebelled against God. The most popular belief for the inception of sin is that which is accepted by Judaism, Christianity, and Islam where Adam and Eve disobeyed God. This is recorded in the Bible (Genesis) and in the Qur'an (7:19:23). It's also in several biblical stories that describe certain sins in more or less detail.

The Bible gives examples of sin and its punishment in different ways. Sometimes it is an individual who commits the sin, and sometimes it is the whole sinful nation in general that is punished. In the Old Testament (before the Persian period), personal punishment is given during one's lifetime, as there was no afterlife or hell. If we search the Old Testament, we see how sins are transferred or continued on to others. "And the Lord passed by before him and proclaimed: The Lord ... the compassionate and gracious God, ... forgiving iniquity, and transgression and sin. But He by no means leaves the guilty unpunished, visiting the iniquity of the fathers on the children and on the children's children, to the third and fourth generation" (Exodus 34:6–7). And also consider the following: "You shall not bow down to them or worship them; for I, the LORD your God, am a jealous God, punishing the children for the sin of the fathers to the third and fourth generation of those who hate me" (Deuteronomy 5:9).

Contrasting those passages, we find, "Instead, everyone will die for his own sin; whoever eats sour grapes—his own teeth will be set on edge" (Jeremiah 31:30). "The soul who sins is the one who will die. The son will not share the guilt of the father, nor will the father share the guilt of the son" (Ezekiel 18:20). We are also told that God does not change his mind. "God is not a man, that he should lie, nor a son of man, that he should change his mind. Does he speak and then not act?" (Numbers 23:19). How do we reconcile these apparent contradictions? We cannot! Only a very clever apologist might come up with something somewhat reasonable. But perhaps there may be other reasons for this that might be reflected by the times, history of events, and conditions that were occurring or had occurred previously to the various authors and their communities.

When Jeremiah and Ezekiel were writing, the Babylonians had or were in the process of destroying Jerusalem. Neither prophet wanted to blame their ancestors for the present-day calamities because that would be redundant. It was only the sins of the people and their leaders that caused God to respond so violently. If they amended their ways, peace and good times would return, as God would then forgive them. It also meant their children would not have to endure the wrath of God because of the sins of the fathers.

Whereas when Deuteronomy and Exodus were assembled or edited by Ezra (as some scholars believe), the situation and conditions he was encountering upon return from captivity revealed pure chaos in every aspect of daily life. As the returnees attempted to reclaim their property, they became engaged in violent opposition from the people who had remained and had now taken possession. In many cases these people were of mixed religions, such as the Samaritans. Marauding bandits abounded, and the authority of returning leaders and priests was not being respected. Thus, Ezra felt the need for greater priestly control and to expand punishments beyond the present generation. He also inaugurated a statute forbidding mixed marriages and the requirement to divorce non-Jewish spouses, and he also demanded them to remarry into the Jewish faith in order to replenish the population of faithful.

Religious fervor had to be reestablished primarily to support civil jurisdiction. This was the time when a formal written book of sacred scripture or the Bible was initially being completed. True, the sacred law of God was already written, though in a very crude and unorganized format, but it was not circulated among the general public except through oral traditions. Therefore, Ezra attempted to attack the problems by using the fear of God through the enactment of a written legal code emphasizing God's laws and focused in on the extreme punishments for violators. When he completed the Bible, he called a general assembly of the people in Jerusalem and read aloud the dictates of the God of Israel (Nehemiah 8:1–8).

The Decalogue or Ten Commandments are often said to be the foundation for defining sin. We find the first two versions of the Ten Commandments in Exodus 20 and Exodus 34. In Deuteronomy 5, we find a third version of the Ten Commandments, one that is similar to the first version in Exodus. Catholics and Lutherans use Deuteronomy as the basis for their Ten Commandments lists. Scholars disagree on which of the two—Exodus 20 or Deuteronomy 5—is older.

Certainly, these statutes constitute a universal standard for moral and ethical behavior as well as making very good social sense. But there are some problems. Wherefore the Bible gives us three different sets of the Ten Commandments. They appear in Exodus 20 and again in 34 also in Deuteronomy 5. Furthermore, the accepted ten for Jews, Catholics, and Protestants have variations, and the order is different. A closer look into these variations would reveal very minor or trivial differences to be sure. However, the alterations set forth between Exodus 20 and 34 undoubtedly show the work of an editor or redactor. Exodus 20 is what God wrote on the tablets of stone, whereas Exodus 34, which is quite different, is what God ordered Moses to write.

This shows that the editor wanted to preserve the older or some more compelling versions but felt the need to modify or reword it to suit the conditions or situation of his day. God's Law was also the civil law, and strict adherence to these laws would ensure a controllable society for the betterment of all the people, especially for the ruling class.

The sin of idolatry was primary as the first two commandments, which is clearly indicated in each case. Here is where we see the priestly influence flexing its political muscle by placing the power and control of the law with the priests. In Exodus 34, we see this as less important because these sins at this time were nearly stamped out, at least for most of the Jewish people, but the old tradition was still well ingrained with most Jews, so it simply could not be eliminated. Therefore, after mitigating the first two statutes, other new commandments were instituted. They are as follows:

> 3. The feast of unleavened bread shalt thou keep in the month when the ear is on the corn. 4. All the first-born are mine. 5. Six days shalt thou work, but on the seventh thou shalt rest. 6. Thou shalt observe the feast of weeks, even of the first fruits of the wheat harvest, and the feast of ingathering at the year's end. 7. Thou shalt not offer the blood of my sacrifice with leavened bread. 8. The fat of my feast shall not remain all night until the morning. 9. The first of the first fruits of thy ground thou shalt bring unto the house of the Lord thy God. 10. Thou shalt not seethe a kid in its mother's milk. (Exodus 34)

When we look to the New Testament, we see a new concept developing in regard to sin. Most Christian denominations believe Jesus died for the redemption of all our sins. It is obvious that the death of Jesus did not change anything relative to the physical world. To put it differently, what actual changes would the people have seen to demonstrate that the death of Jesus had redeemed them? We have all heard that the gates of hell were then opened, but how did anyone know this? Did Jesus tell or teach this? Certainly, this is not found in the Bible.

In the four canonical gospels, Jesus never explicitly states that His death would save humankind from sin. When approached by a person who asked what he must do to gain eternal life, Jesus told him to observe the commandments (Matthew 19:16, 17). Simply put, he had to obey the Law of God as was given to Moses. Based on a similar question put to him by a man versed in the law, Jesus affirms his position to love God and his fellow man (Luke 10:25–28). Jesus also stated that in order to find forgiveness from God for our sins, we first had to forgive one another (Matthew 6:14–15). See also the Sermon on the Mount. It was Paul who preached of a Savior named Jesus Christ, the Son of God, who died and then rose again to save humankind from sin (Roman 5:8–11; 6:8–9). In the Torah, God says that one who is "hanged upon a tree," suggesting crucifixion, is "accursed" (Deuteronomy 21:23). Paul interpreted this by saying that Jesus became accursed in order to take on the sins of man (Galatians 3:13). For the resurrection, Paul says that Jesus "conquered" death and sin for humankind (Romans 6:9, 10), which plays such an important theological part that one who does not believe in it is not considered a good Christian (1 Corinthians 15:14) or one who will ever achieve eternal life.

The first sin, as told of in the book of Genesis, is also known as original sin. Most Christians believe retribution for this sin is inherited by everyone and remission for this sin can only be satisfied through baptism. Original sin is a concept of Catholic Christianity and is embraced by many Protestant sects as well. Orthodox Christians, Jews, and Muslims do not accept this doctrine. Catholics have two levels of sin, which are called *mortal* and *venial*. Mortal refers to a very serious offense, while venial is less offensive. Jews have three levels of sin. They are known as (1) *Pesha* or *Mered* (an intentional sin, an action committed in deliberate defiance of God), (2) *Avon* (a sin of lust or uncontrollable emotion, a sin done knowingly but not done to defy God), and (3) *Cheit* (an unintentional sin).

Different levels of sin are not delineated in Orthodox Christianity or in Protestantism. For most individuals the definition of sin is almost universally understood and is associated with one's personal conscience. But there are those, such as atheists and deists, who see sin as a strictly social offense that has nothing to do with any deity. In other words, they see sin being defined by the mores of each particular society. They believe sin was only added to reinforce these social laws by carrying punishment beyond the grave. It is obvious that the concept of sin has benefited society regardless if one believes it is God-orientated or human-dictated.

THE WORSHIP OF IDOLS

The very first commandment set forth in two of the three sets of the Ten Commandments is paraphrased as "I am the Lord your God you must not worship any other gods" (Exodus 20:1–17;

Deuteronomy 5:6–10). The Ten Commandments are recorded two times in the Hebrew Bible, specifically in the books of Exodus and Deuteronomy, where they are somewhat different in wording and numbering. This notwithstanding the point I make is that the taboo against idol worship was so important that it was God's first order. However, we can clearly establish that its importance had much greater relevance at the time when Exodus and Deuteronomy were written than any other time in history.

Let us look into the Bible and see how this commandment played out. At this point in history, King Jeroboam, ruler of the Northern Kingdom or Israel, was angered because several of his subjects were traveling to Jerusalem to worship in the temple. He would later close the border with Judah and forbid traveling there. The books of Hosea as well as 1 and 2 Kings were written about this time.

"People of Samaria throw out your god that looks like a calf! My anger burns against you. How long will it be until you are able to remain faithful to me? Your calf is not God. A skilled worker from Israel made it. But it will be broken to pieces" (Hosea 8:5–6).

Would you agree that here it appears what the people believed that the golden calf was the actual god?

"'As it now stands,' he said to himself, 'the kingdom will revert to the house of David (in Judah). If these people go to sacrifice in the Temple in Jerusalem, it will revive their allegiance to the King of Judah.' After taking counsel about the matter, he made two golden calves and said to the people, 'You have gone to Jerusalem long enough. Here are your gods that brought you up from Egypt'" (1 Kings 12:26). Now here we have some doubt. Obviously, the two golden calves were manufactured, yet it seems that King Jeroboam fully expected the people would worship them as gods. How else could you interpret this?

Now we go to where the people are clamoring for a god to worship. Aaron then acquiesced and collected the people's golden earrings to be melted down for fabrication of a golden calf. He also erected an altar for the calf, the very next day. The people made offerings and worshipped. They said, "As for this Moses, we don't know what has become of him. Make us a *god* so we can say, 'here are your gods who brought you up from Egypt'" (Exodus 32:1). So Aaron then fashioned a golden calf and gave it to the people saying, "Here are your *gods*, who brought you up from Egypt" (Exodus 32:4).

Notice these are the exact words Jeroboam used in the book of Kings except there is only *one god* (in Kings) instead of the *two gods* (in Exodus). I think that one could conclude that here the golden calf (Exodus) is the object of worship and is the *god* itself!

Now we have the story of Rachel after secretly stealing her father's idols (gods).

"I have the power to harm you; but last night the God of your father said to me, 'Be careful not to say anything to Jacob, either good or bad.' Now you have gone off because you longed to return to your father's household. But why did you steal my gods?" Jacob answered Laban, "I was afraid, because I thought you would take your daughters away from me by force. But if you find anyone who has your gods, that person shall not live. In the presence of our relatives, see for yourself whether there is anything of yours here with me; and if so, take it." Now Jacob did not know that Rachel had stolen the gods.

So Laban went into Jacob's tent and into Leah's tent and into the tent of the two female servants, but he found nothing. After he came out of Leah's tent, he entered Rachel's tent. Now Rachel had taken the household gods and put them inside her camel's saddle and was sitting on them. Laban searched through everything in the tent but found nothing.

Rachel said to her father, "Don't be angry, my lord, that I cannot stand up in your presence; I'm having my period." So he searched but could not find the household gods. (Genesis 31:29–35)

Obviously, idol worship was not a problem or a sin against God at these times in history. Therefore, the biblical dating for the incorporation of the first commandments only began when Moses came down from Mount Sinai for the second time with the stone tablets containing the Ten Commandments. Then it follows that Aaron and the others didn't know that it was offensive to God to worship the golden calf, so why then was Moses so angry when he discovered this? If it was known beforehand, how and by what means did the people and Aaron learn about it?

Just as a side note to this same episode, we have a doublet (in Exodus) with contradictory elements. Ezra certainly must have recognized this but must have believed there was a specific need to include both traditions. However, his blending of them seems to be somewhat incomplete.

1. "Then Moses and Aaron, Nadab, and Abihu, and seventy of the elders of Israel went up, and they saw the God of Israel; and there was under his feet as it were a pavement of sapphire stone, like the very heaven for clearness. And God's arm was not stretched out against the chief men of the people of Israel; they saw God; they ate and drank" (Exodus 24:9).

2. "For no man shall see God and live" (Exodus 33: 20).

We have a later situation occurring during the time of David. "Michal took the household idol and laid it on the bed, and put a quilt of goats' hair at its head, and covered it with clothes. When Saul sent messengers to take David, she said, 'He is sick.' Then Saul sent messengers to see David, saying, 'Bring him up to me on his bed, that I may put him to death.' When the messengers entered, behold, the household idol was on the bed with the quilt of goats' hair at its head" (1 Samuel 19:13–15).

This certainly appears to show that it was common for the people of Israel to have household idols or gods. Now chronologically from Jacob's time (about 1600 BCE) to David's (about 1000 BCE), idol worship was acceptable but by Ezra's time (about 490 BCE) it was condemned.

HISTORY OF THE DEVIL

This history is quite complicated being that there are numerous variations of the word devil (i.e., Satan, Lucifer, Beelzebub, Azazel, Legion, and Belial), which generally refers to the same person or persons. The most common understanding of Satan is that of the chief devil and archenemy of God and of humanity who has numerous evil assistants who work on humanity, trying to lead them into losing their souls and end up with him in hell.

The serpent in Genesis and the Satan in Job, generally believed to be the same, take a more recognizable form in Mark 1:12–13, although Matthew 4:1–11 and Luke 4:1–13 identify him as the devil. However, the earliest Hebrew scriptures use the term *satan*, the Hebrew verb that means "to oppose." In the Greek Septuagint translation, which was almost exclusively used by the early Christian church, translated *satan* as *diaboloc*, which is where we derive our English term *devil* and *diabolic*.

There are no passages in the earliest parts of the Hebrew Bible where Satan is equated to an evil devil as we believe today. He is described as being similar to a prosecuting attorney who simply carries out God's instructions. There is no dualism here between two powerful supernatural entities, such as an all-good God and an all-evil Satan. God is portrayed as performing (directly and indirectly) both kind and evil deeds.

But how did we arrive at our dualistic understanding of an all-good God whose antithesis is the all-evil Satan?

The first Jewish messiah was Cyrus the Great, the founder of the Persian Empire, also known as the Achaemenid dynasty (Isaiah 45:1). Cyrus was highly esteemed by the Jewish people, and they respected Zoroastrianism, which was the faith of Cyrus. The god he worshipped was known as Ahura Mazda the *sovereign, lawmaker, supreme judge, master of day and night, the center of nature and inventor of moral law.* He also was the creator of heaven and earth. Briefly, he had all of the same attributes credited to God by the ancient Israelites but just a different name. However, Ahura Mazda had a twin brother named Angra Manyu, (a.k.a. Ahriman), the god of evil.

The concept of two gods clearly violated the monotheistic principles of Judaism, but this concept did help to explain the responsibility for good and evil, which was appealing. Therefore, the Jews adopted the idea but modified it to fit. The one true God was all good, and Satan now became God's evil adversary. Ezra and his priestly cohorts included this in the first written Hebrew Bible. This was accomplished by assembling sacred oral and written traditions known to them at this time, which then led to a new era in Judaism (Nehemiah 8:1).

One very ancient tradition with several variations regarding atonement was kept by Ezra as he assembled the book of Leviticus (16:8). "He is to cast sacred lots to determine which goat will be reserved as an offering to the LORD and which will carry the sins of the people to the wilderness for Azazel." This is the foundation of the ritual for casting sins onto a scapegoat. The exact meaning for Azazel is lost, and there now are numerous and varying interpretations of it. However, Azazel would later become thought of as the devil and a fallen angel, which would make him one of earliest demons in Judeo-Christian history.

Almost certainly Azazel in pre-Ezra times was not considered a devil as we think of today. Stories spread about him until the author of the book of Enoch (second century BCE) had composed this book. Enoch expanded the Genesis (6:1–8) story to be about fallen angels, creating numerous devils, including Azazel. So we can see how Azazel became the scapegoat that was cast into the wilderness and became a devil by carrying all of the ugly sins of humanity. This is the basis that artists used to portray him as a reddish goat-like creature with a grotesque human face complete with a tail, hoofs, and horns carrying his pitchfork.

Ezra is the likely composer of 1 and 2 Chronicles. His purpose for writing these was to clarify or explain some difficult stories that were part of popular traditions that were necessary portions and that needed to be included in the Hebrew Bible. An example is about the involvement of Satan in the census ordered by David (a practice forbidden in Exodus 30:11–16), which varies from the preexilic account of 2 Samuel from Ezra's later account in1 Chronicles. Second Samuel 24:1 says, "And again the anger of the LORD was kindled against Israel, and he moved David against them to say, Go, number Israel and Judah." First Chronicles 21:1 says, "Satan stood up against Israel and moved David to number Israel." The motivator in the Samuel tradition was God, while in Chronicles, it was Satan. Ezra believed he could not change the accepted words of Samuel, so he clarified the point that it was really Satan who enticed David, justifying it through the application of the newly revised Zoroastrian theology.

Zechariah 3:1 tells how the high priest Joshua was confronted by Satan. Zechariah's vision of the recently deceased Joshua, the high priest, depicts a dispute between Satan and the angel of the Lord. This verse is explained in the book of Ezra (Ezra 4:2–4), which gives a historical account of Joshua's struggle with Satan. Ezra says, "The enemies of the people of Judah and Benjamin heard that those who had returned from exile were rebuilding the Temple," and they "tried to discourage and frighten the Jews and keep them from building." By this we have a clear example of Satan, God's adversary, at work against God's people. From here on all the postexilic prophets would share Ezra's understanding of the relationship between God and Satan.

This theology would then further develop. Around the early second century BCE, the book of Enoch was written to explain in full detail how Satan came to be along with the fall, including actual names of bad and good angels. So popular was the book of Enoch that much of it has become part of Christian thinking. Enoch's devil figures are much more prominent in the New Testament, which became part of Christian theology, much more so than in the Old Testament and theology of Judaism. However, in the last two centuries BCE and the first two centuries CE, or a period of four hundred years, it was very popular among Jews, especially among the Essenes, as many copies of the book were found included in the Dead Sea Scroll cache.

As soon as we turn from the Old Testament to the New, we encounter Enoch's ideas. Now Satan is given another name, "the Devil," and he is mentioned about as often in the very first book of the New Testament as in all Old Testament books put together. Here we have the evil spirits of the New Testament appear to be doing the devil's work, even entering physically into humans and gaining procession of their minds and bodies. However, the devil Lucifer has become a name almost universally used as a pronoun for Satan.

Lucifer is perhaps the most accepted biblical *error* in Christianity. We can show how Satan came to be identified as Lucifer and became part of much biblical confusion. One could ask a logical question. Is it possible that this was just a simple mistake or merely amplification from Jewish Midrash? Let us examine the history behind the term.

Western Christianity generally believes Lucifer and Satan are one and the same. Most people would accept this as factually true. It is generally believed that this rebellious angel was once a member of God's royal court who, out of envy and pride, tried to overthrow the authority of God, or at least this is what most folks have come to believe.

But is Lucifer a biblical person?

Well, certainly not in most of today's modern Bibles. The only place it can be found is in the King James Version and its later related versions, and it occurs only in Isaiah 14:12, which says, "How art thou fallen from heaven, O Lucifer, son of the morning!" Modern translators have recognized this error and its source, resulting in its elimination.

One examples is Isaiah 14:12 (KJV), which says, "How art thou fallen from heaven, O Lucifer, son of the morning! *how* art thou cut down to the ground, which didst weaken the nations!" Now here is how the verse is rendered in some modern translations: "How you have fallen from heaven, O *morning star*, son of the dawn! You have been cast down to the earth, you who once laid low the nations!" (Isaiah 14:12 NIV).

Isaiah 14:12 (NASB) says, "How you have fallen from heaven, O *star of the morning*, son of the dawn! You have been cut down to the earth, You who have weakened the nations!"

And Isaiah 14:12 (YLT) says, "How hast thou fallen from the heavens, O *shining one*, son of the dawn! Thou hast been cut down to earth, O weakener of nations."

So how did the original common noun lucifer become a proper noun that equated to Satan or the devil?

This error was caused by a simple mistranslation by the first translators of the King James Bible, which was then continued in later versions. Lucifer is the English word taken from the Latin word *lux ferre*, which means "bearer of light." Isaiah 14:12, as translated by the KJV writers, were taken from their original source, the Latin Vulgate, where the common noun lucifer actually appears. It also appears in the Vulgate at 2 Peter1:19. However, here the writers of the King James Version got it correct and translated it as "morning star."

A major problem for translators is that some words just do not transliterate or translate very well. Therefore, translators must substitute what they believe is the most appropriate word. This is one reason we have different renderings in the various Bible versions. Such was the problem for Jerome, the fourth-century translator and creator of the Vulgate. In Isaiah 14:12, the Hebrew word *heel* means bright or brilliant, a word that had no Latin equivalent. Jerome selected a very reasonable Latin word "lux ferre," when translated into English is "lucifer," the Latin for "bright one or light bearer."

In the seventeenth century while the King James Version was being assembled, Lucifer had indeed evolved to become a proper noun (in English only). The translators merely assumed that Jerome had intended it that way. Also the KJV translators did not, at least publicly, want to disclose their use of the Roman Catholic Vulgate as one of their sources, as the Protestant Reformation was currently in full swing.

If we study Isaiah 12:14, we can be quite positive that he was referring to the king of Babylon and is obviously taunting him. This is clearly not about a fallen angel. Another reason why it makes no sense to read Satan, Lucifer, or the devil into this passage was that the traditional role of Satan (at least in the Hebrew Bible) is that of an *adversary*. This is exactly what the word Satan means in Hebrew. In fact, in the Tanakh (the Jewish Bible) as translated by "The Jewish Publication Society," the word *satan* appears only in the *first two chapters of Job* and in 1 Chronicles 21:1 and Zechariah 3:1–2. This is also the case in many modern English translations. Likewise, these, too, only show "Satan" appearing twice in Job and Zechariah and once in 1 Chronicles.

Before the time of Ezra, the Hebrews did not have a devil-like power opposed to God. Good and evil came from God. In Isaiah 45:7, God says, "I form light and created darkness, author alike of well being and woe; I, the Lord do all these things." *The Jewish Encyclopedia* confirms that the radical difference between how Satan is conceived in the Old Testament in comparison to the New Testament is that the original role has no basis or foundation for the association of or with a rebellious angel.

"This idea developed from the Persian concepts of two opposing empires, with Satan as God's enemy" (*Valentine's Jewish Encyclopedia* by Hyamson and Silberman, p. 39). There is actually very little in the OT to support the idea of Satan as a rebellious angel and the power opposing God. He is generally detected as a heavenly type of attorney general (accuser) functioning under the authority of God, and this only strengthens the arguments for not reading Satan into the passage about lucifer in Isaiah. This is taken from proto-Isaiah and was certainly written well before the Jewish exile. Chronicles was written or assembled by Ezra while in exile in Babylon under the influence of Persian dualism. Thus, the reason Satan appears in 1 Chronicles.

We can now see that there is no sound biblical basis for associating the Latin word *lucifer* with Satan or even the devil in the Old Testament.

Then where did this idea of a fallen angel appear?

To find the answer, we must look to the pseudepigrapha and the book of Enoch. In 2 Enoch 29, we are told of the angel Satanial's rebellion, ultimate defeat, and his exile from heaven.

Enoch was a very popular book around 200 BCE to 200 CE, as numerous copies were discovered in the Dead Sea Scrolls cache. Looking at the NT, we see an echo in Revelation, most likely taken from Enoch. But we must remember Revelation was a prediction taken from a dream or vision. It is not a factual historical report and does not claim to be. It is clearly a prophecy of events that will occur sometime in the future. There is also a reference to fallen angels in 2 Peter, but no details or histories are given.

Indeed, the King James Version and the book of Enoch inspired John Milton (seventeenth century) to write his classic novel *Paradise Lost*. Here we clearly find our rebellious devil, Lucifer, proper noun and all, along with the story of the great war in heaven. Milton's novel became immensely popular, so popular it became totally confused by many into believing it was biblical. This is not limited to the seventeenth century, as this tale lives on and on even though Milton's classic is no longer popular. Today most people haven't the slightest idea where it came from. Equally, most people believe it originated in the Bible.

THE DEVIL IN THE CHRISTIAN BIBLE

The understanding of the devil in the New Testament is in stark contrast from the ambiguities of Satan in the Old Testament. Here we see he takes on qualities similar to the devil as described in the book of Enoch. The book of Enoch existed in the second century BCE. Some scholars consider this noncanonical book to be more theologically Christian than Jewish. Many early Christians considered it sacred scripture, and the Ethiopian Orthodox church still does today. Some of the earliest literature written by the early church fathers contains several references from this unique book. The book of Jude as well as the early second-century epistle of Barnabus quotes nearly verbatim from of the book of Enoch. Justin Martyr, Irenaeus, Origin, and Clement of Alexandria all make use of the book of Enoch which Tertullian (160-230 CE) spoke of as being part of sacred Scripture (De cultu feminarum 1.3).

Most scholars consider Mark's gospel the earliest written New Testament gospel. It simply states in Mark 1:12–13 that Jesus, immediately after His baptism, went into the desert for forty days where "Satan" tempted him. Matthew 4:1–11 and Luke 4:1–13 expand this story by describing the "devil," presumably "Satan" of Mark's gospel, as the possessor of everything in the entire world, and he offered it to Jesus with the provision that Jesus would worship him. The devil then leaves, and angels come to comfort Jesus. Although Jesus rejected the devil's offer, it would appear the devil failed to recognize that Jesus, being the Son of God, had power and authority over him. In addition, it is clear that Jesus understood the things offered by the devil were, indeed, the devil's possessions to give!

What then was the purpose for Matthew's and Luke's expanding of Mark's story? First of all, Satan and the devil are now one and the same in the eyes of Matthew and Luke. Quite possibly, they were more familiar or more influenced by the book of Enoch than Mark. Very briefly, Enoch tells that Satan (Samyaza) was an angel before creation of the world, one who through jealousy rebelled against God. Satan and his allies were defeated by the archangel Michael and were then expelled from heaven and cast into hell. They now became the source of evil whose penchant was to tempt humans into sinning against God. Look at Matthew 25:41, which says, "Then he will say to those on his left, you are cursed! Go away from me into the fire that burns forever. It has been prepared for the devil and his angels." Also see Luke 8:12, which says, "People on the path are those who hear. But then the devil comes. He takes away the message from their hearts. He does it so they won't believe. Then they can't be saved."

Nothing which Matthew and Luke speak of can be found in the Old Testament. The source of this is in the book of Enoch. It is a fact that Enoch is positively referenced in Jude 1:9, "But even the archangel Michael, when he was disputing with the devil about the body of Moses, did not himself dare to condemn him for slander but said, 'The Lord rebuke you!'"

What makes this important is that the pre-Christian book of Enoch reflected a large segment of the Jewish population's theological understanding of the devil. This concept was clearly part of the Essene perceptions as witnessed by the numerous copies of Enoch found within the Dead Sea Scrolls as well as numerous other similar writings, one of several is the book of Jubilees. The rededication of Judaism after the first revolt (first century CE) witnessed the general rejecting of the devil by the rabbis. Books like Enoch and others were discarded but numerous midrashic references lived on and became to be a part of the Talmud. Christians continued to embrace Enoch right up to the Council of Laodicea (364 CE).

"The whole Jewish and pagan world at the beginning of the Christian era believed in those magic formulas by which the evil powers of the demons could be subdued, and the Jewish exorcists found a fertile soil everywhere for the cultivation of their Essene notions and their magic. This was the atmosphere in which Christianity arose with the claim of healing all that were oppressed of the devil (Acts 10: 38). This passage enforces the recognition by the unclean spirits themselves of the Son of David as the vanquisher of the demons (Mark 1:27; 3:11). The name of Jesus became the power by which the host of Satan was to be overcome, as Jesus Himself had seen Satan as lightning fall from heaven" (Mark 9:38; 16:17; Matthew 12: 28; Luke 10:18)". This paragraph was taken from the *Jewish Encyclopedia* to show how permeated "devil" theology was prior to and early into the Christian consciousness.

Though the belief in demons was greatly encouraged and enlarged in Babylonia under the influence of Parsee notions, demonology never became an essential feature of Jewish theology. (M)any prayers for the warding off of demonic influences have found a place in the Jewish liturgy ... The privies having been in Talmudic times isolated spots which filled the imagination with specters of fear, a special incantation is prescribed invoking the protection of guardian angels against the evil spirits haunting these places.

Here again, we are quoting *The Jewish Encyclopedia*. In it, we see by this that demonic conceptions, though not *officially* recognized by Judaism, have remained to the present day. However, the fact that it became very much a part of Christianity and the New Testament clearly bears this out.

The devil is prominently mentioned in several of Paul's works and is common in Matthew, Luke, John, Acts, James, 1 John, Hebrews, Jude, and Revelation. Even today, most Christian denominations accept the reality of the devil, but several in the mainstream have significantly turned down the rhetoric.

The belief in demons seems to have very primitive roots, as many ancient cultures appear to have accepted evil spirits of some sort. It is quite apparent that the first formal development originated in Zoroastrian society. It became a strong influence on Judaism well before the destruction of the first temple. The Jews exiled to Babylon, especially the ones who chose to remain there, became prosperous and are responsible for writing the Babylon Talmud. Although a formal approval regarding demonology would be later rejected, some of it remains to this day.

Christianity adopted the "fallen angels and Satan theology" straight from the book of Enoch. John Milton's epic novel *Paradise Lost* took Enoch's theme and expanded it into what most Christians believe to be historically true. Of course, Lucifer, which many people still believe to be the devil, is purely a mistranslation taken erroneously from the Latin Vulgate into the King James Version and is certainly not a devil or even a proper noun.

A new nationwide survey of adults' spiritual beliefs conducted by the Barna Group was taken on April 10, 2009. This survey asked questions about God, Jesus Christ, the Holy Spirit, Satan, and demons. Their report states,

> Four out of ten Christians (40%) strongly agreed that Satan "is not a living being but is a symbol of evil." An additional two out of ten Christians (19%) said they "agree somewhat" with that perspective. A minority of Christians indicated

that they believe Satan is real by disagreeing with the statement: one-quarter (26%) disagreed strongly and about one-tenth (9%) disagreed somewhat. The remaining 8% were not sure what they believe about the existence of Satan.

Today 59 percent of people rebuff the concept of Satan or the devil and demons, yet it remains subliminally active in our society.

THE HISTORY OF ANGELS

We move from Satan to angels and ask the following questions: How do we define angels? And how did angels come to being?

In a biblical sense, angels can be defined as a creation of God assumed to be somewhere above the level of humans. They can also be considered messengers of God or those who minister to their Creator. There is no account in the canonical texts of the Bible specifying the creation of angels. Yet there are nearly three hundred references to angels in the Bible with more than 180 in the New Testament. The English word *angel* comes from the Greek word *angelos*, which translates into the Hebrew word *mal'ak*, meaning messenger. In the Hebrew lexicon, angels were often defined as "sons of God" (*ben elohim*) and were thought of as heavenly members of God's army or as part of His royal court.

It is widely assumed by many Christians that Satan was such an angel who, because of jealousy, spontaneously tried to overthrow God and caused other angels to join his revolt. But God's army, led by the archangel Michael, defeated Satan, thus sparking the creation of chaos or evil. However, this is certainly not biblical. Revelation does speak to this somewhat, but one must remember Revelation is a prediction of future events and not something that took place in history.

In the book of Daniel we see Michael as Israel's prince or her patron angel while other angels are called princes or kings of Babylon, Persia, Tyrus, and Grecia. Indicating angels could represent nations other than Israel.

Satan comes from the Hebrew root "STN" (ancient Hebrew did not use vowels), which means "one who opposes, obstructs, or acts as an adversary." As we see in the Old Testament or Hebrew Bible, Satan is never seen as a devil but only as an obstructionist. Books written during the Persian and Greek periods show the influence of Zoroastrianism. Satan then became associated with *Diabolos*, translated from the Greek meaning "one who throws something across one's path." By New Testament times, this came to be considered an evildoer or the very devil himself.

It should be noted that in the book of Job from the Jewish Bible or Tanakh (in the Ketubim), the actual word Satan only appears in the footnotes, using the word *adversary* as being more accurately translated. Several modern versions of the Christian Bible (in Job) use the word Satan only once at the very beginning while using the word adversary in every other case. Many Bible expressions equate human misfortunes as being given by God and caused by Satan because of an individual (or his parents) committing sins.

Ancients thought that angels dwelled in the heavens and that they could see them at night as stars in the sky. Thus, comets, meteors, and shooting stars were believed to be angels on a mission. As we have previously stated, Isaiah 14:12–15 is the only place in the Bible where the name Lucifer is mentioned. (It is never used in the Hebrew Bible.). Most people believe Lucifer is Isaiah's term for Satan, though it clearly is not. This passage is almost certainly the biblical foundation used by the writer of Revelation. However, there is no real basis to identify Isaiah's Lucifer with Satan. The association of a falling star (angel) is in line with the thinking of Isaiah's day, but he never mentions anyone—man or devil—named Lucifer. In fact, the proper noun indicating a name never appears in the original (or earliest texts) Hebrew.

Angels in the Old Testament are simply agents taking on human appearance. They were used by God to deliver messages or act as guards. The serpent in Genesis is never spoken of as a devil or as Satan. He is merely a snake. The cherubim in Genesis are used as guards to ensure Adam will not be able to return back to the Garden of Eden and are assumed to be angels.

The visual image of cherubim, as narrated in Exodus 25:18–22, 1 Kings 6:23–35, and 2 Chronicles 3:7–14, is given to narrate their human appearances, which are described in some detail. Another denomination of angel is called seraphim (Isaiah 6: 2). They had six wings and are supposedly part of God's military forces.

In the New Testament, we are introduced to another rank of angel called the archangel. The Greek *Archangelos* means "chief or first angel." Gabriel (Luke 1: 11, 19) and Michael (Jude 9) are the only two named who belong to this rank. Furthermore, Paul also speaks of this order of angel in 1 Thessalonians 4:16. Assuming that Gabriel (Daniel 8:16) and Michael (Daniel 10:13) are the same angels spoken of in the Old Testament that Luke and Jude speak of in the New Testament, they must have received a promotion to archangel by the time the New Testament was written. Other denominations of angels alluded to by Paul include Thrones, Dominions, Rulers, and Powers (Colossians 1:16).

Most of our information on angels comes from the "interbiblical period." This is the period of approximately four hundred years in which Protestants believe that scriptural writings were interrupted. Written during this period, the Old Testament Apocrypha and the pseudepigrapha books of Tobit, Enoch, and Jubilees offer a good deal more information on angels. In Tobit 5:4, the Angel Raphael serves as a guide and as a matchmaker for Tobias, and he defeats a demon too.

Satan is the one to whom the wicked angels submit, but more than one angel acts as Satan or the chief adversary in 1 Enoch 40:7. Also in 1 Enoch, we are told the serpent (in Genesis) is the wicked angel Gadreel, who led Eve astray (Enoch 69:6). First Enoch expands on the nephilim in Genesis 6 (Hebrew word for fallen ones). They are the evil giants that were the offspring of angels called watchers, whose leader is called Semhazah, and human women.

The personal names of several angels are mentioned in 1 Enoch. Archangels Ueiel and Michael are spoken of along with the standard angel Raguel. Another type of angel that many are familiar with is the guardian angel. Although this expression is strictly not biblical, it is strongly suggested in Acts 12:15 and Matthew 18:10. These passages were used later to develop the guardian angel philosophy by Gregory of Pontus about 250 CE. The Cappadocian Father, Basil, wrote in Eunomius that each member of the faithful has a guardian angel.

By the time of the Council of Nicea (325 CE) an attempt to address the doctrine of angels was required not only because of the Gnostic doctrines but also because of Arianism. Arian vocabulary about the relation of the Son of God as a creature to God the Creator involved their use of the title *angel*. Many inferred that Jesus was an angel. This was based on an interpretation of Proverbs 8: 22–31 and combined with Hebrews 1:4. This interpretation was offered to show that the preexistent one (meaning Jesus) belonged to the category of the angels, although to be sure, He was preeminent among them. Paul (Galatians 3:19) shows an inclination when he said the law of Moses had been "ordained by angels through an intermediary," possibly suggesting Jesus was an angel.

Therefore, Nicea clearly and explicitly declared, "We believe in one God, the Father Almighty, maker of all things, visible and invisible, and in one Lord, Jesus Christ, the Son of God, the only-begotten of the Father and is of the substance of the Father." This then defined the orthodox position on the preexistence of Jesus, the Son, and the creation of the invisible angels. *But ...* they stopped short and left the doctrine of angels completely undefined.

Our knowledge of angels is very obscure. Most of what is believed about angels is based on pure speculation. The fallen angel Satan/Lucifer and the battle in heaven with the expulsion of the rebellious angels are clear examples. Very vague biblical support of this is found in Genesis 6:1–4; Psalm 82, Isaiah 14:12–15, Ezekiel 28, 2 Peter 2:4, and Revelation 12:4–9. Perhaps the most believed or accepted *history* is taken from the seventeenth-century fictional novel by John Milton *Paradise Lost*. Milton defines Lucifer and the expulsion of Satan after the war in heaven.

The Bible claims angels have freedom to make moral choices, but they require judicial supervision (1 Corinthians 6:3; Jude 6). And God is disinclined to trust them (Job 4:18). Angels have limited knowledge (Matthew 24:36; 1 Peter 1:12) and can take on human bodies. Jesus tells us (Matthew 22:30; Luke 10:35–36) angels are not sexual, yet in Genesis 6:4, angels did indeed have sex and fathered offspring. In Zechariah 5:9, we hear of the only occurrence of women angels in the Bible.

Satan was considered the leader of the fallen angels and is also thought of as the devil. This is simply not the case in the Old Testament. Even the name Satan is merely a translation of *adversary*. By the time the New Testament was composed, Satan and the devil became synonymous with the evil fallen angels.

First John 3:8 says, "For this purpose the Son of God was manifested, that He might destroy the devil." Hebrews 2:14 says, "The very object of Christ's assumption … was … through (His) death He might destroy the devil." Are we to infer that Jesus has already destroyed the devil, Satan, and all of our angels? From the New Testament, it is certain that a hierarchy of angels exists. One would assume the archangel (chief angel) ranking would be the highest with cherubs, seraphs, powers, thrones, watchers, dominions, rulers, and just plain angels following somewhat behind. Angels are considered superhuman (Hebrews 2:7). Yet in the end man will be the final judge of the angels (1 Corinthians 6:3).

I would be remiss if I failed to mention a later angel who appeared to the prophet Joseph Smith in 1823. This angel was called Moroni, one that existed as a human in the first century, died, and was later glorified by God and made an angel. This, of course, is found only in the Book of Mormon.

THE HISTORY OF HELL

Perhaps the most contentious word—or should I say place?—in the Bible is *hell*. It is a name or place well known by nearly everyone. It is feared by some, used as a didactic tool by some preachers, and used most often as a simple cuss word. Today there is a growing belief that such a place does not exist. In fact, if my memory serves me correctly, about 28 percent of Americans deny any existence of hell. This number increases to 75 percent for Europeans, according to a recent poll.

For most people this notorious word connotes a place of suffering with fire and brimstone. It is also viewed as a place for punishment generated from our sins as handed down by God. Is hell spoken of in the Bible? Indeed it is, but depending on which translation you have, the number of times varies dramatically. The reason for this is the corresponding Hebrew term *Sheol* and its Greek counterpart *Hades*. This can also be translated (and sometimes is) as a pit, a grave, destruction, disaster, predation, a pod, a rod, death, entombed, and Gehenna.

Referencing the Jewish Bible (Tanakh) as issued by the Jewish Publication Society, the word *hell* does not appear at all. Judaism does not have a clear sense of hell or for that matter even heaven. It stresses the idea that God uses the afterlife to provide ultimate justice and for the wicked to seek some sort of final redemption. In fact, since the Enlightenment, many Jews have given up all concepts of an afterlife.

Tracing the history of the tenet of hell is quite difficult and obscure. The doctrine of hell was thought necessary to keep humankind from becoming corrupt. A little later I will discuss "the history of the soul" by probing the Israelite concept of soul, which originated no earlier than the midsecond century BCE. Dr. Simcah Raphael writes in *Jewish Views of the Afterlife*, "Any doctrine of eternal torment or suffering in the afterlife depends on the doctrine of soul immortality … this doctrine did not develop until the apocryphal period and was a radically new idea that did not exist in Biblical times."

The earliest theological notion that included a vague form of hell and Satan originated from the Hindu sacred writings of the Vedas. This then spread eastward into Persia and developed a religious belief along different lines. About 600 BCE, a seer named Zoroaster expanded the concept of salvation and damnation. Immediately upon one's death, the soul had to cross horseback over a narrow bridge called the "Bridge of the Petitioner." Rashu, an ancient god, would then judge the soul to determine if he was suitably righteous to reach the other side and heaven. An unworthy soul would fall into an abyss-like hell that consisted of fire that emanated an awful stench. Of course, the next logical development would have to be the inclusion of a creature to govern this hell, which set the stage for the devil.

Zoroaster (about 600 BCE) was a Persian prophet. Similar to Jesus, it was said he was tempted by Satan. He performed several miracles. He healed the sick, and his disciples thought of him as a semi divine human similar to Mohammad. Generally, many scholars consider Zoroastrianism to be the world's first established monotheistic religion. Their faith was worshipping a male god, Ahura Mazda, the "sovereign, lawmaker, supreme judge, master of day and night, the center of nature and inventor of moral law." As the creator of heaven and the earth, many basically believed that Ahura Mazda had the same powers as the Jewish God. The exception was Ahura

Mazda, who had a twin brother named Angra Manyu, the god of evil, who had created demons, snakes, and everything evil. Thus, *he* became the world's first devil and the ruler of hell. Zoroaster taught that Ahura Mazda and Angra Manyu would oppose each other until the evil god was defeated. Then the world would end, and all who had died would be resurrected after a final judgment, which would determine who went to heaven and who went to hell for eternity.

Once the perception of a spiritual soul took hold, hell then became a place where the soul received due punishment for being wicked. Of course, this Hellenistic origin of *soul* clashed with the predominant rabbinical Jewish intellection of a bodily type of resurrection/punishment.

The Old Testament use of the term hell comes from the Hebrew word *Sheol*. This means "the grave" or "death" most of the time. The Greek word's rough equivalent is Hades, which has a very different origin but is often interchanged with Sheol (approximately sixty times in the Bible).

In Greek mythology, Hades is the god of the dead who rules over the underworld. The Old Testament usage of these words is never used to signify punishment or retribution after one dies. It cannot be understood as we think of hell today because that would mean that Jacob would go to a place of torture. It would also prove Jesus, David, and Jonah were once subjected to the place of the damned. This is clear when we read the various corresponding biblical stories. In *every instance* in the Old Testament, the English word *grave* may be correctly used in place of or instead of hell.

The ancients believed a dome capped their world. The area above this dome was called heaven, and below the earth was the underworld. When someone died, he was buried and soon disappeared into the underworld or Sheol/Hades. Sheol was a proper noun and in reality is not translatable. Demons and Satan were not committed to writing until after the Jews returned from Babylonian exile, as the returnees had now been exposed to Zoroastrianism. Before this time devils or hell, as we think of it today, was nonexistent.

Previously, I have shown that Satan in the Old Testament is not a devil but merely an adversary. Lucifer is nonexistent in the Old Testament and is a complete misinterpretation taken from the Latin Vulgate. Hell (as we now think of) began to take on serious meaning in the apocryphal and pseudepigraphic books of the Bible.

The book of Enoch (150 BCE) is perhaps the most important. It would certainly appear Jesus was aware of this book, as many of His teachings allude to knowledge of Enoch, although he does not quote directly from it. The final judgment, the concept of demons, the origin of the fallen angels, and the coming of a messiah are narratives that have found their way into our present Judeo- Christian understandings, and they all originated in the book of Enoch. R. H. Charles, a translator and commentator on the book of Enoch, says, "The resurrection, and the nature of afterlife, the origin and punishment for sin … all began with Enoch … and immortality and the price of wickedness."

Hell, as we now understand it, really took shape in the first century BCE through the first century CE. The New Testament, again depending on which translation you have, uses hell, but many Bibles substitute or use the word Gehenna. This is because in Old Testament times Gehenna did not exist. Gehenna is the Greek form of two Hebrew words, GE + HINNOM (this is the English rendering; Hebrew writing was always written in capital letters), meaning the valley of Hinnom. This referred to a ravine on the south side of Jerusalem, now called Wadi er-rababi, a place where pagan deities once were worshipped from the fifth until the second century BCE. It then became a garbage dump that constantly had burning refuge and emitted a horrible smell.

Our understanding of hell in the New Testament is vague and unclear. Matthew's Jesus suggests (Matthew 13:40–42) that sinners at the end of time will be cast into a blazing furnace and that there will be weeping and gnashing of teeth. Also at Matthew 25:41–46, we are told sinners will join the devil and his angels in an eternal fire. Luke 16:19–31 speaks of a man who actually went to hell. He died and was buried and went to hell, where he was tortured by fire. However, he could look up, and in the distance he saw a poor man basking with Abraham in heaven. Mark 9:43 says that hell has an unquenchable fire to torment sinners. These biblical quotations regarding hell are very close to the hell as presented by Enoch.

Paul, however, appears to be a bit different. He actually never uses the word *hell*. It seems that Paul believed souls, which had died merely, fell into a sleeplike death. They would then be awakened and resurrected (as bodies) at the Parousia (second coming). (See Ephesians 5:14, 1 Corinthians 15:51, and 1 Thessalonians 4:14; 5:6). This shows Paul understood that souls simply slept between death and resurrection. This then would occur at the end of time or the end of the world. This concept was quite prevalent in Judea around the time of the first century. Paul avoided expressions for hell, but he certainly reserved some place for the dead until their resurrection, describing this as a peaceful sleep (1 Thessalonians 4:13) or a punishment in fire (1 Corinthians 3:5).

In Second Baruch (about 50 CE), the author teaches that the dead "sleep in the earth" and "all who have fallen asleep in hope of Him shall rise again." This sounds very similar to Paul, doesn't it? Second Baruch goes on, "All the righteous will be gathered in a moment and wicked will grieve because the time of their torment has arrived." Second Baruch was written about the same time as Paul was writing.

Contemporaneously, in Alexandria, Hellenized Jews were reading the Wisdom of Solomon (50–30 BCE). "The souls of the righteous are in the hands of God, and no torment will ever touch them … their hope is full of immortality." The book of Jubilees (130 BCE) teaches that the "bones" rest in the grave while the "spirit" lives independently.

J. Robinson writes,

> Paul's phrase "the mind of the flesh" (Col 2: 18) make no sense to the Greek mind, because mind (nous) was always associated with soul (psyche) and never with flesh. Paul's views of Hell are almost non-existent and his view of the soul is confusing. Epaphroditus risked "his soul for the work of Christ" (Phil 2:30). "I do not account my soul of any value nor as precious … if only I may accomplish my work and ministry" (Acts 20:24).

If Paul believed his soul to be immortal, it is unlikely that he would have viewed it of no value and worth losing for the sake of his gospel. So it would appear Jews, like Paul, both of the Palestinian variety and the Alexandrian variety, viewed hell, resurrection, and the soul differently. In the gospel of John, hell is never mentioned and is not such an issue, although some sort of punishment for sin is alluded to. Obviously, in Revelation, the concept of hell is fully developed although the author claims that after the final conflict death and hell will disappear.

Hell, as it is understood today, simply did not exist in the Old Testament until after the Jewish people returned from exile. The period between the testaments witness the development of hell, as we now know it. Jesus spoke of it while Paul only hints at it. In John's gospel, it is not important. In Revelation, it is fully expressed, but in the end it will evaporate. Christianity still teaches that hell exists, but the emphasis on it has been diminishing. Hell does not exist in modern Jewish thinking. The concept of Sheol is defined as a holding place pending the arrival of the Messiah when the soul will be resurrected in full bodily form.

If there is a hell, presumably there must then be a heaven as well. This presented a very challenging assumption because most religions teach that good people go to heaven after they die and no one has ever come from heaven to describe it. Yet, heaven is usually taught to be a place of ultimate happiness, and those who get there will live joyfully forever. However, taking into account what a wonderful place it is reputed to be, it seems that no one seems to have a great sense of urgency to get there.

Death is the passageway to heaven, yet death is generally thought of as something we must avoid at all costs. Through the use of medical science, we usually do everything we can to put off death as long as possible. Doesn't it appear that most people would prefer the continuation of their present lives here on earth than the option of being in the heaven that we tend to believe in? If heaven was established by God to reward His servants, then why is there *so little information about it found in the Bible?*

Let us look at a few passages that may be pertinent.

In his second epistle to the Corinthians (Corinthians 12:2), Paul writes that he knew a man who was caught in the *third heaven.* Is Paul telling us there are various levels of heaven? This would lead one to think so and possibly associate Paul with a segment of Gnostic theology or at the very least his being influenced by it. Even Matthew seemingly implies various levels of heaven. "Truly I tell you people, among those born of women there has not been raised up a greater than John the Baptist; but a person that is lesser one in the kingdom of the heavens is greater than he" (Matthew 11:11).

Matthew also tells us that heaven is only temporary. "Truly I tell you, this generation will not pass away until all these things have taken place. *Heaven* and earth *will pass away,* but my words will not pass away" (Matthew 24:34–35). Now this adds a new wrinkle to the subject, don't you think? Looking to the book of Revelation, John clearly prophesizes of a future war that will take place in heaven. "And war broke out in heaven; Michael and his angels battled with the dragon; and the dragon and its angels battled" (Revelation 12:7). "Also, the armies that were in heaven were following on white horses, and they were clothed in white, clean, fine linen" (Revelation 19:14). Does this suggest that Jesus was referring to this war in heaven and that there will no longer be a heaven when the war has ended?

We do have a description of both heaven and hell in Luke 16:19–31. Here we see a rich man suffering in hellfire, peering up into heaven and seeing Lazarus basking with the angels and Abraham. Of course, this may be one of Jesus's parables, but Jesus clearly is saying *you suffer from fire in hell and enjoy comfort in heaven.* This is the clearest biblical reference to match our present understanding of heaven and hell. It just does not mention anything relative to time. Is it temporary or eternal? Matthew 13:47 describes it this way:

> Again, the kingdom of heaven is like unto a net, that was cast into the sea, and gathered of every kind: Which, when it was full, they drew to shore, and sat down, and gathered the good into vessels, but cast the bad away. So shall it be at the end of the world: the angels shall come forth, and sever the wicked from

> among the just, and shall cast them into the furnace of fire: there shall be wailing
> and gnashing of teeth.

So biblically, it would seem that heaven must be earned while hell is also earned by being wicked. One will spend some time or perhaps even eternity being *tortured by fire.*

Paul tends to agree in Galatians 6:8. "The one who sows to please his sinful nature, from that nature will reap *destruction*; the one who sows to please the Spirit, from the Spirit will reap *eternal life*." A possible contrast to this is found in Revelation 20:14–15. "And death and Hades (Hell my word) were hurled into the lake of fire. This means the second death, the lake of fire. Furthermore, whoever was not found in the *book of life* was hurled into the lake of fire." This might be suggesting a form of predestination.

The Old Testament writers thought heaven was located above an arching vault (that also had water) supported by pillars at the ends of the earth. While some texts may suggest something different, nowhere in the Old Testament is heaven literally described as being a place where humans are rewarded for being good or for just having faith. We do have a translation problem, though, with the words heaven and heavens. The Hebrew word is *samayim* and is plural, which always means heavens. By being plural and meaning "the heavens" could also be *construed as multiple levels.*

I don't think mainstream Christianity believes in different levels of heaven, and certainly, Judaism does not. Most believe heaven is a spiritual state of being with God. Some believe we will be bodily resurrected at the end of the world and will live on earth in a paradise similar to the Garden of Eden.

The Bible does not give much indication to what heaven is like or what we will be doing once we get there. Getting there is ambiguous. Most believe one has to have lived a good life while others believe you only need to have faith in Jesus. Yet some believe heaven is only for the elect—predestined by God in other words.

Most believe the Bible is the revealed Word or laws demanded by God. One would certainly think that God would have been more descriptive of the rewards for being faithful or good, wouldn't you? Certainly, there is more information on hell or punishment than heaven, but that, too, is ambiguously described in the Bible.

HISTORY OF THE SOUL

The soul is a concept accepted by almost everyone. Yet the words *immortal soul* are never used together in the Bible. In Matthew 10:28, Jesus tells us the soul can and will die in hell. Therefore, there should be no immortality.

This will not be an attempt to prove or disprove the existence of the soul, but I will try to trace the history of the early development of this concept and some problems that many often encountered (and still do).

Homer, who lived around 750 BCE, was perhaps the first person to write of a soul as being a distinct entity from the body. He did not indicate this soul as having an existence outside of the body. In the Hindu writings called Upanishads, also from around 750 BCE, the soul is identified with the real, the immortal, and the life breath (*prana*), which is veiled by name and form for individuality. Therefore, the concept of the soul sprung up in other parts of the ancient world almost simultaneously, at least so it seems.

Orpheus, a mythical Greek of the six century BCE, is said to be the father of the cult called Orphism. Perhaps this cult fostered the original ontological divinity concept of the soul. They taught that the soul was imprisoned in the human body and also of reincarnation. The concept of Hades (meaning the place, not the god) or the nether world (subterranean hell) may have originated with this group. Shades of Genesis 6:5 and the tragedy of Lot's wife are echoed in their stories.

Another Greek philosopher named Pythagoras (590–475 BCE) adopted the thought that the soul can spiritually rise into a union with the divine. He believed the soul had immortal energy completely separate from the living individual. Reincarnation of the soul was expounded. Pythagoras lived for some time in Egypt and in Persia. His philosophy was certainly influenced by these cultures.

Of all the ancients, no one has had a greater influence on the doctrine of the soul than Plato (427-347 BCE) and His followers. He claimed the soul is divine by nature and consists of two different realities—eternal and immortal. Plato believed the association of the soul with the body was caused by a fall from heaven. Therefore, it needed purification by a series of cycles of reincarnations. The body was inferior to the soul, especially its intellectual faculty, and this function was held in contempt. It is Plato who taught our body dies but our soul is immortal.

In 354 BCE, Aristotle wrote *Eudemus*. He advanced the philosophy of the soul from Orphic and Platonic spirit, some twenty years after Plato's writing of *Phaedo*. Later in *De anima* (Latin meaning "the soul"), he develops his full philosophy of the soul. Aristotle completely rejected the mythical thinking of his precursors and the original divinity of the soul, its preexistence, immortality, and imprisonment in the body. The soul became the majority of all belief systems up to the present; whether Christian or pagan, nearly all believe in some type of existence of a soul. My *Franklin/Merriam-Webster* dictionary defines *soul* as immaterial essence of an individual life. There are variations on how or when one receives his *soul*, but most believe it lives on in spirit after the death of one's body. I repeat: The words *immortal soul* are never used together in the Bible. In Matthew 10:28, Jesus tells us the soul can and will die in hell. Therefore, there should be no immortality.

By the fourth century BCE, most cultures understood or believed in a soul of some sort (except Mesopotamians and Hebrews). Genesis 3:19 clearly states that man was created from dust and that to dust he will return. No afterlife, no soul. Jewish Rabbi and scholar Neil Gillman writes in his book *The Death of Death,* "Biblical anthropology knows nothing of this dualistic (soul/body) picture all of a person which claims that a human being is composed of two entities, a material body and a spiritual or non-material soul."

About midsecond century BCE, the Maccabean period, there were two independent developments in Jewish thought concerning the afterlife. Prior to that point, the Jewish tradition had taken death to be the final chapter of human life—no afterlife. One of these developments was the expectation of a bodily resurrection at the end of the world. This is why the gospel writers of the New Testament vehemently emphasize the bodily resurrection of Jesus. Later the early church would label anyone who did not accept this doctrine as being a heretic.

The other development was the adoption of a dualistic account of the individual, according to which the soul survives the death of the body. Neil Gillman says,

> In their original form, the two doctrines of the resurrection of the body and the immortality of the soul appear independent of each other. One knows nothing of bodies; the other knows nothing of souls. One describes personal identity to the body, the other, to the soul. One teaches that at the end of time, the body will be revived. The other insists that the soul is immortal and needs no revival.

By the time rabbinic Judaism took the reins of Jewish thought, those traditions were conflated, teaching that the soul leaves the body at death but receives a resurrected body at the end of time.

But how and when did the concept of the immortality of the soul become a part of Christianity?

It is clearly not in the Old Testament. *The International Standard Bible Encyclopedia* states, "We are influenced always more or less by the Greek, Platonic idea that the body dies, yet the soul is immortal. Such an idea is utterly contrary to the Israelite consciousness and is nowhere found in the Old Testament." The most common Christian belief regarding the afterlife is that people have souls and at death their consciousness in the form of that soul departs from the body and heads for heaven or hell.

Is this found anywhere in the New Testament?

Origen (ca. 185–254) was the first person to attempt to organize Christian doctrine into a systematic theology. He was an admirer of Plato and believed that the soul was immortal and that it would depart to an everlasting reward or everlasting punishment at death. In *Origen De Principiis*, he wrote: "The soul, having a substance and life of its own, shall after its departure from the world, be rewarded according to its deserts, being destined to obtain either an inheritance of eternal life and blessedness, if its actions shall have procured this for it, or to be delivered up to eternal fire and punishments, if the guilt of its crimes shall have brought it down to this." Origen was considered a heretic later in his life.

Almost certainly, Platonic philosophy crept into the Pharisaic sect and also possibly the Essenes, although both sects radically opposed Hellenistic influence. We can see this initially in the book of Daniel (written about 160 BCE). The other development of the soul/afterlife theology can be found in the book of Wisdom (the last book written, about 50 BCE, in the Catholic/Orthodox Bibles). Wisdom allows one to see the chronology and the link between Hebraic Judaism and Alexandrian Judaism permeating into Rabbinic Judaism. Josephus (Antiquities of the Jews 18. 1.5-18) demonstrates quite clearly how this spirituality had percolated into mid-first-century Jewish theology.

Neil Gillman points out that while many Jews since the Enlightenment have given up all concepts of life after death, there is a movement within Judaism to recapture the doctrine of bodily resurrection (rather than immortality of the soul).

There are several references to the soul and the afterlife in the New Testament. But it is not entirely clear whether the soul in spirit or the body is resurrected. Matthew 10:28; 1 Corinthians 15:15, 29 and 45; 1 Peter 1:22–24; Revelation 16:3; and James 1:21 are just a view examples. A major problem is in the interpretation of the scriptures in the New or Old Testament, which is caused by the many different English translations, of which today there are no less than thirty-seven versions.

The English word *soul* in Genesis 2:7, Genesis 9:5, Ezekiel 18:4, Matthew 10:28, Acts 3:23, 1 Corinthians 15:45, 1 Peter 3:28, and Revelation 16:3 are examples of variously translated passages contained in many of these versions where *soul* could be substituted with such words as *life, person, anyone, body, everything, being the, saying, everyone, creature, no one, though this, though one,* or *animal.* In some cases, one could just simply omit the word in its entirety.

The reason for such a variety is that in the extant Hebrew and Greek texts they contain multiple meanings for the words *soul, mind, spirit, wind,* and *breath.* The Hebrew word that comes closest to our English word *soul* is *nephesh.* In actuality, this can mean "essence of life," "breath," and "wind." *Nuah* and *nesharmah* can also refer to the soul. Psyche is the Greek equivalent, which can also mean mind, ghost, or spirit. *Pneuma* can also refer to the soul as well as breath, spirit, or wind. In English, we might associate the soul with spirit or the Holy Ghost, or it may refer to a surprise (such as the expression "upon my soul") or an individual (such as the saying "I didn't see a single soul").

From this one can see the difficult job of the translators. He or she must literally interpret the intention and mind-set of the original authors. Does any of this effect how one perceives his or her faith? The answer is *probably not,* as most people are not sure exactly how their denominational faith defines the soul and the afterlife.

What I find most interesting is this paraphrase taken from Norton Raxort's *Christian Philosophies.*

> Why was the Greek doctrine accepted by the church and the Hebrew Biblical doctrine of resurrection neglected? The reasons go back into history. In the third century CE, nearly every Christian apologist attempted to defend Christianity within the context of Greek philosophy. To the Jews they argued that Christ was the fulfillment of their prophecies and that it was consonant with Greek philosophy, indeed, it was the culmination of it.

Therefore, the Hellenists were able to accept Christianity, which taught the soul's survival, to the whole of the believer rather than resurrection, an idea repugnant to many Greeks. Hence, Paul was reconciled with Plato.

The *soul* cannot be seen or touched. It cannot be explained in scientific vernacular. However, it is spoken of quite often in the Bible and is clearly a profound article of faith.

HISTORY OF REINCARNATION

As an expansion on the "history of the soul" section in this chapter, I will continue with the historical exploration of the theory of reincarnation. Although reincarnation is not accepted by Judaism or most Christians, the idea crops up in both the Hebrew and Christian Bibles. To neglect a discussion of it would diminish a key ingredient of Judeo-Christian philosophy.

In the first book of the Bible (Genesis 1:27), we are told we were created in the image and likeness of God. Most people recognize or believe God as having no body, at least no fleshy bodies like we have. In other words, God is a spirit, and the spirit is the image Genesis is referring to. This is a key to reincarnation as the transmigration of this spirit or soul, which is associated with the divine. Of course, before reincarnation can be set forth, the theory of having a soul had to be established first.

Approximately 20 percent of the world's religious population is composed of Hindus and Buddhists who believe in reincarnation. The Sufi tradition of Islam could possibly be added to this. A Fox News poll recently reported 25 percent of Americans believe in this as well. In Europe, the number is 28 percent. Mainstream Christianity and Judaism do not support this theory and teaches we have just one life and only one life. Resurrection of the body is also held by most, but how and when the soul/body is actually resurrected is mostly ambiguous and not clearly defined. Was this always the case?

Let us take a brief look at history.

Civilization's earliest sacred scriptures, the Hindu Vedas, did not speak of reincarnation, but the somewhat later Upanishads (about 1100 to 850 BCE) clearly do. Shortly thereafter, it also became an integral part of classical Buddhism. Ancient Egypt believed in reincarnation or the transmigration of the soul. Embalming was done to preserve the body for its journey with Ka, an animating force thought to be a counterpart of the body that accompanied the body to the next world or life. Ka is considered to be similar to the soul.

The first Western definer was Pythagoras (590–475 BCE). He taught that the soul was eternal and only resided in the body and that it would go through a series of rebirths in order to achieve perfection. Plato concurred with Pythagoras but claimed the soul tended to become more impure as it migrated from body to body. However, he believed, it was possible that it could return to its preexistence state and union with the divine through doing good works. If the soul continually deteriorates through its bodily inhabitations, Plato believed, it would end up in Tartarus, a hell-like place of eternal damnation (see 2 Peter 2:4).

Prior to the Babylonian captivity, the Hebrews—in fact, all of the Mesopotamian people—did not have a belief in reincarnation or of the soul. No afterlife; God (or their gods) dealt with rewards and punishments in their own lifetime. In 539, Persia conquered Babylon and brought in Zoroastrian theocracy. This had a major impact on the Hebrew, now Jewish people.

They struggled to maintain their ancient beliefs. Over the next few hundred years, the Hebrew religion divided into varying sects. The Sadducees (the original Hebrew religion) remained purists while partially and gradually giving way to the Pharisees (Essenes as well), who dilatorily adopted some concepts of Zoroastrianism, although they did modify them to fit within their monotheistic framework. This dualistic system of "good god and bad god" became to them the one true God, who was superior to all, and His evil counterpart became Satan, who was subordinate to only the one true God (the God of Israel). They also adopted Zoroastrian devils, demons, angels, and hell. Thus, reincarnation, resurrection, and an afterlife became part of the process that caused Hebraism to grow into and become Judaism (see Matthew 22:23).

Josephus (Antiquities 18) wrote that the Pharisees believed in reincarnation and that the souls of good men are "removed into other bodies" and will "have power to revive and live again" while evil men will receive punishment after death. He also states the Essenes believed the soul was immortal and preexistent, offering at least the tenets for belief in reincarnation. In the Talmud, reincarnation, the Hebrew word being *gilgul neshamot*, is often used. This literally means "the judgment of the revolutions of the souls." The Zohar is a Kabbalistic Jewish book of great authority, and it also refers to reincarnation.

Let us look to the Hebrew Bible. Ecclesiastes 1:9; 3:15 says, "What has been will be again, what has been done will be done again; there is nothing new under the sun … Whatever is has already been, and what will be has been before; and God will call the past to account."

Deuteronomy 18:10–11 says, "Let no one be found among you who … is a medium or spiritualist or who consults the dead."

Malachi tells of the return of Elijah before the "great and terrible day of the Lord." Here Elijah, assumed as one who never died, is not actually reborn until the New Testament in Matthew 11:11–15 and 17:10–13, showing Elijah being reborn as John the Baptist. Malachi clearly does not say Elijah will reappear by proxy but that Elijah himself will return.

Hellenistic philosophy and culture added to the mix and caused major resistance from the Essenes and Pharisees and to a lesser degree the Sadducees as well. Greek culture acknowledged empirically the existence of reincarnation from the various cycles of nature. Trees would die in winter and lose all their leaves. They would be reborn in spring and bloom by summer. Thusly, we now look to the thinking and understanding of the people during the time of Jesus.

In discussions between Jesus and His disciples, it appears to show their belief in reincarnation. Matthew 16:15–16 says, "When Jesus came to the region of Caesarea Philippi, He asked His disciples, 'Who do people say the Son of Man is?' 'Some say John the Baptist; others say Elijah; and still others, Jeremiah or one of the prophets.'" It seems obvious people here believed in reincarnation.

Luke 9:7–8 speaks of Herod being perplexed because some people were saying John the Baptist had been raised from the dead and Elijah had returned. Others heard that one of the prophets from long ago had come back to life, confirming the prevalent beliefs of reincarnation.

Paul also suggests the theory of reincarnation in Romans 9:10–13, where he refers to the cases of Jacob and Esau, saying that the Lord loved the one and hated the other before they were born. It so seems that the Lord cannot love or hate a nonexisting thing and this appears to indicate that Jacob and Esau had been in their former lives respectively good and bad. Therefore, the Lord could love the one and hate the other before their birth, and the souls passed this on from the previous inhabitants to the future men, known as Jacob and Esau.

The author of Revelation 3:12 insinuates he believed in reincarnation. In his book we find the verse saying that the voice of the Almighty declared that the man who overcame should "go out no more" from heaven. However, in Hebrews 9:27, we emphatically find the opposite thought, as it says, "And as it is appointed unto men once to die, but after this the judgment." This is more in line with predominant Christian thinking.

Though most Christians reject the idea of reincarnation, traces of it can still be discerned in the notion of physical resurrection. It seems impossible to discover any clear-cut, unambiguous Christian doctrine to explain what death is or what happens after death. What is available does not contradict the idea of reincarnation. However, for every biblical quote I have set forth, a very reasonable Christian apology has been advanced.

Origen has been cited as the early church father who taught reincarnation. Indeed, at least so it seems, he did or some of his followers did. Noteworthy, in 533, the second Council of Constantinople anathematized Origen for being a heretic. But they did not specifically cite any of his inclinations toward reincarnation as a reason. This is the basis used by the supporters of reincarnation who claim early Christian education was indicative of supporting reincarnation. The truth is the extant records of this council are not complete, and what we have gives only ambiguous credence to sustain their assumptions.

We do know that Gnostic Christians did teach various degrees of reincarnation. In his letter to Demetrias, Jerome speaks of numerous (Gnostic) Christians teaching reincarnation.

Epiphanius said that Valentinians, Ophites, Ebionites, and Paulinians were heretics of the Gnostic Christian sects who taught reincarnation.

Some Gnostic Christians believed resurrection was also a spiritual event—simply the awakening of the soul. People who experience the resurrection can experience eternal life or union with God while on earth and then after death to escape reincarnation. Those who don't experience the resurrection and union with God on earth will reincarnate.

Those who advocate the reincarnation theory cite the teachings of Jesus and the early church. They suggest clear and unambiguous teachings were expunged from scripture by the Catholic/Orthodox church at the Council of Nicea in 325. This is clearly not true! We have manuscripts that predate Nicea that are in basic agreement with the present-day texts. This is not to say that some editing and redacting did not take place because it certainly did. But wholesale changes that had profound impact on Christian doctrines have no foundation or substance.

In conclusion I find the theory of reincarnation to be appealing and reasonable. Near-death experiences add to the allure. But to say we can prove it or even offer compelling evidence simply falls short. The same can be said of the predominant Christian views of the afterlife and the soul. But then that is what faith is all about.

HISTORY OF THE FIRST WRITTEN BIBLE

The history of the first written Bible is somewhat obscure. Yet the Bible itself actually tells us exactly when this event took place or at least when it was discovered.

To begin with, the standard understanding of the Hebrew Bible is that Moses is the protagonist in the Torah based on his role. He is the single most important human personality who has been given more space to the account of his life and speeches than to anyone else in the Bible. Moses is also considered closer to God than anyone else in the Bible. By the fifth century BCE, an idea that Moses had written down words that God Himself had spoken on Mount Sinai took on popular acceptance. As time went by, it came to be understood that Moses wrote all of the first five books of the Bible.

Today only staunch fundamentalist believe this to be the case. In the seventeenth century, scholars began in earnest to study the Bible and its development. A study was put forth that we know today as "The Documentary Hypothesis," which is widely accept by most scholars and mainstream religions today. It plots examples from the Bible that strongly indicate numerous authors, editors, and redactors had a hand in writing all the books but particularly the five books of Moses. By careful reading of the Bible, we can find a quite likely beginning for the first written text, starting with a brief history compiled from the books of Deuteronomy, Joshua,1 and 2 Samuel, and 1 and 2 Kings.

After the death of King Solomon (927 BCE), his son, Rehoboam, became king of Israel. Rehoboam was not a strong leader, and soon the nation became divided. The Northern territory (consisting of ten tribes) kept the name Israel and was led by Jeroboam. Their capitol city was Samaria. The Southern kingdom (consisting of two tribes) was now called Judah. Their capital city was Jerusalem and was the site of the temple of Solomon.

Initially, people from Israel continued traveling to and worshipping at this temple in Judah. This caused great irritation to Jeroboam, and he soon restricted this travel. He then built sacrificial altars throughout Israel and consecrated a new line of priests. For the next three hundred years, multiple forms of worship permeated both nations. Passover was not observed. Baal and Asherah were worshipped along with the gods of the sun and moon.

King Josiah of Judah (650–609 BCE) was dedicated to the faith of Yahweh. He became king at the age of eight. During his reign Judah was a vassal state of the Assyrian Empire. However, this empire had grown weak and was battling an open rebellion with its province of Babylon. Assyria was losing its grip on Judah.

Only seventy-two years earlier, Israel was annexed into Assyria, but at this time it was left virtually undefended. Taking advantage of this weakness, Josiah, with the blessing of the Babylonians, sent troops into Israel, hoping to grain reunification.

This was a period that saw a great religious and national revival in Judah. Yahwehist priests had enormous influence with the young king. Remodeling of the temple was given priority. At this time no formalized Bible or Torah existed. Clearly, traditions had been passed on from past generations, and they continued to flourish orally; however, there was no written sacred scripture. This is not to say that some written texts, such as early renderings of Samuel and Kings, did not exist, but clearly, these were not as yet considered sacred or authoritative to the extent that we think of today. Most likely some of the psalms also existed in written form and may have held some semblance of sanctity, but certainly, no Bible or Torah was in place.

While the construction on the temple remodeling proceeded, an old scroll was discovered by the high priest Hilkiah (2 Kings 22:8; 2 Chronicles 34:22–28). He quickly took the scroll to the young king and affirmed to him it was a recording of the sacred law authored by Moses and was the covenant with Yahweh. The contents of the scroll revealed many sins that were ongoing both past and at the present.

Josiah recognized this and quickly issued a decree requiring full civil compliance with these laws. He reinstituted the holy day of Passover and destroyed all the rival religious sites in both Judah and in Israel.

What is important here is the discovery of the law scroll. The passage in 2 Kings and 2 Chronicles describes a biblical discovery of major consequence. From this time forward, this scroll would be copied, and new books would be written. It would become the primary or foundational text of the Bible. By the second century CE, a collection of books would be canonized and declared sacred scripture or the Bible based on this scroll.

Speculation might suggest Hilkiah wrote this scroll to reinforce or further promote religious fervor and the importance of the priesthood. It could also be a genuine article left over from the time of Solomon, and it could have indeed been lost in the temple. Whatever the case, the birth (or at least the rebirth) of the Bible occurred here in 621 BCE.

Another very important detail unfolded here that directly concerns the Bible. King Josiah needed to or wanted to be certain this scroll was authentic. So he ordered the scroll taken to the prophetess Hulda for *her* to decide if it was the work of God (2 Kings 22:14–19; 2 Chronicles 34:22–28) or not. And *she* alone made this final decision!

Now this is clearly an enormous historical event—a *woman* on her own making such an important determination! Even more impressive was the fact that the great prophet Jeremiah (in fact, his father was Hilkiah) was nearby and readily available as well as the other prominent male prophets Zephaniah and Nahum.

But why was a woman given priority in the first place over the three other celebrated males?

Jeremiah was so close to the king that he led the national mourning for Josiah when he was killed. Therefore, we can only speculate on Josiah's reasons for choosing a female prophet over the males. In summation, we can reasonably say that the first written Bible was instituted in 621 BCE and was then granted official status with the imprimatur of a *woman* prophet. *Prophetess Hulda—yes, a woman—is certifiably responsible for having a written Bible today.*

There is more evidence that points to a 621 BCE date for a written biblical book. Let's look at what was actually discovered. Surely, it could not have been the five books or scrolls of the Torah (for reasons we will discuss later). Some scholars believe it was a proto-Deuteronomy scroll. This scroll was taken along during the exile in Babylon and was used for the basis in the other four books. While in captivity it was then edited and revised to suit the current situation. The religious revival by Josiah is also spoken of in the books of Jeremiah and Zephaniah, and it is the same story in 2 Chronicles 34:14–19.

But what is most significant is the story of a *woman* giving this scroll official standing. Women had little if any authority at this time, so this story must have been too well known for anyone to have excluded Hulda's contribution. Excluding it would have surely cast doubts on the whole story. Ezra, the author of Chronicles, written about 480 BCE, obviously had a copy or knew of a strong oral tradition of this event, yet we can see he makes every attempt to downplay the role of Hulda. He likely felt forced to include her in Chronicles. As a high priest and scribe, Ezra clearly wanted men to hold the legal and religious authority of the land.

CHAPTER 2

In chapter 1, we examined the history of several components that form part of the beliefs that make up Judaism and Christianity. The foundation for these beliefs is a written text recorded in sacred literature or scripture, which is called the Bible. Judaism calls their Bible the Tanakh, which contains the Torah or the first five books. Jews also hold sacred the Talmud, which is made up of two units, the Babylon Talmud and the Palestinian Talmud. The Christian Bible consists of two Testaments, the Old and the New. The New Testament is about the ministry of Jesus, whose title is Messiah or Christ, and His followers, covering the years of the first century and early second century. The Old Testament is basically the same as it is in the Jewish Tanakh. However, the majority of Christians (Catholic and Orthodox) have several additional books. In this chapter we will examine the Bible's history.

Modern scholars have given names to describe various terms that I will be using from this point forward. What follows are a few of them.

THE APOCRYPHA AND PSEUDEPIGRAPHA

The canon of the Old Testament varies quite dramatically. The Jewish Tanakh and Protestant Bibles have basically the same thirty-nine books. Catholic Bibles have forty-six books. Catholics use the same thirty-nine plus seven additional, and some of these thirty-nine have longer or additional text. The number of books in the Bible of Eastern Orthodox churches varies from fifty-four to as many as more than sixty. Most have fifty-four. This would consist of the same Protestant thirty-nine plus fifteen additional.

Essentially, Orthodox and Catholic Bibles are the same. The Catholic version does not include 1 and 2 Esdras (Ezra) and the Prayer of Manasseh, which the Orthodox Bible does. Furthermore, it combines several texts with Esther and Daniel that are separate in the Orthodox Bible. The Orthodox Bible is officially the Septuagint (abbreviated LXX). Roman Catholic Bibles are primarily based on the LXX but follow more closely the Latin Vulgate. Protestant Bibles embrace the Jewish Masoretic text. The LXX is the third-century BCE Greek translation of the Hebrew Bible and is the reference Bible used by all the writers of the New Testament. (The possible exception is the book of Jude.)

Strictly speaking, the fifteen additional books of the Orthodox Bible and seven in the Catholic Bible are called "books of the Apocrypha" by Protestants and Jews. However, in most arguments, only the seven are referred to as apocryphal. Orthodox and Catholics officially call these same books "Deuterocanonical."

Numerous biblical-type books exist that are not included in any canon. They tend to be composed prior to the first century CE. These are called "pseudepigrapha." Most of these books are of Jewish origin but were preserved (and sometimes modified) by the early Christians. Pseudepigraphon is the singular and is defined as "writing with a false superscription and false authorship." Apocryphon is the singular and means "something hidden away." Although most people erroneously believe it means "spurious or uninspired."

Much confusion comes from the different use of the terms by Protestants and Orthodox/ Catholics. Pseudepigraphon is a term not *officially* used in Catholic/Orthodox parlance. Instead they are called the books of the Apocrypha. The books Protestants call apocryphal are called Deuterocanonical by Orthodox/Catholics. Adding to this confusion is the fact that most Catholic scholars generally use the Protestant terms. This is because critical biblical scholarship was originally started by Protestant scholars who coined the term pseudepigrapha to distinguish the difference between the two terms.

The Apocrypha was given a pejorative connotation by Jerome (fourth century), the father of the first complete Christian Bible. By this I mean he was *officially* the first person to translate the combined Hebrew and Greek texts into a single book that became known as the Latin Vulgate. He didn't necessary believe these books were inspired by God, but he reluctantly recorded them simply because they were not included in the Jewish canon. However, his sponsor, Pope

Damasus, along with Augustine, insisted they be included because the books were part of the LXX.

Protestants included the Apocrypha in their early Bible translations. This includes the 1611 rendition of the King James Version. Luther's first translation also included the Apocrypha, but he did question their divine inspiration as well as several books from the New Testament. Reformed Christianity did as well, and these Christians were the first to drop the Apocrypha from their Bibles.

Adding further to the confusion is the Gnostic library of biblical books, which consisted of approximately fifty books. Their discovery in the Egyptian desert in 1945 introduced yet another term to the biblical vocabulary. The Gnostics were part of the earliest Christian communities but were declared heretics, and by the late fourth century, they were ostracized by the orthodox into virtual extinction.

The Dead Sea Scrolls entered into the picture in 1947. Several previously unknown texts were discovered along with numerous Apocrypha and pseudepigrapha books as well as every book of the Hebrew canon except Esther and arguably Song of Songs. The significance of this find is the apparent sacred nature of books not included in the Jewish canon. By and large, it now appears that the LXX version, which is not canonized by Judaism, is superior to the Masoretic version, which is the accepted version of today's Jews and Protestants. By this I mean that the LXX is a closer witness to the original writings. The Samaritan Torah or Pentateuch is virtually in agreement with the LXX. An extant Samaritan version claims to be handed down from Aaron's great-grandson, but most scholars date it around the third century CE.

There still are ongoing arguments concerning what faith has the correct Bible. It almost seems futile to quibble over books that have little if any theological support that would show favor of one faith over the other. The one thing that we can ascertain is the fact that the Protestants dropped the Apocrypha from the Christian Bible and not the other way around. Perhaps this is why the Apocrypha is now being included in some modern Protestant Bibles mostly as a separate testament.

Next let us look into how the biblical books were determined as sacred scripture.

FORMATION OF THE HEBREW AND CHRISTIAN BIBLES

At the time, Jerusalem (about 70 CE) was under siege by Roman legions lead by Vespasian. Rabban Yochanan ben Zakkai escaped and appealed to Vespasian for permission to form a rabbinical college at Yavneh (Jamnia). Upon receiving his consent, ben Zakkai and his fellow rabbis set out to establish parameters to rededicate Judaism in the aftermath of their destroyed temple (70 CE). Just what books (out of the many) were to be considered sacred scripture was one item on their agenda.

The Talmud (authoritative rabbinic writings of Jewish civil and ceremonial law that includes the Mishnah and the Gemara) informs us that as late as the days of the Tannaim (200 CE), exactly what books were to be included in the canon was still *fluid*. However, Torah inclusion was positive and without dispute, so it included most prophetic works as well. These rabbis had numerous debates on which of the other books should be excluded from the canon (i.e., Song of Songs, Kohelet, and Ezekiel, which, of course, were finally included).

A Jewish expression called Sefarim Chitzonim, (meaning the Apocrypha—i.e., the books of the Maccabees, the book of Tobit, and the book of Judith) were books they decided not to accept. The primary reason was that they thought all of them were originally composed in Greek and not Hebrew. Of major significance was the rabbis' concern that Christians via the LXX had hijacked their scriptures, which constituted several of the texts in question. Therefore, the rabbis established a timeline cutoff date (about 430 BCE), citing the book of Malachi as a closing point and the requirement that the texts had to be originally written in Hebrew. Another deliberation concerned which books were simply too Christian, meaning that they contained elements that lent support to some Christian theologies.

However, the book of ben Sira (Sirach) was not considered to be a part of this and was allowed to remain, although this was not a unanimous choice. The Talmud has numerous quotations taken directly from the book of ben Sira, so it is obvious that it occupied a very special position among Jews for many centuries. Ben Sira would eventually be dropped from the Tanakh. Some offered reasons for this choice. The date of composition was correctly determined to be 250 CE, which was too late. Second, they erroneously assumed the original was written in Greek and not Hebrew. Third, the religious philosophy it contained was much too close to the Sadducee ideology, which was in opposition to their own, as they were all at this time in history Pharisees.

In Justin Martyr's *Dialogue with Trypho*, written shortly after the bar Kochba rebellion (132–135 CE), we have Justin accusing Trypho or the Jewish community (chapter LXXII) of removing passages from the LXX that were part of the books of Esdras and Jeremiah. At this same time, we know that Jews were in the process of translating their Hebrew Bible into Greek in order to counter the LXX, which was then considered to be the Christian domain. The rabbis sponsored a number of new Greek translations to compete with the LXX for Jewish consumption. Aquila, Symmachus, and Theodotion are the most significant of these translations that were calculated to be used by Jews instead of the LXX. These writings were all completed before the end of the second century, and they omitted the Apocrypha entirely.

Near the end of the fourth century, Western Christians desired the scriptures—now both New and Old—to be translated into Latin, which was their native tongue. Pope Damasus commissioned Jerome to translate the Hebrew and Greek scriptures into Latin. Jerome was a foremost scholar, and he set up his shop in Bethlehem. He had several Jewish scholars assist him in translating the Hebrew Bible. They, of course, showed preference toward the Jamnia canon in deference to the LXX. Initially, Jerome did not translate or include the fifteen books (the complete Apocrypha), which had been deemed unacceptable at Jamnia.

When Damasus, Augustine, and several other Eastern fathers protested this exclusion, Jerome reluctantly acquiesced. The argument was that the fifteen books had always been included in the LXX and that they had been considered scriptural for more than four hundred years. Their contention was that the LXX included the passages of every New Testament writer and therefore had to be included in any Christian scripture.

Jerome, a brilliant but stubborn scholar, argued against the inclusion, and he labeled these books the Apocrypha. Ultimately, he did concede and hastily translated these books. (He may have had two females actually do this work. This will be discussed later.) Jerome then rearranged the order of all the books (exactly as they now appear in the Christian Bibles of today), attempting to place them in chronological sequence. He also combined several books of Daniel, Jeremiah, and Esther that had once been separate books in the LXX, making them one respective unit in each book. This is why the Vulgate and Catholic Bibles contain only seven more books than the Jewish Bible. However, Orthodox Bibles use the LXX as it was passed down originally with all its fifteen books.

The council of Trent (1546) officially approved Jerome's Vulgate but excluded the Prayer of Manasseh and IV Esdras, which were part of the original LXX. The Eastern Orthodox churches have always *officially* included these as they had in the original LXX. Jerome's Vulgate became the Bible for the Western church from the fourth century on, though it was never granted official status until Trent. (There were three minor councils that did approve the Vulgate previously, but these were not considered binding on all Christians).

By the sixteenth century, corruption had permeated the Catholic Church, and the need to change became a challenge. The great reformer Martin Luther attempted to reform the Catholic Church. He saw many problems, one of which concerned the seven books. Therefore, he reinstituted the expression Apocrypha as a pejorative expression for the seven books. Significantly, he did include the Apocrypha in his German translation, but he continued to speak out against its inclusion in the canon. He did not believe the Apocrypha was divinely inspired as the other books were. Later the Protestant Reformers dropped the Apocrypha from their Bibles. To this day, however, no Protestant denomination has officially sanctioned any biblical books except the original autographs.

Archaeology, along with the Dead Sea Scrolls and the Samaritan Pentateuch, have given powerful and compelling evidence showing the superiority of the LXX as being the closest text to the original Bible, which certainly contained the Apocrypha well before the New Testament was conceived or written. While no one can argue for the right of any church to accept or reject any version of the Bible and/or decline any book of the Bible, it is clear that the Apocrypha was part and parcel of Christianity right from its very beginning!

Some prominent Protestant scholars and theologians even today still try to spin the historical facts, confounding the laypeople in this regard. Many of their arguments focus on the historical and geographical inaccuracies found in several books of the Apocrypha, just as similar inaccuracies occurring in the canonical books are surreptitiously glossed over. Yet the simple explanation is quite straightforward. These inaccuracies might merely be fictionalized episodes that were disguised to confuse enemies or to produce a didactic message. This exactly mirrors Arthur Miller's 1953 classic *The Crucible*, which shows a community that ignites and burns people alive with accusations of witchcraft, mass hysteria, and retribution. It's set in the small town of Salem, Massachusetts, in 1692, but it was really about McCarthyism and his activities along with the "House on Un-American Activities Committee" of the early 1950s in disguise.

A major concern of Protestants is their claim that books of the Apocrypha are never quoted in the New Testament. Thus, they cannot be considered to be canonical. Going by that standard of proof, we'd have to throw out Joshua, Judges, Ruth, 2 Kings, 1 Chronicles, 2 Chronicles, Ezra, Nehemiah, Esther, Ecclesiastes, Song of Solomon, Lamentations, Obadiah, Nahum, and Zephaniah because none of these Old Testament Books are quoted in the New Testament.

I have no religious or personal interests in the Apocrypha being included or not in the Bible. Absolutely no one can prove *divine inspiration* in any book. In order to claim such, it can only be based on *faith* and nothing more. Let us now examine a book of the Apocrypha that clearly uses fictional history for strictly didactic purposes.

The Book of Judith

Without a doubt, this is the most pro-feminist biblical book. It is the only book of the Bible featuring a woman in a protagonist role void of any masculine support. She was beautiful, intelligent, religious, and very patriotic. To top it all off, she was very modest and humble.

This book is not found in most Protestant Bibles, but it is included in the Apocrypha section of those that do include it. Moreover, it is not incorporated in the Hebrew Bible either. The earliest Protestant Bibles originally did contain all the books of the Apocrypha as did the original 1611 King James Version, but Judith along with all the Apocrypha was expunged in the late seventeenth century. The Reformers had several good incentives for not accepting the Apocrypha, especially the book of Judith. Let us look into some of them.

The Catholic Bible was (and basically still is) Jerome's Vulgate, which for about a thousand years was *the* Bible of Western Christianity. (The Orthodox Bibles also include the Apocrypha and, of course, Judith.) Jerome did not believe Judith belonged in the Bible but was coerced to include it by Pope Damasus I and Augustine. So he hastily translated it in only a few hours. He wrote that his copies had numerous discrepancies and that he translated only what he believed was the correct understanding of the Chaldaic replicas he had before him.

Jerome knew Judith was not part of the Jewish canon. Therefore, he reasoned the Jews certainly were the best judges on which books should be included in their Bible. If they didn't accept it, Christianity shouldn't either. Judith is loaded with very obvious anachronisms, geographical errors, towns that never existed, and generals no one ever heard of. And a woman, of all things, was the only hero! In other words, it appeared to be nothing but pure fiction. Even Catholic scholars silently raised these same questions. But the Council of Trent (1545–63) approved most of the books of the Apocrypha and included them in the canon of their official Bible, and Catholics had to accept that.

Another group of apocryphal books that bears an important role in Bible history are the books of the Maccabees. There are four books of the Maccabees that exist. However, only the first and second are considered sacred or canonical by the majority of Christians, while all four are rejected by Judaism. Protestant Christianity also rejects all four and considers the first and second to be apocryphal and third and fourth to be pseudepigraphic. We will discuss only the first and second, combined with a summary of the disputed ritual of "praying for the dead."

BOOKS OF THE MACCABEES

First Maccabees is considered by most scholars to be the best history of the entire Bible. Events and geographical descriptions are corroborated by Josephus, while 2 Maccabees is supported to some extent by Polybius of Megalopolis. The unknown author of 1 Maccabees is clearly well educated with a strong penchant for history. Undoubtedly Jewish and quite religious, the author keeps his personal convictions to a minimum. The same is not true for 2 Maccabees. Here the unknown author demonstrates his Pharisaic fervor though frankly describing the events. Actually, the author of 2 Maccabees candidly references his source, which he had condensed from an original five-volume book into his own version. Obviously, the theological portions are that of the author and are perhaps a reason why 2 Maccabees is not included in the Protestant Bible.

Both Maccabees illustrates the history of the Maccabean revolt against the Seleucid Greeks who then controlled Judea, which was then a part of the Syrian Empire that the Seleucids inherited after the death of Alexander the Great. Second Maccabees only covers the period from the high priest Onias III and King Seleucus IV (180 BCE) to the defeat of Nicanor in 161, while 1 Maccabees encompasses the period between the years 175 and 135 BCE. This successful revolution is considered to be one of the most significant events in Jewish history, yet it is not part of their Bible. This is why it is so baffling to historians.

Historian Daniel J. Harrington writes in *Invitation to the Apocrypha*,

> There has been, however, a puzzling ambivalence about 1 and 2 Maccabees in the Jewish tradition. Hanukkah, which celebrates the cleansing and rededication of the Jerusalem temple in 164 B.C.E. … is part of the traditional Jewish calendar of festivals. Since it is likely that 1 Maccabees was composed in Hebrew, its absence from the canon of Hebrew Scriptures is somewhat puzzling. These puzzlements have led some scholars to suspect that at some point in the first century there was a Jewish reaction against the Maccabees and what they stood for, and a deliberate attempt to push them out of the sacred tradition of Judaism. Perhaps in light of a failed uprising against the Romans by Jews claiming to follow the example of Judas and his brothers, the custodians of the Jewish tradition found the Maccabees too controversial and dangerous. The revival of interest in the Maccabees as men of action and noble warriors in the modern state of Israel suggests that these suspicions have some basis in fact.

Late in the first century CE, the Jewish sages living in Mesopotamia sought to lessen the Maccabees' significance in the Hanukah story. These were the scholars who were writing the Babylonian Talmud. Because a recently failed Jewish revolt in Palestine had brought disastrous repercussions, these scholars feared Rome would certainly look askance to any sign of commemorating a Jewish successful revolt. Therefore, they turned their focus on the miracle of the menorah oil indubitably to accentuate the role of God in the legend and to discount the military victory of the Maccabees. Another reason could be that many of these Jewish scholars, who were all dedicated Pharisees, believed that 1 Maccabees was penned by a Sadducee, their once adversaries, and they supposed that the Sadducees were responsible for the failed revolt against the Romans. At the same time, early Christians were actively collecting Jewish and Hebrew writings, thus preserving them for a history that included the Maccabees. The Maccabees were included in the Greek Septuagint of the first century, and the Christians were now proclaiming the Septuagint as their Bible, which also gave purpose to the rejection.

While the Jewish rejection of the Maccabees is difficult to understand, the Protestant reasons are not. The Catholic Church ratified the doctrine of purgatory at the Second Council of Lyon in 1274. This doctrine was formalized over a long period of time, and it stemmed from the belief that purgatory had a foundation, biblical and otherwise, that was based on the practice of praying for the dead. Prayers for the dead carried over from Judaism (as a part of Jewish services) into early Christianity. Even today these Jewish prayers are offered on behalf of the deceased and are known as *Kaddish*, which in Aramaic means "sanctification." Furthermore, the Hebrew Bible distinctly states that a necromancer was able to raise Samuel from the dead because he had expired less than twelve months ago "and the soul stays close to the body for this period." This account very clearly states that it was Samuel and not a demon or spirit deceiving Saul and pretending to be Samuel (1 Samuel 28:3–20). We will go into more of the details on this later.

The concept of purgatory fed a policy of earning *indulgences* so that people could reduce the time a soul spent there, though this was initially achieved by doing good deeds, praying, or almsgiving. Ultimately, this led to the church selling indulgences to finance church projects. This became a major cause in the Protestant Reformation. The sixteenth-century Protestants continued at first with the traditional custom of praying for the dead, but before long, they became opposed to it, mostly because they believed it had no biblical foundation. The Catholic reaction was then to scour the Bible in an effort to disprove this Protestant claim.

Second Maccabees 12:42–46, Tobit 12:12, and Wisdom 3:1–7 were offered as direct proof. A New Testament source given was the apostle Paul talking about baptism for the dead in 1 Corinthians 15:29. Many also offered several other biblical passages (e.g., 2 Timothy 1:16–18) that alluded to the practice. Many Protestants claimed these passages were so ambiguous that they all led to unreasonable conclusions. This became a principal reason for the reformers to reject Maccabees as well as the entire Apocrypha. Another reason for this was it conveniently conformed to the Jewish rejections of the same books.

Praying for the dead was common to early Christianity. Inscriptions on ancient tombstones and on numerous Roman catacombs as well as in writings of several early church fathers bear this out. It is not exclusive to Catholics, as the Eastern Orthodox churches teach prayer for the dead is beneficial for them and is expressed in their divine liturgy. Many jurisdictions that affiliate with the Church of England practice praying for the dead, which often includes offering the Sunday liturgy for the peace, naming departed Christians and keeping All Soul's Day. In Judaism, the Kaddish is said for the dead to keep the memory and good name of the deceased alive.

It is obvious that praying for the dead clearly implies that there is a benefit to be gained for the deceased. However, in an article in the magazine *The Evangelist*, the Reverend Jimmy Swaggart states, "Scripture clearly reveals that all the demands of divine justice on the sinner have been completely fulfilled in Jesus Christ. It also reveals that Christ has totally redeemed or purchased back, that which was lost. The advocates of a purgatory (and the necessity of prayer for the dead) say, in effect, that the redemption of Christ was incomplete ... It has all been done for us by Jesus Christ, there is nothing to be added or done by man." This would be typical of most Protestant understandings.

DEVELOPMENTS IN THE BIBLE

The chronology of the Hebrew Bible does not follow the order as we find it in Christian Bibles. Furthermore, in the Old Testament, there is not one particular and definitely fixed era from which all of its events are dated, though that is the case in Christian history. We should also take note that the Christian Old Testament order of books is different from that found in the Jewish Bible, although the books themselves are the same.

We will now attempt to offer a relative though partial chronological order in which books of the Old Testament were composed or referred to in a particular historical setting.

It is widely accepted that because the Pentateuch (Torah) starts with Genesis, it was the first book to be written. If we closely examine the text, we see that Noah was told by God to "take every clean beast and you shall take by sevens, the male and his female: and of beasts that are not clean by two, the male and his female" (Genesis 7:2). However, we are not told which animals are clean or unclean until God much later gives Moses the exact parameters (Leviticus 11). This would suggest that Leviticus was written before Genesis. Of course, God could have told Noah, but it just was not recorded and then later reiterated to Moses.

Let us take note concerning another interesting series of events that occur in 1 Samuel 19:13 (NIV) and 16. Verse 13 says, "Then Michal took an *idol* and laid it on the bed, covering it with a garment and putting some goats' hair at the head." Verse 16 says, "But when the men entered, there was the **idol** in the bed, and at the head was some goats' hair." As a side note, in some more recent Bible versions, the Hebrew word *teraphim* is substituted for the word *idol*.

Genesis 31:19 says, "At the time they left, Laban was some distance away, shearing his sheep. Rachel stole her father's household *gods* (idols) and took them with her." In some versions *teraphim* is also substituted for the word *gods*. The same holds true in Judges 17:5, which says, "Micah set up a shrine, and he made a sacred ephod and some household *idols*. Then he installed one of his sons as the priest." Idols again are used or are rendered in some versions as *teraphim*. Zechariah 10:2 says, "Household *gods* (*teraphim*) give false advice, fortune-tellers predict only lies, and interpreters of dreams pronounce comfortless falsehoods. So my people are wandering like lost sheep, without a shepherd to protect and guide them."

To clarify my side note, *The Jewish Encyclopedia* writes,

> The word "teraphim" is explained by the Rabbis as meaning "disgraceful things" ... Plural word of unknown derivation used in the Old Testament to denote the primitive Semitic house-gods whose cult had been handed down to historical times from the earlier period of nomadic wanderings. ... It may be noted that teraphim were regarded in early times as representatives of *real gods* endowed with divine attributes (comp. Gen. 31: 30, where Laban, rebuking Jacob for Rachel's theft of the teraphim, asks, "Wherefore hast thou stolen my gods?"), and that evidently the teraphim cult was practically on a plane with YHWH worship.

From this we see that the *idols* at these biblical times were considered to be *gods*. In other words, the idols were actually gods in and of themselves and were worshipped as such. This was very common in greater ancient Mesopotamia. Worship of this type became a very important segment in Hebrew society and was only later considered to be sinful. In fact, it was later looked upon as perhaps *the* greatest sin, as it clearly opposed monotheistic thinking.

Just when did this *later* occur? Back to the Bible!

"I am the Lord thy God; thou shalt not have strange gods before me." This defines strange gods as idolizing material images which were considered gods, to the point they are held in superstition as being a divine gods. This was so important that it was the *first commandment* given by God to Moses. By interpreting biblical chronology, scholars have determined that Moses was born about 1525 BCE, the Exodus was about 1440 BCE, Samuel lived about 1040 BCE, David about 1000 BCE, and Zechariah about 520 BCE. In none of the biblical passages, except that of Zechariah, do we see any concern against idolatry. (Note that Zechariah was a contemporary of Ezra.) Rachael would have lived before the Ten Commandments were issued. Therefore, idolatry would not have been a sin in her time (as it was after Moses).

However, by David's time (well after Moses), this should have been in effect for a long period of time. Yet we can see from the books of Samuel that *idolatry* and even murder does not seem to be of any concern. This would suggest that the books of Samuel were written before the Pentateuch or before *idolatry* was even considered a sin. Taking this a step further, we can then assume that Samuel was known of and was possibly in a written form before the composition of the Pentateuch or Torah.

Moving next to the books of Kings, we see that the Passover had not been celebrated in the past (2 Kings 23:19–24). The high priest Hilkiah discovered an old scroll during the remodeling of the temple (2 Kings 22:8; 2 Chronicles 34:22–28). He quickly took the scroll to the king and declared to him that it was a recording of sacred law and covenant of Yahweh. The contents of the scroll revealed that many sins were ongoing both in the past and at the present. It also becomes obvious that the Ten Commandments were either unknown or had not been written down prior to this discovery. At that time the king was Josiah, who quickly recognized this and issued a decree requiring full civil compliance with these newly discovered laws. He now started or reinstituted Passover and destroyed all the rival religious sites in both Judah and in Israel (2 Kings 23:21–22). Here Josiah's invasion of Israel is significant because the territory was the former nation of Israel. At this time it was part of Assyria and had been since 722 BCE.

These passages in 2 Kings and 2 Chronicles describe a biblical discovery of major consequence. From this time forward, this scroll would be copied, revised, and edited along with new books that would be written later. By the second century CE at the Council of Jamnia, a collection of books would be sorted out, voted on, and canonized. It then would be declared sacred scripture or the Bible.

Now let us examine what was actually discovered. Surely, it could not have been all of the five books or scrolls of the Pentateuch. Most scholars believe it was a proto-Deuteronomy scroll.

This scroll was taken along during the exile in Babylon and was used as a basis for the other four books, which only existed in oral tradition and in varying organized writings from texts that may now be considered "Lost Books of the Bible" (2 Kings 23:28). While at the time of the Babylon captivity, it was Ezra and his priestly cohorts who edited and revised to suit the current theological concerns. So important is the religious revival of Josiah that it is also recorded in the books of Jeremiah and Zephaniah and the same story appears in 2 Chronicles 34:14–19.

What we may be able to assume is that the books of Joshua, Judges, 1 and 2 Samuel, and 1 and 2 Kings were written in their original forms before the Pentateuch and were later edited and revised by Ezra and/or his associates. He then completed this around the time of the return from captivity. Ezra would then add 1 Chronicles, 2 Chronicles, Ezra, and perhaps even Nehemiah, which he wrote and included in his collection of scripture. The books of Esther and Ruth would be written after the death of Ezra as a counter to Ezra's anti-intermarriage edict.

But why Ezra?

Ezra led a group of exiles to Jerusalem under authorization from Artaxerxes (Chronicles 7–8) about fifty-eight years after the second temple was dedicated. Ezra saw a serious problem with mixed marriages. Ezra was very concerned that the Jewish community had not yet the complied with the will of God since it was still under bondage to Persian power (Chronicles 9:7). Within a year of Ezra's departure from Babylon, a purified community was created in Jerusalem. Ezra's actions included a forced divorce of 110 or 111 men who had intermarried with foreign women (Ezra 10:9–44).

Ezra the prophet assembled the Bible, changed the Hebrew alphabet, which was then Paleo-Hebrew (a variant of the Phoenician alphabet) to the current square script, and introduced the synagogue (although it was not actually called a *synagogue* until later) as a substitute place of worship in lieu of the destroyed temple. It was said of Ezra that if the Torah had not been given to Moses, he would have been worthy to receive it (Talmud. *Sanhedrin*. 4–4). He reinvigorated Judaism and scripture, while some considered him to be the father of rabbinic Judaism. With the completion of Ezra's rendition of the Bible, he then read it for the first time to the people of Jerusalem.

As written in Nehemiah 8:1–3,

> All the people gathered together into the square before the Water Gate. They told the scribe Ezra to bring the book of the Law of Moses [this was in 444 BCE], which the LORD had given to Israel. Accordingly, the priest Ezra brought the

law before the assembly, both men and women and all who could hear with understanding. This was on the first day of the seventh month. He read from it facing the square before the Water Gate from early morning until midday, in the presence of the men and the women and those who could understand; and the ears of all the people were attentive to the book of the law. [This likely meant the Torah.]

It is my opinion that Ezra and his staff, while living in Babylon, took the proto-Deuteronomy scroll that was discovered during the reign of Josiah and constructed the Torah. This is not to say that he invented any of the narratives, but quite the contrary. He had several written documents to reference. (See chapter four, "Lost Books of the Bible.") Some of them spoke of the same events but had some basic differences. These differences were traditionally well known and were part of an oral tradition that had strong theological implications. So Ezra rewrote these accounts by weaving the different narratives into a single structure; however, he preserved each version within its own textual framework, even though they could conflict. Scholars call this literary device "doublets."

In the Old Testament, these doublets are repeats with different characters or different emphasis. For example, there are two creation stories (Genesis 1 and Genesis 2). There are three stories of a patriarch traveling among pagans and pretending his wife is his sister. There are two stories of Moses striking a rock to produce water. There are two versions of the Ten Commandments (one in Exodus, and one that is recapped in Deuteronomy) with slightly different wording. Furthermore, the numbers of days of the two flood stories don't add up correctly.

At one point Noah (as I have previously mentioned) takes two of each animal. At another point he takes two of some but seven of others. Joseph is sold into slavery to Ishmaelites in one verse but to Midianites a few verses later. The Mountain of Revelation is sometimes called Sinai and sometimes Horeb. Moses's father-in-law is sometimes called Yitro and sometimes Ruel.

Ezra's purpose was to maintain the sacredness of what he believed were the words of God. He then added didactic stories and other details to elucidate the current circumstances and wrote the two books of Chronicles in an attempt to offer some sort of chronology and to clarify the confusion caused by the doublets. Ezra was not concerned with any kind of set historical chronology, as he only wanted to present a thematic rendering showing the religious integrity of God and emphasizes the role and position of the priesthood. Another interesting fact is that

Ezra was the great-grandson of the high priest Hilkiah, the one who discovered the book of Deuteronomy while remodeling the temple of Solomon.

The majority of Jews and Christians believe the Bible originated with Moses's visit with God at the top of Mount Sinai when he received the Ten Commandments. Afterward, Moses put to writing the first five books we now call the Torah or Pentateuch. The balance of the Tanakh or Old Testament followed as composed over many years by divinely inspired authors who didactically reaffirmed the first five books through various philosophical or historical narrations.

There is another theory that disputes the common authorship of Ezra, Nehemiah, and Chronicles. A majority of scholars once believed that these books formed a consistent harmony and called it "the Chronicler's History." This theory suggests that because the language and theological expressions in Chronicles and Ezra-Nehemiah vary, they must have disconnected origins. The theory asserts that Chronicles has two specific subjects, the reckoning and the prophecy are absent from Ezra-Nehemiah. Furthermore Chronicles conveys a somewhat more positive observation of the people from the Northern tribes which was Israel. This is in contrast to the Israel in Ezra-Nehemiah, which is limited to Judah and Benjamin.

Although their theory implies these books had different authors, they do agree that several common themes pertain to the city of Jerusalem and its temple, their priests, and worship. Furthermore, the period in which they were written occurred during the postexilic or Persian period (539–330 BCE). Another idea to be considered is that Ezra wrote Chronicles while in exile in combination with his fellow scribes and priests, and they did so after they had completed editing and redacting the books of Samuel and Kings. Then they wrote Ezra-Nehemiah after their arrival in Jerusalem, and they later made only minor revisions to Chronicles, changes that reflected the present conditions they were encountering.

It was once believed that the author of Chronicles used a text of Samuel-Kings that was in accordance with the one we now have in our present Bibles. However, scholars discovered some time ago that the Hebrew and Greek texts (Septuagint or LXX) of Samuel in numerous cases differ significantly. The LXX is presently considered to be a closer rendering of the original text. This opinion was enhanced by the discovery of the Dead Sea Scrolls, where three copies of Samuel found in Cave 4, called 4QSam^a, 4QSam^b, 4QSam^c. Here the story in Chronicles about David differs from Chronicles in the present text of Samuel-Kings. The reason for this is the author of Chronicles had a different writing of Samuel and Kings. The variation was not created by the author of Chronicles himself, but it was already part of a text of Samuel and Kings before the author's text of Chronicles was committed to writing.

Asserting prophetic power, the author of Chronicles writes his account of David (1 Chronicles 29:29) by claiming his sources of his information about David are recorded in the history of Samuel the seer (who died before David became king), in the history of Nathan the prophet, and in the history of Gad the seer. (All three books are considered to be lost books of the Bible.)

This could explain some of the inconsistencies found in Samuel. Found in 2 Samuel 21:19, we see that Elhanan, a Bethlehemite, killed Goliath the Gittite. A few scholars have suggested that Elhanan was a different name or nickname for David, whereas others have opined that an act committed by an otherwise unknown Elhanan was used to enhance the image of David in 1 Samuel 17. Whatever the case, the author of Chronicles decidedly has reconciled this problem by declaring that Elhanan killed Lahmi, the brother of Goliath (1 Chronicles 20:5). Accordingly, we know that *Lahmi* is derived from the last two syllables of the Hebrew word *Bethlehemite*.

Another inconsistency in Chronicles states that David's sons were the chief officials in the service of the king (1 Chronicles 18:17), whereas 2 Samuel 8:18 tells us David's sons were priests. Suggesting that the author of Chronicles refused to permit a reference where non-Levites become priests, therefore usurping the divine right granted to the descendants of Aaron.

The author of Chronicles robustly advocates his support for the temple in Jerusalem by declaring that the priesthood and their worship customs had been established by David and Solomon. In 1 Chronicles 10:29, he tells the story of David as the ideal monarch who established Jerusalem as the center of worship as his top priority. In so doing, the author of Chronicles radically reworked the stories of David in 1 Samuel 16 and 1 Kings 2, which had been included in the Deuteronomistic history. That history was probably completed in the sixth century BCE, nearly two centuries before the Chronicles were written.

Moses lived around 450 years before David. It is generally believed God revealed to Moses the events of creation, the great flood, the tower of Babel, and so forth and that Moses put all of this in a written format. The rest of the Old Testament or Tanakh was comprised after Moses, ostensibly ending with the book of Malachi (the Jewish Bible ending with Nehemiah), which scholars assign a date of around 445 BCE. In short, the Old Testament covers history from creation to about 445 BCE, which is incorporated within thirty-nine books (same as the twenty-four books in the Hebrew Tanakh).

Christians adopted these writings (actually using the Greek translation known as the Septuagint or LXX) and composed a collection of new writings now called the New Testament, which basically begins with the birth of Jesus, presumed as the year 1 CE, and ending with the book of Revelation, which was written around the year 95 CE, comprising twenty-seven individual books.

The Hebrew or Jewish Bible was primarily canonized around the year 90 CE shortly after the destruction of the second Jewish temple. At this time, numerous biblical-type writings abounded. Several of these writings were not accepted into this canon for various reasons, but the first Christians chose some to include as part of their scriptures. A number of these more prominent books would become known as the Apocrypha, and they would be a point of contention soon after the Protestant Reformation in the sixteenth century.

In 383 CE, Pope Damasus I commissioned Jerome, an outstanding scholar, to translate the Old and New Testaments into Latin, known today as the Vulgate. This was done in order to establish a canon of sacred scriptures and to make them available in the vernacular of the Western Roman Empire. The Greek-speaking Eastern Empire at this time had the New Testament in its original language, which was Greek. However, a few books of the Old Testament (1 Esdras and the 3 Maccabees) were omitted in the Vulgate. Many rejected Revelation, however, and some had concerns about 2 Peter. They were still questioning the inclusion of a few others too. Their Old Testament was the entire Greek Septuagint. At a later date, they would come to accept all of the books as establish by Jerome.

The New Testament canon was approved in the fourth century through the local synods of Hippo (393) and Carthage (397), and it included all twenty-seven books. Another local synod of Laodicia (350) excluded Revelation, which affected only the Greek or Eastern church. However, the book was finally included in the canon of the New Testament and authorized by the Sixth Ecumenical Council. The Old Testament or Hebrew Bible (the Tanakh) contains numerous genres spread over many segments called books. The basic categories are mythical and legendary, legal, annals, prophetic, genealogic, poetic, allegory, didactic, wisdom, proverbial, and apocalyptic. Myth is found in several of the books. To clarify, I define myth as a written narrative whose source has been lost. It could also be didactic fiction. Let us examine this in the book of Genesis. Our first of two offerings is from Genesis 3.

Metaphor or allegory in the Bible is often used. Now some may dispute this, but the biblical text is quite revealing in this regard. Song of Songs is certainly so, and Genesis has several instances. This first verse is very allegorical, and in my opinion, the story of the two trees is legendary. In order to understand the significance of the two trees, we must explore Genesis 3 to establish a foundation. Let's start with verses 1 through 5 (NWT).

> Now the serpent proved to be the most cautious of all the wild beasts of the field that Jehovah God had made. So it began to say to the woman: "Is it really so that God said you must not eat of every tree of the garden?" At this the woman

said to the serpent: "Of the fruit of the trees (note the plural) of the garden we may eat. But as for (eating) of the fruit of the tree (note the singular) that is in the middle of the garden, God has said, 'You must not eat from it, no, you must not touch it that you do not die.'" At this the serpent said to the woman: "You positively will not die. For God knows that in the very day of your eating from it your eyes are bound to be opened and you are bound to be like God knowing good and bad."

In Genesis 2:17 **of** the Jewish Bible, God states, "But as for the tree of knowledge of good and bad, you must not eat of it; for as soon as you eat of it, you shall die."

First of all, the serpent is not Satan or the devil, although most people assume it is. The text clearly does not say so! Second, most of us believe the serpent is literally lying to Eve, while God is stating the absolute truth. (Keep this in mind.)

Verse 7 says, "Then the eyes of both of them became opened and they began to realize that they were naked. Hence they sewed fig leaves together and made loin coverings for themselves."

Their eyes were now open, and they did not die, confirming the accurate statement of the serpent in verses 4 and 5. The question now is this: Did God lie? Obviously, at least biblically, they lived for several hundred years afterward.

Verse 14 says, "And Jehovah God proceeded to say to the serpent: 'Because you have done this thing, you are the cursed one out of all the domesticated animals and out of all the wild beasts of the field. Upon your belly you will go and dust is what you will eat all the days of your life.'"

Here is confirmation that the serpent is not Satan or the devil, suggesting that the serpent may have had legs before the fall. At this point we must also assume that God has previously explained to Adam and Eve exactly what death was. Does "opened eyes" sound like a literal term or a metaphor? Obviously, Adam would need to have sight in order to cultivate the Garden of Eden. Another question presents itself when they feel it's necessary to sow fig leaves to cover their nakedness. If there were only the two of them in existence, what were they ashamed of?

Verse 22 says, "And Jehovah God went on to say: 'Here the man has become as one of us in knowing good and bad, and now in order that he may not put out his hand and actually take (fruit) also from of the tree of life and eat and live to time indefinite.'" And verse 24 says, "And he drove the man out and posted at the east of the Garden of Eden the Cherubs and a flaming blade of a sword that was turning itself continually to guard the way to the tree of life."

God is speaking as if He was discussing the fate of Adam with another divine person (or persons) and is implying that they feared that Adam would sneak back into the garden and eat from the Tree of Life and then live forever. Thus, He established these armed cherubs with flaming swords to guard the garden as insurance. This also clearly implied that the Tree of Life was not located in the middle of the garden and was not forbidden fruit.

Had Adam eaten from the Tree of Life beforehand instead of eating from the Tree of Knowledge of Good and Evil, it would not have been possible for him to die. Therefore, God's threat of instant death was only true if they ate from the Tree of Knowledge only or at least from it first! This also proves that the serpent did not lie to Eve!

Why was the serpent trying to lead Eve to her death in the first place? This begs another question: What if Adam had refused to eat? Would only Eve then have to die? Furthermore, didn't God give Adam dominion over all the animals? Obviously, He didn't have dominion over the serpent. At this time (was there such a thing then as *time*?) was this the only serpent, or were all the serpents deceivers? And was the serpent the only animal that could speak, or could all the animals speak?

Of course, none of this means anything or needs further exegesis if we assume these passages are only to be taken symbolically or metaphorically. However, there are other explanations. One explanation says that it is only an ancient story that was passed down orally from numerous variant sources and was used to explain the origin of the universe. The variants were then assembled in the fifth century BCE and put to writing, which became the sacred scripture. Today most Christians believe in a figurative or symbolic interpretation of Genesis and do not think that it is actual history. Yet many accept the literal without question, which is exactly what faith is all about. Faith does not require proof. Now we move on to the second part in Genesis.

Genesis 6:1–4 says,

> And it came to pass, when men began to multiply on the face of the earth, and daughters were born unto them. That the sons of God saw the daughters of men that they were fair; and they took them wives of all which they chose. And the LORD said My spirit shall not always strive with man, for that he also is flesh: yet his days shall be a hundred twenty years. There were giants in the earth in those days; and also after that, when the sons of God came in unto the daughters of men, and they bear children to them, the same became mighty men which were of old, men of renown.

This verse, which was taken from the King James Version, has bewildered many scholars and Bible students for centuries. It was so troubling that before the turn of the Common Era, a few pseudepigraphic writings—today called 4QEnochb and 1QGenesis Apocryphon—were in circulation, each attempting to offer explanations. Copies of these were found in the Dead Sea Scrolls cache, which demonstrates how these ancients tried to clarify or expand the text of Genesis to satisfy their concerns.

Just who were these "sons of God?" In the Jewish Bible, they are called "divine beings." Genesis 4 (NIV) calls the giants "the Nephilim" as is the case in the Jewish Bible. The Hebrew words are *ha-nephilim*, and for sons of God, the word is *benei ha-elohim*. Nearly every Bible translation has some variations of the wordings, especially in verse 4. Many speak of the Nephilim as being giants. (This is the case recorded in the LXX.) Several others just omit this term entirely.

Genesis suggests these giants (the Greek word being *gigantes*) were the sons of God who mated with human women and produced an offspring of giants. There are several explanations for who these sons of God were exactly. Some suggest they were fallen angels. But the biblical text clearly does not offer any information to suggest that this may be true. Notwithstanding, some refer to the New Testament and Jude 1:6–12 for support. However, here Jude quotes directly from the pseudepigrapha book of Enoch, which does indeed speak of fallen angels. Enoch was a very popular nonbiblical story in the last two centuries BCE and the first century CE. There seems to be little doubt that the author of the book of Enoch focused especially in on Genesis 6:1–4 by using this to explain how the devil became the force of evil in the world. This would also manifest itself in the psyche of Jude, Jesus, and most of the New Testament writers.

Another explanation offered by some conservative biblical scholars states that the line of Cain ceased to bear male children, producing only female offspring. The line of Seth continued to produce virile males. Though they were considered "the righteous people or sons of God," these males were at any rate "stirred to passion" over the females from the line of Cain. As a result, God gave humankind only 120 years in which to repent or bear the consequences (i.e., the great flood). This theory developed out of the Syriac Peshitta (an Aramaic translation from the third century CE). There is no canonical biblical foundation for this explanation whatsoever, but it has found favor with some conservative instructors.

Of course, the implication in these verses is that the sons of God are nonhuman beings, perhaps angels or semi-divine creatures. This is based on the Hebrew *nephilim*, meaning "fallen ones," harkening to Enoch and his fallen angels. We must remember the ancient written Hebrew language did not have vowels and was written with all capital letters, so its original form would have looked something like NFLM. Therefore, the word *nephilim* did not reach this rendering until the tenth century (916 CE) when the Masoretes began to add vowels where they believed it was appropriate to do so. This means that *nephilim* possibly may not be exactly the correct Hebrew word, meaning while translating from one language to another some words can somewhat obscure its real meaning. For example, the Greek translation, the Septuagint (abbreviated as LXX) of the third century BCE, which translated this word as *gigantes*, meaning giants, clearly not fallen angels or fallen ones. Therefore, it is possible that the original Hebrew could have meant something else.

Josephus, a contemporary of Jesus, believed that the sons of God were angels as he clearly alludes to in Genesis 6. "For many angels of God accompanied with women, and begat sons that proved unjust, and despisers of all that was good, on account of the confidence they had in their own strength; for the tradition is, That these men did what resembled the acts of those whom the Grecians call giants" (Antiquities of the Jews, 1.3.1). In the very next statement, Josephus speaks of Noah and God's plan to save humankind by building an ark, one that God commanded Noah to produce—obviously following the exact same basis and chronological order that was presented in both Genesis and in the apocryphal book 1 Enoch.

My hypothesis theorizes these verses were added to the Genesis text around the time the Jews returned from the Babylonian exile. The intention was to drive home the message concerning intermarriage with foreigners as being offensive toward God. Ezra clearly wants to keep his people *pure* (Ezra 9:1–2, Nehemiah 13:1–2, 23–26). In Ezra's time the Samaritans offered to help rebuild the temple, an offer the Jews totally rejected. Then and even in the time of Jesus, they thought that Samaritans were a polluted people and did not consider them to be among God's chosen ones.

Most scholars believe the Torah or Pentateuch was initially accepted into a Jewish canon during the time of Ezra, perhaps designated by Ezra himself. Before this time written scrolls were few and inconsistent—that is, until prior to the return from exile. Most of the books of the Torah were assembled together in final written form during the exile in Babylon by combining oral traditions with the various writings. Genesis was the last book of the Pentateuch to reach its final written form. God (in Genesis) tells Noah to load the ark with clean and unclean animals, but we first discover which animals were clean and unclean much later in Leviticus during the time of Moses, which suggested a different order (Genesis 7:2; Leviticus 11:3).

Next we should take note that these verses may easily be omitted and that the story line would continue uninterrupted and flow smoothly. This indicates the work of a possible editor. Some could argue that this story is somehow related to the wickedness God was speaking of.

Remarkably, no abominations or violation of laws to that effect are cited in the Bible. However, in Numbers 13:33, we see the *nephilim* again living in the time of Moses, which in this case insinuates they are strong humans or giants. It also makes no reference to "sons of God" or even implying as much.

In ancient Middle Eastern mythology, giants were almost always the product of intermarriage between human beings and their gods. This then is clearly a mythical aspect of the story in Genesis, which was adopted from the cultural context of the ancient world. Now whether or not the Jews believed in the other gods in the myths is not my focus here. The point is that Ezra or his associates took this particular section of myth, namely that these giants were the unsavory result of intermarriage between the gods and human beings, and used that to illustrate the depths to which the disruption in the world had reached. This indicates just how serious the crossing of boundaries had become. Intermarriage now was equally as bad as it was then and had resulted in God destroying the entire world. We can see other didactic stories added to other biblical books, such as the stories of Samson, Delilah, Ahab, and Jezebel, which also emphasize the disastrous events caused by intermarriage, suggesting the work of Ezra.

It is generally believed Ezra was the one responsible for naming, writing, selecting, and forming several of the books that ultimately came to make up the Old Testament canon. Many scholars believe he decided, edited, and arranged most of the scriptures into the general divisions of the Law, Prophets, and Holy Writings, which has survived to the present. In addition to giving Ezra credit for the initial formulation of the Old Testament canon, it is often suggested that Ezra authored the books of Ezra as well as 1 and 2 Chronicles. He was a scholar, a priest, and most importantly, a scribe.

In 2 Kings 22:8, the high priest Hilkiah discovered a sacred scroll of scripture while remodeling the temple a few years before the fall of Judah. It is important to understand that prior to this time, knowledge of the law of Moses, at least in written form, was unknown and certainly was not being practiced (2 Kings 23:1–7). Most scholars believe this book was a proto-Deuteronomy scroll that was then taken to Babylon during the exile. In other words, this was the first written document of the Torah or Pentateuch. In Ezra 7:1, we discover Hilkiah is the great- or great-great-grandfather of Ezra.

Using proto-Deuteronomy as the foundation, Ezra blended together an assortment of the current and obscure religious writings with numerous oral traditions that held sacred meanings. And Ezra diligently assembled the Torah into writing. He was "a ready scribe in the law of Moses" who "had prepared his heart to seek the law of the Lord and to do it, and to teach in Israel statutes and judgments." Ezra was the first well-defined example of an order of men who never ceased in Judaism or the church, men of religious erudition who devote their lives to the study of the scriptures so that they may be worthy to interpret them for the instruction and edification of their religious followers. Ezra was faithful to preserve the oral and written traditions, as there are several puzzling doublets in the Torah that certainly reflect two varying writings or oral traditions. Here we see the creation narrative (Genesis 1–2), the flood narrative (Genesis 6–8), the selling of Joseph (Genesis 37:25–28, 36), Abraham's half-truth, and passing Sarah off as his sister (Genesis 12:10–20; 20:1–18; 26:6–11). Ezra's unscrupulous devotion to recording sacred scripture accurately mandated that he incorporate these doublets. He also felt compelled to didactically expound the will of God as found in Leviticus while regarding the nationalist purity into the text of Genesis 6:1–4.

The Babylon exile (586 BCE) ended with the edict of Cyrus (538 BCE). The first group of returnees was led by Zerubbabel and/or Sheshbazzar about 536 BCE. Enormous problems faced those who returned. The Jews who had remained and had not been taken to Babylon still resided in Judah along with those who the Babylonians had moved in from other areas had now taken over the land. They now considered it their own (Ezekiel 33:24–29). They were resentful of those who had returned and wanted to reclaim ancestral land. Besides, many of those who had remained, especially the Samaritans, saw themselves as the only true heirs of the promises (Ezra 4:1–5). Surrounding tribes saw the return as a new threat to their own local control of the area. For most of the next century, the returned Jews would be harassed by marauding bands of local tribesmen who saw no benefit in having a walled city rebuilt in their territory (Nehemiah 4:1–7:5).

Ezra's return (although he was born in Babylon) occurred in 459 BCE, about eighty years after the edict. He saw the many problems and blamed most of them on the mixing of blood that had been occurring before his arrival. He believed God wanted His chosen people to remain pure and unadulterated. What better example could he give than to show in holy scripture the lessons of the great flood and total destruction of the world, which, as he suggested, was caused by the wickedness of humankind through the mixing of God's people by intermarriage? His assembly of the Torah was completed before he left Babylon. Therefore, upon his return to Jerusalem, he believed the present situation need to be drastically changed because he felt that intermarriage had polluted the faith of the indigenous Jews, which had weakened their Jewish faith. Another reason he saw was the losses inflicted on the previous Jewish population which had to be replenished after the Babylon conquest. He feared that increasing the birth rate was paramount to preserve the continuation of the faith. Thus, Ezra inserted several ancient and well-known didactic stories (i.e., Genesis 6:1–4, Judges 16, and 1 Kings 16) to drive home his point. With that, he presented the Torah to the people of Jerusalem by reading it to them in general assembly (Nehemiah 8:1–18). Torah now included Genesis 6:1–4 just as we now have in all of our Bibles.

The Books of Esther and Ruth

The Hebrew Bible or Old Testament is a collection of writings that basically describe the relationship and history of a people known today as Jews and their God. What is of most importance to Jews is that God directly established a covenant with them by revealing the statutes He demanded of His people to obey. These laws are found in the first five books, and they are commonly called the Torah or Pentateuch. Christians also consider these statutes as binding, but they follow certain divine modifications that they believe came from Christ. The balance of this Bible then is either wisdom literature or history. Many believe that Moses and all the Jewish people were the direct recipients of the Torah. This means all the Jewish people in general not only those past but the present and all in the future, was caused as a direct action taken by God. Many Jews also believe that the other books are part of the Bible because they were divinely inspired. Selectively speaking—I acknowledge there are some who believe God is the actual author—tangible human authorship is not questioned, but only the degree of divine inspiration is disputed by most believers. Modern biblical scholarship has raised this awareness by pointing out obvious multiple authors and numerous redactions that are quite evident. Needless to say, this certainly is not sufficient cause to negate the theory of divine inspiration. Although many believers are uncomfortable with this, there is no reason to deny the divine role was also extended to redactors and editors as well as to the original authors.

Determining just which books are inspired becomes a subjective challenge in and of itself. Historically, we know that the books selected were decided upon by some form of consensus via a number of respected religious leaders. To these early leaders, nearly all of these actual authors were unknown. However, it was deemed important to designate an author for the basis of establishing authenticity and credibility of the source. They then assigned a prominent name to each book that was traditionally recognizable or was conceivably implied through the internal evidence found in the writing.

Modern scholars have focused in on the motivation for these writings. Many believe that they were prompted by current events that occurred during the assigned authors' lives and how that affected the subject matter and the role of God in its presentation. I will offer my historical hypothesis on how this idea was incorporated in two books of the Old Testament.

Many Jewish and Christian scholars believe the Hebrew Bible in its initial written form was assembled by Ezra and his aides using numerous oral along with some written traditions. He was faced with the enormous task of reestablishing religion in the land that was called Judah before the exile. The people who had remained on the land prior to the Babylonian exile and those who were returning home presented huge problems. Ezra believed he needed to find a way to unite all the factions of the faith under the blanket of an all-encompassing religion. He proceeded by using every available sacred tradition and integrated these into the first written Bible. This religion would thereafter be known as Judaism and the people as Jews.

His scheme was to keep the Hebrews faithful and to maintain their purity and loyalty to their past. That is what, he believed, God not only wanted but demanded. This caused a major conflict because some of the people had intermarried with people of other faiths and wanted to remain with their spouses; however, others believed that intermarriage could be beneficial to the faith under certain circumstances. As Ezra indicated, God demanded that they divorce and remarry within Judaism. Those who would not or could not accept this balked. The largest group of these people came to be known as the Samaritans. They were expelled from the faith, and their offers to help reconstruct the temple were rejected.

While many Jews complied with Ezra's laws, there were a few who only acquiesced. Thus, the biblical books of Esther and Ruth were composed and written in response to argue the case showing that Ezra had misinterpreted God's commands. They then attempted to plead with the authorities to rescind this law or at least allow some exceptions.

In the Tanakh, intermarriage presents a legal dichotomy in respect to intermarriage. In one respect, some stories and commandments explicitly forbid it (Deuteronomy 7:3–5; Exodus 34:11–16) and threaten exile or death to the children of these marriages. Examples include Leviticus 24:10–23, Ezra 9:1–3, and Ezra 10:1–44. On the other side, there are two stories that clearly suggest intermarriage as acceptable and mention that the children and grandchildren of these marriages were indeed good for Judaism. The two examples of this approach are found in the book of Ruth and the book of Esther.

Ruth is celebrated as a convert to Judaism who adopted the Jewish faith and took it to heart and became the foremother of Israel's national hero—David. Esther would show how a person living in exile could marry a non-Jew by mustering her courage and love of her people in order to save them from genocide.

The author of Ruth is unknown. Some scholars believe it may have been a woman, a convert to Judaism whose husband was a wealthy Jew. Whatever the case, the response to Ezra's injunction is indicative by the author's focusing on Ezra's acclaimed national hero, David. This fact came to light after one provided a lineage to prove Ruth was David's great-grandmother; thereby establishing that the greatest Israelite hero had been the product of a mixed marriage that had taken place prior to exile. Moreover, he set a historically acceptable scenario to show exactly how it complied with all the current religious requisites.

Esther's author had knowledge of Persian royalty and customs as did Ezra. The author's focus was on driving home the point that Jews should assimilate in order to preserve their faith. In this case, they should capitulate to the Persian power structure in order to share a place in the diaspora. The fact that Esther was married to a non-Jew who was not a convert is only a subtle theme, but its significance to the story defuses any stigma whatsoever by their intermarriage. Clearly, Ruth and Esther each appear to be in conflict with Ezra's edict and share this underlying theme.

Therefore, the authors of Esther and Ruth created didactic stories out of what they believed were a dreadful misinterpretation of the will of God by Ezra. In the Talmud (Baba Bathra 15), we are informed that the men of the great synagogue wrote the scroll of Esther. Tradition dictates that Ezra was the originator of the great synagogue that later became the Sanhedrin. By this we can surmise that the authors were writing after the death of Ezra and were attempting to moderate or repeal the prohibition on intermarriages.

Some scholars would suggest that Ezra redacted the verses in Deuteronomy and Leviticus that forbid intermarriage as well as the story of the nephilim in Genesis 6, Samson and Delilah in Judges 16, and Ahab and Jezebel in 1 Kings 16 to support his position. Certainly, while in exile, Ezra and his fellow priests greatly feared for the survival of their religion. In fact, this was their paramount consideration. During the exile they had worked diligently on the assembling of their religious traditions into a written text. They also wanted to preserve and enhance the authority and respect for the priestly class.

Ezra's great-grandfather, Hilkiah, had started the process with a proto-Deuteronomy scroll (called Deuteronomy 1 by scholars) that was refined during the exile (2 Kings 22:8–20). Upon his completion of Deuteronomy (called Deuteronomy 2), Ezra then combined this with the balance of the traditional Torah and put them into written form. He accomplished this by integrating popular ancient oral traditions with some fragmentary writings using the utmost respect for the sacred traditions and his great religious erudition.

Before Ezra's return the morale of the Jewish population was at an all-time low. Many worried that foreigners were on the increase and were combining their religions with that of the Jews. Many considered this phenomenon a harbinger, and it was further prompted by the fact that many people who had remained during the exile had intermarried and accepted some of their wives'/husbands' religious convictions. Therefore, the need to quickly generate and produce more Jewish children seemed to Ezra to be the only way to assure the survival of Judaism. The problem here wasn't intermarriage per se. It was how this mixing eroded the Jewish sense of nationalism and faith. Of course, racists ever since have used stories like this to defend antimiscegenation laws. Accordingly, it is difficult for us to hear these stories today and not recoil at something that sounds a lot like extreme racism to us. The books of Ruth and Easter were written with the attempt to mitigate this without damaging the faith.

CHAPTER 3

In chapter 2, we looked into the Bible or Tanakh and examined some of the various genres. We will now look a bit closer at the genre of *myth*. The Bible certainly contains real history! However, to better understand some of the stories that may appear to be mythological, we need to explore the evidence from within that particular time in history along with the laws and customs of that day. This is why a number of scholars believe the Exodus narrative to be a blended story mixing a diminutive history together with a great deal of mythology. They may well be correct, but clearly, there is some real history, not only in Exodus but also throughout the Bible. We will try to address only history and will not speculate whether or not the protagonists are actual historical figures. For now we will assume that they are.

This is biblical story of the birth of Moses and his adoption by the daughter of Pharaoh. (All Bible quotes are from New World Translation.)

> 1:6 Eventually Joseph died, and also all his brothers, and all of that generation.

> 1:7 And the sons of Israel became fruitful and began to swarm; and they kept on multiplying and growing mightier at a very extraordinary rate, so that the land got to be filled with them.

> 1:8 In time there arose over Egypt a new king who didn't know Joseph.

1:9 And he proceeded to say to his people, Look! The people of the sons of Israel are more numerous and mightier than we are.

1:10 Come on! Let us deal shrewdly with them, for fear they may multiply, and it must turn out that, in case war should befall us, then they certainly will also be added to those who hate us and will fight against us and go up out of the country.

1:11 So they set over them chiefs of forced labor for the purpose of oppressing them in their burden-bearing, and they went building cities as storage places for Pharaoh, namely Pithom and Raamses.

1:12 But the more they afflicted them, the more they multiplied and the more they spread out. They were grieved because of the children of Israel.

1:13 Consequently the Egyptians made the children of Israel slaves under tyranny.

1:14 And they kept making their life bitter with hard slavery at clay mortar and in bricks and every other form of slavery of theirs in which they used them as slaves under tyranny.

1:15 Later on the king of Egypt said to the Hebrew midwives the name of whom was Shiphrah, and the name of the other Puah,

1:16 yes, he went so far as to say, "When you help the Hebrew women to give birth and you do see them on the stool for childbirth, if it is a son you must also put it to death; but if it is a daughter, it must also live."

1:17 However, the midwives feared the (true) God, and did not do as the king of Egypt had spoken to them, but they would preserve the male children alive.

1:18 In time the king of Egypt called for the midwives and said to them, "Why is it you have done this thing, in that you preserved the male children alive?"

1:19 In turn the midwives said to Pharaoh, "Because the Hebrew women are not like the Egyptian women, because they are lively, they have already given birth before the midwife can come in to them."

1:20 So God dealt well with the midwives, and the people kept growing more numerous and becoming mighty.

1:21 And it came about that because the midwives feared the (true) God he later presented them with families.

1:22 finally Pharaoh commanded all his people, saying, "Every newborn son you shall throw into the river Nile, but every daughter you are to preserve alive." (Exodus 1:11–22)

As bizarre as this story may seem, it does offer some verifiable historical facts concerning abortion and murder, all in the legal framework of Hebrew and Egyptian mores and laws. First of all, we have at least two Hebrew midwives (v. 15), who are ordered by Pharaoh to kill the boy babies and allow the girls to live (v. 16). What the king has ordered is a type of partial-birth abortion that was compliant with Egyptian laws and possibly Hebrew law as well. However, murder was clearly illegal in both societies! Therefore, to meet the exact terms of the law, the baby would have to be killed before it was completely born. That could happen at any time prior to the placenta being discharged, so one could even determine the sex. This was by far the most popular form of abortion exercised in pre-Christian history. However, we must understand abortion in ancient times was rarely exercised as abandonment was socially and legally permitted. This is important to keep in mind.

The midwives disobeyed and offered their excuse directly to Pharaoh that the Hebrew women continually gave birth before they could arrive on the scene (v. 19). Pharaoh absolutely accepted their explanation! (He would not or could not murder innocent humans according to Egyptian law.) He then issued a new edict to throw every Hebrew baby boy into the Nile (v. 22). The Hebrew women now reluctantly complied. Now read Exodus 2:1–10.

2:1 Meantime, a certain man of the house of Levi went ahead and took a daughter of Levi.

2:2 And the woman became pregnant and brought a son to birth. When she saw how good looking he was, she kept him concealed for three lunar months.

2:3 When she was no longer able to conceal him, she took for him an ark of papyrus and coated it with bitumen and pitch and put the child in it and put it among the reeds by the bank of the river Nile.

2:4 Further, his sister stationed herself at a distance, to find out what would be done with him.

2:5 After a while Pharaoh's daughter came down to bathe in the Nile river, and her female attendants were walking by the side of the Nile river. And she caught sight of the ark in the middle of the reeds. Immediately she sent her slave girl that she might get it.

2:6 When she opened it she got to see the child, and here the boy was weeping. At that she felt compassion for him, although she said "This is one of the children of the Hebrews."

2:7 Then his sister said to Pharaoh's daughter, "Shall I go and specially call for you a nursing woman from the Hebrew women, that she may nurse the child for you?"

2:8 So Pharaoh's daughter then said to her, "Go." At once the maiden went and called the child's mother.

2:9 Pharaoh's daughter said to her, "Take this child with you and nurse him for me and I myself shall give you your wages." Accordingly the woman took the child and nursed him.

2:10 And the child grew up. Then she brought him to Pharaoh's daughter, so that he became a son to her, and she proceeded to call his name Moses and to say: "It is because I have drawn him out of the water."

This action was not considered murder because the Egyptians considered the Nile River to be a god. Like the most popular form of infanticide, known as abandonment, the babies were then considered given to or thrown to the gods. They then would become solely responsible for the fate of these babies. This is why Pharaoh's daughter could adopt or become the God-given mother of Moses as a direct gift from the *Nile god* and not be in violation of her father's proclamation.

The Nile River was also considered to be a *god of fertility* as well. Ostensibly, Pharaoh's daughter was bathing in the river with the expectation of becoming fertile and receiving or conceiving a child of her own. Thus, the gods granted her favor.

Of course, the whole story may be just a legend, but it certainly contains real and accurate historical evidence concerning some of the religious beliefs of the ancient Egyptians. (It was also accepted by the Hebrews as well.) For the Hebrews, it became the advent of their religion and clearly has substance in real history.

In summation, Pharaoh's daughter desired to have a child of her own, so she practiced the fertility ritual by bathing in the waters of the Nile, the Egyptian god of fertility. The princes surely had a luxurious pool in the palace, which was far more comfortable for bathing. The river was actually dirty and contained harmful fish and animals, especially crocodiles and hippos. In other words, it was not the safest place to just go for a swim.

Moses's birth was not aborted because he was fully born. Thus, he escaped Pharaoh's orders to kill every Hebrew baby boy because Egyptian law strictly forbade murder. Throwing him into the Nile, the Egyptian god of fertility, was merely a method of submitting an offering to the gods while staying in compliance with the edict of Pharaoh.

The partial-birth abortion was necessary because the midwife needed to determine the sex of the child. Therefore, it had to be out of the birth canal tube; however, as long as the umbilical cord was still attached to the baby and the placenta was still inside the mother, the child was not considered born. Thus, killing it at this time was not acknowledged as murder.

In our next case, we will see how myth, legend, and folklore blend with actual history.

IS DAVID A REAL HISTORICAL FIGURE?

Some scholars who question the historicity of the David/Solomon period are known as minimalists. In a nutshell, they claim the David/Solomon eras are unsubstantiated history.

They don't deny their existence. They merely claim that it cannot be proven to satisfy the standard requirements established by modern historians. By this strict criterion, the minimalists are right. These are highly respected scholars who are established biblical sages, but they are considered controversial in this field of endeavor. While it is generally assumed David was an actual historical figure, this presumes a line of reasoning that the Bible shows him to be a larger-than-life hero without trying to hide all his flaws and shortcomings.

Now one may start to believe the books of Samuel and Kings were written before the exile and Ezra. Yet we see that Chronicles, written by Ezra, paints David quite differently. He omits most of the "history of David's rise to power" (1 Samuel 16:14–2 Samuel 5:10) by opting to start his narrative with the death of Saul (1 Samuel 31). He also omitted other major passages from Samuel, most of which contained deeds that would be harmful to the reputation of David and therefore would disparage his reputation as the founder of the temple and the priesthood. By this, it would appear that Ezra (when he wrote Chronicles) had not assembled all the books of the Tanakh into a single unit yet, or perhaps he wrote it before he even endeavored the formulation of a Bible. (More on this will follow later.)

Furthermore, from this, we can piece together Ezra's motives and what writings may have been available to him. Without a doubt, he either had some written text of Samuel and Kings or strong oral traditions that may have gained written form earlier than the Pentateuch. I believe he wrote Chronicles to strengthen religious nationalism and to bolster respect for the priesthood. He laboriously lays out the ancestral genealogy to excite pride and purpose for the establishment of a new understanding of Israel in light of the disastrous recent past. Ezra wanted David to be reaffirmed as the national hero, this time without most of the character flaws.

When Ezra assembled Genesis, it was then important to show how God selected the Jews and established His covenant with David as His chosen people. Therefore, they had to remain *pure*. Thus, he believed intermarriage needed to be condemned. One clue appears that suggests the use of more than one author in the Bible from the numerous doublets that occur in the books of Genesis and Samuel.

I believe David was historical, but some of the stories that surround him scream of legend. The books of Samuel and Kings are considered to be among the earliest biblical books committed to writing. We know Ezra certainly had a copy of some sort upon his return from Babylon. But it is not clear who the author was or when it was actually written. There's a strong possibility that Ezra had at least two popular sources, which may have involved a strong tradition that was preserved orally. Ezra then combined these oral or written sources, blending them into one written scroll.

The evidence for this is very compelling. In the two books of Samuel, we see numerous doublets with contradictions and discrepancies. Succinctly, some of these include the following: David was a skilled warrior (1 Samuel 16:18). Then he was a person untrained for war (1 Samuel 17:33). He lives at home with his father, but he lives with Saul. However, Saul doesn't know of him until after he slays Goliath (1 Samuel 17:55). He is Saul's personal harp player (1 Samuel 17:15). David killed Goliath (1 Samuel 17:50), or Elhanan killed Goliath (2 Samuel 21:19). We then see (in 1 Chronicles 20:5) Ezra's attempt to correct this last problem by claiming Elhahan killed Lahmi, the brother of Goliath. In 2 Samuel 21:19, the King James Version adds these same words, which do not appear in the Hebrew Bible or any other modern translation as the translators believed the problem needed to be further explained.

David and Goliath is pure hyperbole at best and clearly legendary. Think about it! Has there ever been a time when two opposing armies positioned for battle arbitrarily selected two champions to settle it by individual combat? Next, under these circumstances, who in their right mind would then send a young boy to face a seasoned warrior? David's subsequent victory causes the Philistines to panic and flee. Then what was the purpose for individual confrontation in the first place?

What did David do with Goliath's head? "David took the head of the Philistine and brought it to Jerusalem, but he put his armor in his tent" (1 Samuel 17:54). This is impossible because Israelites had not yet captured Jerusalem from the Jebusites (2 Samuel 5:6–10). Jerusalem was not captured from the Jebusites until after David became king. So David was already king when Goliath was killed. Then Ezra's version of the story where Elhanan killed Goliath could only be possible if David was already king and Elhanan was an Israeli soldier.

Now let us look at the various texts that exist. There are at least five—the Masoretic, the Old Greek LXX, the Lucianic (old Latin) version of the LXX, the Hebrew texts from the Dead Sea Scrolls, and the account from Josephus. We should also look at the stories found in Psalms 89 and 132. Each has substantial differences in the story line, particularly in regard to the Goliath episode. This indicates that after the initial blending by Ezra, later editors made attempts to correct or smooth out the discrepancies.

My point here is to show some basis for the minimalist position and the problems encountered through biblical historical criticism, even though I personally don't agree completely. Their discipline is to simply seek to verify the history of the Bible by an accepted scholarly process. What could be wrong with that? Conservative Christians label these positions destructive criticism and condemn all their suspected preconceived motives. Their attitude simply is that anything written in the Bible or at least what was written in the original manuscripts must not be questioned because it was written by God. Surely, when one reads the Bible, he or she will encounter ambiguities and will need to make an interpretation. Some believe they must listen to what some other person or church has determined sections to mean. If that is the case, then one is accepting another human's opinion, certainly not God's. Why then should that opinion not be examined from its source to see if indeed the other source was correct? If the fundamentalist position had always been the accepted norm, we would still be compelled to believe the Earth was the center of the universe and everything revolved around us.

Next we will investigate the *myth* genre a bit further.

THE WITCH OF ENDOR

A majority of people read the Bible to bolster their religious experience or to enhance their spirituality. In several cases certain historical and theological information falls outside of the popular erudition. Because of this, most readers casually pass over or ignore several passages that seem unimportant. The only thing wrong with this is ignoring what was really intended by the biblical writer. What is lost by this is the failure to correctly comprehend the author's theological conception altogether.

I will now endeavor to explore one such example of this without theological predilection. My selection is commonly known as "the witch of Endor," taken from the book of 1 Samuel. Here we learn about the first king of Israel, Saul, his rise to power, and his eventual fall, which coincided with the story of the last judge of Israel, Samuel. The book also narrates the rise of David, and it is the only Old Testament biblical account of a deceased person being raised from the dead, someone who actually was seen and spoke to an audience.

Succinctly, the twelve (or thirteen) tribes of Israel clamored for a king to unite them. A reluctant God worked through Samuel, the last judge and a prophet, to anoint Saul as their first king. Saul was handsome, hardworking, and courageous, and he was dedicated to defending the nation. He was loved by the people. Yet he was forsaken by God and killed. Some reasons for Saul's demise are described in the Bible (1 Samuel 13:8–15). One explanation is that Saul offered a sacrifice but intruded upon the exclusive duties of the priest as commanded by God (Numbers 8:19). Furthermore, he also disobeyed God by failing to kill every man and woman, infant and suckling, ox and sheep, camel and ass (1 Samuel 15:1–9).

The downfall of Saul occurs shortly after he violates his own decree and God's commandment concerning necromancy (e.g., witchcraft, conjuring with the spirit world). "There shall not be found among you anyone who makes his son or daughter pass through the fire, or who uses divination, or is a soothsayer, or an augur, or a sorcerer" (Deuteronomy 18:10; Leviticus 19:31; 20:6, 27).

Fearing impending defeat from the Philistines, Saul disguised himself and consulted with a necromancer only to be told of his own impending death by Samuel, who had been summoned from the dead by the witch of Endor (1 Samuel 28:3–25).

Let us now look at the actual Bible story of 1 Samuel 28:3–20 (NWT).

28:3 Now Samuel himself had died, and all Israel had proceeded to bewail him and bury him in Ramah his own city. As for Saul, he had removed the spirit mediums and professional foretellers of events from the land.

10:4 Subsequently the Philistines collected together and came and pitched camp at Shunem. So Saul collected all Israel together and pitched camp in Gilboa.

10:5 When Saul got to see the camp of the Philistines, he became afraid his heart began to tremble very much.

10:6 Although Saul would inquire of Jehovah, Jehovah never answered him either by dreams or by the Urim or by the prophets.

10:7 Finally Saul said to his servants, Seek for me a woman who is a mistress of a spirit mediumship and I will go to her and consulter her. Then his servants said to him: Look! There is a woman who is a mistress of spirit mediumship in Endor.

10:8 So Saul disguised himself and clothed himself with outer garments and went, he and two men with him; and they came to the woman by night. He said: "Employ divination, please, for me by spirit mediumship and bring up for me the one whom I shall designate to you."

10:9 However the woman said to him: "Here you yourself well know what Saul did, how he cut off spirit mediums and the professional foretellers of events from the land. Why, then, are you acting like a trapper against my soul to have me put to death?"

10:10 Immediately Saul swore to her by Jehovah, saying: "As Jehovah is alive guilt for error will not befall you in this matter!"

10:11 At this the woman said: "Whom shall I bring up for you?" To this he said: "Bring up Samuel for me."

10:12 When the woman saw Samuel, she began crying out at the top of her voice; and the woman went on to say to Saul: "Why did you trick me, when you yourself are Saul?"

10:13 But the king said to her: "Do not be afraid, but what did you see?" And the woman went on to say to Saul: "A god I saw coming up out of the earth."

10:14 At once he said to her: "What is his form? To which she said: "It is an old man coming up, and he has himself covered with a sleeveless coat." At that Saul recognized that it was Samuel, and he proceeded to bow low with his face to the earth and prostrated himself.

10:15 And Samuel began to say to Saul: "Why have you disturbed me by having me brought up?" To this Saul said: "I am in very sore straits, as the Philistines are fighting against me, and God himself has departed from me and has answered me no more, either by means of the prophets or by dreams so that I am calling you to let me know what I shall do."

10:16 And Samuel went on to say: "Why, then, do you inquire of me, when Jehovah himself has departed from you and proves to be your adversary?

10:17 And Jehovah will do for himself just as he spoke by means of me, and Jehovah will rip the kingdom away from your hand and give it to your fellow man David.

10:18 As you did not obey the voice of Jehovah and you did not execute his burning anger against Amalek that is why this is the thing that Jehovah will certainly do to you this day.

10:19 And Jehovah will also give Israel with you into the hand of the Philistines and tomorrow you and your sons will be with me. Even the camp of Israel Jehovah will give into the hand of the Philistines."

10:20 At that Saul quickly fell his full length on the earth and became very much afraid because of "Samuel's" words. Also there happened to be no power in him, because he had not eaten food the whole day and the whole night.

10:21 The woman now came to Saul and saw that he was greatly disturbed. So she said to him: "Here your maidservant has obeyed your voice, and I proceeded to put my soul in my palm and obey the words that you spoke to me.

10:22 And now, please, you, in turn, obey the voice of your maidservant; and let me set before you a piece of bread, and you eat, that power may come to be in you, because you will be on your way."

10:23 But he refused and said: "I am not going to eat." However his servants and also the woman kept urging him. Finally he obeyed their voices and rose up from the earth and sat on the couch.

10:24 Now the woman had a fattened calf in the house. So she quickly sacrificed it and took flour and kneaded dough and baked it into unfermented cakes.

10:25 Then she served them to Saul and his servants and they ate. After that they rose up and went away during the night.

Note verse 6, "Jehovah never answered him either by dreams or by the Urim or by the prophets." Urim is defined by the *Jewish Encyclopedia* as "objects connected with the breastplate of the high priest, and used as a kind of divine oracle." This means that it was a device used to see into the future. Also take note that Saul had violated God's law by offering a burnt sacrifice, which was emphatically the duty of the priest, Samuel at the time. This act greatly angered Samuel, and he condemned Saul for it.

To understand these passages, we need to accept that Samuel, although departed, was in some form alive because of his protest, "Why have you disturbed me by having me brought up?" (v. 15). This begs the question. By whose authority did the witch receive this power to raise the dead, Satan or God? Samuel was the voice of God while he was alive! "A man or a woman who has a ghost or a familiar spirit shall be put to death; they shall be pelted with stones—their bloodguilt shall be upon them" (Leviticus 20:27). "Do not turn to mediums or spiritists; do not seek them out to be defiled by them. I am the LORD your God" (Leviticus 19:31). It would certainly seem that dealings in the occult were an ongoing concern that enjoyed popularity at that time in history.

Later Christian writers would reject any idea that a human could bring back the spirit of a dead person, although some critics have tried to interpret that these events were actually disguised demons by conflating necromancy with demon-summoning. Yet the account very clearly states that it was Samuel and not a demon or spirit who was deceiving Saul by pretending to be the real Samuel. The text is quite clear that it was indeed Samuel who was raised and he foretold that Saul would be routed and that his sons and he would die the next day. Incidentally, one of Saul's sons did not die. Ish-bosheth became king (though with little backing) for a few years—until he was killed and David took over (2 Samuel 2:8–9).

Theologians are divided in their opinions whether the apparition of Samuel was genuine or deceptive. Some believe that the witch of Endor only cast a spell on Saul that deceived him into believing he had actually seen or heard Samuel. Others expound that God had explicitly forbidden witchcraft and that He would not have allowed someone to use witchcraft to summon one of His prophets. Then there are also those who insist that all of this could only have been the work of the devil.

A more reasonable possibility could be that Ezra, believed by many scholars to be the redactor of the Hebrew Bible, compiled this story for didactic reasons to promote his religious agenda. It is quite obvious that Ezra's program was to promote the priesthood to the top of the social and political ladder, especially while living under the authority of a foreign power. He was successful, and the results would prevail until the Roman period. During the Maccabean period, this emphasis was placed on the role of the high priest. He also was the king, but this role was downplayed. Prior to this, the high priest did not have much power, but during and after the exile, he apparently attained greater importance. In fact, much of the paraphernalia of the monarchy were transferred to the high priest, not merely the clothing but also the duties of government.

The expressed theology revolving about the witch of Endor and concerning the various Christian denominations is quite diverse and is complicated based on the following: Many believed that when one died (in Samuel's time), his or her body would be buried and then went directly to Sheol. This was where the righteous and the unrighteous reside after death as recorded in Job. "Just as a cloud dissipates and vanishes, those who go down to Sheol will not come back" (Job 7:9).

Many Christians believe that before Jesus, everyone who had previously died slept in the earth (Acts 13:36; Revelation 6:9–11). The original Apostles' Creed states that Jesus descended into hell (although some denominations have eliminated this phrase). This would imply that Jesus went to hell to open the gates and to allow the righteous to enter heaven (Matthew 27:52–53; John 11:11–14). However, Paul seems to indicate that everyone would sleep in the earth until the parousia and final judgment (1 Thessalonians 4:13–17; 1 Corinthians 15:51).

This seems to be in conflict with the story of the *good thief.* "Truly I tell you today, you will be with me in paradise" (Luke 23:43). Jesus clearly implies that they were going to go to paradise on the same Friday when they died, the criminal accompanying Him. Therefore, they would only be asleep until the Sunday He was resurrected. Therefore, they wouldn't have to wait for the second coming.

Is the witch of Endor a story to be taken literally or allegorically, or is it plain mythology? And how does it fit with Christian theology? And finally, do Christians or Jews still believe there is a spirit world, and can the dead still be summoned and brought up?

We will now look into a book that has an apocalyptic genre, one that the writer possibly intended to be allegory but could perhaps be considered pseudepigraphic.

THE BOOK OF DANIEL

The book of Daniel is one of the most controversial books of the Hebrew Bible or Old Testament. It is a favorite of the prophetic folks. Without a doubt, the dating of its origin is the most argued point among scholars. Both sides vigorously offer evidence to support their cases. The facts are many and can be convincing in either direction. Another argument is that some claim

Daniel's prophecy is about to unfold in the very near future; however, others believe Daniel was allegorically writing for the people of his own time and place.

Originally, the earliest writing had to have caused some reprisals from the government, which undoubtedly spurred on revisions, perhaps by the initial author. These reprisals caused the writer to encrypt his message so that only his designated audience knew exactly what he was saying. Of course, this occurs in several cases in other books of the Bible as well.

One example of the revisions is evident in the striking differences in style, suggesting multiple authors. For example, Daniel 2:4 to 7: 28 is originally written in Aramaic, but the preceding and following portions are written in Hebrew. Fragments from the Dead Sea Scrolls bear this out. Certainly, one could reasonably argue that a single author still could have written the text, but it is still very suspicious and bizarre. All scholars generally agree that "Bel and the Dragon," "Susanna," and "the Song of the Three Holy Children," books which are included in Orthodox and Catholic Bibles (not Jewish or Protestant) and are attached to Daniel, are clearly later additions by different authors. These Greek additions were added to the Septuagint in an attempt to clarify or fill in details of the famous person Daniel and to complement certain oral traditions.

Daniel 11 is the most controversial, according to most scholars. It gives a very detailed account of the battles of the Seleucid king Antiochus IV Epiphanies. The author implies that the book was written in the sixth century BCE, and he seems to express real prophetic skills with his formless historical predictions. In the third century CE, Poryphyry wrote a work titled *Against Christians*, here he questioned the authenticity of Daniel and a few scholars began to take notice. Porphyry's contention is that the book must have been written in the second century BCE. But the general consensus until modern times was that the book was written by Daniel in the sixth century BCE and that it was an inspired prophecy from God.

Modern scholars have alleged that there are numerous historical errors or inaccuracies in Daniel. Conservatives counter this argument by using recent archaeological findings to prove that Daniel is right. The most outstanding historical disagreement concerned Belshazzar. Daniel claimed he was the last king of Babylon (Daniel 5:30) and that Nebuchadnezzar was his father (Daniel 5:2, 13, 18). This appeared to be an irreconcilable error for most historians and critics. Several nonbiblical sources have, since ancient times, stated that Nabonidus was the last king of Babylon. Then the discovery of a cuneiform tablet called the "Nabonidus Chronicle" proved Daniel was correct. It states that Nabonidus "entrusted the 'camp' to his eldest son 'Belshazzar' … entrusted the kingship to him and himself." However, it falls short of actually proving Belshazzar became the last king and that his father clearly was Nabonidus, not Nebuchadnezzar.

The counterclaim is that Nabonidus did live in Arabia for eight years (552–545 BCE), but no evidence that Belshazzar was assassinated exists. Daniel claims Belshazzar was killed after he saw the writing on the wall, at which time Darius the Mede allegedly took over Babylon (Daniel 5:30). A good deal of existing non-biblical evidence shows that Cyrus took Babylon in 539 BCE and captured Nabonidus. Furthermore, Darius was the second successor to Cyrus after Cambyses, and he (Darius) ascended to the throne of Persia in 522 BCE. Daniel also shows no knowledge of the "Edict of Cyrus" (538 BCE), which allowed the Hebrews to return to Israel. This was one of the most monumental events in Jewish history.

Daniel alludes that the Jews in Babylon were persecuted. He also suggests that several attempts were made to destroy their religion. Yet many Jews seemed to do well there, and many chose to remain since they had prospered. The synagogue originated there, and the Torah was also finalized, not to mention the (Babylon) Talmud.

Predictions by Daniel are remarkably accurate—that is, up to a point where they suddenly fail to hold up. The ascension of the four kingdoms, Alexander the Great, the division of Alexander's empire, and hostilities between Seleucid (king of the north) and Ptolemy (king of the south) are uncannily correct. This continues with Epiphanes IV, who performed pagan sacrifices in the temple (Daniel 9:27) and committed a "desolating sacrilege" in the temple (Daniel 12:11), which actually did occur in 167 BCE.

From here to the end of the book, Daniel is prone to historical errors. He describes the kingdom as being divided between the Medes and the Persians, which never happened (Daniel 5:28). Another inaccurate description is that of the downfall of Antiochus IV, of which he seemed unaware (Daniel 11:40–45). Antiochus did not conquer Egypt (Daniel 11:42–45) as he predicted, but they actually suffered from a humiliating withdrawal on Roman orders in 167 BCE after his initial attack. This is a well-known historical record. And Antiochus (king of the north) is not attacked by the king of the south (Daniel 11:40). Rather he died in Persia from an unknown illness, not as claimed by Daniel (1 Maccabees 6:1–6).

Since Daniel seemed to know everything about the history of the Seleucid kingdom except for the final days and death of its most despised tyrant, we might reasonably assume that the book of Daniel was compiled sometime between the last accurate *prophecies* (i.e., the temple desecrations and Jewish uprisings in 167–165) and the death of Antiochus Epiphanes in 164 BCE.

Notably, the book of Daniel is not included in the Nevi'im (the prophets) of the Hebrew Bible, but it is included in the Ketuvim (the writings). So too, Daniel is not considered to be a prophet in Judaism. However, Josephus (writing about 95 CE) does include Daniel as one of the prophets in his description of the Hebrew canon. (See *Contra Apion* (*Against the Jews*) I, 38–39 [8] and *Antiquities*, X, 11, 17) This suggests that the Hebrew Bible was still fluid at the time of Josephus.

As another point that some bring up, Daniel is not mentioned in the prologue (by the grandson) or the text of Sirach (Greek or LXX version), which was written by Jesus ben Sira "near the start of the second century BCE" and is the earliest reference to a Hebrew canon. It is noteworthy that ben Sira refers to all the Hebrew heroes but fails to even mention Daniel.

Many scholars believe the original story of Daniel comes from a poem originating from Syria dated 1500 BCE. It is part of the Ugarit texts recovered in 1930–1. It is sometimes titled the "Epic of Daniel" or "The Tale of Aqhat." The protagonist in this story is similarly named Daniel. This would point to the Daniel referred to by Ezekiel 14:14, 14:20, and 28:3.

I have touched on only a small portion of evidence, but I think it is heavily tilted in favor of Daniel being composed just before the Maccabean revolt. He wrote to encourage his people to rise up and defeat the oppressor Antiochus. He disguised the language to confuse the enemy just as the book of Judith did, which was written about the same time.

THE BOOK OF EZEKIEL

The book of Ezekiel is another example of apocalyptic genre, and it also is excellent rendition of history in the Bible. It is brimming with details revolving around a specific time with events surrounding the period of captivity the Jewish people experienced in Babylon. Through the prophet, who is also a priest, we are given an actual sampling of the concerns, fears, and mood of the exiles. He appears to be writing didactically for future generations while justifying why God has subjected His people to such sufferings.

Ezekiel mentions his name only once early in the book (Ezekiel 1:3). Thereafter, he refers to himself as "son of man" eighty-eight times. He says he's a messenger of God speaking not of his own solicitudes but trumpeting the Word of God. He is preaching from 593 to 563 BCE. The book discusses the fall of Jerusalem in 586 BCE and contains many oracles of warning. He sometimes symbolically acted out his prophecies. He spoke about the restoration of Israel and the destruction of empires that sought to destroy Israel.

This valuable historical writing has some issues that have caused concern from within the Jewish rabbinical community. Solomon B. Freehof writes,

> The Book of Ezekiel has always been a problem book. As early as the second century C.E., in the time of the Mishnah, there were doubts and concern about it. These doubts were strong enough, in those early days, to raise the question of whether Ezekiel should be one of the biblical books. The Talmud (Sabbath 13b) relates that Hananiah ben Hezekiah (one of the teachers of the Mishnah) labored to harmonize the laws in Ezekiel with those given in the Torah. If not for this effort, some believed, the book would have been kept out of the Bible. The phrase used was: "The Book of Ezekiel would have been hidden away" (nignaz Sefer Yehezkel).

> The rabbis were greatly troubled by the fact that the Book of Ezekiel gives certain laws, chiefly as to the Temple procedures, which actually contradict the laws given in the Book of Leviticus. They had a further objection: The opening chapters (chapters 1-3) of the Book of Ezekiel present a detailed picture of God coming in a chariot, surrounded by retinues of angels, etc. This picture, called "the arrangement of the chariot" (ma'aseh merkavah), became the starting point of special mystical studies. Though deemed important by the rabbis, such studies were considered dangerous for the uninitiated, and therefore the rabbis said that these chapters should not be studied, except by the learned few (Mishnah Hagigah 2: 1). How then, could they permit such a book to be part of the Bible, to be read by anyone?

Another troubling dubiety occurs in Ezekiel 20:25; God gave Israel laws that He knew "were not good and judgments they could not live by." He also states that the Israelites were corrupt through their entire history. He claims they were evil from the beginning of their relationship with God in a manor expressed by no other prophet. The only canonical book to describe the whole history in significant detail as totally decadent and sinful is Ezekiel (chapters 16, 20, and 23).

There are numerous other distressful segments in Ezekiel that I will ignore. However, I will focus only on prophetic significance and Ezekiel's defining what constitutes a "false prophet." Ezekiel 13:1–10 basically defines a false prophet. Verse 7 read, "'Have you not seen false visions and uttered lying divinations when you say,' The LORD declares, 'though I have not spoken?'" In other words, false prophets are making prophecies that are not or will not come to pass. If this is the criteria, then let us examine prophecies Ezekiel made and see how they meet this standard.

Consider Ezekiel 4:3–6 and 37:15–21. *Ezekiel predicted when Israel would be reestablished and united again with Judah.* Although some might consider that he was reasonably accurate with the length of time, the state of Judah and the state of Israel in combination were never again united. In fact, the people or tribes of the state of Israel have long been considered *lost* (the ten lost tribes).

Consider Ezekiel 11:17. *The Jews would have Israel as their country again!* In 163 BCE, this did come true but only lasted about a hundred years and returned again in 1948. Somehow I don't think the events just described are what Ezekiel had in mind when he made this prediction, but let us say that this is an accurate prediction.

Consider Ezekiel 25:14 and 35:1–9. *The Jews would avenge the Edomites, and Edom would become a wasteland.* Five years after the destruction of Jerusalem, Nebuchadnezzar conquered all the states around Judah, particularly Edom (later known by its Greek name, Idumea), though he did not carry them away as captives. About 130 BCE, John Hyrcanus drove the Edomites from Southern Judea, where they had settled, conquered them, and obliged them to accept circumcision and Jewish law. They remained subject to the later kings and queen of Judea till the destruction of Jerusalem by the Romans. Josephus informs us that twenty thousand of them were summoned to aid in the defense of that city but that they gave themselves up to plunder and murder.

Therefore, the Jews did gain revenge as Ezekiel had predicted. However, this took about 430 years to accomplish! Did Ezekiel intend for such a long period of time to lapse? Why would such a prediction be relevant at the time of Ezekiel only to happen 430 years later? Edom lived on even through Roman times, and Herod the Great even became king of Judea.

Consider Ezekiel 26:7–14. *Tyre would be destroyed by Nebuchadnezzar* and never be rebuilt. Without any doubt, here Ezekiel was *absolutely wrong!* Nebuchadnezzar did destroy Tyre's dependent towns but failed to take the island city. Alexander the Great did a few hundred years later. But that is not part of his prophecy. And Tyre was rebuilt after Alexander and is still in existence today.

Consider Ezekiel 29:19–20. *Egypt would be conquered and plundered by Nebuchadnezzar!* This also never happened. Ezekiel 29:11–12 says, "For *forty* years not a soul will pass that way, neither people nor *animals*. It will be completely uninhabited. I will make *Egypt* desolate, and it will be surrounded by other desolate *nations*. Its *cities* will be empty and desolate for *forty* years, surrounded by other desolate cities. I will scatter the *Egyptians* to distant lands." Nebuchadnezzar did invade Egypt in 568 BCE and ravaged the desert town of Tahpanhes on the eastern frontier, but he was repulsed and retreated without carrying off the wealth of the nation!

In Ezekiel's time the false prophets were causing much confusion among the exiles. Some of these prophets said everything would be all right and the Babylon captivity would soon end. Ezekiel claims he was speaking the truth as he received the revelation directly from God. We only know the gist of what the false prophets were saying (from Ezekiel), but it seems likely that they were trying to mitigate the traumatic experience of being forcibly relocated to a foreign land through words of encouragement. After the captivity ended, many exiles refused to return to Judea because they had become quite prosperous.

Ezekiel only differed in that he condemned the Jewish people for being sinful and claimed that this was the reason God was causing their sufferings. He required the people to repent and to reconfirm their faithfulness to God and obey His laws. His prophesized future events were issued to reinforce his points and to offer some form of hope. Some of them came to pass while others failed or took place hundreds of years later. Of course, making correct prophecies are not the only criteria used to measure a prophet. His or her message is the most important issue, and Ezekiel qualifies in that regard. Bearing this all in mind, how could the people distinguish between those prophets who were true and those who were false? What proof do we now have today that Ezekiel was a true prophet?

Wisdom literature genre lies ahead now, beginning with a book that attempts to answer a difficult question. Why do bad things happen to good people?

THE BOOK OF JOB

Because of its highly social and theological context many scholars consider the book of Job as an ancient literary masterpiece. It addresses the age-old question of why bad things happen to good people. Scholars are at odds about the origin date and who the author(s) was/were. What everyone seems to agree on is the fact that it definitely belongs in the Bible.

Job contains the longest recorded speech by God anywhere in the Bible. It is loaded with theology and theological implications. The questions it answers only seem to open the doors to more questions. There is little doubt that this poetic tale was written didactically just as is the case with several biblical stories. Therefore, it would be appropriate to assume that it was not intended to be explicit history.

After all, the author would have had to have been present during the conversations between God and Satan in order to record them. Of course, the author could have obtained a direct message or vision from God, which is not uncommon in the Bible. It does seem to be challenging the accepted belief that God punishes those who do wrong and rewards those who do good. At least it attempts to offer some kind of reasoning for when the opposite takes place.

We must notice the role that Satan plays. He appears to be an adviser to God (certainly not an evil devil) who is suspicious of Job's devotion toward God. He recommends a series of tests to determine Job's true nature. God then orders it. The scene is set in heaven, and Satan is there beside God. This means that at the time the book of Job was written, there was no knowledge of devils or hell, which would suggest that it was composed before the Persian period.

Perhaps the most troubling theological implication is it claims that God is *not* omniscient. God believed He needed to test Job to make certain His opinion of Job was correct and Satan's opinion was wrong. A similar story also occurs in the narrative of Abraham and Isaac. God stopped the slaying of Isaac after He was satisfied that Abraham was loyal to Him. Obviously, if God required these tests, He didn't know or wasn't sure what the final outcome would be.

The next question to ask would be this: Are all the attributes we assign to God correct? Is God all powerful? One would think so. He did create everything, didn't He? Is He all-just and all-merciful? The book of Job certainly calls that into question.

PRAYER

A feature used in almost every biblical genre is prayer.

Several years ago when I first delved into this subject, it seemed that tracing the history of prayer would be quite easy. It seemed to me that a common source had to be buried somewhere in the historical record. I quickly discovered tracing this origin was very difficult, as it appears that every society from the earliest of times indulged in some form of praying to a higher from of life. This would even include prehistoric times. Therefore, I concluded that prayer had to be a secondary instinct following the acceptance of a supreme creator.

Primitive man realized he was powerless to control several conditions and circumstances that were affecting his daily life. He soon recognized that he would one day die and that there was nothing he could do to prevent it. Reason suggested to him that a higher form of beings or gods were controlling the world along with everything in it. His next step was to try to understand what these gods wanted and then attempt to please them or try to manipulate them for his own benefit.

His first prayers were merely verbalized wishes, the expression of personal requests. Prayer next became a technique for achieving cooperation with these gods. The gods were anthropomorphized and given comparable human desires. These were then interpreted to find appropriate actions for pleasing the gods. With this method, people could achieve some kind of divine-human working relationship. In the very beginning he believed the gods could hear his prayers but could not read his mind. Therefore, prayers had to be expressed orally or visually. Soon afterward this changed when people accepted the belief that the gods had the power to see into a man's mind, which meant that mental prayers were equally as effective, dispelling other beliefs.

Our earliest known description of an organized religious mythology can be found in the Sumerian pantheon consisting of a multifaceted format of more than 2,500 deities that covered nearly every aspect of nature and human endeavor. They had gods of sunshine and of rain. There were vegetation gods, fertility gods, river gods, and animal gods. There were also great gods—Enlil (prince of the air), Anu (ruler of the heavens), Enki (the god of water), and so on. Just below these gods existed a sublevel of deities—Nannar (the moon god), Utu (the sun god), and Inanna (the queen of heaven). In ancient Egypt, several writings from pharaohs exist. These were often written or commissioned prayers that were fashioned out of the tales of their gods.

Prayer and sacrifices along with magic then became the most used methods of reaching the gods. This practice seems to have universal acceptance throughout the planet, and it is still in use in backward areas today. Both prayer and magic arose as a result of man's primitive reactions to his environment. But aside from this generalized relationship, the two have little in common. Prayer has always indicated positive action by the praying ego. It almost always is psychic and usually spiritual. Magic has typically signified an attempt to manipulate reality without affecting the ego of the manipulator or the practitioner of magic.

As societies aged, they established more sophisticated prayers and rituals. Soon each god needed a special place to be worshipped. Temples would be constructed and priests or priestesses became necessary to supervise and lead the worship. Most of this was ceremonial, and prayer was the cornerstone of the services. Along with this, the steady and reliable movements in the sky led to a general understanding that the heavens were the residence for most of the gods.

In the writings of nearly every civilized nation, a description of the major stars in the heavens—which might be called the *constellations of the zodiac* or the *signs of the zodiac*—is evident. If you go back in time to ancient India, China, Rome, Greece, Egypt, Persia, Assyria, or Babylonia, regardless of how far back you go, there is a remarkable phenomenon. Many of these nations had twelve signs representing the analogous twelve things or cryptograms.

In a past issue of *Biblical Archaeology Review*, Archaeologist Zeev Weiss features and describes a mosaic recently uncovered in an ancient Jewish synagogue in Sepphoris in which a zodiac surrounds a striking portrayal of the Greek sun god, Helios. Curiously, similar artwork depicting the zodiac has been discovered in synagogues at Tiberius, Khirbet Susiya, Na'aran, Husifa, Yafia, and Beit Alpha. In several instances the characters of the zodiac were looked upon as gods, but in the case of Israel, it appears they were not worshipped and were not the recipients of prayers. Ancient Jews were part of the larger society, although with some distinguishing customs, notably the worship of a single God and a scorn for the use of religious images. During the Hellenistic period, Jews adopted the practice of astrology enthusiastically, but they gave the principles of astrology their own Judaic interpretation.

Prayer may be performed by an individual or group as either formal or spontaneous, silent or spoken. In one or more forms, it is at the center of all worship. It is an inseparable accessory of sacrifice in most primitive religions. Prayer occupied a central position in Jewish religion from earliest days. The temple was "a house of prayer" (Isaiah 56:7), and the book of Psalms or psalter became the prayers of liturgy of the temple and the synagogue and formed the very heart of prayers in early Christianity. We can pray for others, ourselves, or thanksgiving or we can pray simply to demonstrate adoration to God. The latter is an anthropomorphic assumption that God desires to be adored. We also assume that He wishes that we thank Him for granting our requests. Most of our prayers are generally an appeal for something we desire.

History seems to support the human belief that some form of deity exists and that this deity requires adoration, and prayer becomes a significant part of that ritual. Since the Enlightenment, the influence of religion in the Western world has diminished, and religious values have come under scrutiny. Prayer involved in any part of government has moved to the forefront of our minds. Some people applaud this move, while others think it is an attempt to take God out of society. However, the vast majority believe that prayer is good and that a small minority is trying to force their will on the majority.

Exploiting this controversy, the media has found that featuring prayer as a subject improves their ratings. Magazines and television programs have been mostly favorable toward prayer, and many have extolled the healing power of prayer. There have been a number of shows that have offered scientific evidence that prayer has produced affirmative therapeutic results. The accuracy of this science has been vigorously challenged. Some have even accused the studies of being seriously flawed. Yet television faith healers, although popular in their own right, have often been exposed as charlatans. A 1997 *Newsweek* survey reports that 92 percent of Americans believe prayer is beneficial. The same report claims that 85 percent are willing to accept failure in getting requests granted without abandoning their faith. They rationalize that God does sometimes say no for reasons that may not be presently evident.

In my lifetime I have heard hundreds of miracles produced through prayer. I accept most of the stories as truth, although I am usually very skeptical. How can a person be sure this miracle occurred as the result of prayer, and was it really a miracle? A miracle by definition means that it is an event that cannot be explained through natural means. In other words, it has to be supernatural. How often do we witness supernatural occurrences? Several of my prayers have produced positive results, and many have not. I've noted that the more ambitious my request is, the less likely it is to occur. Certainly, someone who has lost an arm or leg will not miraculously grow a new one, no matter how long or hard he prays. Haven't we heard of countless stories where good and caring parents are charged with neglect in the death of their children when they failed to get proper medical treatments because their faith prohibited it and their prayers failed?

There is no doubt that prayer is consoling and that it clearly generates hope. Prayer is obviously a major component of every religion. By praying for a sick loved one, prayer can afford some satisfaction and even offer a degree of comfort in doing something positive to help. Community prayer reinforces solidarity. Certainly, prayer can be a last resort and is often embraced by atheists stricken with serious illnesses. In the final analysis, prayer is a positive force in human behavior, but it does have its doubters, including deists, who believe that God created the universe and programmed it to run without any interference until its conclusion. They would ask, "Is prayer a request begging God to change His mind?"

CHAPTER 4

Although most people accept the established books of the Bible to be a complete work, we know that some Bibles have more books and that the canonization process segregated books deemed as inspired and uninspired. Rumors have abounded for centuries about lost books. We will examine some of these in this chapter.

What exactly do we consider a lost book of the Bible? The answer to this is not as simple as we may think. There are hundreds of biblical-type books that are not included in any Bible today. The mere fact that we know of them verifies that they are not lost at all. They are just books not included in any of our known Bibles. As a first task, we need to explore the sources where a lost book is mentioned and where it might exist. Next we will look into following documents:

1. New Testament Apocrypha
2. Old Testament Apocrypha
3. New Testament pseudepigrapha
4. Old Testament pseudepigrapha
5. Gnostic library
6. Noncanonical writings
7. The Book of Mormon
8. Miscellaneous books

LOST BOOKS OF THE BIBLE

Therefore, lost books of the Bible must be books that were once considered to be part of sacred scripture but became lost for one reason or another. The only legitimate records we have of these lost books can only be found in the canonical books we have today. Only the canonical books are deemed sacred scripture. We will look into the Bible and examine where and which books these are listed in along with any other information available that may show any information regarding these texts.

Many people of deep faith, particularly our fundamentalist friends, would say there are no lost books of the Bible. God inspired only sixty-six books and designated only these sixty-six books found in the King James Version of the Bible. This is a minority position, but most Christians and Jews believe their Bibles are complete without any missing books.

Defining lost books of the Bible can be confusing and certainly ambiguous. I will use the definition accepted by most scholars (as mentioned earlier). The only confirmation we have for this claim is that the lost books specifically are referenced in the canonical books as we read them today. We will look into the Bible and show just where they are recorded along with any other outside information available regarding the particular lost book.

There are eighteen—but perhaps as many as twenty-four—books mentioned or implied as scripture in the Old and New Testaments that are definitely not included in any Bible. These are the ones that at least appear to be lost books. Variation in the quantity could be the result of duplicate mentions using differing names to reference the same book. Of the twenty-four, eighteen are found in the Old Testament or Hebrew Bible and six in the New Testament.

The most important factor concerning these lost books, especially in the Hebrew Bible but only somewhat less in the Christian Bible, is that they represent a documented record of tangible evidence that gives us an explicit source manuscript that was available to the writers of the canonical books. Simply stated, the Bible states that a book of Jasher is a reliable source. Therefore, these lost books most likely were some of the actual written sources used by the biblical authors when they wrote their stories. That is the reason the biblical author recorded the reference at all. Pointing out the name of the lost book gives us positive proof that written material was used to assemble their written sacred document. It was then combined in consort with the oral traditions to complete their present canonical text. Why the lost books were not passed down for future generations is a mystery that we may never know, but at least we do know of their identity.

Perhaps the most famous example is the book of Jasher, whose source is found in Joshua 10:13, which says, "And the sun stood still, and the moon stayed, until the people had avenged themselves upon their enemies. Is not this written in the book of Jasher?" Another reference is also found in 2 Samuel 1:18, which says, "And to say that the sons of Judah should be taught 'the Bow.' Look! it is written in the book of Jasher." It is obvious that Jasher was once considered authoritative and worthy as some form of scriptural reference. After all, it is used by the authors of two separate biblical books. It should be pointed out that some scholars believe the same person authored Samuel and Joshua.

An actual book of Jasher certainly exists today, but nearly every biblical scholar agrees that these copies are the concoctions of writers from a time much later than Samuel or Joshua. Highly respected Professor Edgar J. Goodspeed did extensive research on Jasher and came up with three known books. The earliest are from medieval times, but there's no evidence whatsoever of anything earlier. The first is a 1391 version by Rabbi Shabbatai Carmuz Levita that is now in the Vatican library. The second is a book used as the introduction to the Hexateuch, which was probably written by a Spanish Jew in the thirteenth century and was published in Venice in 1625. Lastly, there's is a treatise on Jewish ritual written by Rabbi Tham, who died in 1171. It was printed in Italy in 1544.

The second of these (the thirteenth-century version) was translated into English by a Mr. Samuel of Liverpool, England, and published in 1840 in New York by Nash and Gould.

The version of the book of Jasher most people would be familiar with is likely the one that was produced by a man named Jacob Ilive, a London printer who published his own version of the book of in 1751. This version has been reprinted and circulated by the Rosicrucian order. Goodspeed calls this rendition a "shameless literary forgery."

Perhaps the greatest proponents for the authenticity of the book of Jasher are the Mormons. Unofficially, they seem to have shown (in the past and present) a good deal of interest in Jasher. So much so that American Jewish officials became irritated by Mormon activities early in the nineteenth century. The following article about early Mormonism was taken from the *Spalding Studies*:

> Mordecai Noah was not unaware of the Mormon activities in building a temporary city of refuge at Kirtland in the 1830s. In a late 1835 issue of his Evening Star, Noah protested the Mormons' calling their nearly finished house of worship at Kirtland the "Temple of the Lord." The Jewish editor and would-be American Zionist seemingly had no patience with what he termed the Mormons'

"unhallowed purposes" in gathering around a "heathen temple." The Mormons never quite lose sight of Mordecai Noah's work, though they have long since forgotten his name. In 1840 the Jewish scholar translated into English and published the extracanonical Book of Jasher. The Mormons became fascinated with the book and have kept it in print and circulation wherever they congregate. The first of their reprinting of this strange volume was published by J. H. Parry & Company in Salt Lake City, Utah, in 1887 and modern printings are always kept in stock at the LDS Church's Deseret (original name of the theocratic state founded by Brigham Young) Book Stores.

All the Mormon sources that I have read claim that the LDS church takes no official position on the authenticity of the book of Jasher.

OTHER LOST BOOKS

Consider the book of the covenant referenced in Exodus 24:7, which says, "And he took the book of the Covenant, and read it in the audience of the people: and they said, all that the Lord hath said will we do, and be obedient." Some scholars believe excerpts from this lost book are incorporated in Exodus 20, 21, 22, and 23; but clearly, this is just speculation with no factual evidence.

Consider the book of the wars of the Lord (Jehovah) referenced in Numbers 21:14, which says, "Wherefore it is said in the book of the wars of the Lord (Jehovah), what He did in the Red sea and in the brooks of Arnon."

Consider the manner of the kingdom, also known as book of statutes, which is referenced in 1 Samuel 10:25, which says, "Then Samuel told the people the manner of the kingdom, and wrote it in a book, and laid it up before the Lord."

Consider the book of Samuel the seer referenced in 1 Chronicles 29:29, which says, "Now the acts of David the king, first and last, behold, they are written in the book of Samuel the seer, and in the book of Nathan the prophet, and in the book of Gad the seer." Here are three sources that were available to Ezra at the time he was writing Chronicles.

Nathan the prophet also appears in 2 Chronicles 9:29, which says, "Now the rest of the acts of Solomon, first and last, are they not written in the book of Nathan the prophet, and in the prophecy of Ahijah the Sholonite, and in the visions of Iddo the seer against Jeroboam the son of Nebat?"

Acts of Solomon is also referenced in 1 Kings 11:41, which says, "And the rest of the acts of Solomon, and all that he did, and his wisdom, are they not written in the book of the acts of Solomon?"

Shemaiah the prophet appears in 2 Chronicles 12:15, which says, "Now the acts of Rehoboam, first and last, are they not written in the book of Shemaiah the prophet, and of Iddo the seer concerning genealogies?"

There's the story of Prophet Iddo in 2 Chronicles 13:22, which says, "And the rest of the acts of Ahijah, and his ways, and his sayings, are written in the story of the prophet Iddo."

Consider the book of Jehu referenced in 2 Chronicles 20:34, which says, "Now the rest of the acts of Jehoshaphat, first and last, behold, they are written in the book of Jehu the son of Hanani, who is mentioned in the book of the kings of Israel."

Consider the sayings of the seers referenced in 2 Chronicles 33:19, which says, "His prayer also, and how God was intreated of him, and all his sin, and his trespass, and the places wherein he built high places, and set up groves and graven images, before he was humbled: behold, they are among the sayings of the seers."

Consider the acts of Uzziah referenced in 2 Chronicles 26:22, which says, "Now the rest of the acts of Uzziah, first and last, did Isaiah the prophet, the son of Amoz, write."

The annals of King David are then referenced 1 Chronicles 27:24, which says, "Joab son of Zeruiah began to count the men but did not finish. Wrath came on Israel on account of this numbering, and the number was not entered in the book of the annals of King David."

Clearly, all of these lost books should not be taken or understood to be—necessarily—part of an original definition of *sacred scripture. But* ... it is quite obvious that some of them were considered so by the ancient canonical writers. That is the reason they are mentioned. Simply put, they were recorded in the written sources writers used. Ezra is thought of by many biblical scholars to be the author of the books of Chronicles, which contain most of the references of the lost books.

The New Testament book of Jude definitely cites and quotes directly from the book of Enoch. Jude recites it as if it were sacred scripture. Jude 1:14 says, "And Enoch also, the seventh from Adam, prophesied of these, saying, behold, the Lord cometh with 10 thousands of His saints."

Today the book of Enoch is positively not a lost book but is not found in any Bibles except in the Christian Ethiopian Orthodox Bible. The Dead Sea Scrolls have provided several copies written in Hebrew. Prior to this, Coptic/Ethiopian versions of Enoch existed, but these were considered to be only of little value and certainly pseudepigraphic. Perhaps of all the disputed pseudepigrapha or apocryphal books, it is by far the most important. Many of the sayings and expressions by Jesus allude to His obvious knowledge of Enoch. The author of the book of Revelation clearly alludes to this book, and many Christian traditions are taken directly from Enoch. Seven copies were discovered in different caves at Qumran, proving the popularity of this book in the early first century.

Consider the missing epistle of Jude. Jude 1:3 says, "Beloved, when I gave all diligence to write unto you of the common salvation, it was needful for me to write unto you, and exhort you that ye should earnestly contend for the faith which was once delivered unto the saints." This indicates that Jude had a previous epistle which is no longer in existence.

Consider the Nazarene prophecy source. Matthew 2:23 says, "And he came and dwelt in a city called Nazareth: that it might be fulfilled which was spoken by the prophets, He shall be called a Nazarene."

There are many cases in the Pauline Epistles where he alludes to letters he wrote that for some reason were not preserved. Yet we can clearly see these letters in 2 Corinthians, which is a composite of perhaps as many as three separate letters conflated into one.

Consider the epistle to the Corinthians (missing perhaps the third letter or part of the conflation of 2 Corinthians). First Corinthians 5:9 says, "I wrote unto you in an epistle not to company with fornicators."

Consider the epistle to the Ephesians (missing). Ephesians 3:3 says, "How that by revelation he made known unto me the mystery; (as I wrote afore in few words, four whereby, when ye read, ye may understand my knowledge in the mystery of Christ)."

Consider the epistle from Laodicea to the Colossians. Colossians 4:16 says, "And when this epistle is read among you, cause that it be read also in the church of the Laodiceans; and that ye likewise read the epistle from Laodicea."

These *lost* books I just delineated are the only *lost books of the Bible* considered by most biblical scholars. However, some other books are often confused with the lost books. Some of these appear only in some Bibles, but others do not appear in any Bibles at all and are technically not considered lost books. The terms or categories generally used to describe these books are Apocrypha and/or pseudepigrapha. A good deal of confusion exists with these terms. Protestants and Jews use the expression pseudepigrapha to classify several books that Orthodox and Catholics would call the Apocrypha. (What follows is an expanded explanation of some of the same material as found in chapter 2.)

It works this way. Critical study of the Bible began in earnest in the eighteenth century by Protestant scholars. Likewise, Catholic scholarship did not start until the mid-twentieth century. As a result, Protestants (for about two hundred years) exclusively applied and used the term pseudepigrapha to reference any biblical book (usually restricted to the Old Testament) that was considered false or unauthentic and was never considered scripture by any church. Apocrypha was then used to represent generally the fifteen books that only appear in the Old Testament of Orthodox and Catholic Bibles.

Today scholars sometimes apply the term Apocrypha to any Christian writings that are not part of the sixty-six book canon which is accepted by all. Orthodox and Catholics use only this term for all books that are not included in their canon. They do not officially use the term pseudepigrapha at all. Historically, Protestant scholarship established the groundwork in this area of study, and many but certainly not all Orthodox and Catholic scholars usually just follow and use the same terms. Thus, we can see how this confusion may have set in.

The pseudepigrapha books originated at about the same general time as the Apocrypha emerged, roughly 250 BCE to 90 CE; however, the later date may be and is often extended into the Middle Ages. Literally, this term means "pseudonymous writings." These typically are books that were falsely attributed to a real character in the Hebrew Bible, but this reference sometimes applies to late New Testament writings as well.

For example, many scholars today believe the book of Daniel should belong to the pseudepigrapha. They believe this book was written about 170 BCE, about the same time the Maccabean revolt began, obviously well after the time period referenced in the book of Daniel. Clearly, there is strong evidence to support this theory, but it cannot be conclusively proven.

The earliest understanding of the term Apocrypha applied to a very sacred group of valuable writings that had to be kept secret or hidden from the general public. The secrecy was set up so that only the experienced membership and not novices or outsiders could read the books. Historically, the philosophers of ancient Greece distinguished between the doctrines and rites that all of their pupils could learn from and those that could be taught only to a select circle called the initiated. Judging by this we can understand that the very early Christian usage of the word Apocrypha was considered as being analogous to gold and silver (something very precious but hidden away for only those who knew how to find it and utilize its value). Also from this, we can see how the Gnostic influence was prevalent even among the Orthodox. Perhaps this is one reason Jerome viewed these writings adversely.

The pejorative expression Apocrypha (meaning "spurious or dubious authenticity") was first used by Jerome, the fourth-century Christian father of the New Testament. He used it to represent fifteen books he believed were spurious because they were not considered *inspired* by the Jewish scholars of his day. He had also actively used Jewish scholars to assist him in his translation. Jerome translated the Greek and Hebrew texts into the Latin Vulgate. This became the first complete Christian Bible (combining the Old and New Testaments together in one book) and the standard for all Christianity for more than a thousand years afterward. At this point the sequence and order of the books as they appear even to this day in every Christian Bible was established too. Please be mindful that most Protestant Bibles do not contain the books of the Apocrypha. The reference Deuterocanonical is the term used in Orthodox and Catholic parlance representing these fifteen books.

There is a wide variation in the number of books that are included by the various Orthodox synods. The number of Old Testament books range from sixty-three to fifty-four of the most common books. Some do not accept the book of Revelation, while most include it but do not use it in any of their services. Catholic Bibles contain forty-six books of the Old Testament. That is seven more than Protestant Bibles, which have thirty-nine. However, Catholic Bibles have what are called additions to or longer versions of several canonical books. Daniel, Jeremiah (actually attributed to the Letter to Baruch), and Esther combined with several books that appear in the Orthodox Bibles as separate books, and they are incorporated within these canonical texts, therefore making them much longer.

Factually, the Christian Bible (as we now know it) was the idea of Pope Damasus, who commissioned Jerome's work. He and Augustine pressured Jerome to include the books of the Apocrypha in the Vulgate. The petulant Jerome acquiesced, but his term and definition of apocryphal quietly lingered until actively revived during the Protestant Reformation.

The Protestant reformers discarded the Apocrypha mainly because the Jews, who they believed were the divinely ordained custodians of the Hebrew Bible or Old Testament, did not accept them. They also knew of the numerous historical and geographical errors that were prevalent in several of these books. But perhaps the greatest reason was that 2 Maccabees lent *scriptural* support for the Catholic doctrine of purgatory.

Another misconception of these lost books is the Gnostic Christian library of biblical books. The Gnostics made up a large segment of early Christianity. Because of their theological practices, they came to be considered heretical by Orthodox Christianity and were persecuted into extinction. However, a very tiny segment of Gnostics did survive and lingered quietly in Armenia and still exist today.

The Gnostic writings, also known as the Nag Hammadi Library, are a collection of thirteen ancient codices containing more than fifty texts. These books were actually unknown until a major discovery was unearthed in the Egyptian desert in 1945. This immensely important discovery includes a large number of primary Gnostic scriptures—texts once thought to have been entirely destroyed during the early Christian struggle to define orthodoxy—such as the gospel of Thomas, the gospel of Philip, and the gospel of truth, the apocryphon of John, the hypostasis of the Archons, the origin of the world, the apocalypse of Adam, and the paraphrase of Shem, to name just a few. Many of these writings originated in the first and second centuries. Notice the apocryphon of John. The early usage of the word apocryphon, the singular of apocrypha, in the first century was not considered inferior or secondary but a sacred writing so important that it had to keep secret and available only for the confirmed membership.

The early struggle between Gnostic and Orthodox Christianity did not become hostile until the early third century. Valentinus, a major second-century Gnostic bishop, was a legitimate candidate for the pope of Rome. In the fourth century, Saint Augustine was a convert from Gnosticism. After the Council of Nicea (325 CE), Gnostic scriptures became anathema to the newly organized orthodox church, and imperial decree ordered that these be destroyed.

The earliest complete Bibles contain books that are not found in any of our Bibles today. The earliest and the most important of these books is codex Vaticanus, which is dated to the early fourth century. It contains all the books of the Apocrypha as do all the earliest codices, except 1 and 2 Maccabees. Another fourth-century codex is called Sinaiticus. In addition to all of the canonical books, there's the epistle of Barabbas and the shepherd of Hermas, not to mention 1 Maccabees and 4 Maccabees (not 2 or 3 Maccabees). This clearly indicates these books were considered, at that point in history when they were written, the equal to the others within the community where Sinaiticus was first published.

The last of the big three codices is called Alexandrinus and is dated to the mid-fifth century. It is the most complete of the three; most of its pages are preserved. It embodies the *extra* books of 1 and 2 Clement (of Rome) and all four books of Maccabees.

Summarizing the *extra books* of the New Testament that are encompassed within the earliest codices, we find the epistle of Barabbas, the shepherd of Hermas, and the epistles of 1 and 2 Clement. Those people in the communities from where these books derived must have considered them sacred scripture. Most believe all three codices originated in Alexandria, Egypt.

SECRET GOSPEL OF MARK

Another recent discovery that possibly could qualify as a lost book is what's known as the "secret gospel of Mark." This discovery caused a major scandal within the scholar community. The discovery was made by a man named Morton Smith. In 1958, he was a young graduate student working in a library in Jerusalem. He came across a letter written by Clement of Alexandria, a third-century bishop. He spotted a formal letter inscribed on the backside of a much later document. The letter was very faded but still readable. Clement writes "to Theodore," congratulating him for his success in his disputes with the Carpocratians. They were a heterodox sect about which little is known. Apparently, in their conflict with Theodore, the Carpocratians had appealed to Mark's gospel for support. (Mark is the patron saint of Alexandria.)

Clement responds by recounting a new story about the gospel. He writes that after Peter's death, Mark brought his original gospel to Alexandria and wrote a "more spiritual gospel for the use of those who were being perfected." Clement says this text is kept by the Alexandrian church for use only in the initiation into "the great mysteries." However, the heretic Carpocrates, by means of magical stealth, obtained a copy and adapted it to his own ends. Because this version of the *secret* or *mystery* gospel had been polluted with "shameless lies," Clement urges Theodore to deny its Mark authorship even under oath. He advises, "Not all true things are to be said to all men."

Theodore had asked questions about particular passages from the special Carpocratian gospel of Mark, and by way of reply Clement transcribes two sections that he claims have been distorted by the heretics. The first fragment of the secret gospel of Mark was meant to be inserted between Mark 10:34 and 10:35. It reads,

> They came to Bethany. There was one woman there whose brother had died. She came and prostrated herself before Jesus and spoke to him. "Son of David, pity me!" But the disciples rebuked her. Jesus was angry and went with her into the garden where the tomb was. Immediately a great cry was heard from the tomb. And going up to it, Jesus rolled the stone away from the door of the tomb, and immediately went in where the young man was. Stretching out his hand, he lifted him up, taking hold his hand. And the youth, looking intently at him, loved him and started begging him to let him remain with him. And going out of the tomb, they went into the house of the youth, for he was rich. And after six days Jesus gave him an order and, at evening, the young man came to him

wearing nothing but a linen cloth. And he stayed with him for the night, because Jesus taught him the mystery of the Kingdom of God. And then when he left he went back to the other side of the Jordan.

Then a second fragment of the secret gospel of Mark is to be inserted into Mark 10:46. This has long been recognized as a narrative snag in Mark's gospel, as it awkwardly reads, "Then they come to Jericho. As he was leaving Jericho with his disciples … This strangely construction sentence is not present in Secret Mark, which reads: 'Then he came into Jericho. And the sister of the young man whom Jesus loved was there with his mother and Salome, but Jesus would not receive them.'"

Just as Clement prepares to reveal the *real interpretation* of these verses to Theodore, the copyist discontinues, and Smith's discovery is despondently complete. Notice the similarity to Lazarus's story and the disciple whom Jesus loved as written in the gospel of John.

Morton Smith later became professor of ancient history at Columbia University. (At the time of his discovery, he was a graduate student at Columbia.) And his translation was called "Secret Mark," an expansion or early version of the canonical gospel of Mark.

While working at the monastery of Mar Saba, which was a few miles south of Jerusalem, Smith discovered on the back of an eighteenth-century document a portion of a letter allegedly written by Clement of Alexandria, though it was in very faded condition and barely visible. Smith surmised that the later document was written over an existing erased text. (This was common practice at the time.) He photographed the document but was not allowed to take the original out of the monastery. Mysteriously, the original letter subsequently became lost.

Because no one besides Smith had seen the document, the scholarly community refused to accept it as authentic. Smith underwent long and harsh criticism, and he was met with skepticism from all quarters. However, by 1991, shortly before his death, most scholars had come to view the document as genuine.

As the news of this document became more widely dispersed, Christian leaders became disturbed and began to voice opposition. As a result, today there is a complete split in the scholarly community all over again. One of the main points of contention involves the fact that the text refers to some suspect conduct by Jesus. Some scholars and church leaders believe the text might allude to homosexual behavior.

At present, society has come to accept homosexuality, but it wasn't long ago that this issue was viewed in a negative light. In ancient pagan times, it was an accepted lifestyle. In *The Naked and the Nude*, Rabbi Bradley Shavit Artson states, "Ritual nudity was not uncommon in the ancient Near East, yet the Torah fuses bodily modesty with divine service. Therefore initiation ceremonies, such as Baptism, probably did require some kind of nudity without the slightest inclination toward sexual activity."

Perhaps the following excerpt by David Fideler from the *Journal of Western Cosmological Traditions* presents a good example of what is being described in Secret Mark:

> [F]rom the scattered indications in the canonical Gospels and the secret Gospel of Mark, we can put together a picture of Jesus' baptism, "the mystery of the kingdom of God." It was a water baptism administered by Jesus to chosen disciples, singly and by night. The costume, for the disciple, was a linen cloth worn over the naked body. This cloth was probably removed for the baptism proper, the immersion in water, which was now reduced to a preparatory purification. After that, by unknown ceremonies, the disciple was possessed by Jesus' spirit and so united with Jesus. One with him, he participated by hallucination in Jesus' ascent into the heavens, he entered the kingdom of God, and was thereby set free from the laws ordained for and in the lower world. Freedom from the law may have resulted in completion of the spiritual union by physical union. This certainly occurred in many forms of Gnostic Christianity; how early it began there is no telling.

As was the case in refusal to share with other scholars by their early reluctance toward publishing the Dead Sea Scrolls, scholarly egos and petty jealousy has confused and bewildered the general public, and the same holds true for Morton Smith and Secret Mark. Fideler continues,

> Secret Mark's plight constitutes a warning to all scholars as to the dangers of allowing sentiments of faith to cloud or prevent critical examination of evidence. When seen in light of the massive literature which has been produced by the other major manuscript finds in the 20th century, the Dead Sea Scrolls, Nag Hammadi codices, the comparative dearth of good studies on this piece in particular cannot be explained in any other way that a stubborn refusal to deal with information which might challenge deeply-held personal convictions. It is good to keep in mind an unofficial directive of the Jesus Seminar: "Beware of finding a Jesus entirely congenial to you."

Many scholars condemned Smith's find as a fraud, and perhaps some maintain that attitude even to this day. Although it is still being debated, Smith's discovery is generally accepted as authentic. It should be noted Mark's gospel had been considered incomplete or unfinished by many scholars even as far back as Eusubius, the author of *The History of the Church*, which was written in the fourth century. Reasoning for this is in some of the later ancient texts include different endings while the earliest texts in Mark's Gospel end at chapter 16 verse 8. Many of these endings still circulate in some of today's Bibles, but they were not included in the earliest manuscripts. This shows strong evidence that pious Christians believed there was a need to correct, clarify, or complete Mark's gospel to satisfy their present understandings or doctrines. They also did this in an attempt to appeal to pagans and counter-heretics.

Certainly, the Book of Mormon is not a lost book. Most Christians consider it to be a fictitious collection fabricated by Joseph Smith. Mormons believe Smith found some sacred gold plates that contained writing in scripture, and then he translated them into English. Let us now look into these books.

THE BOOK OF MORMON

Here we will reflect on the Book of Mormon. This is considered a separate scriptural document in addition to the Christian New and Old Testaments. This is similar to how some modern Protestant Bibles include the Apocrypha as a third or separate testament.

The Book of Mormon is viewed as a lost book of the Bible by people who are Mormons. According to the Mormon faith, their founder, Joseph Smith, received a vision from the angel Maroni telling him the location of lost ancient plates containing sacred scripture. Smith found them and translated them into English, calling it the Book of Mormon.

As the Apocrypha is made up of several books, so is the Book of Mormon. It consists of eleven books written in the style of English quite similar to that found in the King James Version. They include 1, 2, 3, and 4 Nephi, Jacob, Mosiah, Alma, Helaman, Mormon, Ether, and Maroni.

To be sure, numerous other biblical books do exist, many of which I have not mentioned, which may have at one time been though of as a lost book are clearly fictional and have no basis to be considered as being part of any Bible. These are books that clearly (and undisputedly) belong in the pseudepigrapha or Apocrypha because they were written later than the fifth century.

Many questions and problems concerning the canonical books clearly have some validity, but even the most skeptical would have to admit the books the ancients selected to be in the Bible are clearly the best from a historical and theological point of view. Next we will look into another Bible very similar to the Torah in the Hebrew Bible. It is called the Samaritan Pentateuch.

THE HISTORY OF THE SAMARITANS

The New Testament mentions Samaritans a number of times. Most memorable are the clearly positive examples showing them as kind and good people (e.g., the Good Samaritan in Luke). We also see the implication that many of them converted to Christianity. Surprisingly, the Old Testament mentions *Samaritan* only one time at 2 Kings 17:29.

Acts and the Gospels fail to describe just who or what a Samaritan is while only vaguely indicating their home was Samaria. Of course, any additional information would not have been pertinent for the evangelist's agenda, but some facts certainly would help modern readers to better understand. We must keep in mind that the Gospels and Acts were written at least thirty years after the Easter event. No one immediately wrote down the events as they happened. When they did commit something to writing, most of their sources were oral traditions that were then didactically combined in concert with present events. Therefore, exact accuracy simply could not be maintained. Take the recordings of the last words of Jesus on the cross—certainly a most important and memorable episode for Christians. Yet all four gospels transcribe different words. This doesn't mean the writers lied or tried to mislead, only that the passing of time causes memories to fade. They simply wrote what they thought best suited the occasion. The Samaritan story is an excellent case in point.

Samaritans got their name from the word *Samerim*, which means *keepers* (of the Torah). Basically, they were and are a sister religion to Judaism. During the time of Jesus, they had a sizable population. Like the Sadducees, Samaritans only accepted the Torah/Pentateuch as binding scared scripture. Scholars use the Samaritan Pentateuch when trying to determine the original text of the Torah and the development of the Bible. The Dead Sea Scrolls are considered to be in close accordance with the Samaritan Pentateuch and the Septuagint. In fact, the Abishua Scroll, which is still used in the Samaritan synagogue at Nablus, was allegedly written by Abishua, the great-grandson of Aaron, and claimed to be the most ancient biblical text in existence. However, most scholars agree this text dates to the thirteenth century CE.

Around 930 BCE, Jeroboam led the revolt of the Northern tribes and established the kingdom of Israel, opposing Rehoboam, which left him the kingship of only Judah (1 Kings 11–14; 2 Chronicles 10). Israel then fell to the Assyrians in 722 BCE. Assyrian records tell us that they took 27,290 captives, mostly people of the leadership class, into exile in Assyria. The majority were allowed to remain but were forced to accept Assyrian immigration and sovereignty.

This is in conflict with the story in the Old Testament, which declares that the entire population was removed. Conceivably, that cannot be correct. Second Kings 17:18 says, "Therefore the Lord was very angry with Israel, and removed them out of his sight: there was none left but the tribe of Judah only." Samaritans claim they are the remnant that was left as well as those who returned later. However, there is no record of any return as was the case with the Jewish/Babylon return. Certainly, before the fall of Israel, many who anticipated the invasion fled south to Judah and may have returned after Judah fell.

Why then would the Old Testament contend total evacuation in view of the Assyrian records and Samaritan claims? Even Josephus (*Antiquities of the Jews*, book IX, chapter 148) states that "Shalmaneser, the king of Assyria … transplanted all the people into Media and Persia." It would appear that the Judean writers/editors believed the ten Northern tribes had fatally alienated the God of Israel, thus leaving the covenant in sole position of the Jews.

Ezra believed that only Jews were exiled to Babylon and that they remained pure and faithful (Ezra 16:6). But some of those Jews who had remained in Judea during the exile had become corrupted through foreign marriages. Ezra, who wrote Chronicles, states that the Israelites "transgressed against the God of their fathers, and went a whoring after the gods of the people of the land, whom God destroyed before them" (1 Chronicles 5:25).

It was Ezra's religious fervor that inspired him to compile an all-encompassing Bible that spelled out the written will of God as it applied throughout all of Hebrew history. This, of course, left out the Samaritans because Ezra was certain they were rejected by God. Needless to say, this caused an immediate estrangement, especially when the Samaritans offered to help with building the new temple in Jerusalem and were turned down.

This dislike for one another intensified as time went by. In about 409 BCE, Manasseh, the son of the high priest, was expelled from Jerusalem by Nehemiah because he was married to a Samaritan woman. He then went to Samaria, and with permission from the Persian king Darius Nothus, he built a rival temple on Mount Gerizim (Josephus, *Antiquities* 11.7–8). In 333 BCE, Alexander the Great laid siege to Tyre. Sanballat, governor of Samaria, sent eight thousand troops to Alexander's aid, and so he received permission to build a temple on Mount Gerizim. While Alexander was on campaign in Egypt, the Samaritans rebelled, causing Alexander to return and destroy the city of Samaria and turn it into a Macedonian colony. The historical records I have mentioned in this paragraph all have other conflicting stories, but the Jewish-Samaritan problems are real.

Just prior to the Maccabean uprising, Jesus ben Sirach wrote that the Samaritans, Idumeans, and Philistines were the three greatest enemies of the Jewish people (Sirach 50:25–26). Josephus tells us about the Samaritans requesting the rededication of their temple to Jupiter Hellenius at the time of the Maccabee insurrection. Perhaps this is an embellishment, but "Antichous sent Gerontes the Athenian to force the Jews of Israel to violate their ancestral customs and live no longer by the laws of God; and to profane the Temple in Jerusalem and dedicate it to Olympian Zeus, and the one on Mount Gerizim to Zeus, Patron of Strangers, as the inhabitants of the latter place had requested" (2 Maccabees 6:1–2).

John Hyrcanus destroyed the Samaritan temple in 128 BCE. The exact reasons for doing so are lost in the religious polemics of both sides, but the Jewish hostility that expressed itself in the destruction of the Samaritan temple was a fact. The most likely reason was probably that the Samaritans supported the Seleucid Greek occupation of Palestine and opposed the Maccabean revolt.

About the time of Jesus, stress between the Jews and the Samaritans was at a high point. During the period between 6 CE and 9 CE, a group of Samaritans scattered bones in the Jerusalem temple at Passover. In 52 CE, Samaritans killed a group of pilgrims from Galilee near the town of En-gannim. The Samaritans throughout history were inhabitants of central Palestine, and they were not the most peaceful of subjects. In AD 36, a mob of them led by a messianic agitator, in spite of a Roman injunction, made a march on Mount Gerizim. Pilate's forces blocked them there, killing the leaders and imprisoning many. Jews traveling between Galilee and Judea made a point to avoid Samaria by crossing east of the Jordan River.

At the time of the first Jewish revolt, they adopted the same attitude toward the Romans and took up arms with the Jews. The Roman general Cerealis opposed their march toward Jerusalem, but shortly before they set off for Jerusalem the Romans confronted them on Mount Gerizim, and ended the march by massacring eleven thousand people on 27 June 67, according to Josephus (*Antiquities of the Jews*). Perhaps we can see how and why this enmity toward Samaritans was prevalent in the first century, yet the New Testament clearly shows Jesus openly accepting them and also reveals their willingness to embrace Christianity. Clearly, this ran contrary to the customs of the time.

Could Jesus have really reached out to the Samaritans and risked alienating His Jewish followers? Of course! Jesus was insultingly accused of being a Samaritan possessed by a demon

(John 8:48–49). He, indeed, traveled through Samaria a number of times, one time staying for two days with the villagers of Sychar. However, on His last trip to Jerusalem, people in a Samaritan village refused Him admittance because His destination was Jerusalem (Luke 9.51–56).

But a more likely scenario might be found by a close examination of the religious and political circumstances evolving at the time the Gospels were being written. The woman at the well (John 4:1–42), the tenth leper (Luke 17:11–19), the Great Commission (Matthew 28:19–20), and the Good Samaritan (Luke 10:30–37) all stemmed from a time when Christians were separating from Judaism in a way similar to undergoing a bitter divorce.

Because the Jews had always rejected the Samaritans and Christians did as well, perhaps a dialogue between the rejects could find some mutual acquiescence. Jesus had accepted the Samaritans. Then it was clearly acceptable, even desirable, to recruit Samaritans. Obviously, these events were taking place as the evangelists wrote.

In summation, the Jewish people returning from Babylon exile had committed themselves to God through the reforms incorporated by King Josiah. Ezra was the chief priest in charge of the rededication of their faith. He had spent his lifetime faithfully organizing the religious traditions and writings into the masterpiece we now call the Bible. Although today it seems unjust, Ezra insisted on uncompromised religious/ethnic purity to assure the salvation of his people. The Samaritans just didn't fit Ezra's template.

After the destruction of Jerusalem, the Jewish nation once again had to try to understand why God had allowed it to happen. How had they gone astray this time? Strict compliance with the law seemed to be the best answer. So like the Samaritans of Ezra's time, now many were disassociating from the Christians. In response, the Christians quickly offered brotherhood to the old Jewish enemy, the Samaritans. This required the approval of Jesus, and the writers of the Gospels incorporated this approval too.

CHAPTER 5

I n chapter 2, we discussed how the Bible came into existence. Now we will look into the development of the Jewish Bible and how we receive it today.

HISTORY OF THE MASORETIC TEXT

This name is derived from the Hebrew scholars who copied earlier biblical manuscripts and added vowel points and standardized pronunciations. They are called the Masoretes. The name is derived from the Hebrew word *masorah*, which means *tradition*. The earliest existing manuscripts were copied and edited by the Masoretes beginning about 600 CE. Later a more accurate edition produced by leading Palestinian Masoretes during the first half of the tenth century (Ben Asher and Ben Naphtali) became what is known today as the Masoretic Text (abbreviated MT). This text has been considered to be *the* superior rendering of the original Hebrew Bible for at least the past five hundred years. The Masoretes gained the reputation of being most excellent scholars. Their almost superhuman, disciplined fortitude and extreme diligence in the creation of this interpretation also enhanced their renown. Previously, the original Hebrew texts had been written in Paleo-Hebrew (consonantal text), which contained no vowels. Thus, accurate verbalization of the original text was very difficult or next to impossible to vocalize in a straightforward way.

The astounding accuracy of their work is recognized by comparing the numerous existing texts, the earliest (about 850 CE) to the later ones. Errors of any kind are almost nonexistent. Without question, even the most critical savants accept the scholarly work of the Masoretes. Most famous of these was produced by the Ben Asher family (ninth to the eleventh century), and their version has become the official Jewish Bible.

The ancient historian Josephus (first century CE) claims in *Contra Apion*, "And how firmly we have given credit to these books of our own nation is evident by what we do; for during so many ages as have already passed, no one has been so bold as either to add anything to them, to take anything from them, or to make any change in them." Although Josephus preceded the Masoretes, the mystique of a single unified and accurate text had already been in existence.

Was Josephus correct?

Well, from the early Middle Ages to the last quarter of the twentieth century, most scholars believed so! Although the Septuagint (LXX) and the Samaritan Pentateuch (SP) clearly expressed numerous differences, these texts were considered inferior to the MT. Perhaps this subordinate view of the LXX by the sixteenth-century reformers influenced their decision to omit certain books from the Christian Bible that did not appear in the MT.

Today we have a plethora of evidence indicating that the superiority of the MT may have been misplaced. The discovery of the Dead Sea Scrolls (DDS) clearly proved this, as numerous scrolls produced many variants from the MT, as most but certainly not all of these variants favored the LXX, and some favored the SP.

Some MT supporters claimed the pacifistic Essene Jews instigated these changes. This was dispelled when more ancient scrolls were also discovered at the fortress of Masada which was defended by zealot Jews, that contained similar variations. We now know that a single unified Bible did not exist prior to the first century.

How can we explain this?

Since the Septuagint is not a Hebrew text and the Samaritan version reached us through a breakaway sect, their value to reflect the early stages of the biblical text was debatable. But the majority of the DSS clearly supported the LXX and even the SP over the MT. Today's scholars believe variant texts abounded and no single unified text existed until after the rabbinical council of Jamnia in about 90 CE.

Jamnia's rabbis needed to codify the texts that they believed accurately represented Pharisaic Judaism. They clearly believed Christians had stolen their sacred books because the Christians had adopted the Greek LXX and claimed it as their own. Because overwhelmingly more Jews understood and spoke Greek than Hebrew, Jamnia's rabbis promoted and produced Greek versions of their own. Aquila's version was the preferred one, but the Symmachus and Theodotion versions were also acceptable. Of course, these versions were based solely on the MT. (This was what should be called the proto or pre-MT.) It is important here to recognize that the Hebrew language at this point in history was not used at all except in religious circumstances. Aramaic was the standard language with Greek as a secondary language.

From about the time the Jews returned from Babylon captivity, the people spoke and read Aramaic. Therefore, the Hebrew Bible had to be translated into Aramaic for the community to understand it. For Bible study purposes, the texts translated from Hebrew to Aramaic would be called *targum* (the plural being *targumim*). When Ezra read the first written Bible in Jerusalem, he almost certainly read it in Aramaic.

The Kaige Recension of the LXX is an extant text created to agree with the proto-rabbinic or pre-MT in the Greek language. This recension or revision included the book of Baruch and the longer addition of Daniel, clearly showing the stamp of Pharisaic influence in these apocryphal books. This recension indicates a time when Jews still considered the Apocrypha as part of their scriptures (or at least some of the books). The Kaige Recension was a Greek copy of the Hebrew Bible produced by Palestinian Pharisees in the first century BCE. This bears clear proof that a fixed canon of the Hebrew Bible did not exist until after the first Jewish revolt (70 CE).

These events caused Christians to accuse Jewish translators of deliberately corrupting the LXX text. Justin Martyr (140 CE) wrote in *Dialogue with Trypho*, "Here Trypho remarked, 'We ask you first of all to tell us some scriptures which you allege have been completely cancelled'" (LXXI–LXXII). Justin claimed Jews removed major parts from Jeremiah and Ezra. Remarkably, the DSS copies show these two books were not reduced but expanded. In fact, they were considerably expanded.

The earliest evidence of the MT comes from the discovery of remnants of scrolls in the Judean desert (Wadi Murabba'at and Nahal Hever). Soldiers of Bar Kochba (around 135 CE) used these scrolls. Around this time Aramaic translations, such as Onqelos, Targum Jonathan, and the Palestine Targum, also sprang up, bearing the MT base. Therefore, we can safely say the MT, as we now know it, came to life between Jamnia (90 CE) and the Bar Kochba revolt (135 CE). In fact, Bar Kochba reverted back to using Paleo-Hebrew script, reversing the block Aramaic lettering designed by Ezra.

Today most scholars—Protestant, Catholic, and even Jewish—agree that several variant versions of sacred scripture existed well into the first century CE and that the LXX represents our closest text to the originals. Catholic Bibles are loosely based on the LXX. It is the official

Bible of the Greek Orthodox church and most other Orthodox churches. The MT is the official Bible of Judaism.

WHEN WAS THE COUNCIL OF JAMNIA HELD?

The Council of a Jamnia (Yavne) is a consensus theory and not an established historical fact. Accordingly most scholars, Jewish and Christian, believe it took place at Jamnia around 100 CE. We do have knowledge of several recognized sacred books prior to this from Josephus and the prologue of ben Sira, showing that a group of Jewish books had a special status and suggesting that a canon of some sorts was commonly acceptable in their time. However, the author of ben Sira (Sirach), the grandson of the Hebrew author, strongly implies that his grandfather's work should be included, indicating that the canon was still open. This happened in about 120 BCE.

The Talmud informs us that as late as the days of the Tannaim (200 CE), exactly which books were to be included in the canon was still *fluid*. Books of the Torah and some prophetic works as well were without dispute. Between 125 BCE and 125 CE (and even much later), the rabbis had numerous debates on which of the other books should be excluded or included in the canon (Song of Songs, Kohelet, and Ezekiel, which, of course, were finally included). Of course, no *official* proclamation has ever been formally declared.

Today we know without a doubt that the Dead Sea Scrolls clearly show a closed canon did not exist at a time prior to the destruction of Jerusalem in 70 CE. Numerous scrolls from what we now call the Apocrypha and pseudepigrapha make up a good portion of these scrolls. From this we can tentatively conclude a fixed Jewish canon was not recognized until after the rabbinical college at Jamnia was established.

The Jamnia rabbinical school was established by Rabban Yochanan ben Zakkai shortly after the destruction of Jerusalem. Judaism at this time was in complete disarray. Hebraic Judaism was ending, and rabbinic Judaism was now in place. This transition began in the Maccabean period, so this shifting of authority slowly developed during a period of about two hundred years.

In that span of time, the Jewish nation gained enormous status in the Mediterranean world for a number of reasons. I'm only listing here three of many. First, their religion had an ancient written text or bible. This bible was given the highest recognition by King Ptolemy of Egypt, as he included copies of it in the famous library of Alexandria. Second, the Maccabean revolt had shocked the world by achieving victory over an overwhelmingly superior Seleucid Greek force, and this resulted in their independence. Third, their religion became most appealing because of its ethics and emphasis on reading and writing.

The written text was translated into Greek for Ptolemy and is called the Septuagint or LXX. Here is where history becomes muddled by conflicting theologies that come later. At first, the LXX became a sense of pride to the Jewish nation. But after the Romans took over the country and a new offshoot of the faith came into play (Christianity) by confiscating the LXX and calling it their own, the attitude changed to actual hatred of the LXX.

Indeed, the rabbis recognized the importance of a Greek translation of their prestigious Bible and attempted to offer alternative versions in Greek to counter the LXX. The Christians busily collected most of the Jewish writings and thus preserved them, including all the books of the LXX. When this became evident to Jamnia (remember after the revolt), the rabbis began in earnest to completely reorganize their faith, and thusly, they began work on the Mishnah, which became part of the Talmud. Jews consider the Talmud to be equal in authority to the Bible. Many books of the Bible were reviewed, and a preliminary approval of which books constituted sacred scripture was loosely established.

By the late first century, Christianity considered the LXX to be their sacred scripture— well before there was even a New Testament. This was to remain so until after the Protestant Reformation when some of the reformers decided to drop several books of the LXX. Their reasons for the most part were valid, considering their knowledge of history that was available at the time. The idea of omitting books came about by the reformers' need to establish a foundation for their new faith which then was the Bible. To add emphasis they used the Latin term "Sola Scriptura" as their mantra. In short, if it was not specifically written in the Bible, it was not binding to Christians.

Until the late eighteenth century, the historical accuracy of the Bible was undisputed. It was here that German Protestants began to study the Bible in depth. These were scholars who believed everything in the Bible and were looking to gain knowledge to corroborate the truth of their Bible version. As it turned out, they found discrepancies and inconsistencies that gave birth to historical criticism.

Herein lies our problem with the Apocrypha. If you are a Protestant, you will be biased toward the Protestant Bible. If you are Catholic or Orthodox, you will be biased toward that Bible. The undisputable fact is the Apocrypha was basic to first-century Christian scripture, and as a result, the Jewish rabbis attempted to expel writings (that they thought were of Greek origin) from their scriptures—pure and simple! So the Christian scriptures or LXX became the undisputed property of Christianity, while the Jewish scriptures were still under intense consideration.

Protestants were certain they had theological and political advantage by ousting the Apocrypha. After all, several of the books contained obvious historical and geographical errors. This was fitting until historical criticism examined them in earnest late in the twentieth century when scholars began to uncover the reasoning behind the stories.

Notwithstanding, the confusion of just when, where, and how the various canons of the Bible actually took form still is in place today, most likely because the Council of Jamnia theory has not been proven and the authority for confirmation is widely disputed.

Let's us now turn to the Bible again to see how we may have encountered the climate conditions that could have had bearing on Israel's foundation in relation to her neighbors.

CLIMATE CONDITIONS AND THE EFFECTS

The current debates relative to global warming have prompted some scientists to look to history for possible answers. I believe the Bible is packed with pertinent information that could prove valuable in understanding this phenomenon. We will examine this history and offer the evidence particularly in regard to the data found in the Bible and from later historical events.

Around 2300 BCE, several of the major civilizations of the world inexplicably and simultaneously collapsed—the Akkadian Empire in Mesopotamia; the old kingdom in Egypt; the early Bronze Age civilization in Palestine, Anatolia, and Greece; the Indus Valley civilization in India; the Hilmand in Afghanistan; and Hongshan in China. The first urban civilizations in the world all fell about this same time.

About a thousand years later (1200 BCE), many civilizations of these same regions collapsed again. The Mycenaeans of Greece, Hittites in Anatolia, the Egyptian new kingdom, late Bronze Age Palestine, and the Shang Dynasty of China all seemingly imploded. The reasons for these apparently concurrent disasters coincided with changes of cultures and societies and have puzzled historians. Most common explanations include wars, natural calamities, diseases, famine, and more recently, "system collapse," but the apparent absence of direct archaeological or written evidence for these causes as opposed to effects has led many archaeologists and historians to concede that no definitive explanation can be found.

For more than three hundred years during the late Bronze Age and early Iron Age (1300–1000 BCE), Egypt ruled Canaan. Deities, arts, and technologies were intermingled between the two cultures. Many of the Old Testament writings are purported to have taken place in this period. There is a serious paucity of archaeological evidence to completely support the biblical account of the Israelites' occupation of Palestine. Archaeologists have demonstrated that certain cities allegedly taken by the Israelites were indeed destroyed just about this time. Another explanation might be that they could have been sacked by invading Egyptian armies. On the other hand, modern scholarship has suggested that the *conquest* took place more gradually than presented in the biblical account—the course of action more like a series of ethnic migrations rather than a long, drawn-out military campaign. Of course, it is possible that the Bible stories, in order to be more succinct, condensed a number of small battles into one, thus making several skirmishes appear to be a major battle to later readers.

Exodus reports that the Israelites were refused passage through Edom, forcing them north to the Amorite country near Madaba, where they battled and were victorious. Continuing on, they triumphed over the Moabites and then the Midianites as well. Some of the tribes then settled in the conquered territories. Here is where Moses died, and Joshua then led the remaining tribes across the Jordan River into Palestine. About two hundred years later, the tribes of Israel would take over Canaan and unite with Judah and Benjamin along with other territories to form the United Kingdom (about 1000 BCE).

This remarkable accomplishment could only have taken place because Israel's larger and more powerful neighbors were all experiencing serious internal problems at this time. After 1200 BCE, significant social and economic upheavals disrupted the eastern Mediterranean world. From Greece to Palestine, many important cities were abandoned or burned, possibly by the people displaced by the collapse of the Mycenaean palace system in the Aegean. Many of these people were called "sea peoples." Many believed that some of these peoples were the Philistines. Even Egypt was put under siege as the pharaohs Mernepthat and later Ramesses II struggled to fight back attacks from maritime invaders.

We know the facts of all these disintegrations, but we don't know the causes. It seems only one major factor could have reeked such havoc simultaneously on so many nations for such a prolonged period of time. Plagues certainly occurred, and their effects could have lasted a long time; however, it could not have lasted hundreds of years as the record shows. *Only a major climate change would have had these long-term results.* There are no historical records concerning Europe's weather conditions (the exception being Greece) for these times. But we may look for evidence from a more modern period when similar occurrences took place.

During the years 800 to 1200 CE, Iceland and Greenland were settled by the Vikings. The very warm climate during this period allowed this great migration to flourish. Drift ice posed the greatest hazard to sailors, but reports of drift ice in the old records do not appear until the thirteenth century. The warmer climate resulted in greater harvests in Iceland than would be experienced today, so this land must have looked much more inviting in the past than it does today.

The Norse peoples traveled to Iceland for a variety of reasons, namely to search for more land and resources to satisfy a rapidly expanding population and to escape raiders and harsh rulers. Animal bones and other materials collected from archaeological sites reveal Icelandic Vikings had large farmsteads with dairy cattle, pigs, sheep, and goats. Farmsteads also had ample pastures and fields of barley used for making beer, and these farms were located near bird cliffs (providing meat, eggs, and eiderdown) and inshore fishing grounds.

Eric the Red sailed west to Greenland, which had been discovered earlier. Here he found a welcoming area, a deep fiord on the southwestern coast. Warmer Atlantic currents met the island there, and the conditions were not much different from the way they were in Iceland. He called this new land "Greenland," in his opinion, "people would go thither if the country had a beautiful name." According to one of the Icelandic chronicles, although Greenland as a whole could not be considered *green*, it certainly was capable of supporting a harsh but substantial existence. It did also mention the land was not very good for farming. However, archaeological evidence has shown an abundance of domesticated animal bones from the earliest settlements and fish bones from later times, indicating a slow cooling period after 1200 CE. Consequently, their diet changed from one based on agriculture to one based on seafood. This leaves no doubt that Greenland was obviously much warmer then than it is today.

Eric's son, Leif, sailed from Greenland to the North American coast and named this new land "Vineland" because it was covered with vines. This would be the coasts of Labrador and Newfoundland, which is much colder today than it was when Leif Ericson explored the region. Archaeologists have recently discovered that during this same period, New Zealand's South Island experienced much warmer temperatures then than the place sees today, indicating that what we now call "the Medieval Warm Period" (or MWP) was occurring in both hemispheres.

All the records indicate that Western Europe experienced a gradual cooling between the years 1150 and 1460. Then it increasingly got colder from 1560 to 1850. This brought dire consequences to the people. This is now known as the "Little Ice Age," by most historians and scientists. It would then seem that a climate shift, warming or cooling, moving 350 miles (as the evidence appears to indicate) or so north would have had a profound effect in the biblical lands as well. If the warmer weather did move north, this would have brought conditions to the lands similar to that of the Sahara. This would explain the numerous droughts and famines spoken of in the Bible. Conditions around 1200 BCE caused Egypt to evacuate Canaan. For several years, the ordinarily reliable Nile floods failed to take place, causing even Egypt to experience famines. Did this impact the Exodus story? By restricting the shrinking food supply to favor native Egyptians, the Hebrew population would have certainly been forced to react.

The apogee of the climate change occurred about 1200 BCE, and about the time the United Kingdom of Judah and Israel was being established, every major power in the area was at its most weakened point, thus allowing time for the new state to form and grow. Then as the climate slowly turned, populations again grew, and soon the Israelites began to once again experience the pressures from their larger neighbors. The lesson we learned from the MWP shows the population explosion of Europe led to abundant food supplies and provided for more people to enter the military. There was now a surplus of manpower to use for the Crusades. The Crusaders and their livestock clearly suffered in battling with temperatures much higher than those at home. As history repeats, we can see how climate change affected past civilizations as witnessed by the Bible.

Some excellent resources on this subject are the following: *Ancient History and Culture* by W. H. Stiebing Jr., *The Late Bronze and Early Iron Ages of Central Jordan* by P. McGovern, *The Archeology of the Israelite Settlement* by Israel Finkelstein, and *Is It Possible to Write a History of Israel without Relying on the Bible?* by J. M. Miller.

What follows next is an examination of biblical inspiration and how it is applied by religion.

BIBLICAL INSPIRATION

The Bible is considered by many to be the written revelation of God that has been passed down to humankind. In short, God inspired a particular human to put His dictates into written form. These divine revelations were spread out over many centuries through a multitude of authors. This scenario is universally accepted throughout most Judeo-Christian faiths. Just how divine inspiration relates to each word of the text is an issue that does vary significantly and is vigorously debated by the numerous denominations.

Sacred scripture is a term most often used to describe the divinely inspired Bible. There is no doubt that the Bible dates back to ancient times and has been remarkably and quite accurately preserved. Variations are mostly minor in nature. But there are some areas that are problematic.

Divine inspiration is a nebulous term. It has several varying definitions. Divine biblical inspiration by fundamentalist Protestant terms means God actually took the hand of each biblical author and caused the person to write exactly what He dictated. They use the expression "God breathed." Mainstream Protestants and Catholics view this process very differently. In their view God conveys His revelation to the author but allows the author's human elements to enter into the text. Simply put, the Bible *contains* the Word of God as opposed to *being* the Word of God.

Fundamentalists essentially deem only the original autographs as being inerrant and *God breathed*. This could explain some of the ambiguities that have crept in during transmission. *The Chicago Statement of 1978* confirms this. However, modern scholarship has proven that numerous books contain the works of multiple authors. Does inerrancy then apply to these later authors as well as the original?

I offer a simple analogy to reasonably pose an answer to this question.

HOW BIBLICAL CRITICISM BEGAN

The Bible is the cornerstone of Christianity. For Judaism, it is the very foundation of the faith. Similar holy books exist for every major religion. Where you were born has a significant effect on your religion. If you were raised in India, you would most likely be Hindu, and the Dhammapada would be your equivalent of the Bible. Likewise, if you were raised in Indonesia, you would be Muslim, and the Qu'ran would be your Bible.

In general, these sacred books are believed to contain revelations from God for humans to use as a way to live good lives. Obviously, each religion believes their book is the *true book*. Needless to say each religion has written numerous articles and even books defending their faith, and some even attack the books of other faiths.

All Christians view the Bible as sacred, but the degree to which the divine and human participation interacts is widely diverse. For Jews, the Torah is God's revelation of His laws and the establishment of a covenant with them. Over the most part of the first 1,500 years of the Common Era, the Bible was interpreted by the church in harmony with tradition. The

Protestant Reformation emphasized the importance of the Bible and rejected the use of tradition to determine doctrine. Basically, they declared that the Bible was the Word of God while tradition was the word of man.

Surprisingly, it was Protestant scholars who instigated historical biblical criticism, while Catholics were forbidden to interpret the Bible and were discouraged from even reading it. Initially, Bible critics applied scholarly study to substantiate and support the text. However, the Enlightenment produced skeptics who used their scholarship to diminish or remove the divine role in scripture. This then became known by fundamental evangelicals as "destructive criticism." Many suggest that this distance is the cause of the terrible harm that unbelievers do when they ignore or deny the plain statements of scripture and arrogantly think that they know more than God does.

However, several Protestant scholars think otherwise. Carl F. H. Henry says, "What is objectionable is not the historical-critical method, but rather the alien presuppositions to which neo-protestant scholars subject it." When it is "freed from the arbitrary assumptions of critics," it becomes "highly serviceable as a disciplined investigative approach to past historical events." These scholars were then able to share and explore their theories along with archaeological evidence to enhance history. This would give us the widely accepted *documentary hypothesis* of the nineteenth century.

Catholic scholars were restricted from this study until 1943 when Pope Pius XII issued the encyclical *Divino Afflante Spiritu*. The pope encouraged scholars to pursue knowledge about the biblical writers, their venues, and their purpose in pursuit of improving spiritual knowledge. No doubt Pius believed that a deeper understanding of the Bible would prove the veracity of the Bible and strengthen the faithful.

At present it appears Pius was correct. Although many of the legendary aspects are now seen in a different light along with a better comprehension of authorship and transmission, the basic faith remains unscathed. Historical criticism has numerous Christian adherents today who are not seeking to undermine the faith. Certainly, there are other scholars whose motives may be suspect, but even they have not be able to discredit the essential principles of Christianity.

Here is what former episcopal bishop John Shelby Spong has to say.

> What we need is maturity in religion not childlike dependency. We don't need to be "born again," we need to grow up! But religion encourages childishness by proclaiming there is a super parent in the sky ready and willing to take care of us. So we seek to please this God with proper worship and proper living.

We flatter the God in worship (listen to the words of our hymns: "How great thou art!" for example). Because we learned as children that flattery works with authority figures, we assume that it will also work on the ultimate authority figure! That is why I have argued that "theism" as a definition of God has got to go. That does not mean that there is no God, no holiness, and no "otherness." It does mean that the old definitions do not work any longer. I see God as life, love and being. I worship God by living, loving and being. I serve this God by seeking to build a world in which all people have a better chance to live, love and be. That seems so simple to me and yet it constantly fills me with wonder. When I live into this meaning of worship, religion and life flow together as one. That is the heart of mysticism. It makes sense to me and it places God in the center of all that is. That is where I always meet holiness.

What Spong is saying may be controversial, and his views may be hard for many to accept; however, his love for Christianity has forced him to motivate Christians toward modern philosophy in line with history. Next, we must listen to the Jewish reaction to historical criticism. Rabbi Dr. Charles H Middleburgh says,

To the Progressive Jew, Biblical Criticism has underpinned what for us is an obvious reality, that the Bible, and particularly the Torah, is a human document. We feel free to say that there is much in it that is inspiring, timeless, and beyond reproach; but biblical scholarship's analysis has also encouraged us to say that there is plenty that is flawed, petty, and rooted in ancient politics and culture. We refuse to accept that the God in whom we believe propounded some of these latter concepts and laws, such as the stoning to death of a rebellious son or the permanent ostracism from the community of Israel of the members of ancient Canaanite tribes; we can only comprehend them as emanating from a human mind, and being rooted in the culture and morality of their time.

This does not mean to say that we necessarily discount the possibility of divine inspiration behind the Biblical text, far from it; the Bible is, after all, a remarkable document, replete with great wisdom and insights and expressing timeless thoughts and ideals that cannot easily be conceived as emanating from other than an extraordinary intellect. For many, the acknowledgement of the Deity behind this pre-eminent book is nothing less than a statement of the obvious, but it in no way diminishes the feeling that it is the work of human beings and should be responded to as such.

Scholars of Biblical criticism, and the archaeologists and others whose work complements their own, have liberated modern Jews and Christians from the shackles of fundamentalist dogma, have enhanced the Bible's worth even while demonstrating that it is a richly composite work owing its inspiration to God, and have shown the historicity of many of its texts to an unparalleled degree. Their theories may be disowned by traditionalists for whom scientific analysis and religious dogma are incompatible bedfellows, but they are hard to reject on any other grounds. We owe much to the courage of those whose search for the truth led them to take a stand against the received, uncritical wisdom of the ages, and from the fruits of whose research we are all the beneficiaries.

Rabbi Middleburgh certainly speaks the mind-set of modern Reformed Jews and probably would agree to some extent with Bishop Spong, but Conservative Jews—or more accurately, fundamentalist Jews—would not. The very same could be said about liberal and conservative Christians. Let's us move on to a closer look into the history of biblical criticism.

Critical investigations of the Old Testament in Europe began in the seventeenth century. By the nineteenth century, they produced a much greater interest in scholarship as this field sprung up, particularly by Protestant German theologians. The driving force was the inherent desire to understand the foundations of Christianity. The majority of scholars took a more conservative attitude in studying the New Testament because they believed critical investigations of the Old Testament would prove more favorable toward their Protestant core beliefs and detrimental to Judaism, perhaps finding proof that Jesus was the predicted Messiah.

Along the way several theories arose on how to classify literary irregularities and textual concerns in some of the books of the Hebrew Bible. This was achieved by comparing the various books to one another, particularly comparing the historical books with the prophetic ones and the Pentateuch. The most important and greatest discord among the critics was regarding the historicity of the Pentateuch. Nevertheless, they did not attempt to devise any alterations concerning the history of the Israelite religion or a dissimilar understanding of ancient Israelite society as well as any devaluation of the Pentateuch, which some nineteenth-century German scholars certainly attempted. It appeared no one seriously questioned whether or not the existing texts of the Old Testament were inspired by God.

When historians began to date the documents of the Pentateuch, a new narrative was created through this methodology that priestly authors used. They embraced anachronisms to bolster a semblance of their authority on history. This notion of religious development quite often came along with an implied if not overt anti-Semitism. Rabbinic Judaism was seen as the culmination of their overly tortuous, self-serving religious authority.

Another argument accelerated the ongoing battles between Protestant and Catholic Christians, which centered on ecclesiastic authority (and its misuse, from the Protestant point of view). This dichotomy was manifested by the special position these biblical scholars held as Christian theologians, and to a large extent, they considered themselves enlightened scholars, a combination that clearly fueled further skepticism toward priestly or rabbinical control. Anti-Judaism was no doubt a factor all throughout these times. It did not originate from the biblical analysis, but it contributed to the idea that Orthodox Jews held regarding their traditional biblical study. Catholic and Protestant scholars were aggravated by the ridged rabbinical viewpoint by which conservative ideas of the ancient rabbis and medieval exegetes were applied. In general, Jewish Bible study was limited to the Torah because of the prominence on Talmudic study.

To these Jews, using the biblical texts was secondary to the expansion of Jewish law, mysticism, and pietism. Few Jewish scholars had any interest in historical criticism whatsoever. In Orthodox Jewish circles, the belief regarding the foundational, canonical nature of the Bible as promoted by rabbinic thought was the only accepted method.

In the middle of the eighteenth century, a swing began among some Jews who had become more assimilated in Christian society. They began looking into the Bible to increase their understanding of contemporary Judaism and its practice—at least theoretically—from their traditional understanding of Jewish teachings. Now scientific research in Jewish areas of historical biblical study was being accepted and promoted. They lagged in the area of biblical studies, especially those scholars who were more conservative in their religious position and those who did not recognize the new Reformation movement.

Protestant scholars began advocating a change in their thinking, especially in the areas where they had determined the content leaned heavily on mythology. Their scrutiny was more open to questioning the Bible, especially the Old Testament. This resulted in a surge in academic research and institutions in Germany in the nineteenth century. Now German Protestant scholars examined the Bible and produced a range of pioneering methods. Thus, tension between anti-Jewish scholars clashed with mild Jewish resistance, which produced a view that

Judaism had been supplanted by Christianity in a way that made Christian triumphalism seems more believable.

Most non-orthodox scholars in the early twentieth century came to accept the *documentary hypothesis* in their understanding of Judaism and the Bible. On the other hand, Orthodox Judaism was totally disinterested since these scholars had no doubt that biblical critical theories were incorrect and had no inclination to even examine them. Catholic Christianity prohibited its members from any form of free interpretation of the Bible until the midcentury. The Orthodox Christian doctrine of infallibility rests on their doctrine of the Church as the guardian of the spiritual and doctrinal revelation of God and is free from error. Similar to the Catholic view, these believers, too, showed little interest in Bible criticism until after World War II.

By the last quarter of the twentieth century, historical biblical criticism grew exponentially after numerous archaeological discoveries. The Dead Sea Scrolls cache stirred up public interest for Jews and Christians as well as many with secular interests. At the close of the century, this subject was offered by most colleges and universities in the Americas and Europe.

CHAPTER 6

U p until now we have only skirted around Jewish history. Now I will try to give a succinct chronological history starting with the first king and ending in the early second century CE.

The Bible tells us that the Israelite monarchy was formed around 1000 BCE. This monarchy began with Saul. He was succeeded by King David, who was followed by Solomon, one of David's many sons. David conquered the Jebusites, who were the indigenous people of the city of Jerusalem. He then made it the national and spiritual capital of Israel. The first temple built on Mount Moriah in Jerusalem was erected by Solomon. After Solomon's death, a civil war erupted between the ten Northern Israelite tribes, against the tribes of Judah (the tribe of Simon was previously absorbed into Judah) and the tribe of Benjamin. The nation split into the kingdom of Israel in the north and the kingdom of Judah in the south. The Northern Kingdom was conquered by the Assyrian ruler Tiglath-Pileser III in the 722 BCE and then became the legendary ten lost tribes.

Mathematically, the ten lost tribes of Israel may seem to be wrong when listing them by name. Reuben, Simon, Levi, Judah, Dan, Naphtali, Gad, Asher, Issachar, Zebulun, Joseph, and Benjamin are the original twelve tribes. The Promised Land was divided and given to each son of Jacob (God changed his name to Israel) by Moses as God had ordered (Joshua14:5). Levi did not receive a portion because he (and his descendants) was consecrated by God to be His priest. That leaves eleven tribes. If you subtract Simon, Judah, and Benjamin, that leaves nine tribes;

however, Joseph had died in Egypt before the Exodus, so his sons (Ephraim and Manasseh) were adopted by Jacob in his stead (Genesis 48). Now we have the ten lost tribes.

Upon the death of Sargon II, king of Assyria (705 BCE), several countries, including Judah (a vassal state that was subject to Assyria), thought this was their chance to gain a greater form of independence from Assyria. During the reign of King Hezekiah (715–686 BCE), Judah became quite prosperous. He decided to stop paying the tribute that his father, Ahaz, had agreed to. He then joined Judah in an alliance with Egypt. In 701 BCE, Sennacherib, Sargon's son, began to strike back at the rebel states. Hezekiah believed the Egyptians would come to his aid. Egypt reneged, so Hezekiah had to face the invasion of Judah without foreign help.

The Bible states that during the reign of Hezekiah, Sennacherib, king of Assyria, came and conquered most of Judah and laid siege to Jerusalem. Then an angel of the Lord (the Lord Himself) slew 185,000 Assyrian troops, which then lifted the siege (2 Kings 18:13; 19:32–37). In 2 Kings 18:7, the writer suggests his approval for Hezekiah's decision to join the rebellion. While in sharp contrast, Isaiah speaks out against Hezekiah and Jerusalem's leaders in particular forming an alliance with Egypt. Isaiah prophesied that God will protect Jerusalem and cause Assyria to fall by the sword (Isaiah 31:5, 8; 30:31). Even though Judah has "deeply betrayed" the Lord, Isaiah promises their rescue (Isaiah 31:5–6). At the same time in the book of Micah (Micah 1:12), he bemoans Sennacherib's invasion as divine judgment.

So too, 2 Kings 18:14 says, "So Hezekiah king of Judah sent this message to the king of Assyria at Lachish: 'I have done wrong. Withdraw from me, and I will pay whatever you demand of me.'" Furthermore, in 2 Kings 15–16, Hezekiah gave the Assyrian king all the silver that was found in the house of the Lord and in the royal treasury. He also stripped the gold from the doors of the temple and from the doorposts of his palace and gave them to the Assyrians.

Sennacherib left written records of his exploits. There are three existing cuneiform prisms known as *Sennacherib's Annals*. They are found inscribed with the same text—the Taylor Prism, the Oriental Institute Prism, and the Jerusalem Prism, all of which describe these same events in the Bible. In these prisms Sennacherib brags about how he had King Hezekiah shut up in Jerusalem "like a caged bird." He also mentions Hezekiah's mercenaries and the Arabs deserting him. Therefore, Hezekiah sued for peace. His tribute gave Sennacherib antimony, jewels, ivory-inlaid furniture, his own daughters, a harem, and musicians. It states that Hezekiah became a vassal king. Although we see conflicting events in the Bible and from our other sources, it appears that Judah and Hezekiah survived the invasion.

Hezekiah ruled for about twenty-nine years and died of natural causes at the age of fifty-four. His son, Manasseh, succeeded him (2 Kings 20:21). Hezekiah was a strong religious reformer. He commanded strict laws for the sole worship of God and prohibited venerating other deities in the temple. His first order was to repair and reopen the temple by reinstituting the Passover holy days. He also destroyed a brazen serpent said to have been the one used by Moses in the miraculous healing of the Israelites (Numbers 21:9). The Bible clearly has high praise for Hezekiah, and he is spoken of in 2 Kings 16:20–20:21; 2 Chronicles 28:27–32:33; and Isaiah 36:1–39:8. He is also mentioned in Proverbs 25:1; Isaiah 1:1; Jeremiah 15:4; 26:18, 19; Hosea 1:1; and Micah 1:1.

Manasseh succeeded Hezekiah and became the first king of Judah who did not have a direct acquaintance with the former state of Israel. He allowed polytheistic revivals and reversed many of the religious reforms made by Hezekiah. In the Bible, he is considered to be the most evil and worst king of Judah. He died in 642 BCE.

Manasseh began his fifty-five-year reign (the longest of all the kings of Judah) as a subject king to Sennacherib of Assyria. Assyrian records show him to be a loyal vassal of Sennacherib's son and also to his successor, Esarhaddon. Manasseh supported Ashurbanipal, the son of Esarhaddon, who died in 669 BCE, in a successful war with Egypt. Archaeological evidence agrees with Assyrian records that seem to indicate Judah's economic stability was fostered by positive foreign relationships throughout Manasseh's reign. Despite the criticisms of his religious policies in the biblical texts, it appears Manasseh was popular with the common people but not with writers of the biblical texts. In the Talmud and in *the ascension of Isaiah*, a book that is part of Christian pseudepigrapha, Manasseh is accused of executing the prophet Isaiah. *The prayer of Manasseh*, a book included in the LXX, is a prayer of penance attributed to Manasseh, and it is considered an apocryphal writing by Jews, Roman Catholics, and Protestants.

Babylon was a province of Assyria, and in 626 BCE, it revolted. By 616 BCE, they succeeded in establishing their independence. This revolt was one of the key factors leading to the fall of Assyria. In the coming years, Babylon grew stronger. In 605 BCE, Babylon defeated Egypt at the Battle of Carchemish. King Nebuchadnezzar II then attacked Judah, which was an ally with Pharaoh Necho of Egypt. In his third year, King Jehoiakim of Judah quickly rescinded his alliance with Egypt and switched to Babylon. He had to pay tribute, and he gave up some members of the royal family and nobility as hostages.

In 601 BCE, during the fourth year of Jehoiakim's reign, Nebuchadnezzar invaded Egypt, which resulted in defeat with staggering losses of manpower. The aftermath spurred on rebellions among the vassal states of Nebuchadnezzar. King Jehoiakim then stopped paying tribute to Babylon and entered into a new alliance with Egypt. Nebuchadnezzar regrouped his forces in response to the rebellions, and in the month of Chislev in 598 BCE (November/December), his reassembled army invaded "Hatti land" (or Syro-Palestine and Judah). On the second day in the month of Adar (March 16), he succeeded in conquering Jerusalem. He then took King Jeconiah to Babylon as prisoner. Nebuchadnezzar then placed Zedekiah (uncle of Jeconiah) to serve as his pawn king.

Jehoiakim died during the siege. Nebuchadnezzar looted the city and the Jerusalem temple. The new king of Judah was the young king Jeconiah. (His reign lasted only about forty days.) He and his court and other leading citizens, craftsmen, and about ten thousand residents of Judah were deported to Babylon (597 BCE). The prophet Ezekiel wrote about this event. "None remained except the poorest people of the land." They also took to Babylon the treasures and furnishings of the temple. This included the gold vessels that were once dedicated by King Solomon (2 Kings 24:13–14).

Following the 597 BCE campaign, Nebuchadnezzar made the twenty-one-year-old Zedekiah the puppet king of Judah. Against the advice from the prophet Jeremiah, Zedekiah formed an alliance with Egypt and revolted against Babylon. Enraged by this, Nebuchadnezzar attacked Judah and began another siege of Jerusalem in December of 589 BCE. The siege lasted about two years. "Every worst woe befell the city, which drank the cup of God's fury to the dregs" (2 Kings 25:3; Lamentations 4:4, 5, 10). Then in 586 BCE, Nebuchadnezzar ruptured Jerusalem's walls and took the city. Although Zedekiah escaped, he was soon captured. He was forced to watch them murder his sons, and then they poked out his eyes. He was then bound in chains and taken captive to Babylon, where he remained a prisoner to the day of his death. (How long he remained there is unknown.)

Babylonian general Nebuzaraddan next set forth to completely destroy Jerusalem, and he tore down Solomon's temple. Most of Jerusalem's upper class and priests were taken into captivity to Babylon. Only a few people were permitted to stay in order to care for the land. Gedaliah was made governor of what remained of Judah. Jewish refugees and Jews who lived in neighboring countries now began to return to Judah. Within two months the governor was assassinated, and the people who had remained and many of those who had reentered the country fled in fear to Egypt.

Nebuchadnezzar died in 562 BCE. His son Amel-Marduk (called Evil-Merodach in Jeremiah 52:31 and 2 Kings 25:27) became king and was overthrown in 560 BCE by Nergal-Sharezer (Jeremiah 39:3). After a short period, Nergal-Sharezer was then deposed, and Labashi-Marduk replaced him only to be taken out by Nabonidas in 556 BCE. With all this turmoil, the Babylon economy turned downward and a serious famine occurred. Nabonidas moved to Arabia and left his son Belshazzar in charge.

Cyrus II, king of Persia, invaded Babylon in 539 BCE. His army was led by one of his generals named Ugbaru, who was victorious in the battle of Opis. He was then able to enter the capital city unopposed as Nabonidas fled as detailed in the famous *Stele of Cyrus* or the *Cyrus Cylinder*. Cyrus announced his son Cambyses as the viceroy and claimed the title king of Babylon for himself in 538 BCE. The Middle East was now at peace until the death of Cyrus in 522 BCE.

For the Jews in exile, Cyrus was their hero who had freed them, and he encouraged them to return to Judea (Chronicles 36:22; Ezra 1:1–4). He also allowed them to take home the treasures plundered from the temple, and he contributed funding for the construction of a new temple. Cyrus is the only foreigner in the Bible specified as a messiah or anointed one of God. Isaiah tells us that God spoke "to his messiah, to Cyrus, whom I took by his right hand to subdue nations before him" (Isaiah 45:1). In fact, the hallmark of Cyrus was his religious tolerance. His religion was Zoroastrianism, which had a significant impact on Judaism.

Judea was once again conquered this time by Alexander the Great in 332 BCE. This former Persian state would now become part of the Hellenistic world. After Alexander conquered Tyre, he then passed through Judea on his way to Gaza in route to conquering Egypt and Babylonia. The Samaritans assisted Alexander during the siege of Tyre while Judea remained loyal to Persia. Therefore, Alexander agreed to permit the Samaritans the authorization for construction of a temple to be built on Mount Gerizim near Shechem, which became the center for Samaritan worship.

A rift between Jews returning from the Babylon captivity and the Samaritans had opened up because the Samaritan people were considered religiously polluted by the returnees. Thus, they reject the Samaritan offer to help build the new temple in Jerusalem. Angered by this rejection, the Samaritans then proceeded to prevent or delay the project (Ezra 4:1–6). When the Jewish exiles began to rebuild the walls of Jerusalem, the Samaritans protested to the authorities in Persia (Artaxerxes) that this constituted an act of rebellion and the work was stopped until the arrival of Nehemiah, whom King Artaxerxes had commissioned as governor (Ezra 4:7–24).

They continued their hostile actions directed against Nehemiah's governorship (Nehemiah 6:1–13). This effort proved unsuccessful, but the hatred now was intensified. The Jews forbade the Samaritans the right to offer sacrifices at the Jerusalem temple and forbade them to intermarry with Jews. This drove the Samaritan desire to build their own temple on Mount Gerizim.

There is a legendary story in the Talmud (Yoma 69a) about the first meeting between Alexander the Great and Simon the Just (the high priest of Jerusalem). Simon had come to welcome Alexander with his cohorts of priests and sages of the Sanhedrin. They met at the gates of Jerusalem. Amazingly, when Alexander drew close to Simon, he got off his horse and bowed to him. Alexander's troops were shocked that he would lower himself to another conquered leader. He explained to them that whenever he prepared for a battle, he would dream about an angel leading him to victory. The face of Simon was the face of the angel he had seen in his dreams, and that was the reason he had bowed down to him.

Aristotle was the famous teacher to Alexander. He suggested to Alexander that he take a favorable position toward the Jews. His plan was to be conciliatory as an alternative to destroying and vanquish them. If they (the Jews) would be loyal vassals and pay their taxes, he would allow them to live in peace. In recognition to Alexander, the Jews promised to name every male child born the next year "Alexander." This is why the name is so popular with Jewish families even in the present.

However, it allowed this culture to spread Greek names and customs quite readily. Many Jews gave their children Greek names. Several of these Greek names are found in the Talmud. As luck would have it, the unexpected consequences were that they inadvertently opened the door to the Greek language. And with the Greek language automatically came the Greek culture, which would later result in acrimony among the Jewish people. They also agreed to a tax system, but its methods of collection would lead to dreadful corruption. An example appears in the Talmud, which casts any tax collector as an alleged thief. This insidious tax system shattered the unity of the Jewish community long after Alexander was gone.

Alexander suddenly died in Babylon in 323 BCE at the age of thirty-three. His empire was divided into three large kingdoms—Antigonus, Ptolemaic, and Seleucid. Geographically, Antigonus received the Greek homeland and Turkey, while Ptolemy received Egypt and southern Syria plus part of Cyrene and Nubia (Northern Sudan). Alexandria became his capital city. At its greatest, Seleucid included central Anatolia, Persia, the Levant, Mesopotamia, and what today we would consider Kuwait, Afghanistan, Pakistan, Turkmenistan, and northwest parts of India. Over the upcoming years there would be many battles over territory with some areas going back and forth.

When Ptolemy IV (221–204 BCE) died, Antiochus III (the Seleucid king who lived from 241 to 187 BCE) saw a chance to expand his territory. Antiochus and Philip V of Macedon became allies and defeated Ptolemy V (infant king) and divided the Ptolemaic territory outside of Egypt. This was called the Fifth Syrian War, which gained them control of Syria and Judea. Antiochus III moved some two thousand Jewish families from Babylonia to Anatolia (modern Turkey) for reasons unknown. However, Josephus (Antiquities 3:3–4) describes Antiochus III as a man who was kind to the Jews of Jerusalem. He goes on to say Antiochus even lowered their taxes and gave money to the temple. He let the Jews live "according to the law of their forefathers." His successor, Seleucus IV, was assassinated in 175 BCE, and Antiochus IV became king. This would be the advent of the Maccabean rebellion. Some modern historians believe that this rebellion was actually a civil war between traditional or Conservative Jews and Hellenized Jews, the king supporting the Hellenists. However, we know from the biblical books of the Maccabees that Antiochus IV desecrated the Jerusalem temple and tried to force traditional Jews to comply with Greek laws and abandon their own.

The Maccabean Revolt (167–160 BCE) began with a Jewish rebel group called the Maccabees. From the book of 1 Maccabees, which describes Antiochus ordering decrees outlawing Jewish traditional religious practices, we see he ordered the worship of Zeus as the supreme god (2 Maccabees 6:1–12). A Jewish priest from Modiin (a small town seventeen miles northwest of Jerusalem) set off a revolt against the Seleucid Empire by refusing to worship the Greek gods. Mattathias killed a Hellenistic Jew who was commanded by Antiochus to force the people to make sacrifices to a Greek god. With his five sons, Mattathias fled to the wilderness. Mattathias died a year later, and in 166 BCE, his son Judas Maccabee took over the clan and formed a guerilla army of Jewish dissidents. He then led them to an unimaginable victory over the Seleucid Greeks. This was an underdog victory of epic proportions. The word Maccabees is taken from the Hebrew word for *hammer*.

After this victory the Maccabees gloriously entered Jerusalem and ritually cleansed the temple, reestablishing traditional Jewish worship there. Jonathan Maccabee, the youngest brother, was then made the new high priest, laying the basis for a future controversy over the inherited position. Enraged, Antiochus sent a large army commanded by Lysias to put down the revolt. He laid siege to Jerusalem, but the death of Antiochus IV then forced Lysias to quickly respond to Antiochus's commander-in-chief Philip, who saw his opportunity to become king and was about to enter Antioch to seize power. Now Lysias quickly agreed to a political compromise with Judas, which included the restoration of religious freedoms and customs.

Prior to this, Antiochus had several problems which required military attention. On his eastern frontier, King Mithridates, the Parthian king, attacked in 167 BCE, disrupting the major trade route to India. In the east Rome was looming as a threat, so he needed to keep a large force there. When the Maccabee revolt forced him to split his forces, and he sent Lysias to Judea while the king himself led the main Seleucid army against the Parthian king. He had his last successful campaign in the east, retaking Armenia, but then suddenly, Antiochus became ill and died (164 BCE). Antiochus V Eupator became the new king at the age of nine and reigned only two years (163–161 BCE.).

In 163 BCE, Demetrius I Soter, the nephew of the late Antiochus IV, who at this time was being held as a hostage by the Roman Senate, escaped to Syria. He laid his claim to be the rightful king. He gained some military support, killed Lysias, and became king. Demetrius appointed Alcimus as the new high priest to appease the Hellenistic Jews in Jerusalem with the guarantied protection of the army. The army was led by General Bacchides with forces of twenty thousand men. Judas didn't have an army to compete with Bacchides, and so he withdrew and fled Jerusalem. Thus, Judas went back to wage guerrilla warfare. Judas turned to Rome for help. He negotiated the Roman-Jewish Treaty, which was an agreement with the Roman Republic (161 BCE). The treaty required each party to aid the other if it was attacked and to abstain from helping the enemies of the other party. Josephus recorded the contact between the Jews and Rome (Josephus's *Antiquities of the Jews* 12. 417–419; 1 Maccabees 8:17–20).

The treaty clearly was a mutual defense agreement. It also shows that Rome recognized Judean independence. A few months later, Judas was killed in battle against the well-known Demetrius I Soter, who was fighting Jewish rebels. Rome did not help the Jews in any respect whatsoever. This is why some scholars question the authenticity of the treaty.

Just before Judas was killed, the army of Demetrius had to return to Antioch. Judas's forces then reentered Jerusalem. As soon as he was able, General Nicanor advanced on Jerusalem and met Judas in the Battle of Adasa, which was fought on the thirteenth of Adar (February–March) in 161 BCE. Nicanor was defeated and slain along with every man in his army. In a victory celebration, the Jews declared the thirteenth of Adar a holiday (1 Maccabees 7:39–50; 2 Maccabees 15:1–36; Josephus, *l.c.* xii. 10, § 5). "Nicanor Day" is also mentioned in the rabbinical sources (Meg. Ta'an. xii.; Ta'an. 18b; Yer. Ta'an. ii. 13 *et seq.*, 66a).

After the death of Judas, his Helene-Jewish opponents preached their rhetoric everywhere in Judea. At that time there was also a severe famine, and many people went over to the side of the Hellenists. Bacchides deliberately appointed some Hellenist Jews as rulers over the country. These Jews hunted down friends of Judas and brought them all before Bacchides, who punished them. It was a time of great trouble for Israel (1 Maccabees 9:23–27).

The supporters of Judas came together and offered the leadership to Jonathan. "Since your brother Judas died, there has been no one like him to lead us against our enemies, against Bacchides and those of our own nation who oppose us. So today we choose you to succeed him as our ruler and commander to carry on our war." "Jonathan accepted the leadership that day and took the place of his brother Judas" (1 Maccabees 9:28–31).

Upon hearing this, Bacchides decided to kill Jonathan. With his brother Simon, Jonathan dodged several attacks. But the Jambrites of Medeba attacked John (Jonathan and Simon's younger brother), took him captive, and killed him. Outraged, the brothers took revenge, ambushed an entire wedding party of Jambrite dignitaries, and killed many of them. Bacchides heard about this, and with a large army, he cornered Jonathan in the wilderness. The Jews soundly defeated him, and he fled back to Jerusalem. When the high priest Alcimus suddenly died, Bacchides feared he had lost the support of the Hellenist Jews, and he went to Damascus to see King Demetrius, who decided to rescind the order to attack the Jews, thus giving Judea a peace that lasted for the next two years. Never again did he come into Jewish territory. When the war came to an end in Judea, Jonathan settled in Michmash, and he governed the people and dealt with the Hellenist Jews, killing many of them as traitors.

In 143 BCE, Diodotus Tryphon, now the regent Seleucid king, invited Jonathan to a meeting in the town of Scythopolis for an amicable political conference and tricked him into believing he would give him Ptolemais and other fortresses. When Jonathan entered Ptolemais with a thousand of his men, Tryphon was waiting and captured Jonathan and killed all his men. Jonathan was taken prisoner, and they wanted to use him as a hostage. After the capture of Jonathan, Simon was elected leader in Jerusalem. He quickly shored up the fortifications of the capital and Joppa. He expelled all Gentiles, replacing them with Jews (1 Maccabees 13: 8, 10, 11). Simon then prevented Trypho from returning to Damascus, which stalled him from taking the throne of Syria. Trypho then demanded a ransom for Jonathan and exacted Jonathan's sons as hostages. Simon complied with the demands, even though he knew Trypho was trying to trick him. Jonathan was killed, and the hostages were not returned. Jonathan was buried at Modin, and Simon erected a monument to him (1 Maccabees 13:25–30 and Josephus, *Antiquities of the Jews* 3:6, § 5). We know nothing of what happened with his two captive sons.

Simon brought peace and security to Jerusalem and gained full independence for Judea. He was the second Maccabean high priest and established the Hasmonean dynasty. In 135 BCE, Simon Maccabeus was assassinated in Jericho by his son-in-law Ptolemy. Next in the succession of the Maccabees was Simon's son John. His name was changed to Hyrcanus I because he was the general who defeated the Syrians in a major battle. Thus, John was given the surname *Hyrcanus* because of his victory. He also became the high priest in Jerusalem until he died (104 BCE). Hyrcanus was clearly the king, but he avoided making a big deal about it. He had a long reign, and he expanded Judean territory to it largest size since Solomon. He crushed the Samaritans and destroyed their temple on Mount Gerizim. As for the Idumaeans (who lived southeast of the Dead Sea), Hyrcanus forced them to be circumcised and convert to Judaism. One of the forced converts was Antipater, the father of Herod the Great.

The reign of Hyrcanus became a turning point in the history of Judaism. It exacerbated the political contentions in religious ideology between the Sadducees, Pharisees, and Essenes. We also see the advance of rabbinic Judaism and the decline of Hebraic Judaism. Hyrcanus began his career as a Pharisee but then joined the Sadducees. He did not persecute the Pharisees but he did rescind the Pharisaic rules and made the Sadducean laws the standard of the nation. When compared to his grandfather Mattathias's political ideas, his political ideas were rotated 180 degrees. The intensely conservative religious and patriotic zeal (such as they saw in the beginning) gradually changed as Hyrcanus slowly took on an upper-class attitude and became a Sadducee who accepted only the written law as the divinely revealed and authoritative text. He was worldly and genteel, which was quite the opposite of his grandfather.

John Hyrcanus was at first *a disciple* of the Pharisees, but he soon became their enemy (Josephus, *Antiquities of the Jews* XIII: 10, 5 [288–98]). The Pharisees then became opponents of the Hasmonean rulers from then on. This was mainly due to the Hasmonean disregard of the sacred traditional rules concerning the heritage of the high priesthood, and they also took the unprecedented role of de facto king as well. Jewish tradition forbade combining the high priesthood with the kingship.

This was the time when Jewish life revolved around two centers—the temple and the Torah. The Jerusalem temple was the one place where sacrifices could be offered. But away from Jerusalem there was an increasing number of *synagogues* where Jews could learn to read and write scripture and pray together. Synagogues helped Jews everywhere maintain a sense of community and tradition, while they became sanctuaries for travelers. As time went on, they would grow in popularity and become very attractive to Gentiles as well as Jews.

After the death of John Hyrcanus, his eldest son and leader of his army, Aristobulus I became the fifth Hasmonean priest to rule Judea (104–103 BCE). The will of Hyrcanus I stated that Aristobulus was to be the next high priest, and his mother (her name is unknown) was to become the ruling queen. However, Aristobulus seized the throne, threw his mother in prison, and let her die from hunger (Josephus, *Antiquities of the Jews* 13:302). He also threw all of his brothers (except Antigonus) in prison. Although later Aristobulus had Antigonus put to death when he suspected Antigonus was plotting against him. Aristobulus was the first of the Hasmonean to accept the title of king (Josephus, *Antiquities of the Jews* 11:301).

Aristobulus called himself *Philhellene*. This title designated that he had accepted Hellenistic philosophy just as other Eastern rulers had adopted Hellenistic culture. This adds credence to the adage that the cultural animosity between Conservative Jews and Hellenist Jews was intensifying. It was the Pharisees who threatened to revolt over the official adoption of the title of king by Aristobulus. He was a Levite and not a descendant of David; however, before anything got going, Aristobulus died.

Next in line would be Alexander Jannaeus, who reigned from 103 to 76 BCE. He was the third son of Hyrcanus I, and it seems he was married to his brother's widow (Aristobulus) Salome Alexandra, according to Josephus. As the oldest living brother, Alexander inherited the throne, but he also inherited Salome through Jewish tradition because she was childless. Thus, Alexander married her despite the fact she was thirteen years older than him. They had two sons—Hyrcanus II, who became high priest (62 BCE), and his younger brother, Aristobulus II, who was high priest from 66 to 62 BCE. Their rivalry led to another bloody civil war that ended the Hasmonean dynasty.

When Queen Alexandra Salome died, her two sons, Hyrcanus and Aristobulus, battled for the kingdom. Aristobulus ousted his elder brother from both the throne and the high priesthood. In 63 BCE, both Hyrcanus and Aristobulus visited the Roman consul Pompey in Damascus, asking him to resolve their dispute (Josephus Ant. xiv 12–15).

Alexander Jannaeus persecuted the Pharisees and crucified eight hundred of them according to Josephus. (However, there exists a very favorable memorial writing that was discovered at Qumran, indicating he was respected and loved by his subjects.) A civil war broke out under Alexander Jannaeus between the Sadducees and Pharisees. This war was just as bitter as our American Civil War. The Sadducees prevailed, and they were in control until the death of Alexander, when Salome Alexandra, who was a Pharisee, became queen regent. After her death Hyrcanus became high priest, and the younger son, Aristobulus, struggled to become king. Hyrcanus put together an army with the aid of the Nabataean kingdom, and he marched on Jerusalem, besieging Aristobulus and his Sadducee supporters in the temple. Scaurus, the Roman general from Syria, intervened and sent the Nabataean troops home. Pompey decided in favor of Hyrcanus, whose supporters opened the gates of Jerusalem to the Romans. After a three-month siege, the temple was taken, and in 63 BCE, the whole of Judea was annexed by the Roman Republic. Aristobulus along with his son Alexander was eventually killed in the turmoil during the Roman civil war about ten years later.

As we look back into this history, it is apparent that the clash of cultures between Jews and Greeks was monumental. While the melding of Jewish-Persian (Zoroastrianism) culture blended reasonably well, the Greek influence actually split the Jews culturally and religiously into different camps.

Many Jews gravitated to the Hellenic arts and sciences and quickly learned to appreciate such disciplines as literature and philosophy in combination with the Greek emphasis on physical culture and beauty. The religion of the Greeks was another story. Conservative religious Jews vigorously refused to accept paganism and strongly defended and promoted their traditional religion, which actually contributed to the Maccabean revolt. Certainly, most Jews did not simply absorb Hellenism. They modified it and reinterpreted their traditional values in view of the appealing *modern* civilization, which had now become the ruling regime. The practice of reinterpretation led to emergence of several varieties of Hellenistic Judaism.

Adopting the Greek language became a sign of Hellenization. People from all over Judea found they could quickly gain legal and economic advantages afforded by accepting the language and culture. This would include exemption from certain customs and duties and even participation in some of the municipal governments. In the Greek cities, some Jews could join the upper classes, and some had access to the schools and other institutions of the Hellenistic world.

This was a time when there was a cultural decline in the native civilizations around the entire region. The pervasive and widespread interest in new religions indicated a built-up hunger for a new means of gaining spiritual fulfillment. As the Greeks pushed eastward, their religious philosophy gained acceptance even in Judea. However, Jews did not only resist religiously. They also had a profound impact on the pagan Greek religion. Monotheism in consort with Jewish traditions and ethics penetrated deeply into the Greek philosophy. This would later become a contributing factor in the birth of Christianity.

Christianity was born to Hellenistic Judaism, and it remained thoroughly the Jewish tradition until Paul of Tarsus initiated bold reforms that made conversion to Judaism more alluring to Gentiles. These reforms did bring about several hostile reactions from mainstream Jews, causing the expulsion of these Christians from Judaism. After the first Jewish revolt against Rome (66 CE), Christianity began a campaign to legally divorce itself from Judaism. This accelerated after the second revolt (132 CE), and by the fourth century, Christianity became legal and the official religion of the Roman Empire. Historically, this was a time when Christians everywhere else were attempting to disassociate themselves from Judaism for political reasons (the consequences of the first Jewish revolt). As the early persecutions of Christians by Rome became more intense, editors and writers of Christian literature vehemently attempted to show the loyalty of the members of the new faith to the empire while exclusively blaming the Jews for the revolt along with all the resulting problems.

In Judea, Christians were being expelled from the synagogues, the result of a Jewish benediction concerning heretics (called Birkat Ha-Minim) issued around the year 85 CE. Because these Jewish Christians observed the Torah, they were now considered to be a heretical sect of Judaism. This action instigated the expulsion of these Christians from Jewish synagogues. Thus, this set off deep resentment from Jewish Christians, and the Christian Bible clearly displays their sentiments.

John 9:22 says, "His parents said this because they were afraid of the Jewish leaders, who already had decided that anyone who acknowledged that Jesus was the Messiah would be put out of the synagogue." John 12:42 says, "Yet at the same time many even among the leaders believed in him. But because of the Pharisees they would not openly acknowledge their faith for fear they would be put out of the synagogue." And John 16:2 says, "They will put you out of the synagogue; in fact, the hour is coming when those who kill you will think they are offering a service to God."

This would signal the beginning of Christian attacks on Judaism, and these would only intensify, resulting in a series of tragic events for Jews that would last until the present day.

So if the first Christians were Jews and Jesus was a Jew, how and why did the two faiths become separated?

Christianity in its earliest day consisted entirely of Jews who believed that they were an inseparable part of Judaism. We are told in Acts 2:46 that they continued to worship on a daily basis in the temple after the death of Jesus. This is important because it suggests that Jesus never intended to start a new religion and that He never taught anyone to discontinue worshipping there. Therefore, something happened that prompted a schism between Judaism and Christianity, and it clearly wasn't triggered by Jesus.

Acts 6 tells of friction between Greek-speaking Jews and Hebrew-speaking Jews. It seems reasonable to assume that the Greek speakers consisted of Jews who came to Jerusalem from outside of Judea, and the remainder, which were probably the larger, included converts and/or those who feared God. "God fearers" were Gentiles who were members of the synagogue but had not converted to Judaism. The God fearers did not share a nationalistic loyalty to the land of Judea that their Jewish co-religionists did because they were predominantly Greeks.

It appears that the earliest Christian community outside of Jerusalem developed in Antioch. Strong evidence suggests that Antioch may have had the larger Christian population by the midforties. From there it rapidly spread to other parts of the empire, including Rome. These Christians communities shared the belief that Jesus was the Messiah and was scheduled to soon return and establish a universal kingdom of God with Jerusalem as its capital. Otherwise, they shared in the traditional Jewish religion.

It is clear that the apostle Paul had great success in uniting together many of these assorted Jewish-Christian communities, many of which were beginning to practice various ceremonies and rituals under the blanket of his gospel. Paul's missionary strategy was to go first to the local synagogues to deliver his message. He quickly found success among gentile God fearers. Because of its outstanding social and religious appeal, the synagogue excited many Gentiles and made membership more desirable. However, in order to be full members of Judaism, they had to undergo circumcision and obey all the dietary laws. Paul's scheme was to circumvent these laws for only Gentiles and allow them full membership, and it worked. This was the major step in the separation.

Some Jews reacted negatively toward this decision, while others just thought it was a passing phase that would soon die off (Acts 5:27–42). As time went on, however, more and more Jews began to reject this concept. Some began to actually attack Paul, but for the most part, these were only localized issues. His main adversaries were Jewish Christians, including some of the closest followers of Jesus. Initially, the early leadership discovered Paul's ability to recruit new members and particularly his capacity to increase their treasury. These clearly mitigated his deviations, which they believed could be reined in later. Thus, Pauline Christianity was allowed to take root.

The first Jewish revolt (66–70 CE) was a major factor in the separation. At first, Jewish Christians supported their countrymen, but apparently, they later abandoned the cause. Eusebius, quoting Hegesippus, wrote, "The people of the church in Jerusalem were commanded by an oracle given by revelation before the war to those in the city who were worthy of it to depart and dwell in one of the cities of Peraea which is called Pella. To it those who believed in Christ migrated from Jerusalem" (Eusebius *The History of The Church* EH III: 5, 1 ff).

Both these writers lived in the fourth century nearly three hundred years after the events. I believe the Christians who abandoned Jerusalem were mostly Gentiles and perhaps a few Greek-speaking Jews, whereas the native Jewish Christians remained loyal. There is strong evidence that suggests that following the war, many Jewish Christians (which was a small group) from outside of the city relocated there and tried to regain their fellowship. Talmudic and other Jewish sources indicate the presence of such groups throughout Judea, not to mention the contempt and hatred directed toward them by their non-Christian countrymen. Of course, these are the facts, but it would seem much more likely that the Jewish Christians who abandoned the uprising were part of the second or the Bar Kochba revolt (132 CE), when Rabbi Akiva declared Bar Kochba to be the Messiah. Jewish Christians already had their Messiah in Jesus and would not have been interested in promoting a rival messiah.

Eusebius and Epiphanius disagree about the size and importance of the postwar Jewish Jerusalem church. Eusebius states that "there was a very important Church, composed of Jews, which existed until the siege of the city under Hadrian" (*The Proof of the Gospel* III: 5,124[d]) and gives a list of bishops who reigned in the city during that time (EH V:5). Epiphanius (De Mesuris et Ponderibus IV) implies that there was nothing more than a struggling, insignificant church on the site of old Jerusalem between 70 and 132 CE.

The actual split occurred after the war but was isolated for the most part to Judea. The Gospels of John and Matthew clearly reflect the animosities as the Jewish people expressed their derision by expelling them from the synagogues. In other areas of the empire, this attitude was not as prevalent. For example, as late as the fifth century, we have evidence of Christians still living within Jewish communities, and we have data that shows members of Christian communities still participating in Jewish festivals. The famous leader of Antioch and later of Constantinople, John Chrysostom, complains through a series of sermons to his membership that "you must stop going to the synagogue, you must not think that the synagogue is a holier place than our churches are." This clearly indicates that the break between Judaism and Christianity (even as late as the fifth century) was not universal.

In all of his epistles, the social separation in the communities founded by Paul seems to have already taken place. Paul was writing in the fifties, and Christians weren't congregating with Jews. They were meeting in various household. So it's a varied change. Separation doesn't happen all at once or at the same time, and it doesn't occur in the same manner everywhere. So it appears that in Jerusalem or Judea, before and immediately after the revolt, the local Jewish Christians wanted to remain a part of Judaism, whereas in regards to the empire, the separation was already taking place as Pauline Christianity pervaded.

Paul used the Greek word *ecclesia*, which modern translators now define it as "the church." This is an honest rendering, but it fails to communicate the true meaning the word had in the first century. No one would have then known what a *church* was. They would have understood ecclesia as just a meeting of free citizens who had organized to discuss relevant community concerns. Religion had no part of its meaning. Obviously, the word did evolve to mean church later.

In reaction to Emperor Hadrian's decision to build a pagan temple for Jupiter on the site of the destroyed Jewish temple, Simon Bar Kosiba instigated a revolt (also known as the second revolt of 132 CE). Bar Kosiba's revolt initially had great success. Many started to believe that he could be the expected Messiah as a result, especially Chief Rabbi Akivia. Akivia nicknamed him "Bar Kochba" or "Son of Star," a reference to Numbers 24:17, which says, "There shall come a star out of Jacob." This star is believed to refer to the Messiah. Of course, Jewish Christians had to reject Bar Kochba, and most of them then fled to Alexandria.

The Romans annihilated the Jews and sought to extinguish any Jewish presence in Jerusalem by renaming it Aelia Capitolina and by changing the name of the country from Judea to Palestine. Jews were now forbidden from entering the city. The only day that Jews were allowed to enter the city was on the ninth of Av to remind them of the disaster and weep over the ruins of the temple. Hatred for Jews then spread throughout the empire. Christians now felt the need to *officially* divorce themselves from Judaism. An apologetic campaign started unfolding which would reveal that Christians were loyal and peaceful citizens of Rome, hoping the Romans would see that Christians were the complete opposite of the rebellious Jews.

Now separation was complete! This is not to say that some areas did not remain friendly or at least sociable, but from here on, Christians would begin persecuting Jews, especially the few remaining Jewish Christians.

CHAPTER 7

I n the previous chapters, we were concentrating on Judaism and Jewish history while only referencing Christianity's effect on the subject. Moving forward, we will now explore the beginning of Christianity and its effect on history. This chapter will deal with the personalities that appear to have made a significant impact on the early church.

EARLY CHRISTIANITY

The Bible gives little information on the development of the very early church. Tradition also is very ambivalent in this respect. There seems to be a mysterious void of information concerning the Palestinian church's development. The Bible vaguely alludes to a conflict between the Pauline branch and the branch led by James or the Jerusalem church, which was possibly later called the Ebionites. Why was the church of James cast into a secondary status so soon after the birth of Christianity?

History is packed with personalities and events from the cities of Alexandria, Damascus, Antioch, but surprisingly little of Jerusalem. Another very vague biblical/tradition account is that of James, the leader of the church of Jerusalem. Just who was this James, and how does he fit in the biblical accounts?

In order to detail the history of the early church, we need to understand the social climate of the first century. We must also particularize the church leaders immediately after the death of Jesus and into the early second century.

Here are a few of the obstacles for us: First, our primary sources are the books of the Bible, whose history is questionable. Second, writings by Josephus, a Jewish historian of the first century, have been edited, interpreted, and reproduced by biased early Christians. Third, there's the lack of written Jewish evidence that makes reference to Christianity. Fourth, the New Testament Apocrypha generally contains late writings that are extremely biased. Fifth, pseudepigraphical writings by obviously pseudonymous authors which are unreliable and by and large late information. Sixth, there's the issue of the accepted license of ancient writers who reported on some events as they believed or wished to have occurred as factual.

Evidence of these early Christian forms is found mostly in polemic writings opposed to the numerous ostensible heresies that we must sift through carefully. We must also examine the numerous writings of the Apocrypha and pseudepigrapha that may shed some light on the subject, especially because some of them tell an utterly different story than the canonical works.

Firstly, exactly when did Christianity start? Presumably Christianity began when Jesus recruited Andrew and then started his ministry (about 30–33 CE); however, the term Christian was first used to describe the followers of the deceased Jesus, who lived in and about the city of Antioch, approximately 40 CE.

The term Christian obviously refers to the followers or believers of Christ. Christ means Messiah, the Aramaic-Hebrew word corresponding to the Greek word *Christos*. Consequently, when we say, "Jesus Christ," it really means "Jesus Messiah."

To the Jews, *Messiah* referred to the prophesied Anointed One. King David (1013 BCE) was the original anointed one and king of a then powerful and prosperous Israel. Cyrus, king of Persia (525 BCE), was referred to as a messiah in the book of Isaiah (Isaiah 42:1–17). Therefore, the Messiah was associated with a king of some sort. The yearning for a Jewish messiah began in earnest after the Maccabees (166–163 BCE) gave way to the conquering Romans. This is when the Jews beseeched this kind of a messiah. This yearning continued to build to a fever pitch, culminating with the second Jewish revolt or the Bar Kochba rebellion of 135 CE. Certainly, the Messiah was also expected to be a military leader, one sent by the God of Israel to defeat her enemies and to place Israel into a paramount position over all the nations.

Judas Maccabeus (166 BCE) led a revolt against the Seleucid Greeks who at this time ruled Judea. Judas overcame enormous odds and returned the land of Judea to the Jews. This type of man was what the Jews of the first century expected as their presaged Messiah. His exploits are celebrated even today in the Jewish feast of Hanukkah, the festival of lights. However, Judas's regime did not completely satisfy all Jewish expectations. The reasoning behind this has no bearing on our present subject, so I will not explore it any further here.

Most Jews firmly believed that their Hebrew Bible, which they referred to as the scriptures (the Christian Old Testament), predicted this coming Messiah. Some Jews believed Jesus of Nazareth was the fulfillment of those prognostications, and therefore, they formed the first Christian community.

When the Romans crucified Jesus, some of His followers were disappointed, abandoned the cause, and looked forward to a future messiah. The next Messiah was Bar-Kochba, who failed their expectations. However, the closest followers of Jesus believed that the God of Israel had raised Jesus, His Son, from the dead and had taken Him up to heaven after forty days. During those forty days, they believed Jesus appeared to many Jews, especially His apostles.

The twelve apostles, as understood by most Christians, formed the church on Pentecost (the fiftieth day after Jesus's resurrection). This date coincided with the Jewish Feast of Weeks (Shavuot), which is considered by many rabbis to be the birth of Judaism since it was the day Moses received the Torah from God on Mount Sinai.

The number twelve is significant in its symbolic reference to the original twelve tribes of Israel. The four gospels and the book of Acts have slightly different lists of the twelve persons, with Acts naming Matthias as Judas Iscariot's replacement. The author of Acts most positively wants to convey the significance of the number twelve representing the apostles. The book of Revelation predicts the New Jerusalem will be built on the foundation of the twelve apostles.

Paul became an apostle presumably on his own assumption (Galatians 1:1–5). He claimed his authority or apostleship came directly from Jesus through a vision or dream. The book of Acts gives a brief history of some of the apostles, but the protagonist is definitely Paul. Nearly all Jewish scholars and many scholars in general believe the real founder of present-day Christianity was Paul. We will discuss more of Paul later. Now let us explore the three pillars of the early church—James, John, and Peter—as well as Paul and perhaps the female apostle, Mary Magdalene. We will also try to sort out and describe the various apostles named James.

JAMES

A major leader (perhaps the successor to Jesus) of the first Christians was James, the brother of Jesus. This James was called an apostle but was not one of the original twelve. It appears that James became the leader of the Christian church shortly after the death of Jesus. Acts 12:17 tells us of Peter specifically reporting to Him after his escape from prison. Acts 21:18–26 apprises us that Paul displayed his subordination and submitted to the orders of James. He apparently decided to permit uncircumcised Gentiles to become full members of the church (Acts 15:13–21), while the rest of the apostles obediently approved.

Paul refers to this James as the "Lord's brother" (Galatians 19). We know he is not either James, son of Zebedee, or James, son of Alpheus. He is possibly the presumed author of the biblical epistle bearing his name (the twentieth book the New Testament) and the likely brother of Jude (the twenty-seventh book of the New Testament). It is important to note that Jude and James (in their epistles) do not claim to be apostles. Therefore, the most logical explanation for this James is just as Paul declared in Galatians 19 (and also Matthew 13:55 and Mark 6:3), namely the half brother of Jesus. "Half brother" here infers that Joseph is the father of James and God is the Father of Jesus, the Virgin Mary being the mother of both. This would also reconcile with some Jewish traditions where the blood brother is expected to pick up the duties and responsibilities of his deceased sibling.

James became the first bishop of Christianity and also the first bishop of Jerusalem. Clement, the fourth bishop (pope from 92 to 101CE) of Rome wrote in *Outlines Book VI*, "Peter, James, and John, after the Ascension of the Savior, did not claim pre-eminence because the Savior had specially honored them, but chose James the Righteous as Bishop of Jerusalem."

Subsequently, this James presided over the Jerusalem Council (50 CE) (Acts 15:13). This is evident in the fact that although Peter (in all the Gospels) was the leader of the apostles before Jesus's death, James then assumed that role (Galatians 2:11–12; Acts 21:17–18), and Peter became his first lieutenant just as he had been under the leadership of Jesus.

Eusebius, the first church historian (born about 260 CE), quotes again from Cement's *Outlines*, "James the Righteous, John, and Peter were entrusted by the Lord after his resurrection with higher knowledge. They imparted it to the other Apostles, and the other Apostles to the 70, one of whom was Barnabas. There were two Jameses one the Righteous, who was thrown down from the parapet and beaten to death with a fuller's club, the other James who was beheaded."

James, the brother of Jesus, must not be confused with the other two original apostles—James, son of Alpheus, and James, brother of John, both the sons of Zebedee. The son of Zebedee was beheaded shortly after the death of Steven (40 CE) and was said to be the first bishop of the Syrian church. Nothing is known of the son of Alpheus or what happened to him (outside of the New Testament). There are some who believe that Alpheus is an unknown or erroneously proper noun that really means Joseph. Thus, these people believe there were only two people named James—James (son of Zebedee) and James (the brother of Jesus). There is nothing to substantiate this claim.

The epistle of James is attributed to the brother of Jesus; however, this is not universally accepted. It is difficult to date its origin. Some scholars date the book to the very late first century or about 90 CE, while others believe it to predate some of the Pauline epistles. A few scholars believe James wrote this epistle in response or rebuttal to Paul.

In his book *St. Peter*, Michael Grant declares James is inadequately described in the New Testament and is afforded especially little justice in the book of Acts. Could the reason possibly be that James supplanted Peter as leader of the Christian church? What would the reason be for the New Testament or church tradition to be so reticent of this earliest leader?

Much is said of him in the New Testament Apocrypha and pseudepigraphical writings. Eusebius gives him high praise and lists him as the first leader of the church. Perhaps the reason for this silence is James led the church of Jerusalem. Plus his theology was prone to Judaism and included the belief that Jesus was the Messiah. James also practiced full obedience to the Torah, circumcision, dietary laws, feasts, and all.

In the gospel of Thomas, the disciples of Jesus are instructed by the master (Jesus) to seek out James to be their leader after His death. "Go to James the Just, for whose sake heaven and earth came into being" (verse 12 of the gospel of Thomas).

One branch of Christianity that claimed James was their leader would later be called the Ebionites. Like all the earliest Jewish Christians, they did not believe that they had founded a new religion. In fact, they considered themselves still a branch of the Pharisees. The only difference was they considered Jesus to be the Messiah, who was resurrected by God and was expected to return very soon. With the power of God, He will lead the Jews to victory over Rome. Because of this belief, James, the Lord's brother, was killed by Ananaas, the chief priest under Herod Agrippa in 62 CE. This James was also said to be the first bishop of Jerusalem. (This is probably only a legend.) The Ebionites were later considered to be a heretical group and were excommunicated by the Orthodox church, and they soon died off after that.

Another explanation for the lack of information about James could be that Gentile Christianity or Pauline Christianity expanded in the Hellenized areas of the Jewish Diaspora, such as Greece and Asia Minor. This theology mingled with Neoplatonic thinking and developed into the Christianity we know today. This branch grew rapidly under Paul and alienated many Jewish Christians, specifically in the areas where James served as the head. Pauline Christianity was originally subordinate to James, but he seemed unable to completely control Paul. When he did discipline Paul, it was too late. Paul was arrested by the Romans and taken to Rome for trial, and James was killed (Acts 21:18–26). Thus, James became a liability to Pauline Christianity and needed to be toned down or relegated to the shadows of history.

Why did this, the very earliest Christian church, fade into oblivion? The extant fragmentary apocryphal gospel of the Ebionites sheds a great deal of light on this subject. It describes a major hostility toward Paul. He is described as a heretic and a betrayer of Jesus. We can also see the same hostility in reverse through the Pauline epistles and also from the book of Acts, although the betrayers are called "the Jews" (most likely referring to Jewish Christians and the earliest Jerusalem church).

To further demonstrate this point, the canon of the New Testament was collected, assembled, and edited by Pauline Christians. Furthermore, when this branch of Christianity deified Jesus, it ruptured the relationship with the James branch. James died in 62 CE, and Jerusalem was destroyed by the Romans in 70 CE. These calamities decimated the Jewish Christian ranks. They also created a great deal of animosity from the Jews that clearly restricted their ability to recruit new members and left them without a strong leader.

Many Jews and Jewish Christians believed that the destruction of Jerusalem was God's punishment for the murder of James. We find evidence of this in numerous ancient writings. This, of course, shattered James's Christianity, and its descendants soon became heretics and small divergent minority groups. Paul's Christianity became the Orthodox.

Civil war broke out between these Jewish Christians and the pedigree Pauline Christians. The victor was, of course, the church of Paul, and thus, a new divine Jesus surfaced and became the paramount theology of this new Orthodox church. This theology blended nicely with Greek thinking and fit well with platonic philosophy. The Pauline church merged with the Petrine community about 90 CE as evidenced by the gospel of John.

The four gospels of the Bible were selected to be part of the Christian canon, most likely because they were closer to Pauline theology than the many other gospels that existed at the time when the New Testament was being assembled (fourth century). All other existing gospels were then declared spurious and heretical. They were condemned, and authorities ordered them destroyed.

If we closely examine these four canonical gospels and study the theology directly attributed to Jesus, we will find a great deal of current theology missing. We must turn to Paul's writings to discover the basis of modern theology. Paul's initial theology would be later expanded and modified, most significantly by the first Ecumenical Council or the Council of Nicea in 325 CE. There Jesus was declared the equal to God the Father. (John 14:28 is contradictory. Jesus said, "For the Father is greater than I am.") The Council of Constantinople (381 CE) created the divinity of the Holy Ghost and thus the Trinity. The human and divine nature of Jesus was declared in 451 CE at the Council of Chalcedon.

Evidence of the theology of the Jerusalem church is located in the modern city of Tiberius, a city on the Sea of Galilee, which is next to some natural hot springs. There are the ruins of a first-century synagogue. Beautifully preserved is the mosaic tile mural on the floor, and it depicts the zodiac and several other images. Images of this kind were always forbidden by Jewish law, but not by Hellenistic Jewish Christian law. Evidence exists throughout present-day Israel of the Jewish Christian community. This faith still required circumcision and obedience to Jewish dietary laws up to the fifth century.

The Pauline-James clash is described in Acts 15, although it seems the author is cautiously minimizing the dispute. The failure of the James branch to compete with Paul seems to have been effected from the Jewish tradition of placing of secondary status to Gentile Christians. When the Jews revolted against Rome in 66 CE, all Judea was destroyed, and Rome placed harsh restrictions on all Jews, including Jewish Christians. The secondary status forced the Gentiles to migrate to the Pauline branch. Another reason for this failure was that many Jews died in the war, and their ranks were slow to expand. The war caused many Roman reprisals, which affected reforms within Judaism and the persecution of Jewish Christians. These results caused the Jews to expel Christians from their synagogues, and as a consequence, they lost their exempted status from worshipping the Roman emperor. This persecution further thinned the ranks of the James Christians as the *Letter 96* by Pliny (governor of Bithynia) from 112 CE bears this out.

Still, another reason for the quietude—at least regarding James in the New Testament—was perhaps that James, a true blood brother of the deified Jesus, caused abrasiveness to Pauline thinking causing them to obfuscate his real identity. The gospel of Matthew quotes an Isaiah passage from the Greek Old Testament translation (Septuagint) referencing Mary, the mother of Jesus, as she had performed a virgin birth. This led to the dogma of Mary being a virgin, and James became a problem to her perpetual virginity. Therefore, many apologetic scenarios were written to explain this awkward situation, and many avoided referencing James by not having any prayers to him and quietly allowing him to be overshadowed by two others named James. The Orthodox church also became deeply interested in displaying a presence of Christian unity. Hence, it played down the many early divergences.

Without question, James set forth written rules and instructions for the Gentile converts, and thus, he inadvertently helped create a separate and distinctive branch of Christianity (Acts 15:13–21). He did this with his authority as the leader, and he was certainly motivated by a degree to accommodate Gentiles and expand the ranks of his followers. Historically, James, "the brother of the Lord," became the head of the Jerusalem church. The endeavor to shunt James into the background of Christianity has not escaped the careful eyes of modern scholars. Jewish scholars especially exploit the inconsistencies of the New Testament and its treatment of this James.

In his book *The Mythmaker*, Hiam Maccoby states,

> For example, we find immediately after Jesus' death that the leader of the Jerusalem Church is Jesus' brother James. Yet in the Gospels, this James does not appear at all as having anything to do with Jesus' mission and story. Instead, he is given a brief mention as one of the brothers of Jesus who allegedly opposed Jesus during his lifetime and regarded him as mad. How it came about that a brother who had been hostile to Jesus in his lifetime suddenly became the revered leader of the church immediately after Jesus' death is not explained, though one would have thought that some explanation was called for.

James's branch of Christianity worshipped in the temple and obeyed the law. This is why Jewish scholars are quick to point out that Acts, the Gospels, and Paul openly write about the apostles after Jesus's death frequenting the temple, following the Torah, and attending the synagogues. According to Luke (Luke 24:45, 50–53), after Jesus's death, He opened the minds of the apostles so that they understood the scriptures and sent them to pray in the temple. Jesus did not instruct them to do otherwise. What caused this to change, and by whose authority? They believed it was Paul.

Several years after the death of Jesus, Paul adopted the faith of Jesus's followers. In the letter to the Galatians (Galatians 1:17–20), the apostle reports that after he had become a follower of Jesus, he had made several journeys between Damascus and Arabia and then journeyed to Jerusalem to meet Peter. In Jerusalem at this time, he also made the acquaintance of Jesus's brother James.

To explain the unpleasant association of James, the sibling of Jesus, with Mary, the virgin, the early church wrote numerous apologies. "Now Joseph had his first wife from the tribe of Judah, and she bore him six children, four boys and two girls," as the Gospels of Mark and John explain (Mark 6:3; John 19:25). His firstborn was James, surnamed Oblias, meaning *wall*, and also surnamed Just, a Nazarite, which means *holy man*. He was the first to receive the bishop's chair, the first to whom the Lord entrusted His throne upon earth. He was also called the brother of the Lord, and the apostle also agrees, as he says, "I saw no other Apostle except James, the brother of the Lord" (Galatians 19). He was called the Lord's brother because he was reared with Him. It was a matter not of nature but of grace.

"Joseph became the father of James when he was about forty years old, more or less. After James the boy called Joses was born, after him Simeon, and then Judas and the two daughters called Mary and Salome, and then his wife died. After many years he took Mary when he was a widower, being then over 80 years old." These statements are taken from a writing in the fourth century by Epiphanius, bishop of Salamis. Of course, this would make James the older stepbrother of Jesus. Is this historically factual? Probably not, but it is just one of several apologies explaining the relationship between Jesus, James, and Mary.

After the death of James, Symeon, a cousin, became bishop of Jerusalem. Symeon is said to have received a revelation (from God) to leave Jerusalem before disaster befell the place and to instead settle in a town in Peraea called Pella. This story is taken from *The History of the Church* by Eusebius, written in the fourth century. By the time Eusebius wrote his history, the church was under full control of the Paulines. While the Pella story smacks of fabrication, Eusebius's aim was to show the smooth continuity of Christianity and to play down any conflicts.

Eusebius fails to harmonize Paul's doctrine with that of James. This is evident in his chapter 23, which describes "the martyrdom of James, 'the Lord's brother.'" Here the villains are called the Scribes and Pharisees who force James, the righteous one, to make the facts about Jesus clear to all people attending the temple for Passover. James does not attribute divinity to Jesus or even call Him the Son of God. He calls Him the Son of Man and also the Son of David. He also declares, "He (Jesus) is sitting at the right hand of the great power, and he will come on the clouds of heaven." This omission of the Jesus Godhead gives credence to this story, as it opposes Paul's claiming Son of God and the divinity of Jesus as part of Paul's theology. Eusebius was in attendance and played a major role at the Council of Nicea, where Jesus was declared as equal with God the Father.

The effort to erase the James Christians is also apparent in Eusebius's attempt to downplay the epistle attributed to James. This epistle is possibly the first written of its kind, and it consists of the epistles of Jude, Hebrews, and John 2 and 3. Eusebius questions their authenticity. It is not surprising that Eusebius calls the gospel of John the greatest gospel and the most authoritative. It is in the gospel of John that the esoteric facts of the James-Paul conflict occur.

In *The Mythmaker*, Hiam Maccoby states,

From the Acts of the Apostles, from Josephus and from early Christian historians, there emerges a coherent, if still incomplete, portrait of James, "the Lord's brother." He appears as an exemplar of "righteousness"—so much so that "the Just," or "the Righteous," is appended as a sobriquet to his name. He is the acknowledged leader of a "sectarian" religious community whose members are "zealous for the Law." He must contend with two quite separate and distinct adversaries. One of these is Paul, an outsider who, having first persecuted the community, then converts and is admitted into it, only to turn renegade, prevaricate and quarrel with his superiors, highjack the image of Jesus and begin preaching his only doctrine—a doctrine which draws on that of the community, but distorts it. James' second adversary is from outside the community—the high priest Ananaas, head of the Sadducee priesthood. Ananaas is a notoriously corrupt and widely hated man. He has also betrayed both the God and the people of Israel by collaborating with the Roman administration and their Herodian puppet-kings. James publicly challenges Ananaas and eventually meets his death at the hands of Ananaas' minions; but Ananaas will shortly be assassinated in turn. All of this takes place against a back drop of increasing social and political unrest and the impending invasion of a foreign army.

Summing up the history of James, the brother of the Lord, we find him somewhat in opposition or disagreement early on with Jesus (Mark 3:33; Luke 8:20; Matthew 12:46–50). He apparently does not participate in his brother's ministry. After the death of Jesus, he joins the apostles, and by about 45 CE, he becomes the leader of Christianity, supplanting Peter. Tradition claims that he was the first bishop of the church and Jerusalem. Eusebius and Josephus make this assertion; however, many scholars are skeptical. In Acts and Paul, he is certainly a major leader.

Josephus writes that James was stoned to death in 62 CE. High Priest Ananaas, who was in office for only three months, ordered this execution. This caused the indignant inhabitants of Jerusalem to rise up in anger and bring about Ananaas's resignation from office. He was replaced by Jesus, the son of Damascus. James was highly respected by the Jews, especially the Pharisees, and was called James the Just. Some of the branches of Christianity that survived his murder were called Nazoraeans, Ebionites, and Cerinthians, and there were numerous others; however, in general, the name Jewish Christians could be applied to them all.

Four years after the death of James (63 CE), the Jews revolted against Rome, and soon most Jewish Christians abandoned Jerusalem for Pella, although some scholars are skeptical of this move. Pella is a town in the province of Peraea, part of the Greek region of the Decapolis. This action created a schism between the Jews and their cousins, the Jewish Christians. Some factions of Jewish Christians survived until the fifth century.

JOHN

Our next main character of the earliest church is John. Along with his brother James (who was also an apostle but played a minor role), they were the sons of Zebedee.

John Zebedee was a fisherman and could have been a cousin to Jesus (Matthew 20:20; Mark 10:35). He was also called Boanerges, an Aramaic word meaning "the son of thunder." Traditionally, many have said that he wrote the fourth gospel, the three epistles, and the book of Revelation. Surprisingly, John, the son of Zebedee, is not mentioned by name in the gospel he is purported to have authored. John 21:2 speaks of the sons of Zebedee in the third person. In fact, all of chapter 21 mysteriously fails to tell us who the "beloved disciple" is, and it clearly does not identify him as the son of Zebedee.

Mark 10:39 and Matthew 20:23 strongly suggest that these evangelists thought both James and John Zebedee were martyred. Tradition claims John was imprisoned on the island of Patmos (Revelation 1:9) and died of natural causes at nearly a hundred years of age in Ephesus, which is now Turkey.

Much confusion exists about John Zebedee. His natural death is in conflict with Polycarates (about 189 CE) in his letter to Victor (the bishop of Rome). It states, "John, who leant back on the Lord's breast, and who became a sacrificing priest wearing the mitre, a martyr, and a teacher; he too sleeps in Ephesus." Papias (150 CE) claims that John Zebedee and another person named John the presbyter both are buried in Ephesus, and this John authored the book of Revelation. Virtually nothing is known of John Zebedee, and it is certain that he was mistaken by the ancients for numerous others named John. Today only fundamentalist scholars believe he authored the gospel, Revelation, and the three epistles.

This confusion among the authors who were called or called themselves John originates early in the second century as Christianity began to blossom and multiply. Many early church leaders confused the many Johns and recognized this in their writings. Further evidence of this is demonstrated in the apocryphal writing Acts of John, which is part of what is called the Apocryphal Acts of the Apostles. The existing text describes John's death and burial in

Ephesus in a fashion that is similar to Eusebius's account, and it is probably the writing he used to reference John in his book *The History of the Church*.

In perpetuating the early tradition of John, Modestus, the bishop of Jerusalem (634 CE), writes, "After the death of our Lord, the Mother of God and Mary Magdalene joined John, the well-beloved disciple at Ephesus. It is there that the myrrhophore ended her apostolic career through martyrdom, not wishing to the very end to be separated from John the Apostle and the Virgin."

John, like Peter, was uneducated and ignorant (Acts 4:13) and was certainly unable to read or write. Therefore, he could not have written the fourth gospel, the book of Revelation, or the three epistles. Fundamentalists are quick to point out that John could have (or did) dictate his recollections to a scribe or several different scribes. This, of course, is a good possibility. Therefore, we must then look to the writings that the early church fathers claim were written by John Zebedee and see if we can glean anything about this man.

His gospel was popular with Gnostic Christians, and the early Orthodox fathers felt that it had to establish an apostolic origin for it. Because many early Christians questioned its accuracy, many considered it to conflict with the synoptic Gospels. The community that established the Johannine theology (early second century) also split into two groups. One was Gnostic, and the other merged into the Orthodox church (see 1 John).

The fear of Gnosticism even brought the fourth gospel under distrust. "You shall know the truth and the truth will make you free" (John 8:32). Some Gnostic schools thought this summed up their whole system, and the first fourteen verses of John's gospel would be especially relevant for them. In the gospel we detect at least three groups that are responsible for hostilities toward John or the Johannine community. The first group would be the followers of John the Baptist (John 1:35–37; 3:22–30; 4:1–3; 10:40–42). The second group and possibly the most hostile were *Jews* (John 9:22–23; 16:1–4). And the third group was composed of Jewish Christians or followers of James.

We can date the writing of the gospel to no earlier than 90 CE. That is about the time of the Jewish benediction against heretics (birkat ha-minim), expelling all Christians from the synagogues. Before this time only Gentile Christians were unwelcomed. Many scholars believe the birkat ha-minim was inaugurated by Rabbi Gamaliel II (80–115 CE) specifically to expurgate the Jewish Christian group known as the Nazarenes from Jewish synagogues. The writer (or writers) of the fourth gospel was almost certainly from this sect.

The vitriolic language used toward the Jews in this gospel probably exaggerates Jewish conduct. First-century Judaism was quite tolerant of diversity within their faith. An example would be the Pharisees believed in a life after death, but the Sadducees did not. The Essenes rejected the priests and the temple. The Zealots were revolutionists. There were also subdivisions of each within these factions. Yet all were embraced within the framework of Judaism.

The reason for the confusion concerning the expulsion of Jewish Christians from the temple perhaps is that this sect was beginning to adopt some of the Gentile Christian and Gnostic deification theology of Jesus. Therefore, these Christians would have been considered blasphemers and were an anathema to the core of Jewish faith. This deification theology found in the fourth gospel is very evident of the Johannine communities' thought evolution, and one can see why this ran contrary to Jewish thinking.

The Jewish scholar Samuel Sandmel, who discerns this same text as being anti-Semitic, says,

> From a general non-acceptance of Jesus by people in the early chapters (of John), the opposition becomes more and more identified with a (specific) group ... the Jews. Ultimately the group stands for the forces opposed to Jesus, which are the forces of darkness. It is obvious that we are not dealing with an ethnic group, but with a dramatic theological symbol ... we would miss the full significance of this symbol if we considered the Jew in John only as an historical figure ... "The Jews" are an ever-present reality and threat to any worship of God in spirit and in truth.

Sandmel points out that John does not charge "humanity" or "the world" in general for actively seeking Jesus's execution, but he specifically signals it out in "the Jews."

The first epistle of John discloses a rift within the membership of this community of Christians (1 John 2:10). Christians probably separated into a Gnostic faction and into what later amalgamated into a Gentile-Christian branch that claimed Peter as its leader. It soon blended into the descendant Orthodox church. In reconciling with this division, the author of the fourth gospel pejoratively describes Peter in such a way as to show that John's community was special or at least equal to the community represented by Peter as its leader (John 13:21–26; 20:2–10).

Second and third John also alludes to a breach within the community and warns about what seems to be a Docetist (Gnostic) villain. He is former member-preacher leading others astray. In the three epistles and the gospel, we cannot make out John Zebedee. The author or authors do not identify themselves. Although the gospel alludes to the author being "the disciple who Jesus loved," it does not point directly to John Zebedee.

Revelation certainly states it was written by John. However, he does not claim to be an apostle, disciple, or even a prophet. He only says he is a servant of God. However, tradition states that the author is John Zebedee. There are no facts or documents to substantiate this claim. Surprisingly, the word *apostle* does not appear anywhere in the writings attributed to John Zebedee.

Justin Martyr, writing about 160 CE, was the original church father to credit John the apostle as the author of Revelation. Perhaps when Irenaeus and Origen supported this assertion, Revelation, the twenty-seventh book of the New Testament, was accepted by the Orthodox church. However, only 2 Peter was more disputed by the early church fathers. Eusebius, who wrote in the fourth century, told of many church leaders who did not accept John Zebedee as its author.

In summarizing the apostle John, we discover a man who became a legend. Many stories circulated about John, placing him in several different places and showing him performing miracles, being a martyr, and surviving as a centenarian. He became the proponent of the Gnostics and also the Orthodoxy. Factually, we know little to nothing about John Zebedee. Just as modern legends contain only a little truth, so is it with this apostle. Many writings are said to have been authored by this John—the fourth gospel, 1, 2 and 3 Epistles, Revelation, the secret book of John, the Apocryphon of John, the Acts of John, and two apocryphal books of Revelation to John.

Although John Zebedee probably was not responsible for any of the writings, a very distinct Christian community sprung up with John as its focal point. This community fractured early in the second century, forming a Gnostic sect, and the other fused with another Christian sect that had Peter as its focal point. This new compounded faith then merged with the Pauline branch and became the Orthodox Catholic church.

MARY MAGDALENE

As was the case with James (the Lord's brother), Mary Magdalene played a prominent role in early Christianity but was placed in a pejorative role by the Orthodox church. In first-century Judaism, women had no legal rights. They belonged to their husbands and were strictly obliged to obey. Women were considered unreliable witnesses and were not allowed to testify in any legal cases. Their future and stature rested on their ability to marry and produce children, especially males.

Mary, whom we assume was from Magdala, existed in this patriarchal climate. She undoubtedly commanded high respect from Jesus's disciples. However, the leaders of the early male-dominated Orthodox church were embarrassed by a woman's preeminence with Jesus and the apostles, resulting in their playing down her significance. The four canonical gospels speak of her only because she was so prominent that their stories would be incomplete if they had not mentioned her. She was very well known among all of Jesus's supporters and probably His enemies as well.

Mary was the first to see the risen Jesus (Mark 16:9; John 20:16–18), and she alone was given the responsibility to notify the other disciples. Yet Paul, the most prolific New Testament writer, fails to even mention her name. Eusebius, bishop and author of *The History of Church* (fourth century), does not even speak her name. Even Luke in the book of Acts totally eliminates Mary, making it seem as though she never existed.

It certainly appears that the earliest church or churches accepted women as leaders. Several of the New Testament apocryphal texts now substantiate this. But as the churches organized into Orthodox churches, the once lofty position of women deteriorated. As the orthodox church solidified its accepted writings, it also condemned all other writings (e.g., gospels, acts, revelations) as heretical and ordered them destroyed.

As the Orthodox church grew, it became increasingly opposed to sex. In 305 CE, the Council of Elvira decided those involved in the ministry of the altar were to maintain sexual abstinence under the penalty of the forfeiture of their office. In 352 CE, the Council of Laodicea considered women ineligible to become priests. Celibacy soon became the norm, and by the fifth century, it became mandatory for all bishops not to marry. Pope Gregory VII (1021–85 CE) issued a decree forbidding marriage for all clergy in 1073 CE. This decree remains in force even to today. This was the environment while the New Testament canon was being compiled and edited. Certainly, references to celibacy were expanded, and positive references to sex diminished as the New Testament entered into its final form.

First-century Judaism required its rabbis to be married, and it was socially of the utmost importance that men take wives and produce children. The religion did not approve of sex outside of marriage (especially for women) and required unmarried women to remain under the protection or guardianship of a male relative.

What then prompted the rush by the organizing Orthodox church to total celibacy? Although Paul's writings clearly state preference to celibacy, he definitely does not require it. There is no indication of this ideal whatsoever from Jesus toward His preference in today's Bibles. By that, it was virtually unthinkable that a thirty-year-old, first-century male Jew would not be married.

Yet there are no statements or even allusions that Jesus was anything but unmarried in the entire Bible.

An interesting hypothesis is presented by Episcopal bishop John Shelby Spong in his book *Born of a Woman*. Bishop Spong declares,

> The female figure that first appeared to be the primary woman in Christian history was Mary Magdalene. But she was soon relegated to inferior status in favor of Jesus' mother. Mary Magdalene was certainly a more prominent figure, in the New Testament, than the mother of Jesus. In fact by the end of the second century the image of Mary Magdalene had deteriorated into being a prostitute, a sinner, and was considered a lusty individual representing the dangers of the flesh. The virgin became the figure head of ideal womanhood: understanding, virtuous, faithful, cooperating, and docile.

To establish his hypothesis, Bishop Song says, "Suppose Jesus were married." It's a difficult question for today's Christians to comprehend because two thousand years of church tradition leans heavily toward the contrary. Yet throughout history there has been a undercurrent that linked Jesus with Mary Magdalene. Shows like *The Last Temptation of Christ*, *Godspell*, and *Jesus Christ Superstar* certainly emphasize this theme.

Are there any real facts to substantiate this subtradition? The answer is no, but the Gospels record several allusions. The apostle Paul says, "Do we not have the right to be accompanied by a wife, as the other apostles and the brothers of the Lord and Cephas (Peter)?" He was essentially stating that the apostles were married and traveled with their wives.

The Gospels record that groups of women traveled with Jesus's entourage, which certainly included Mary Magdalene. As stated earlier, Jewish custom required unmarried women to travel under the guardianship of a male relative or husband. Throughout the Old and New Testaments, only Mary Magdalene is referred to without a male counterpart (except in the book of Judith). Could Jesus be this counterpart? Why do all the Gospels name Mary Magdalene as the first person to experience the first Easter? This strongly suggests that she was related to Jesus, perhaps through marriage. Another hint comes from the wedding feast of Cana in the gospel of John. Bishop Spong implies that this wedding either involved Jesus or a member of His immediate family. The reasoning is as follows: Jesus appears to be living with his mother. This must occur early in Jesus's ministry because only four disciples were in attendance. Has anyone attended a wedding where one of the guests was asked to supply the wine? Only a host or hostess would be considered. The mother of the bride or groom certainly would be.

The next clue is found in John 1:49. The apostle Nathaniel addresses Jesus as Rabbi. Marriage was a prerequisite for becoming a rabbi. Other references include John 1:38, 3:2, and 6:2. In John 20:15, Mary lays claim to the body of Jesus. In first-century Jewish society, claiming the body of a deceased person could only be done by the next of kin or the wife. Continuing with gospel quotes, Jesus said, "Mary, do not hold me" or "do not cling to me." This expression is one of intimacy. Women did not embrace or even touch men in Jewish society outside of wedlock, even in the privacy of one's own home. Bishop Song's arguments strongly show the possibility of Mary Magdalene being the spouse of Jesus.

If we look into the New Testament Apocrypha, we find much more information about Mary. The gospel of Philip (63:34; 64:5) states, "And the companion of the Savior ... Mary Magdalene ... (Jesus) loved her more than (all) the disciples (and used to) kiss her (often) on her (lips). The rest of (the disciples) said to Him, 'Why do you love her more than all of us?' The Savior answered them, 'Why do I not love you like her?'" Could it be that they were husband and wife?

The gospel of Philip also states, "There were three who always walked with the Lord: Mary his mother and her sister and Magdalene, the one who was caned His companion." Or perhaps she was his concubine? The gospel of Mary is a New Testament apocryphal writing that was in circulation until the end of the second century, when it was declared to be heretical. This gospel has many familiar characters and words that invoke language similar to Matthew, Mark, Luke, and John.

The story contains nothing that would upset orthodox theology, but it does deal with apostolic quarreling. Most importantly, it confirms what the canonical gospel alludes to about Mary Magdalene. She and Levi are the only disciples to understand the risen Savior's teachings. Mary instructs them but is jealously attacked and put down. However, Levi then defends her.

The astounding fact that a gospel was written about a first-century Jewish female in a starring role defies tradition and must certainly contain some historical facts. This gospel exists today only in fragments. Writings were discovered in Coptic and Greek, possibly indicating widespread usage in the second century. Scholars estimate the date of its authorship as the late first to early second century.

Further evidence of Mary's prominence is found in two Gnostic books called *Questions of Mary—Greater* and *Questions of Mary—Lesser*. These books do not exist today, but we know of them through the writings of opposition to heresies by Epiphanius (*The Panarion of St. Epiphanius Bishop of Salamis* written in 310 CE).

> They have many books. They display some questions of Mary, while others based themselves on many books supposedly from the aforementioned Ialdabaoth and in the name of Seth. Others they call the revelations of Adam, and they have dared to compose other gospels in the name of the disciples. They do not blush to say that our very Savior and Lord Jesus Christ revealed this shameful practice of theirs. For in the so-called greater questions of Mary (they have also made up some called "Lesser") they suppose that he made a revelation to her, having taken her to the mountain, prayed, taken out of his side a woman, and begun to have sex with her, and so having partaken of his secretion he showed that thus we ought to do, that we may live. Mary fell to the ground, shaken, but he raised her up again and said to her: "Why did you doubt, you of little faith?" They say that this is what is said in the gospel: "If I have spoken to you of earthly things and you do not believe, how will you believe heavenly things?"

To summarize the story of Mary Magdalene, we almost certainly find a major cover-up that is unfortunately shrouded in a diminutive amount of writings. But this small amount of evidence does suggest that Mary Magdalene was the primary female of Jesus's disciples. She very likely was also a prime disciple ranking above many of the men. She was later called "the apostle to the Apostles" by Hippolytus of Rome (170–235 CE), which was in agreement with the many writings that existed at that time, although they later were labeled heretical and destroyed.

Without question, Mary's role in early Christianity was deliberately downplayed because of her sex. Yet all the canonical gospels tell of her loyalty and devotion, and of all the disciples, she alone was fearlessly present at Jesus's crucifixion. She was also the first human to witness the resurrection of Jesus.

Some scholars believe she was married to Jesus and that she had a prominent role in His ministry. This is nothing but speculation and cannot be proven. In modern times archaeology has enhanced our knowledge of Mary Magdalene, although most of the information comes from writings of dubious accuracy. Almost certainly, some truth is present. Some of the writings are mostly contemporaneous with the New Testament but are considered apocryphal: *Dialog of the Savior; Pistis Sophia; The Gospel of Mary, Thomas, Philip and Peter.* All these writings exist today, at least in fragments.

These writings show Mary Magdalene's role in Christianity as something quite different from that spoken of in the canonical gospels. Though it probably will never be proven, the apocryphal writings certainly have a strong ring of truth to them regarding Mary Magdalene and women's role in early Christianity.

PETER

The most prominent of Jesus's apostles or disciples certainly was Peter. Without a doubt, Jesus chose Peter to be the leader of the twelve apostles. The New Testament is quite clear that he also was the handpicked successor to Jesus. We envisage Saint Peter with his keys in hand at the golden gate, deciding who shall be let in.

Catholics see him as the first pope and the apostle who founded the church in Rome. Protestants prefer to put him in a subordinate position to Paul. The Bible positively places Peter as the prime apostle of Jesus throughout His ministry.

Peter, of course, was originally named Simon. He was renamed by Jesus. *Petros* (Greek) means rock or stone, and in the New Testament, he is sometimes referred to as Cephas. This name is then taken from the Aramaic word *Kefa* (also meaning rock or stone). Aramaic was the language spoken in Judea at this time. Jesus renamed Simon "the rock" most likely because of his personality. No doubt Jesus fully intended to compliment Simon for his rock-solid devotion, zeal, and strength of character. Jesus had nicknames for all his closes associates. While he was alive, Jesus named Peter to be the very foundation of His movement. Every ancient writing—apocryphal, pseudepigraphical, or canonical—shows Peter to be Jesus's choice for His successor.

Peter was married and had at least one daughter, Petronilla. He came from Bethsaida and had a home in Capernaum. John and James Zebedee were his partners in a fishing business, and they appeared to do quite well. Eusebius records Peter as the first bishop of Antioch and also of Rome. The tradition of Peter's founding the church in Rome cannot be proven either way. However, there is a solid basis that he did indeed visit the city and probably died there.

Protestant Christianity takes a very skeptical view of Peter founding the Roman church. They cite Paul's letter to the Romans, which does not acknowledge Peter being in the city or having been there. Acts and 1 Clement are also mute in this regard. Designated as the fourth pope or bishop of Rome (96 CE), Clement should have known that Peter, his predecessor, was residing or had resided in the same city. Even the written verification of Peter's presence in Rome as stated in a letter from Dionysius to the church in Rome (166 CE) is brought into question. It declares that the Roman church was founded by Peter. However, Protestants correctly point out that Dionysius's letter made several statements that were not true and thus negate the whole letter.

This incredulous view by Protestants regarding Peter's role in Rome is certainly strong but fails to prove anything to the contrary. In Romans 1:13, Paul says he never met the Christians of Rome. So if Peter was there, he quite possibly would not have known. It is certainly feasible the author of Acts did not know the whereabouts of Peter at the time of his writing. Clement says nothing at all about where Peter lived or even mentioned that it mattered. It is not impossible that he did live in Rome.

It is certain that Christianity existed in Rome well before Peter or Paul's arrival. At best, Peter became the leader of an existing branch of Christianity in Rome. According to a number of writings pertaining to Peter, in Rome, he is said to have arrived somewhere about 54, 58, or possibly as late as 63 CE.

Peter's burial in Rome is stated in the epistle of Clement to the Corinthians. Ignatius's letter to the Romans and the unanimous tradition of second-century writers strongly support this claim. Ignatius tells them besides a memorial monument at the cemetery on the Vatican hill, which was built about 160–170 CE, there is the tomb of Peter.

Recently excavations under Saint Peter's church have disclosed a pagan necropolis of the second century. In the middle of this structure, there stood a monument in honor of Saint Peter constructed in that decade. A Roman writer (200 CE) named Gaius mentions both this monument on Vatican hill and one for Saint Paul on the road to Ostia.

The identification of this (Peter's) tomb under Saint Peter's church in Rome is accepted by several scholars as authentic and was affirmed by Pope Paul in 1968. Today almost all biblical scholars agree that it is a historical fact Peter lived and died in Rome.

Jewish scholars are skeptical of Peter's moving the church of Jesus to Rome. They call this a myth predicated by power politics. Hyam Maccoby, a British Talmudic scholar and author of the book *The Mythmaker*, states,

> The Roman Catholic Church's claim to supremacy over Christendom is a second century legend. Peter was conceived to have been the first Bishop of Rome or Pope and, since Peter had been declared by Jesus to be the rock on which the church was to be built, this made Rome the center of Christendom, and the papal succession the true hierarchy founded by Jesus himself. This is of course

mere power politics and not to be taken seriously as historical fact. To Jesus, a Jew, the idea that his teaching would have its administrative center at Rome, the capital of military power against which his whole life was directed, would have seemed astonishing and dismaying.

But to return to historical realities, what was the relationship between Peter, evidently the leader of the Apostles during Jesus' life time, and James, the brother of Jesus? Why was it that Peter did not become the unchallenged leader of the movement after the death of Jesus?

Some scholars take the position that when Herod Agrippa I had James Zebedee executed in 44 CE, this caused Peter to flee Jerusalem. Then James, the brother of Jesus, took over the leadership of the church. James was a very popular leader and was respected by all the Jews except possibly the Sadducees. They are said to have killed James in 62 CE while Peter was most likely in Rome. Therefore, Peter probably regained the leadership of the church, and it is said he died in Rome about 65 CE.

Eusebius acknowledges Peter as the foundation of the church, but he does not establish Rome as the seat of Christianity. Nearly every ancient writing agrees to Peter being the apostle whom Jesus designated to build His church. However, none of them claim He declared or moved the primacy of the church to Rome. In fact, no one considered Rome superior to Jerusalem, Antioch, or Alexandria until after the Moslem conquests in the seventh century.

The gospel of Mark is said to have been dictated to Mark (possibly Peter's son) by Peter. Eusebius, Clement of Rome, and Irenaeus all state that this is true. However, most modern scholars do not accept this claim. Scholars are more unanimous in their rejection of the two epistles, which many claim Peter wrote. One reason is the late date of their production. First Peter internally claims to be authored by the apostle Peter. Of course, this is impossible because the churches to which 1 Peter was sent did not exist until after Peter was dead.

The most deprecated book of the New Testament is 2 Peter. Its authenticity was seriously doubted by nearly every early church leader; however, Jerome (fifth century) accepted it. Therefore, it became part of the Christian canon. The value of these epistles is in the fact that they establish the time of acceptance of Peter as the foundation of the church regardless of who the real author was. It also shows the pervading Pauline theology creeping into the Petrine community.

Peter's life is an enigma shrouded by myths and legend. How did he become Jesus's favorite and designated successor? He then lost the supreme leadership to James only to win it back. He is reviled by Paul in Galatians 2:11–14, and he demonstrates intimidating subordination to James. Paul's statements in Galatians show a definite conflict within the early church that is mentioned in the book of Acts. No place in Acts is there any criticism of Peter or any hint of disagreement between Peter and Paul. Many scholars point out conflicts between Acts and Galatians pertaining to the Jerusalem Council. By gathering corollaries from both, many conclude that Paul was admonished by James and was given a strong penance, which ultimately caused him to be condemned to death. People respond to Peter with only favorable language.

Besides the two epistles of Peter, some of the New Testament apocryphal and Gnostic texts in existence include Apocalypse of Peter, the gospel of Peter, the Acts of Peter, and the Twelve Letters of Peter to Philip. Each of these texts are basically in agreement with the details concerning Peter in the canonical works, although some are expanded and have more detail.

In summary, we discover Peter accepting the call of Jesus to become His first lieutenant. Jesus gives Simon the keys to His church and renames him Peter, Petros, the rock-solid foundation. After the death of Jesus, he presides over the remaining eleven apostles and establishes a replacement for Judas Iscariot. He is imprisoned by Herod, but he escapes and flees to Antioch. While he is in prison, James, the brother of Jesus, becomes the leader of the Jerusalem church. Peter becomes the bishop of Antioch. When James is killed (62 CE), Peter is reestablished as the supreme leader while he resides in Rome. Tradition says he was martyred in 65 CE by crucifixion. (By his request, he was hanged upside down.)

THE EARLIEST CHRISTIANS

Without a doubt, the earliest Christians were Jews. Every follower of Jesus (while He was living) was Jewish. According to Acts 2:46, the disciples after His death worshipped in the temple just as they had traditionally in the past. In other words, nothing had changed, at least in their worship.

In Acts 5, we see this new Jesus/Judaism was granted toleration within the ranks of Orthodox Judaism, thus creating a new separate branch of this faith coalescing with the likes of Sadducees, Pharisees, and Essenes. Chapter 6 tells of Hellenists joining the movement. It would appear these Hellenists had become full Jews or were accepted as God fearers. This suggests that they were considered as having a secondary status.

Most likely before the destruction of Jerusalem, Gnostic Christianity was quietly taking form and establishing its roots. Actually, Gnosticism was born before Christianity. This birth occurred shortly after the Jews returned from exile. It did not gain a great of popularity until after the death of Jesus and the Christian variety burst on the scene. Two major branches of Jewish Gnostics were known as Sethian and Hermetic. Epiphanius's *Panerion*, written in the fourth century, records numerous heresies, several of them Jewish Gnostic in origin.

Gnostic Christianity grew alongside of Orthodox/Gentile Christianity and along with Jewish Christians, and it was tolerated for about the first hundred years. Thus, from about 35 to 135 CE, three distinct variations of Christians lived for the most part harmoniously as fellow Christian brothers. By the middle of the second century, the message or gospel of Jesus had clearly become very dynamic and appealing throughout the pagan Roman Empire. The first Jewish revolt (66 CE) seriously reduced Jewish Christian ranks. The aftermath of the second revolt (132 CE) all but finished them. They then became outcasts of both Judaism and Orthodox/Gentile Christianity, but not from the other Gnostic Christians who were more tolerant.

Between the revolts, Gnostic and Orthodox Christianity rapidly grew, and this incredible growth escalated hostilities between these two. During this era it was hard to distinguish between the two sects. A few scholars estimate the Gnostic population of this period to be 45 percent of Christendom. Some Roman writings speak of Christian rituals that sound more Gnostic than Orthodox, but they clearly refer to Christianity as a solitary cult.

The first Ecumenical Council at Nicea (325 CE) rang the death knell for Gnostic Christians. This was not because Orthodox Christianity vigorously persecuted them, although some persecution did occur, but because the lack of imperial funding and taxation choked them to death. This, of course, then made Orthodox Christianity much more desirable to the masses.

From early on, both Christians organized their ranks and developed a hierarchy. The Orthodox sect was more uniform and better systematized and was clearly easier to understand. Gnostics had a good amount of diversity and were seriously divided and very complex. Though generally minor, several theological differences existed as well. However, these individuals were extremely tolerant of variant Gnostics and even of the Orthodox faith.

Most surprisingly, they accepted women as equals, allowing them to take leadership positions. The supreme God was considered sexless while wisdom was defined as feminine. In her book *When God Was a Woman*, Professor Merlyn Stone wrote of frescos in the Roman catacombs depicting women wearing the bishop's mitre, many of which were defaced in order to disguise their gender. But through infrared photography, the original clearly is visible, proving the high rank that women achieved within Gnosticism.

Mary Magdalene was considered to be an apostle who was equal to Peter and superior to most of the others. God (the supreme God) was viewed as androgynous by most Gnostics and both male and female by at least a few. This stirred great anger among several male Orthodox leaders. In *De Praescr,* Tertullian wrote concerning Gnostic women leaders, "These heretical women—how audacious they are! They have no modesty; they are bold enough to teach, to engage in argument, to enact exorcisms, to undertake cures, and, it may be, even to Baptize."

Granting women high positions would appear (to today's modern readers) to give Gnostics an advantage in recruitment. Actually, the results had quite the opposite effect. Patriarchal society was so dominant, and most men considered women inferior. Many thought Gnostic Christianity then was inferior. So much so that many Orthodox fathers wrote treatises outlining male superiority and female inferiority. Several of Paul's epistles were edited to show feminine subordination. These same editors wrote in Paul's name in the epistles to Timothy. First Timothy was perhaps the most antiwoman book. Again, the motive was to embarrass Gnostic egalitarianism.

This resulted in vigorous attacks coming from the Orthodox. The Gnostic defense failed, and shortly after Nicea, they became castaways and soon died out. At Nicea, they were forced to acquiesce and compromise with the Orthodox or face exile. Their writings became heretical, and the order for their destruction was issued by imperial decree.

So thorough was the Orthodox victory that our understanding of Gnostic Christianity has long been hampered by a lack of historical evidence. Until Nag Hammadi (1945), our only information came from the early Orthodox father's polemical writings against them, most notably from Irenaeus, Hippolytus, Epiphanius, and Tertullian. Today our knowledge has vastly increased. The Nag Hammadi cache of twelve codices plus one loose tractate provides fifty-two extant tracts in total, of which forty were completely unknown before.

The early close association between Orthodox and Gnostics is apparent in some of the writings of Paul and the Gospels. So much so that later editors expunged several passages that contained too much Gnostic inference. Prolific Orthodox writer Justin Martyr (140 CE) refused to reference Paul in any of his numerous apologies. Even Tertullian labeled Paul the "apostle of the heretics," not because he considered Paul an untrue apostle but because Gnostics were vigorously citing him to support their doctrines.

Here are a few examples of details that escaped these editors. First Corinthians 2:6–8 says,

> Yet among the mature we do impart wisdom (sophia), although it is not a wisdom of this age or of the rulers of this age, who are doomed to pass away.

But we impart a secret and hidden wisdom of God, which God decreed before the ages (aeons) for our glorification. None of the rulers of this AGE understood this; for if they had, they would not have crucified the Lord of glory.

Second Corinthians 12:2 says, "I know a man in Christ who 14 years ago was caught up to the third heaven—whether in the body or out of the body I do not know, God knows." A large segment of Gnostics believed there were seven levels of heaven. Each level was represented by the seven planets in the sky. These were the seven planets known to the ancient astronomers. The sun and moon were also considered to be part of the seven planets.

Matthew 4:8–9 tells of Satan offering Jesus all the kingdoms of the world if only He would bow down and worship him. This indicates they (Jesus and Satan) believed the world was Satan's possession to begin with, an idea that coincides with most Gnostic beliefs. They believed this world was created by an inferior god (Demiurge, the Greek word meaning *public craftsman*) or the evil antitheses of the true God.

Jude 4:19 reveals "certain men" who "have secretly slipped in among you." This passage resembles pre-Carpocratian Gnostics almost to the letter. The fourth gospel has numerous Gnostic passages, and many others were removed or modified by a later editor.

The early Gnostics had great diversity in their belief systems, although generally, the fundamentals were in agreement, however loose that agreement might have been. We must keep in mind the Roman persecution of the early Christians included Gnostic martyrs in equal proportion.

CHAPTER 8

GNOSTIC CHRISTIANS

Immediately after the death of Jesus, His followers were dismayed and disorganized. We know that at least some of them quickly took up the cause and eventually achieved world renown. Clearly, something about the circumstances concerning Jesus was compelling as it soon became the planet's most populous religion. Over the centuries many have tried to explain this phenomenon; however, these explanations vary widely, and most are quite controversial.

As the new faith was being organized, most scholars agree that three distinct segments took shape. Today they are called Orthodox, Jewish Christian, and Gnostic Christian. Of course, the earliest of these were the Jewish Christians. Ultimately, the Orthodox won out, and it is the Christianity we have at present. As most of us believe, early Christianity struggled through several persecutions until the early fourth century when it became the official religion of the Roman Empire.

The New Testament also alludes to the battle with Gnostics and Jewish Christians. This is understandable because the New Testament writers certainly desired harmony and unity within their congeries. Therefore, little was known of these rivals until the Nag Hammadi discovery in 1945. Actually, it took more than thirty years for this repository of books to rise to the surface of academia and become public.

Initially, the writings were classified as a Gnostic library of sacred scripture. We now know that most of the writings are exactly that, but not all of them qualify as Gnostic Christian (e.g.,

Plato's *The Republic*). Before Nag Hammadi, our only knowledge of Christian Gnosticism came from the early church fathers who wrote treatises denouncing them. The texts are written in Coptic, and copies were translated from the original Greek. Some of the books, meaning their original manuscripts, arguably have been dated to the first century, placing them contemporaneously with the canonical books of the New Testament.

We have learned that ancient Gnosticism was not well organized and had many variations in belief and rituals. In fact, so many mutations developed it is impossible to offer a standardized Gnostic denomination. Therefore, it could be said that the death of ancient Gnosticism was caused more by its inability to appeal to the masses than by the persecution by the Orthodox. The Council of Nicea did consolidate the numerous diversities within the Orthodox church and thus interdicted Gnosticism in general. But to say the church after Nicea actively persecuted Gnostics would be an exaggeration.

The common thread in Gnostic Christianity was the belief that an inferior god created the universe. This god was called Demiurge (Greek meaning *public craftsman*). Demiurge was subordinate to the supreme God of truth, an androgynous being. This subaltern god was believed to be the God of the Hebrew scriptures (Old Testament) also acknowledged as the creator of the earth and all of its life forms. The characteristics of Demiurge are fundamentally evil, jealous, rigid, lacking in compassion, and prone to genocide.

Most Gnostics believed the supreme God sent Jesus (out of pity for humankind) to show the path to escape the evils of the flesh and ultimately achieve communion with this supreme Being. They classified Demiurge with the Hebrew God and offered as proof numerous quotations from the Bible. I will list only a few of them.

First Samuel 15:3 says, "Go now and put Amalek to the sword, putting to the curse all they have, without mercy: put to death every man and woman, every child and baby at the breast, every ox and sheep, camel and ass."

First Samuel 16:14–15 says, "Now the spirit of the Lord had gone from Saul, and an evil spirit sent from the Lord was troubling him. And Saul's servants said to him, See now, an evil spirit from God is troubling you."

Numbers 13:17–18 says, "Now therefore kill every male among the little ones, and kill every woman who has known man by lying with him. But all the female children, that have not known a man by lying with him, keep alive for yourselves."

Leviticus 21:16–23 says,

And the LORD spoke unto Moses, saying, "Say to Aaron, If a man of your family, in any generation, is damaged in body, let him not come near to make the offering of the bread of his God. For whatever man he is that has a blemish, he shall not draw near: a blind man, or a lame, or he who has a flat nose, or any deformity, or a man who has an injured foot, or an injured hand, or hunchbacked, or a dwarf, or one who has a defect in his eye, or an itching disease, or scabs, or who has damaged testicles no man of the seed of Aaron the priest, who has a blemish, shall come near to offer the offerings of the Lord made by fire. Since he has a blemish, he shall not come near to offer the bread of his God. He shall eat the bread of his God, both of the most holy, and of the holy. He shall not come near to the veil, nor come near to the altar, because he has a blemish; that he may not profane my sanctuaries, for I am the Lord who sanctifies them."

Deuteronomy 2:30 says, "But Sihon king of Heshbon would not let us pass by him: for the LORD your God hardened his spirit, and made his heart obstinate, that he might deliver him into thy hand, as appeared this day."

Deuteronomy 2:33–36 says,

And the Lord our God gave him into our hands; and we overcame him and his sons and all his people. We took all his cities at that time, and utterly destroyed every inhabited city, with the women and the little ones; we left none remaining: only the livestock we took for a prey to ourselves, with the spoil of the cities which we had taken. From Aroer on the edge of the valley of the Arnon and from the town in the valley as far as Gilead, no town was strong enough to keep us out; the Lord our God gave them all into our hands.

Deuteronomy 6:15 says, "For the Lord your God who is with you is a jealous God who will not let his honor be given to another; or the wrath of the Lord will be burning against you, causing your destruction from the face of the earth."

Most Gnostics believed Demiurge was cruel to the extreme because he designed all living creatures so that they had to eat other living things in order to survive. The supreme God took pity on man and sent Jesus to introduce to humanity the path to the Pleroma (heaven). This dualism was very similar to Zoroastrianism's "good god and bad god" concept.

Gnosticism is assumed by many to be a product or by-product of Christianity. For the most part, this is true; however, it really sprung to life in the last century before the Common Era (BCE) as a splinter group of Judaism in Egypt. Today this brand is called "Sethian Gnosticism." The history of this original small sect was virtually unknown before the Nag Hammadi discovery in 1945. This discovery and the translations of the various books have revealed much about this unusual proto-Gnostic faith. Several of the books have been categorized as being Sethian. This label has been given by modern scholars because their identity has been recognized through the Nag Hammadi library and mentioned briefly by Epiphanius in *Panerion*, where Seth is considered to be their focal point.

The entire Nag Hammadi library was written in Coptic, although some scholars believe the original manuscripts were penned in Greek. Coptic is a Semitic language that was the tongue spoken in Egypt before Islamic Arabic. After the conquest of Egypt by Alexander the Great, the Egyptians blended their language (Demotic) with Greek and adopted the Greek alphabet and script in their writings. Greek and later Christian philosophy greatly influenced Sethians, especially that of Plato, who also had a profound impact on Gnosticism in general.

The earliest Sethians' primary focus was on a Jewish purification ritual or a pre-Christian baptismal rite. They believed that by the practicing of this custom, they would derive the wisdom of Adam via his descendant or third son, Seth. They believed that Seth would soon be returning in an apocalyptic (a prediction of a cataclysm but not necessarily the end of the world) messianic fashion. Seth would be a type of savior that would then make accessible the knowledge of a wisdom path to the spiritual world. The *Paraphrase of Seth*, which Hippolytus (Refutatio V 19.22) attributes to the Sethians, suggests that baptism was a washing in and drinking from a cup of living springwater by which the believer, like the savior, takes on the role of a servant, escapes earthy bondage, and is redressed with a heavenly garment.

When the news of Christ reached these people (late thirties to early forties), they found several similarities and began to embrace Christianity. This was loosely associated with the Jewish Christian segment of the new faith. Seth then became transformed into a supernatural being. We must keep in mind that there was no eschatology (end of the world) involved in their belief systems.

Generally, all Gnostics gravitated toward Jesus from the stories they heard about Him. They then developed their own theology to suit. This is typified in many of the Gnostic gospels offering esoteric or secret teachings of Jesus. These teachings were rationalized in such a way as to reveal how Jesus taught special knowledge exclusively to His disciples while His general or public teachings were accomplished through the use of parables. Sethians, in particular, used the Apocryphon of John as sacred scripture, which is very likely inspired from the canonical fourth gospel (at least in part). This development is reflected in Acts 17:23–24, regarding the "unknown God" as delivered by Paul.

As Marcionism (a heretic from the middle of the second century) deviated away from the mainstream (I use this term very broadly) of Gnosticism, the Sethians began to almost simultaneously separate from Christianity. We can trace this transformation through the texts Melchezidec and the gospel of the Egyptians. The former shows Jewish influences, while the latter offers evidence about the beginning of the breakdown with Christianity. In both the Coptic (not to be confused with the Greek version, which is quite different) gospel of the Egyptians and the Trimorphic Protennoia, the final discourse of salvation is the second coming of Seth in the form of the Word or of the Logos as is in the image of Christ, who also appears in the person of Jesus. The salvation of Jesus is obviously implied in the two books. These polemical abstractions place Seth as their savior while Jesus becomes one of the saved. In view of this Sethian Christological reinterpretation, one would characterize the present form of these two texts as reacting to rather than merely submitting to Christian influence.

We can find additional Sethian information from Epiphanius (Panarion 40.2.6–8) concerning the Archontics. He presents them as an offshoot of the Sethians who have come to completely reject baptism (a mainstay of the early Sethians) and the sacraments of the church, which they view as a being a derivative from the inferior lawgiver Sabaoth (the god of Israel or Demiurge in other Gnosticisms). They believed that the shunning of baptism and the sacraments would enhance their prospects for acquiring the gnosis, enabling their return to the supreme God, the androgynous Mother-Father of all.

Sethian Gnosticism seems to have gone into serious decline around the end of the third century. As is the case with nearly all forms of Gnosticism, they failed to attract new membership because Orthodox Christianity was becoming more attractive and was much better organized. *The Three Steles of Seth*, another Nag Hammadi text, offers insight to changes that their faith may have been undergoing, and this may have fostered this degeneration and drop-off in membership. Orthodox Christianity did eventually attack Gnostics verbally and relentlessly but did not revert to killings or violence to any degree.

Sethianism was one of the earliest forms of Gnosticism and was Jewish-based. It later migrated to Christian Gnosticism and eventually fell away into a mixed Neopythagorean and Neoplatonic conceptualism. Their communities were located in Egypt and failed to spread to other areas to any great degree, although they did influence other groups, such as the Archontics. Their writings make up a significant portion of the Nag Hammadi library.

Although we have copious information concerning other people and events of the early Christian era, very few facts are left in respect to the lives of the Gnostic teachers, for their personal remains were destroyed as thoroughly as their written ones. Only archaeological discoveries of their ancient manuscripts have opened a beginning for the reconstruction of a more accurate picture of their lives and thoughts.

THE TWELVE APOSTLES

Christianity is the world's most popular religion. It is based on the historical person we all know as Jesus. Christ is not His last name. It represents basically the English rendering of the Greek word for the Hebrew word in English as messiah. And messiah was understood to mean a redeemer who would elevate the Jewish people to stature among the nations of the world.

This is exactly what Jesus did! It may not have happened the way the earliest followers of Jesus thought, and it certainly did not happen the way the Jewish people thought or expected; however, it most certainly has become a historical fact.

The plain fact is that Jesus was Jewish and was nurtured in a Jewish environment. Christianity has inherited many Jewish characteristics and has expanded by incorporating these characteristics within its basic structure, making Judaism also world-prominent.

Jesus began His ministry as a member of John the Baptist's troupe. He gained followers, several of whom had been followers of John, who believed in Jesus or in His ability to bring about a positive change. Most likely, this anticipated change was believed to be a social or political change and not religious change.

The New Testament Gospels, Revelation, and Acts allude to a distinct twelve—very close followers of Jesus who are commonly known as the twelve apostles. In the first epistle of Paul to the Corinthians (15:3–8), Paul specifies the number twelve alluding to the original apostles and particularly mentioning Peter in the first position. The earliest writer in the New Testament, Paul is keenly aware that the number twelve is significant, and this is proof that this fact was well known, at least by the early fifties. Revelation, which was written in the late nineties, also specifically speaks of the twelve apostles. Hebrews 3:1 also mentions apostles, which include Christ in the original meaning, a delegate sent from God.

Taking in the whole context of the New Testament, it seems that Jesus did not choose twelve apostles haphazardly. For most Christians the old Israel (the twelve tribes) was replaced by the new Israel (the church), and the twelve apostles were the foundation of that church. The apostles themselves must have understood this, since the first thing they did after the ascension of Jesus was to find a replacement for Judas Iscariot, someone they knew had been a witness to the resurrection of Jesus. In Matthew 19:25–30, Jesus tells the twelve that they will sit on thrones and judge the twelve tribes of Israel, reinforcing the importance of these twelve original apostles. Incidentally, Paul and James (the Lord's brother) were not part of the original twelve.

Therefore, it would seem that the twelve people who were appointed personally by Jesus as His special assistants are indeed historical individuals. Furthermore, these individuals have specific names and should be labeled as such in the New Testament. Alas, here we have some discrepancies. For example, several more than the original twelve apostles are named.

Matthew 10:2–4 says, "These are the names of the twelve apostles: first, Simon (who is called Peter) and his brother Andrew; James son of Zebedee, and his brother John; Philip and Bartholomew; Thomas and Matthew the tax collector; James son of Alphaeus, and Thaddaeus; Simon the Zealot and Judas Iscariot, who betrayed Him." The Bible also lists the twelve apostles in Mark 3:16–19 and Luke 6:13–16. In comparing the three passages, there are differences in the names. It seems that Thaddaeus is missing while "Judas, son of James" (Luke 6:16) is an addition, and Lebbaeus (Matthew 10:3) in some translations is used in place of Thaddaeus. Simon the Zealot was also known as Simon the Canaanite (Mark 3:18). Judas Iscariot, who betrayed Jesus, was replaced in the twelve apostles by Matthias (Acts 1:20–26).

The fourth gospel adds the name Nathaniel. Amazing, the gospel of John makes no mention of any apostle named John. But then John's gospel has no Bartholomew either. It doesn't have any Matthew, James (the son of Alphaeus), or Simon the Canaanite. Neither does he have Simon the Zealot, Levi (the son of Alphaeus), or any Levi or Matthew. Through the centuries numerous Christian apologies offer explanations for these discrepancies, and while some are reasonable, others seem to be quite a stretch.

The truth of the matter is Christianity is not predicated on the actual names or number of these apostles. It is merely a minor detail used to describe the events surrounding the life of Jesus. The birth of Christianity arises with the crucifixion and resurrection of Jesus. At that time there was only a very small number of people who actually knew Jesus. His death would not have caused anything to alarm the general population whatsoever. So it began with a small group, which included the eleven or twelve who worked at convincing others that Jesus and His teachings were something very special and should be emulated.

Three years after Paul's epiphany in route to Damascus, he went to Jerusalem to meet with Peter. In the fifteen days he stayed, he did not see any of the other apostles, but he did meet

James, the brother of Jesus. Fourteen years later he came back. This is sometimes referred to as the Jerusalem Council. Here he meets with John as well as Peter and James. Acts 4 describes the early workings of the apostles. Here it seems Peter was the clear leader, and John was next with no mention of James. Chapter 12 informs us of the death of James (the brother of John Zebedee). This took place before the Jerusalem Council, which would then leave James the son of Alpheaus (Mark 3:14–19; Matthew 10:2–4) as the only remaining apostle named James. We then find that Peter is imprisoned, but an angel of God frees him. His first impulse is to report to James. It does not seem likely that this was James the son of Alpheaus but rather was the brother of Jesus, who appears to be the leader of the Jerusalem Christians.

Of course, James could have been the leader only while Peter was in prison and now Peter was forced to leave town for fear of being recaptured. The earliest historian of the church, Eusebius, indicates Peter went on to Antioch and became their first bishop. This would mean that Peter must have returned later in time to attend the Jerusalem Council. My point here is James, the leader, was not an apostle or at least not one of the original twelve.

Numerous pseudepigrapha and apocryphal books offering many additional details of the apostles exist, but none of them have reliable credibility. Basically, all historians have to work with is the New Testament. Perhaps the most famous—or I should say infamous—apostle is Judas Iscariot. He is named in all four gospels and Acts as the betrayer of Jesus. Yet the circumstances surrounding his death significantly differ in Matthew and Acts. More surprising is that Paul never mentions Judas even though he acknowledges Jesus was betrayed, but he doesn't say by whom. Judas was the son of Simon Iscariot (John 6:71). "Iscariot" is interpreted as meaning "dagger man" (meaning that Judas was a Zealot) or "man of Kerioth," which was a town near Hebron. If the latter is correct, then Judas was the only non-Galilean among the twelve. This Simon apparently is not the same person as the apostle Simon the Zealot.

Only in the Gospels of John and Luke as well as Acts do we hear of another apostle also named Judas who was the son of James. We are not told which James that was either. The apostle Thomas also presents a problem. The word *Thomas* at this time in history was not a proper noun. This word in Hebrew meant *twin*, and the equivalent in Greek would have been Didymus. Both renderings are used in the New Testament, and in several early manuscripts, "Didymus Thomas" is used. In Syriac tradition, he is referred to as Judas Thomas.

In Mark 2:14–15 and Luke 5:27–29, we are told of an apostle named Levi, the son of Alpheaus. This presents two problems in that it would make Levi the brother of James. This is, of course, not impossible; however, family relationships have been generally acknowledged when speaking of the original twelve, and nothing is mentioned associating these two. The other problem is there is no apostle named Matthew in Mark and Luke's list. Apologists assert Levi was just another name or nickname for Matthew. This seems to be unlikely but possible.

There's much debating in regards to the apostle Peter. Catholic, Orthodox, and Protestants view Peter very differently. Catholics believe he was the first pope, the leader designated by Jesus to carry on His church, and doubtlessly the prime apostle who established the seat of the new church in Rome.

Orthodox Christians view Peter as a major apostle and believe he did die in Rome and was buried there. The Orthodox church has consistently expressed its readiness to accord the bishop of Rome a primacy of honor. However, this is similar to the respect now given to the bishop of Constantinople, who is called "first among equals." They do not and surely would not accept this as approval of universal jurisdiction. They believe it is perfectly acceptable to consider the pope Peter's successor just as they believe the bishop of Constantinople is the successor of Andrew the first-called (who actually brought Peter to the Jesus).

Protestants have a myriad of opinions relative to Peter depending on their denomination. Some recognize him as the bishop of Antioch and later as the bishop of Rome and nothing more. Most submit that his primacy was indeed given to him by Jesus but was never intended to be passed on to his successors or create a hierarchy. Some view Peter as never having held the office of bishop or ever residing in Rome on the grounds that this office was a later development of the Catholic church. A few Protestants refuse to use the title of *saint* in reference to him. Although opponents of Peter's commission, as articulated by Catholicism, present some strong and reasonable objections, it seems clear that the passages in Matthew 16:18 and John 21:15–16 do indeed tend to support the Catholic position, at least to an impartial reader.

It has been stated that there is no reliable documentation regarding Peter moving to and living in Rome. This is true indeed. He was an uneducated, Aramaic-speaking Jew with a strong Galilean accent. He almost certainly would not have spoken Latin and very little Greek, the primary and secondary languages of Rome.

Christian tradition states that Peter was crucified and buried in Rome about 65 CE. This assertion has been loudly expressed by the Roman church from the earliest of times, and there never were any challenges brought up by any of the other Patriarchates to their claim. This is significant because the early Christian communities cherished relics and traditions of the apostles and were eager to lay claim or dispute any assertions of authenticity. Therefore, it is reasonable to treat the idea that Peter did travel to and die in Rome as an historical fact.

In summation, I believe, Jesus did have a close cabinet of friends as well as more numerous supporters or disciples. The number twelve became prominent only after His death when people began to recognize or believe He was someone special as the stories about Him circulated. No doubt these stories added details to make the religion more acceptable in light of its Jewish roots. Twelve then made sense historically to some Jews and Greeks who respected Judaism. The names of the apostles became important when the need came to put the stories into written form. The gospel writer's sources listed many names, and the writer needed to consolidate these numerous individuals into the special twelve.

The important names like Peter, John, James, Andrew, and perhaps Philip were well known, but the others weren't in comparison. Even Judas Iscariot was most likely consigned to be the betrayer, as it is obvious even Paul did not know the name of this traitor. Perhaps the most important aspect of the twelve is the early church's concern to fill in the blanks of history. These were important details to the curious but not to the faith.

THE APOSTLE JUDAS ISCARIOT

Judas Iscariot is perhaps the most infamous human mentioned in the Christian Bible. He is considered a thief who stole from the apostles and betrayed Jesus for thirty pieces of silver. We associate him with potter's field or the "field of blood" and as one suffering a terrible and horrific death. With a few minor variations, all four gospels and Acts speak of his deeds as being the epitome of evil treachery. His very name has become synonymous with disloyalty, and he is thought of as the woeful rejecter of the Messiah.

We know nothing about him outside of the Christian Bible. Therefore, we must look closely at what we do have to see what history might be extracted. Judas is the Greek word for Judah, which means *praise*. Iscariot means "man from Kerioth," a town in the Negev region near Hebron in Southern Judea. This would then imply he was the son of the apostle Simon Iscariot (John 6:71; 13:2, 26). Simon is also known as "the zealot" (Acts 1:13; Luke 6:15), which could possibly indicate Judas was also a "Zealot." This term suggests they could be rebels that were struggling against Roman domination. Simon and Judas then would be the only apostles who did not come from Galilee.

By collectively piecing together the information from the New Testament, we can obtain evidence about Judas that perhaps has not been ardently evident. Only Matthew 26:15 tells of the thirty pieces of silver. (Mark 15:11) mentions silver but not the exact amount as the reward for Judas's betrayal. In today's dollars, this is about $50 to $75. Their silver coins were then about the same size as our quarters (*American Tract Society Dictionary*). A slight problem arises here in that thirty pieces of silver was not a form of currency in use at this time. In fact, since the Maccabean era, only minted coins were used in Judea.

Another problem in Matthew (27:9) is the fact that he specifically quotes Jeremiah's prophecy, referring to the thirty pieces and the "field of blood." However, Jeremiah never made such a prediction. Matthew obviously intended to actually quote from Zechariah 11:12–13. Matthew (27:7) and Acts (1:18) have conflicting reports concerning who actually purchased the "field of blood" and how Judas died (Matthew 27:5; Acts 1:18). These discrepancies clearly are not a major stumbling block, but they strongly suggest that Matthew was not familiar with the story of Judas and relied on his sources for the information.

We can see a growing progression of information regarding Judas when reading the Gospels ranging from the earliest written (Mark) to the latest (John). Mark only has 169 words concerning Judas, while John contains 489. Most significantly, the earliest New Testament documents, Paul's epistles, say absolutely nothing whatsoever about Judas. This demonstrates that there was a rapidly developing tradition hostile toward Judas, paralleling the growing hostility between Christians and Jews at the time the Gospels were being written.

Considering the loathing toward Judas expressed in all the Gospels, especially that of John, and the preaching style and material used by Paul, it is extraordinary that he fails to even mention Judas. This could only mean that Paul deliberately ignored Judas or that he didn't know anything about him. In 1 Corinthians 11:23–24, Paul speaks of Jesus being betrayed but does not say by whom. Obviously, this betrayal could have been alluding to Judas without saying his name, but it could also have been referring to the Jewish leaders or the Jewish people in general. (See 1 Thessalonians 1:14–16.)

Further exploring Paul's lack of familiarity with Judas, look to 1 Corinthians 15:3–5, which says, "For I delivered unto you first of all that which I also received, how that Christ died for our sins according to the scriptures; And that he was buried, and that he rose again the third day according to the scriptures: And that he was seen of Cephas, then of the twelve." Paul is saying the risen Jesus appeared to all twelve apostles, which had to have included Judas. Of course, this appearance could have happened after Matthias was elected to replace Judas, but as we know from Acts, this event apparently occurred sometime around Pentecost (fifty days after), certainly not on the first day as all the Gospels say. This would offer compelling evidence that Paul knew nothing about the person Judas.

The gospel of John 20:19 says, "Then the same day at evening (note! the day of the Resurrection), being the first day of the week, when the doors were shut where the disciples were assembled for fear of the Jews, came Jesus and stood in the midst, and spoke unto them, Peace be unto you." Next in John 20:24 says, "But Thomas, one of the twelve, called Didymus, was not with them when Jesus came." Therefore, upon this first encounter with the risen Jesus, we know Thomas was missing, leaving a maximum of eleven apostles (or ten if we eliminate Judas) present. Now let us look at Luke 24:33, which says, "And they rose up the same hour, and returned to Jerusalem, and found the eleven gathered together, and them that were with them." Luke and John (and similar passages in Matthew and Mark) all agree on the eleven. This must include Judas because we know from John that Thomas was not there.

What I'm trying to show here is Judas, at least in these particular examples, was not yet considered to be the betrayer of Jesus. Yet even in Mark, the earliest gospel, Judas is clearly the traitor. Paul, who was writing up to 64 BCE, did not know anything about Judas, but by 70, Mark allegedly did. We are quite certain Mark was not an eyewitness as he clearly is not familiar with Judean geography. His source or sources must have contained material relative to a betrayal of Jesus because Paul mentions this in 1 Corinthians 11:23–24 but does not say who this person or persons are. In other words, Mark's account, the base source for Matthew, Luke, and John (at least in this case), of this traitor was probably very sketchy. Also it most likely did not name the person or persons.

Using the accepted writer's license of his day, Mark simply substituted the name of the territory where the event took place. *That place was Judah, the Greek word for Judas.* Therefore, Mark unilaterally labeled the entire Jewish population as the betrayers of Jesus. I do not believe Mark intended to calumniate all the Jewish people. But at the time he was writing, it certainly looked as though the Jewish nation was going to be totally destroyed and would cease to exist so any future ramifications therein could certainly be considered redundant.

The gospel writers who used Markan materials (Matthew, Luke, and John) simply embellished the Judas story, believing it to be actual history. They did this to conform to the political climate in which they were writing. The fourth gospel's community was undergoing a bitter divorce from Judaism, and John's community was being expelled from the local synagogues. The results of this bitter antagonism were expressed in this gospel.

In summation, the most prolific and earliest New Testament writer, Paul, knew Jesus was somehow betrayed but did not know the betrayer's name. Considering Paul's style of preaching, this would have fit within Paul's template very nicely. He could have enhanced his message by using Judas as an example of treachery. In consideration of his statement in 1 Corinthians 15:3–5, we can conclude that he did not know anything about this person named Judas.

Mark, the source for the other three gospels, used a name that represented the territory where Jesus lived and died as being the person who was the betrayer. Judas is the Greek name for the land of Judea. The later evangelists expanded on this theme as relations worsened between Christians and Jews. Of course, there is some speculation in my presentation, and the evidence falls short of being conclusive proof. But by closely scrutinizing these details with honesty and an open mind, one can interpret Judas symbolically just as we have seen in several similar episodes so frequent in history.

THE APOSTLE PAUL

In the last fifty years, critical scholarship has focused in on Paul. His alleged contradictions have been voiced and widely written. Five of his epistles have been disputed, and some have claimed they are forgeries. Jewish scholars consider him to be a traitor, a recreant rogue, and the prime source of persecution by Christians down through the ages.

Are these allegations fair based on the established information we have?

Criticism such as this, whether one agrees or not, flies in the face of many Christians. Paul's theology is the very basis for Protestantism. Orthodox and Catholics consider him to be a great apostle and early pioneer of their church. It is my position that Paul was a true Jew and dedicated Christian who has been misinterpreted by many critical scholars. This is not intended to be an apology for Paul but only a historically fair and impartial interpretation of the evidence.

Each epistle has been scrutinized, and the apparent contradictions have been exposed. In some instances apocryphal texts critical of Paul are used to demean him. Many scholars consider him to be the real founder of modern Christianity and not Jesus.

To understand this, the reader must try to place him or herself in the context of the time when Paul was writing and completely disregard knowledge of anything that occurred later. Remember the name *Christian* was just beginning to be used. Jewish Christians were still considered Jews, and most people, including the Romans, considered Christians also to be Jews. Most Jews considered the new Christians as merely an anomaly or a passing fad. Think of how Paul would have addressed Jewish Christians. He would have called them simply Jews. Christian Gnosticism was barely a scattered bunch of ideas and not a factor at this time.

When Paul became a Christian, there still was no such thing as Christianity! The original followers of Jesus were all Jews—everyone with no exception! These disciples saw Jesus as the expected Jewish Messiah. He would be the kind of Messiah the likes of Judas Maccabeus, David, or even Cyrus. He would be the one who would gather forces and overthrow the yoke of Roman oppression and restore Israel to the forefront of all the nations.

However, Jewish Christians realized Jesus had died and believed He was taken by God up to heaven. As promised, He would return very soon with an angelic army with massive power and glory. The timing was supposed to be within the lifetime of most of His followers (1 Thessalonians 4:15–18; 1 Corinthians 7:29–33). The only difference between ordinary Jews and Jesus Jews was this expectation. These presumptions clearly were accepted by Paul. In his early missionary career, Paul recognized the strong interest coming from Gentiles about Judaism as well as to the new Jesus Judaism, and he believed he could win them over to Christ.

First-century Judaism was very attractive to many Gentiles. The synagogues afforded an excellent social atmosphere. It taught reading and writing, something the average poor Gentile could not receive any other place. Study of the ancient sacred scriptures, devotion, monotheism, and Jewish religious ethics was desirable to many. Then and even now, Judaism stressed social justice, a burning desire of Jews and Gentiles alike. The downside, however, was the strict dietary laws, and the circumcision ritual clearly proved to be a serious obstacle. Paul quickly picked up on this and sought a way for Gentiles to become full Jesus Jews in lieu of being subordinated members in regular Judaism. Gentiles who attended synagogues without circumcision were called God fearers. You were not considered a full Jew until you were circumcised and you obeyed all of the dietary laws.

Paul usually began his mission by going first to the synagogues and preaching this Jesus sect form of Judaism. He focused on Jews, but he also converged on the God fearers. By offering full membership in Jesus Judaism without requiring circumcision and dietary regulations, the religion became very attractive, and many Gentiles joined. In fact, they soon became the overwhelming majority. At about this time, members of the Jesus Judaism sect were beginning to be called Christians. All through Paul's career, he considered himself to be a full Jew who believed Jesus was the Messiah or Christ.

In several of his epistles, he encounters hostilities from the Jews. Who these Jews were is confusing because Paul and most of his entourage were also Jewish. At this point in history, Judaism was tolerant of deviant sects within their ranks. Sadducees, Pharisees, Essenes, and the new Jewish Christians all gathered under the same umbrella, even though they had many differences. But Jewish Christians especially were antagonized by Paul's apparent violation of granting full membership to Gentiles without first becoming full Jews.

Of course, the other sects would have found this unacceptable as well but not to the same degree. Pharisees, who developed the synagogues as an alternative to the temple worship of the Sadducees, simply would not change any of their customs regarding full membership. They were now starting to look at the Jewish Christians and question their membership. The Jewish Christians also feared Pauline Christianity was beginning to lean toward what they saw as the apotheosis of Jesus.

Sadducees were not messianic. Therefore, Jesus or Christ meant nothing to them. Most likely Paul's antagonists then were Jewish Christians, whose concern with losing their particular identity and acceptance by fellow Jews fueled their enmity. Their fear of being blurred with Pauline Christians would lead them to lose their Jewish status, and many would see them as polytheists.

We now have a good idea where the principal opposition to Paul was coming from. The Jewish Christians were also concerned about Paul's assumed authority. They recoiled that his only contact with Jesus was through a vision (Galatians 1:12–15). Even though he may have received instructions from James and Peter, most Jewish Christians could not reconcile what they saw as abrogation of the laws given by God to Moses.

Now let us look into some of the problems some scholars see with Paul.

An underlying problem—one that Acts seems to downplay—occurs at a meeting in Jerusalem with James (Acts 21:17–26). Many believe James was punishing Paul by making him go through a purification ritual in the temple. The gospel of the Ebionites appears to shed more light on this confrontation.

If Paul knew or thought he was doing something contrary to Christian or Jesus Judaism, why then would he voluntarily return to Jerusalem and confront the leader of his church, James? He did have a large sum of money for James, one that he could easily have kept for himself. Or he could have sent the money to James via messenger. Therefore, it seems logical Paul must have been performing his missionary work within the parameters set forth by James and the elders at the Jerusalem Council. But the question lingers. Why did James subject Paul to the long and expensive purification ordeal? Could it be that James was only attempting to appease Paul's detractors?

Paul's exclusive use of the Septuagint (LXX) and not the Hebrew Bible is very puzzling. Ninety-four percent of Paul's quotations from holy scripture are taken from the LXX. In view of this, Paul claims, "I advanced in the Jews' religion beyond many of mine own age among my countrymen, being more exceedingly zealous for the traditions of my fathers" (Galatians 1:14). From Acts, we read, "I am a Jew, from Tarsus in Cilicia, a citizen of no ordinary city." "I was circumcised on the eighth day, of the people of Israel, of the tribe of Benjamin, a Hebrew born of Hebrews, as to the Law a Pharisee." "I have been a Roman citizen 'since I was born.'" "The Jews all know the way I have lived ever since I was a child, from the beginning of my life in my own country, and also in Jerusalem." And I was "taught at the feet of Gamaliel" (Acts 22:1–30).

Clearly, he was brought up in the Hebrew traditions and should have been more familiar with the Hebrew Bible than the LXX. Yet all his epistles reflect only the LXX. Of course, these letters were sent to Greek-speaking people, and the LXX is written in Greek; however, these people would not have known or cared which Bible Paul was quoting from. Therefore, it would only seem logical that Paul was taught scripture from the LXX and not the Hebrew Bible.

Paul's use of the LXX is difficult to understand. His early training could have been in Hebrew, perhaps even in Jerusalem from Gamaliel. The chronology sure seems to fit. Then until adulthood he could have trained in Greek and the LXX. Hebrew, even in Judea, was a forgotten language by the first century. The LXX was not viewed unfavorably until after the destruction of Jerusalem when the rabbis then considered it too Christian and began to speak out against it. Therefore, the usage of the LXX was quite proper and maybe even preferred.

It is clear from the record in Acts that Paul claims several times to be a Roman citizen (Acts 16:37–38; 22:25–28), and he gained this though birth (Acts 22:28). So why did he allow himself to be three times beaten with Roman rods and once stoned, dragged out of the city of Lystra, and left for dead, not to mention many of the other indignities that could not have been lawfully forced upon a Roman citizen, and yet nowhere did he so much as mention his Roman citizenship, which would have spared him several beatings and imprisonments (2 Corinthians 11:24–25). Suddenly, when he was in the hands of the Roman officers and authorities and they were about to beat him as they did at Jerusalem, he said, "Is it lawful for you to scourge a man that is a Roman, and un-condemned?" (Acts 22:25). Or when he was held by the Romans at Caesar's judgment seat, some proposed to subject him to the judgment of the Jews to please the Jews who were clamoring for his life, but then he said, "I stand at Caesar's judgment seat, where I ought to be judged; … no man may deliver me unto them. I appeal unto Caesar" (Acts 25:10).

Paul says that he and his companions "suffered" and were "shamefully treated" at Philippi (1 Thessalonians 2:2). Acts 16:19–24 supports this statement by claiming that Paul and his companions were whipped by command of city officials and thrown into prison. Some scholars suggest Paul used some of the money he had collected for the Jerusalem church to purchase Roman citizenship and did so just before he was arrested. This, however, does not agree with Paul's statement that he was born a Roman citizen. These scholars state that the claim of citizenship was only made in Acts, which is a secondary source, but there is no mention in any of the genuine Pauline writings.

Feminists consider Paul to be a misogynist and cite several biblical statements to prove it. "Let the women keep silent in the churches, for it is not permitted them to speak, but let them subject themselves, just as the Law also says. And if they desire to learn anything, let them ask their own husbands at home; for it is improper for a woman to speak in church" (1 Corinthians 14:34–35).

We must view this within a first-century context, not today's! Paul certainly had to oblige the customs of his day, and the women of his day would have certainly understood this. In all of Paul's letters, we hear of numerous women to whom Paul gave responsible and respectable positions. This far exceeded the normal role for women. In fact, Paul's egalitarianism made Christianity very attractive to women, and it was the women who lead the charge to obtain new recruits.

Elsewhere in 1 Corinthians, Paul takes women prophesying and praying out loud in church for granted. When they do this, he says that they must be wearing the head covering (now called chador), which was once a uniform worn by respectable women throughout the Mediterranean. From this we can see women in Paul's churches had important positions. For the times Paul was clearly egalitarian.

The anti-Jewish language in several of Paul's epistles is also troubling. However, if we exclude the Deutero-Pauline or pseudo-Pauline epistles and Acts, we find only 1 Thessalonians 2:13–16, which is virulently anti-Jewish. Although it cannot be proven, many scholars believe this passage was added to the text shortly after the second Jewish revolt of 132–135 CE. Let us look further into this and see if there are any clues.

> And for this reason we also give thanks to God constantly, that when you received the word of God that you heard from us, you did not receive it as a human word, but just as it truly is, God's word, which is also at work in you who believe. For you, brothers and sisters, became imitators of the churches of God that are in Christ Jesus in Judea, for you suffered the same things from your own kinsfolk as they did from the Jews, who killed the Lord Jesus and the prophets, who drove us out, who are displeasing God, who are hostile to all people, and who are forbidding us to speak to the Gentiles so that they might be saved; thus they always fill up the measure of their sins. But His wrath has come upon them finally. (1 Thessalonians 2:13–16)

BOYD GUTBROD

The last sentence, "But His wrath has come upon them finally," strongly suggests that the wrath of God represents the destruction of Jerusalem and the annihilation of the Jewish people. This first Jewish revolt started in 66 CE. Paul wrote 1 Thessalonians about 50 CE. Around 50 CE, there was no particular danger or disaster generated toward Judaism, so the work of a late editor here becomes very possible. Also, verse 15 indicates that Paul's people were being "driven out," which could only mean expulsions from synagogues. We know these expulsions did occur from John's gospel and from Jewish records that date to about 85 CE, again well after 1 Thessalonians was written.

Lastly, the accusation of the Jewish people killing their prophets is not supported by any historical evidence, and Paul certainly would have known this. During Paul's lifetime his opposition came mainly from Jews who were Christian. Afterward, hostility toward the Christians came from Jews but clearly not around 50 CE.

In Romans, Paul makes every effort to reconcile Judaism with Christianity (his version of Christianity as opposed to Jewish Christianity). He makes a good case for associating his Christianity with Judaism with solid reasoning for compatibility between the two branches of God's chosen people. Therefore, Paul was not antiwoman. He was not anti-Jewish. He was a true and loyal Jew and a true believer in Christ. Sadly, circumstances caused by editors and pseudonymous writers who were only trying to promote the new Christian faith have made the real Paul look bad to the people of the present generation.

THE WOMAN APOSTLE—JUNIA

The Bible story of Junia shows the first and only female apostle (Mary Magdalene excluded). Paul, I think, references her in Romans 16:7, which says, "Greetings to Andronicus and Junia, my relatives, who were in prison with me. They are very important apostles. They were believers in Christ before I was." Junia is and was a very popular feminine name in ancient Rome, and here she is clearly called an apostle by Paul. This passage from Romans is taken from the New Century Version.

The Greek word for apostle, *apostello*, occurs more than eighty times in the New Testament. Since apostles did not exist in Old Testament times, we have to understand the word to mean someone who was sent and/or was a messenger, and that is exactly what the word *apostle* means, "sent one." So an apostle is someone who has been sent to transmit a message per the instructions of the sender.

We know Paul was not one of the original twelve apostles. He was considered an apostle later on as was Barnabas (Acts 14:14). Even Jesus is called an apostle in Hebrews 3:1, and we learn that there were also false apostles (2 Corinthians 11:13). This would indicate that the term *twelve apostles* must have taken on greater importance later or at least after Paul used the word to reference himself (Galatians 1:1). Prior to the Gospels, apostle merely means "sent one," of which there could be several, and the number twelve would be considered to be only that specific number. The others then would be thought of as disciples including Paul who was not part of the original twelve.

Like Paul, Junia as well as a number of others who are referred to as, let us call them, small "a" while opposed to the Twelve as capital "A." Obviously the small "a" as was Paul still signified a very important position of authority in the new church and that Junia was his equal, at least superficially.

It appears as though this understanding was true until the thirteenth century when the name Junia suddenly became Junias and masculine. From the inception of Christianity and through the second century, women contributed a major part in the growth and administration of the new faith. After that there appears to be a distinct effort on the part of the early church fathers to channel the role of women to secondary status.

By the year 200 CE, there is no evidence of women taking prophetic, priestly, and episcopal roles in Orthodox churches. In the middle of the second century, women and men no longer sat together for worship. Instead they were separated, and they adopted the synagogue custom. Groups that had leadership positions held by women were branded heretical. These groups commonly came to be known as Gnostics.

In the earliest recordings of Romans 16:7, Junia is feminine. Then from around 1225 CE till the mid-twentieth century, Romans 16:7 had the masculine interpretation. "Greet Andronicus and Junias, my relatives who have been in prison with me. They are outstanding among the apostles, and they were in Christ before I was." This rendering from the New International Version is a typical example. Most new translations, however, are reverting back to the feminine word, as modern scholarship is leaning in that direction.

A number of historians claim Junia was erased from the Bible because it was unimaginable that a woman could have been considered an apostle. The very idea "offended the monopoly of church offices and honors" reserved for males only.

Some scholars recognize Junia was a woman but reject the proposition she was an apostle. Others argue there is no decisive evidence to prove Junia was a woman or an apostle. And there are those who see that the whole disagreement that Junia was a female apostle stems from nothing more than a justification to support a feminist schema.

Most biblical scholars are of the belief that the second named individual in verse 7 is a female named Junia. It clearly was a very common feminine name at that time. "All early sources attest Junia as female, especially Jerome (340–420 A.D.) and John Chrysostom (345–407 A.D.). Although the name often appears in masculine forms in English translations, they are unattested in ancient times. Junia is the only woman called an 'apostle' in the NT" (*Eerdmans Dictionary of the Bible*, 757).

Another consideration has to do with the rate of recurrence of this word used as a man's or a woman's name. No cases of *Junias* as a man's name have surfaced to date in Greek literature, while at least three instances of *Junia* as a feminine name have appeared in Greek. Accordingly, *Junia* was a common enough Latin name. Since this was Paul's letter to the Romans, one might expect to see a few Latin names on the list, even though the text was written in Greek originally.

Andronicus and Junia are thought of by most biblical scholars to be a husband-and-wife pair (like Priscilla and Aquila) or possibly a brother-and-sister team. Paul clearly has often praised several women who were held in high esteem within the early church. So elevating a special woman to apostle status should not be astonishing.

But … the most convincing reference would be that of John Chrysostom, a doctor of the church and a most famous misogynist, to put it mildly. "O how great is the devotion of this woman that she should be counted worthy of the appellation of apostle!" (homily on Romans 16). Chrysostom was a master of the Greek language, and he certainly had access to some of the earliest writings of Paul. His exegetic style for detail and his penchant toward male superiority makes his feminine assertion most convincing.

"For those things which I have already mentioned might easily be performed by many even of those who are under authority, women as well as men; but when one is required to preside over the Church, and to be entrusted with the care of so many souls, the whole female sex must retire before the magnitude of the task, and the majority of men also" (*Concerning the Priesthood*, book II, § 2).

> If it be asked, what has this to do with women of the present day? It shows that
> the male sex enjoyed the higher honor. Man was first formed; and elsewhere he
> shows their superiority. "Neither was the man created for the woman, but the

woman for the man" (1 Corinthians 11:9). Why then does he say this? He wishes the man to have the preeminence in every way; both for the reason given above, he means, let him have precedence, and on account of what occurred afterwards.

The woman [Eve] taught once, and ruined all. On this account therefore he saith, let her not teach. But what is it to other women, that she suffered this? It certainly concerns them; for the sex is weak and fickle, and he is speaking of the sex collectively. For he says not Eve, but "the woman," which is the common name of the whole sex, not her proper name. Was then the whole sex included in the transgression for her fault? As he said of Adam, "After the similitude of Adam's transgression, who is the figure of Him that was to come" (Rom. v. 14); so here the female sex transgressed, and not the male. (Homily 9)

These are only three quotes out of many showing Chrysostom's bias to emphasize my point. Although there are several scholars who still would argue for Junias (masculine) with some convincing rhetoric, I believe the evidence favors the female.

THE MYSTERY OF THE APOSTLE PAUL

Saint Paul is clearly the most prolific writer in the New Testament. He is also the earliest and greatest contributor to spreading the faith. I use the title *saint* here to signify the honor bestowed upon him by the church. Nearly every segment of Christianity approves of the use of that title. There is no doubt that Saint Paul was the most important person for Christianity next to Jesus. His theology is the very foundation for Protestant Christianity and is also a major part of Orthodox and Catholic theology as well.

But when we read the New Testament, many confusing problems stand out. The most troubling is the apparent friction between Paul and the other apostles. Most of the details come directly from the epistles that were written by Paul, which everyone agrees are genuine. In Acts, Peter plays an important role, but Paul is the main character. We learn from Acts that Paul never met Jesus while He was alive. Jesus, we also learn, carefully selected the twelve apostles, which obviously did not include Paul.

What was the purpose for Jesus to choose these particular apostles if Paul, who wasn't chosen, was destined to be the main propagator of the teachings of Jesus shortly after His death? In fact, there seems to be some downright hostility between Paul and the original apostles. We will now explore some of these apparent conflicts.

We know from both Galatians and Acts that a meeting between Paul and the apostles took place in Jerusalem. This is called the Jerusalem Council (50 CE). Paul and Barnabas present their case and make a financial contribution to the church, and then Peter offers his opinion. James then voices the final decision. It is implied here that James is the leader of the church. He quotes a passage from scripture, specifically Amos 9:11–12 from the Greek LXX (not the Hebrew Bible). He then declares, "Therefore I judge that we should not trouble those from among the Gentiles who are turning to God, but that we write to them to abstain from things polluted by idols, from sexual immorality, from things strangled, and from blood" (Acts 15:19). Paul also adds that he was instructed to collect money for the poor of Jerusalem (Galatians 2:9).

This decision was basically standard Jewish practice (Noahide Covenant) required for Gentiles desiring to be participants in the synagogue and in Judaism without actually converting. Paul was given authority to undertake a mission to the Gentiles. His first encounter occurs in Antioch. Here Paul has a meeting with Peter that seems to be very strained, to say the least (Galatians 2:11–14) In fact, Paul's first comment in Galatians is chastising his readers for following a different gospel other than the gospel Paul had previously preached to them. This other gospel must have been coming from the Jerusalem apostles because for most of chapter 2, he sarcastically tries to minimize the reputation of these apostles while defending his own apostolic standing. Galatians was written about five years after the Jerusalem Council.

First Corinthians suggests further tensions endured by Paul. Here again he seems compelled to defend his apostolic title (1 Corinthians 9:1–3). Paul mentions two others who are preaching a gospel, Apollos and Cephas (Peter) (1 Corinthians 1:12). In chapter 3, Paul alludes to the fact that he and Apollos are of equal standing or at least that Apollos is following in Paul's footsteps. But … there is no conciliatory rhetoric offered or even suggested to Peter. This strongly implies that it was Peter or followers of Peter who had been questioning Paul's apostleship.

It is the opinion of many literary scholars that 2 Corinthians is a composite of two or more letters combined into one. This becomes quite obvious when reading and looking for the breaks and insertions in the text. Here again we see Paul defending his gospel and apostleship. As in Galatians, he sarcastically refers to the "superlative apostles" as preachers of a different gospel than his (2 Corinthians 11:4–5). He called his opponents "servants of Satan" (2 Corinthians 11:5), "false apostles," and "deceitful workers" (2 Corinthians 11:13). Obviously, these are the same "superlative apostles." Further evidence comes from 2 Corinthians 11:22–23, which says, "Are they Hebrews? So am I. Are they Israelites? So am I. Are they descendents of Abraham? So am I. Are they servants of Christ? I am a better one." Clearly, his attackers are from the Jerusalem church who carried letters of recommendation (2 Corinthians 3:1). "Are we beginning to commend ourselves again? Surely we do not need, as some do, letters of recommendation to you." Another important note is Paul—or at least Paul's assistant, Titus—was collecting money for the Jerusalem church, a topic that will be addressed a bit later.

Paul clearly has issues with the apostolic church, but this was not the case with Gnostic Christians. They saw him as being *the* true apostle of Christ. Marcion (140 CE), the father of the New Testament, included only Luke's gospel along with most of Paul's epistles in his canon. So it is not surprising to see encouraging Gnostic language coming from Paul. Second Corinthians 12:2–5 says,

> I knew a man in Christ who fourteen years ago, (whether in the body, I cannot tell; or whether out of the body, I cannot tell: God knows ;) such a one caught up as far as the third heaven. And I knew such a man, (whether in the body, or out of the body, I cannot tell: God knows ;) How that he was caught up into paradise, and heard unspeakable words, which it is unlawful for a man to speak of. Of such a one will I glory: yet of myself I will not glory, but in my infirmities.

There are several clear Gnostic references, especially the various levels of heaven, such as the third heaven. Another Gnostic passage is found in 1 Corinthians 2:7, which says, "But we speak God's wisdom in a mystery, the WISDOM that has been HIDDEN, which God foreordained before the worlds for our glory, which none of the rulers of this world has known. For had they known it, they wouldn't have crucified the Lord of glory." I am not implying that Paul was a Gnostic, just that Paul spoke a theological language that pleased many Gnostics, which offended Jewish Christians.

The letter to the Philippians tells us Paul was in prison, probably in Rome. Once again he rails against false teachers who advocate circumcision (Philippians 3:2–6). This surely is indicating opposition, once again, from Jewish Christians lead by the apostles of Jerusalem. I would suspect that Paul believed James or the Jerusalem church had a role leading to his arrest and imprisonment. So I think it is very evident that Paul and the original apostles of Jesus were at odds, to say the least.

Leading up to Paul's final trip to Jerusalem, several disciples warn him (Acts 21:4, 10–12) of impending danger. He, too, believed that danger was possible (Acts 20:23). Now he did have with him a good deal of money for the Jerusalem church. Yet the tension and anxiety is very apparent concerning his visit (Acts 21:17–40). His meeting with James seems to be downplayed in Acts, but the result is that Paul is instructed to take four men who are "under a vow" to the temple and to pay for their expenses (Acts 21:22–26), an order that Paul then accepts. At the end of the seven-day period of the purification ceremony of the four men, some Jews from Asia recognized Paul in the temple and accused him of transgressing the law with his teachings. A commotion followed, which led to Paul's arrest by the Romans (Acts 21:27–40).

The collection for the Jerusalem church must have been important to Paul because he obviously knew he was headed for trouble there and could have avoided it. So it would appear that Paul believed his explanation of the events along with his financial offering would be sufficient to smooth or at least greatly mitigate the problems. This would lead us to believe that in Paul's mind he was convinced that he did not violate to any great degree the accord of the Jerusalem Council. What is confusing is his actual arrest. According to Acts, it was the Jews from Asia who caused the riot, not Paul. I can understand the Roman authorities taking Paul into protective custody, but to keep him in prison seems to suggest something more serious.

Paul's internment alludes to a possible capital crime that caused him to invoke his Roman citizenship. Now this brings up another difficult question. With all the previous beatings and imprisonments Paul endured, why didn't he use his citizenship before now? Is it possible that Paul could have used a portion of his collection to purchase this citizenship, even though he had stated he was born a citizen?

In the Gospels Peter is given the keys of the church by the living Jesus. There is little doubt that the living Jesus selected Peter to be His steward after He died. We know from history that it was Paul who is mostly responsible for developing and organizing Christianity into what it is today. Is it possible that Jesus after His resurrection changed His mind and made Paul the primary spokesman for His new faith? Or could it simply be that God just works in strange and mysterious ways?

CHAPTER 9

In chapter 8, we discussed the apostles of Jesus. We will now examine the historical Jesus and try to determine the source of Christianity. Delving into the archives to discover the historical Jesus has never been considered tremendously successful. There has been some progress in determining numerous facts about the geography and environment in which Jesus lived but still the only sources that offer personal details remain to be found in the New Testament and some apocryphal and pseudepigrapha writings. The historical reliability of these documents remains somewhat questionable.

I purpose a hypothesis that in my opinion offers a realistic picture of Jesus and His mission. The foundational supports I will be using are the New Testament and various writings from contemporaries. This hypothesis is strictly based on history and will be devoid of any theological implications except to explain a certain aspect of Christian belief. This is not intended to disprove or approve any of the supernatural characteristics or events concerning the life of Jesus.

First-century Judea was under the firm control of the Roman Empire. Rome used this nation to extract tribute in the form of heavy taxation. She did not demand military manpower from the Jews and allowed most Jewish laws to prevail in this territory. Yet the yoke of supporting Roman occupation was very consuming and overpowering.

From about 167 to 63 BCE, known as the Maccabean or Hasmonean period, the Jewish state was basically free and independent. In its later years, it became imperialistic and even forced conversions to Judaism in conquered lands. Only through a dispute for supremacy between the last two Hasmonean brothers—one brother invited Roman assistance and afterward took over—did they lose their freedom. So from 63 BCE to about 66 CE, much of the produce of the Jewish people went to Rome. Their civil liberties were also strictly curtailed by their Roman masters. In short, the overwhelming population of Judea was very poor, and their lives had deteriorated into a meager existence at best during the time of Jesus.

Earlier after the successful Maccabean revolt, which overthrew the controlling Seleucid Greeks about 167 BCE, the hero Judas Maccabaeus became a major personality. He became a source of great pride from this recent history, which certainly had a strong influence on Jesus throughout His life. Although the Hasmonean dynasty would be downgraded by the later Jewish leaders, Judas especially was quite popular for the most of the first century. In fact, the Messiah that the people longed for would have been more applicable to Judas at this time than to David.

When the Jews revolted against Rome (66–72 BCE), the results caused the destruction of Jerusalem in epic proportions. All privileges the Jews had previously enjoyed were taken away and many people were crucified or sold into slavery. Throughout the Roman Empire, the Jews now were looked down upon and even despised. Anything Jewish was mistrusted. The early Christians were considered Jews by the Romans and were treated accordingly. Around the year 80 CE, Judaism underwent a reorganization or redefinition of their faith. Jewish Christians soon came to be considered heretics and were expelled from the synagogues. Of course, this angered the Christians. Coupled with widespread Roman antagonism toward Judaism and Roman misunderstandings of the new faith, the early church did everything they could to dispel their association with Judaism and to show they were separate and good subjects of the empire.

Some of the New Testament writers struggled to demonstrate that they were an autonomous religion and were not a branch of Judaism. The Gospels themselves clearly reflect these animosities that existed at the time of writing. As Judaism was in the process of excommunicating Jewish Christians from their synagogues, Christians realized the need to change the Roman perception of them so as to see Christians as peaceful, taxpaying, and law-abiding members of the empire (John 9:22; 12:42; 16:2). The problem was that Christianity was not a recognized religion by Rome. (Therefore, it was an outlawed religion.) However, Judaism was still considered legal. This friction was more intense in the geographic areas nearest to Judea, and it had a tenacious influence on the New Testament.

In the aftermath of the fall of Jerusalem, the Sadducee sect was literally eliminated, leaving the Pharisee branch as the lone survivor. In turn, they would reinvigorate their faith by emphasizing Pharisaic understandings regarding Torah through new rabbinical literature. Thus, the Pharisees, who were now in complete charge of Judaism, vicariously became the villains of Jesus in the Gospels. The New Testament writers attempted to conceal any Christian negativity toward Rome while venting their frustrations on the Jews. The epistles of Paul offer good examples of this (Romans 13:1-7; Matthew 27:25).

In the late part of the first and nearly all of the second and third centuries, Christian literature tried to appease the Romans by downgrading Judaism, careful not to say anything that might incur the wrath of Rome. When they did attack Rome—and they certainly did so—they did it in such a way as to disguise their Roman enemies. (e.g. the author of Revelation anachronistically using Babylon to symbolize Rome).

Now let us look into Jesus as conditions were during His lifetime. His nation was groaning under the oppressive domination of Rome. His people had tried to revolt and failed several times within His lifetime. The Galileans, who had rebelled against Rome only two decades before His public ministry, wanted to fight. Jesus and many of His followers would have seen two thousand of their countrymen crucified by the Romans along the roadsides. They would have known some of the inhabitants of Sepphoris (a mere three miles north of Nazareth) who had been sold into slavery for aiding the insurrectionists' assault on the arsenal there. Jesus was a true and loyal Jew who knew and understood His faith and its history. Both David and Judas Maccabaeus were immense heroic warriors who in the past had led their nation to freedom. Without a doubt, Jesus would have been very familiar with this history and would have approved of the methods they used to attain that freedom. In fact, it would have been crystal clear to Him that some sort of military action would be necessary.

Jesus truly believed that God had an invincible heavenly army of angels and could use this resource to aid His people as described in the book of Enoch. (Several copies were found in the Dead Sea Scrolls cache, and the New Testament often refers or alludes to this writing.) John the Baptist (Jesus as well) preached language alluding to Enoch during the time when Jesus was one of his followers. When John was killed, Jesus became the leader of John's flock or at least a segment of it.

Nowhere in any literature of this time is there any indication that Jesus wanted to form a new religion to replace Judaism. Therefore any disputes Jesus actually had with the Pharisees, at the very worst, were only to the extent of interpreting the accepted Jewish laws or customs and not with the faith itself.

The vast majority of Jewish people followed and believed in their faith as they were taught from early on. They worshipped in the temple and supported all their Jewish traditions just as Jesus did. The major dissatisfaction nearly every Jew felt involved the excessive burden of paying tribute to the Roman oppressors. True, they had religious freedom, but the religious leaders were all appointed by Rome and were clearly under their control.

After slightly less than a hundred years of Roman occupation, the Jewish people had fallen into the depths of poverty. All hope for a better life seemed out of reach as long as Rome dominated their nation. So powerful was this occupier that many thought only the Almighty could intercede and create a kingdom of God on this earth. The suggested formula to achieve this kingdom of God, as we see in the New Testament, meant that all the people had to turn to God and repent while abstaining from their evil ways. But just what was their evil behavior? They were not worshipping idols, and surely, they were praying to God. This kingdom of God was a prime subject preached by both John and Jesus, and at the very least, it must have alluded to some form of appropriate militant action.

Jesus loved His people and had deep feelings for their sufferings equally as He had for His personal family. His human nature experienced all the pain and deprivations just the same as the people were enduring. He must have despised the Jewish leaders (mostly Sadducees but also a few Pharisees) who appeared to be doing nothing to help. Just what was the human Jesus to do?

Keep in mind that I am employing the determination of the Council of Constantinople (May 5 to June 2, 553) to explain how Christians should understand the two natures of Christ. They state in article VII,

> If anyone using the expression, "in two natures," does not confess that our one Lord Jesus Christ is made known in the deity and in the manhood, in order to indicate by that expression a difference of the natures of which the ineffable union took place without confusion, a union in which neither the nature of the Word has changed into that of the flesh, nor that of the flesh into that of the Word (for each remained what it was by nature, even when the union by hypostasis had taken place); but shall take the expression with regard to the mystery of Christ in a sense so as to divide the parties, let him be anathema. Or if anyone recognizing the number of natures in the same our one Lord Jesus Christ, God the Word incarnate, does not take in contemplation only the difference of the natures which compose him, which difference is not destroyed by the union between them—for one is composed of the two and the two are in one—but shall make use of the number two to divide the natures or to make of them persons properly so called, let him be anathema.

The implication here is that Christ has two inseparable natures but is one distinct person, both human and divine, but neither interfered with or contradicted the other. He was a true human like all of us. Therefore, while on this earth, He experienced pain, hunger, anger, love, and all the other human emotions like all of us, while His divine nature did not contradict or interfere with this earthly life.

I believe Jesus wanted to impart a strong religious message to His people. But only that would not have been enough for the majority to trek into the wilderness to hear His preaching, not unless the message included something on the order of offering some relief from Roman domination (Matthew 15:32–33).

In His human capacity, did He have the power to summon an angelic army? Or as a human, did He believe God, His Father, could only to do so? Ponder Matthew 24:36–37, which states, "No one knows about that day or hour, not even the angels in heaven, nor the Son, but only the Father. As it was in the days of Noah, so it will be at the coming of the Son of Man." Clearly, Jesus the Son while on this earth and while in His human nature had and confessed to not having knowledge of the plans of the Father. Accordingly then, the angelic army mentioned in Matthew 26:53, which says, "Or do you think that I cannot appeal to My Father, and He will at once put at My disposal more than twelve legions of angels," required an appeal to the Father before any deployment.

My hypothesis here is the human historical Jesus believed He could rally His people to rise up and expel the Roman occupiers. Many commonly believe the kingdom of God in heaven was defended by many legions of angels who were invincible. Not even Rome could withstand such a force. Jesus preached this kind of message to his audiences, and this preaching drew the large crowds the Gospels speak of. But how could the gospel writers report any anti-Roman rhetoric without incurring the wrath of Rome upon the author and his community?

WAS JESUS A REBEL AGAINST ROME?

The Bible presents a historical detailing of the ministry of Jesus through the four gospels. It shows Him as a peaceful teacher who came to earth to usher in the kingdom of God. The early church gave Him titles such as our Savior, Son of Man, Son of God, and Prince of Peace. For two thousand years this has been the only rendition and is accepted by all Christians as factual history.

We will not dispute these assertions, and this section is not intended to demean the Gospels or the Bible. It will explore the possibility that Jesus may have been more active politically than what the Gospels portray. I will take rarely cited passages from the Gospels and try to show how they may fit within the historical framework of the first century.

Through the synagogues many first-century Jews had learned to read. A somewhat lesser amount could also write. Their intense Jewish faith and love of their sacred writings found in Torah urged them to learn these skills. Nationalism was prevalent along with a vehement hatred of their Roman oppressors, who had occupied their Promised Land for nearly a hundred years. The burden of Roman taxation was overwhelming and affected every segment of Jewish society. They yearned desperately for a liberator, which they labeled *messiah*.

As a young boy, Jesus would have been constantly exposed to Jewish history. Like most young boys, He would have heard about Jewish heroes and dreamt of emulating them. He would have also been susceptible to His elder's rancor toward the despotic Romans.

Today we think of Jewish heroes such as Abraham, Moses, and others but little or nothing of Judas Maccabaeus. Judas (actually through his successors) brought about the first Jewish independent state in five hundred years. Judas led a successful revolt against the Seleucid Greeks in spite of the overwhelming odds against him. Clearly, first-century Jews believed God would send a messiah like Judas who would redeem their Promised Land.

Could Jesus have been this type of messiah? Is there any evidence to support such an idea? Let us look to the Bible.

In Matthew 10:34–39, Jesus says, "Do not think that I have come to bring peace on earth; I have not come to bring peace, but a sword. For I have come to set man against his father … and a man's foes will be those of his own household. He who loves father or mother more than me is unworthy of me … He who finds his life will lose it, and he who loses his life for my sake will find it." How should we interpret this? A sword was then an ultimate weapon used in warfare. Like in the early Maccabean revolt, many Jews were fearful of the consequences of losing. So Jewish families were at odds with one another about whether to support the Maccabees or not. Therefore, fighting for Jesus was emphasized. As momentum for independence grew, the partisans purged those who did not assist or aid the revolutionists. The beginning of Matthew 10 sounds eerily like Jesus is dispatching the twelve (though Luke 10:1–12 claims there are seventy-two) to recruit new followers. This was very similar to the recruitment methods used by Judas Maccabaeus in forming his guerrilla army 130 years earlier.

What was Jesus intending (Matthew 10:5) in His message to the town and villagers about the kingdom of God being close at hand? What would the people have expected to happen? Did they think the kingdom of God would bring about supreme happiness on this earth, in this life, or perhaps the next after death? I don't think anyone thought that this new kingdom would soon bring Jesus into the hands of the Romans to be crucified. No one would have expected this, and Jesus did not tell them that would happen. Is Matthew 10:11–23 a threat similar to the tactics used by Judas? Let us look at it in light of how the Maccabees solicited their help from the countryside.

Matthew 10:11 says, "Whatever town or village you enter, look for a worthy person in it, and stay there until you leave." Matthew 10:14–23 then says,

> Whoever will not receive you or listen to your words—go outside that house or town and shake the dust from your feet. Amen, I say to you, it will be more tolerable for the land of Sodom and Gomorrah on the Day of Judgment than for that town. Behold, I am sending you like sheep in the midst of wolves; so be shrewd as serpents and simple as doves.

> But beware of people, for they will hand you over to courts and scourge you in their synagogues, and you will be led before governors and kings for my sake as a witness before them and the pagans.

> When they hand you over, do not worry about how you are to speak or what you are to say. You will be given at that moment what you are to say.

> For it will not be you who speak but the Spirit of your Father speaking through you.

> Brother will hand over brother to death, and the father his child; children will rise up against parents and have them put to death.

> You will be hated by all because of my name, but whoever endures to the end will be saved.

> When they persecute you in one town, flee to another. Amen, I say to you, you will not finish the towns of Israel before the Son of Man comes.

Judas marched on Jerusalem and cleansed the defiled temple. Jesus marched on Jerusalem and cleansed the temple. For three days He held the temple. The people who lined the streets on His triumphal entry spread their garments on the road. They shouted, "Hosanna to the son of David," a clear signal that He was the expected and long-awaited Messiah in the Davidic tradition.

All the Gospels are referring to the prophecy of Zechariah 9:9–11, which says,

> Daughter of Zion, rejoice with all of your heart; shout in triumph, daughter of Jerusalem! See, your King coming to you, his cause won, his victory gained, humble and mounted on a donkey, on a colt, the foal of a donkey. He will banish the chariot from Ephraim, the war-horse from Jerusalem; the warriors' bow will be banished, and he will proclaim peace to the nations. His rule will extend from sea to sea, from the river to the ends of the earth. As for you, because of your blood covenant with me I shall release your people imprisoned in a waterless dungeon.

Zechariah 9 is most certainly speaking of an expected military encounter to usher in a new kingdom, a kingdom of God. If this was not to be the role of Jesus (meaning peaceful methods only), then why do all the evangelists quote this Zechariah prediction? It surely does not apply to our conception of the Messiah that most of us have been taught.

Jesus went directly to the temple and drove out the entrepreneurs. This temple represented the sacred traditional seat of Jewish government. No one stopped Him! Think about that! Why? Perhaps He had too many troops or supporters. Matthew 21:45 says, "They feared Him (Chief priests and Pharisees) because of the multitudes." Were these multitudes armed?

After the Last Supper, Jesus tells the twelve apostles to sell their cloaks and buy swords (Luke 22:36), implying that this action was required to fulfill a prophecy. Perhaps the one from Zechariah? What else could Jesus have been referring to? What did Jesus anticipate from His edict that His apostles had to be armed?

He retreats to Gethsemane and is joined by Peter, James, and John (Matthew 26:37). When Jesus was arrested, Peter drew his sword and cut off the ear of Malchus (John 18:10–11). Obviously, Peter at least was armed. Jesus called James and John Zebedee *Boanerges*, meaning "sons of thunder." What significance does this represent?

Luke 6:14 and Acts 1:13 refer to Simon "the Zealot" as a member of the twelve apostles. A first-century understanding of the term *zealot* referred to a rebel. Judas Iscariot was another member of the twelve. Iscariot was certainly not his last name nor a village or town. So what could it mean? Some scholars believe it meant assassin or dagger man. Why did the Romans crucify Jesus? The Gospels suggest the reason was that He claimed to be the Son of God. The

Jews may have thought He blasphemed and should have been killed for that reason. If that were the case, the prescribed punishment would have been death by stoning. Jews were not allowed to crucify anyone. Only Rome had that authority. Rome reserved this form of punishment, the most horrific of all, for seditionists and perpetrators of the most heinous crimes.

Josephus wrote that after the death of Herod the Great (about 4 BCE), his son, Archelaus, was appointed by Caesar to succeed him. When Archelaus was in Rome, an insurgent named Judas, the son of Ezekiah, started a revolt in the city of Sepphoris in Galilee. (Sepphoris was a Greek city near Nazareth, where Jesus lived.) Josephus wrote that Judas had "an ambitious desire for royal dignity," meaning he desired to become the king of Israel. During his time there were several mini revolts against the Romans. Josephus named a few other revolts instigated by Athronges and then Simon. He goes on to say that there were ten thousand other disorders in Judea, which were like riots all prior to Jesus.

What did all of these disturbances have in common? The people held secret meetings in the desert. They all spoke in deeply religious or nationalistic terms. They were all armed. They all tried to recruit others to their cause, and each one was crucified.

Rome crucified Jesus for sedition! No doubt about this! They placed a sign above His head on the cross, one that read, "King of the Jews" (Matthew 27: 37). The scarlet robe and the crown (of thorns) signifies what the Romans considered or believed was proper punishment for sedition. This treatment was intended to serve as an example to any others who would consider revolting against Roman rule.

Ponder the large crowds that continuously gathered to hear Jesus speak. Would first-century Jews travel great distances to only listen to a wise man speak of peace, loving for their enemies, and turning the other cheek? The people desperately wanted the Roman oppressors expelled from their lands. They could have heard religious messages any Saturday in the local synagogues. The yoke of Rome was very heavy! Compare this to how our founding fathers reacted to excessive British taxation.

It is hard to imagine first-century Jews not reminiscing with pride on the successes of Judas Maccabaeus. He was a genuine hero who struggled mightily but brought about home rule and peace. By his triumphs, he demonstrated that action and the help of God could achieve victory. Even then people recognized that history repeated itself.

Consider the gospel writers' dilemma. They felt compelled to tell the story of Jesus in written form as true and honest as they could. Certainly, they could not have written about His rebellious side out of fear the Romans would come down on them and their community. In fact, they were so intimidated by Roman might and spy systems that they consciously avoided writing anything Rome could conceive as being negative toward their regime. Keep in mind Rome had just butchered and crucified many thousands for revolting at the time the earliest gospel was written.

If Jesus did preach of revolution and Jewish independence, would that be contrary to any Christian doctrine? I don't think so! Mainstream Christianity teaches He had two natures, divine and human. The two completely separate natures never came into conflict. This then would suggest Jesus would have been unaware of His divinity as long as His human life existed.

He surely preached of love, mercy, justice, and charity, especially toward His fellow countrymen (Matthew 10:5–8; 15:24). He was a real man with every human emotion, and He certainly was a great speaker. No one would doubt this man changed the world.

What I have suggested here is clearly not conclusive evidence, but it does offer the distinct possibility of a facet of Jesus deliberately overlooked by the evangelists and the early church out of fear of Roman reprisals.

THE GEOGRAPHY OF JUDEA AT THE TIME OF JESUS

The search for the historical Jesus has generated only limited success. While a good deal of evidence has been exposed, solid new facts are hard to come by. The majority of information still comes from the New Testament, which was written as a theological treatise. It clearly was never intended to be a scholarly work of history.

In most case archaeological evidence has supported the New Testament, and what has not supported the text can be reasonably defended. We have broadened our knowledge of early Christianity, its history, and its geographical confines. We will now explore some history focusing on the geography at the early stages in the life of Jesus.

Although the Gospels of Matthew and Luke agree that Jesus was born to Joseph and the Virgin Mary in Bethlehem, their records of the other events cannot be reconciled. Biblically, it was deemed necessary for the Jewish Messiah to be born in the city where the birth of David occurred, and He should also be of his lineage. The evangelists who could not confirm Jesus's birthplace assumed it had to be Bethlehem, obviously to fulfill a prophecy in Micah 5:2, namely that a ruler born in Bethlehem would deliver the Jewish people.

Many scholars, therefore, believe the actual birth took place in Nazareth and not Bethlehem. The greatest obstacle to the Nazareth assertion was the historian Josephus, commander of

Jewish forces in Galilee during the first revolt. He apparently transcribed the entire region's main towns and villages. Remarkably, he makes no mention of Nazareth. The earliest mention of Nazareth spoken in Jewish literature is in a poem dated about the seventh century CE.

An archaeological discovery in 1955 uncovered evidence that seems to be from the middle of the first century BCE. The discovery yielded solid evidence which was found under the Church of the Annunciation in the present-day town of Nazareth. This strongly implies that the site was inhabited in the first century CE. Also, in 1962 at Caesarea, where the first-century Romans had their managerial headquarters, archaeologists discovered an inscription incorporating the name Nazareth, which probably formed part of a marble tablet displayed on a synagogue wall dating to no later than the third century.

Where Jesus was born is not exceedingly important. However, from the evidence we have, it is reasonable to assume He grew up in Nazareth, which was considered a satellite village of Sepphoris. Sepphoris has been virtually ignored until the twentieth century, mainly because it is not mentioned in the Bible. Yet this once splendid city thrived throughout Jesus's lifetime, and it was only an hour's walk (three-quarters of a mile) from Nazareth. Sepphoris sat on top of a four-hundred-foot hill overlooking the Bet Netofa Valley. Its Hebrew name, *Zippori*, meaning "bird," reflects its spectacular view. The city had a fantastic sight of Lower Galilee, including the towns of Cana and Nazareth, which are three to four miles south.

The historian Josephus called it "the ornament of Galilee." Sepphoris was located about halfway between the Mediterranean coast and the Sea of Galilee. Its position was on a busy highway that connected the port city of Ptolemais, which was seventeen miles northwest, and the Sea of Galilee. This road also connected Sepphoris to Tiberius via the Turan Valley. Throughout the early years of Jesus, Herod Antipas (the tetrarch of Galilee and Perea) was restoring, developing, and fortifying Sepphoris. It served as his principle residence and the administrative center of Galilee until he built Tiberius in 18–20 CE (to honor the emperor).

Herod Antipas constructed a four-thousand-seat amphitheater, possibly while Jesus was a teenager. The stage covered approximately 156 feet in width and had a depth of twenty-seven feet. He completely rebuilt the city and erected a spacious palace, an upper city, and a lower city with a new city wall. He also built a large marketplace, synagogues, and a colonnaded street with a substantial residential area. Several large cisterns were built to supply the water requirements for the city. About 7 CE, Antipas started his rebuilding of the city and renamed it Autocratis or the "Ornament of the Galilee."

Jesus and Joseph are said to be carpenters. The New Testament Greek word *tekton* means "builder," and it was inaccurately translated as "carpenter" in English Bibles (see Matthew

13:55 and Mark 6:3). This could mean that they were experienced in construction and skilled at working with wood and/or stone. Therefore, it would be very likely that Joseph and Jesus would have been involved in the reconstruction of Sepphoris since it was close by and this vast project was ongoing throughout most of the life of Jesus.

Sepphoris was destroyed about 6 CE after a revolt instigated by Judas the Galilean. The new procurator, Coponius, ordered a census and levied new taxes on the population, which is what sparked the revolt. Publius Quirinius, governor of Syria, and Coponius stamped out the revolt and killed Judas (Luke 2–2, also see Acts 5:37 and Josephus, *Jewish Antiquities* 18.7–9). At this time the population of Nazareth would have swelled because of the refugees fleeing Sepphoris. Jesus would have been in His most informative years when these events took place.

Before this time Nazareth was only a very tiny village and lacked the kind of construction projects that would provide sufficient work for skilled builders. Antipas's project was only an hour's walk away and undoubtedly attracted workers from all around the area. The distinct possibility exists that at some point Joseph and Jesus would have been employed in Sepphoris.

Here Jesus would have had a good deal of contact with Greek-speaking tradesmen, supervisors, engineers, and architects, and He possibly would have learned their language as well as their religious, social, and political leanings. The Protevangelium of James (a very early second-century apocryphal writing) along with early Christian traditions hints that Sepphoris was the home of Joachim and Anna, the parents of Mary, the mother of Jesus. This would also support the Jesus-Sepphoris connection. Jesus apparently did not have a positive opinion of the theater as He often used the word "hypocrite," thinking of the meaning the word had in the theater at Sepphoris, namely "one acting under a mask," as an analogy for religious pretense (Matthew 6:15). The Gospels show Jesus used this expression seventeen times.

Although Sepphoris was considered a Gentile city, it certainly had a reasonably large Jewish population because it had at least two synagogues, and after the fall of Jerusalem in 70 CE, Sepphoris became the home of the Sanhedrin. About 200 CE, it was in Sepphoris that Judah Hanassi (the prince) codified the Mishnah.

Shortly after Jesus assumed His ministry from John the Baptist, Antipas set out to have Jesus killed as well (Luke 13:31). This caused Jesus to flee the area. Antipas disposed of John the Baptist (according to Josephus) for political reasons, and he also saw Jesus as the new leader of a seditious movement. He would tolerate none of that in his territory.

Here one could argue that the birth of Jesus occurred just as any other normal human births and that He grew up with the same needs, illnesses, and desires as any ordinary child of His time would have. The political and geographical environment of the day certainly had influence on

His adult life. Many of His parables and phrases are clearly responding to the experiences that prevailed in and around Sepphoris.

The parable of the unforgiving servant (Matthew 18) arranges its backdrop in an accounting office of the king, one like Antipas, in a great banking center, and it resembled the one in the city of Sepphoris. There's also the parable about the king who receives a kingdom and returns to execute his opponents (Luke 19) and the one about the ten servants with whom are entrusted a sum of money to invest (Luke 19; Matthew 25). The image of a sovereign king and the mention of a bank paying interest suggest a cultural milieu similar to the affairs going on in the capital city at Sepphoris or Tiberias.

This brings us to the apocryphal literature describing the childhood and preadolescence period of Jesus. Books such as Pseudo-Matthew, James, and Thomas (infancy gospels not to be confused with others with similar names) detailed events not mentioned in the canonical gospels. The latter two have been the most popular. No early Christian writer considered the infancy gospels to have any scriptural authority for believers or any place among the canonical works. It is quite obvious these stories are pious fiction designed to satisfy the curiosities of the interested faithful.

Only Luke's gospel offers details of Jesus's childhood years. Luke records two stories about Jesus's childhood—His presentation in the temple as a newborn (Luke 2:22–39) and His visit to the temple for Passover when He was twelve years old (Luke 2:41–52). Both stories are dubious history. Luke by his own admission is not an eyewitness (Luke 1:1–4). Therefore, in the opinion of numerous scholars, the stories are at best secondhand and belong in the category of pious embellishment. Of course, much of this is based on speculation, but I believe it develops a reasonable path toward a better understanding of the historical Jesus.

We will now look into the forerunner of Jesus, the man who began a movement that Jesus essentially took over after his death—John the Baptist.

JOHN THE BAPTIST

Some scholars have questioned the historicity of John the Baptist. Although he is mentioned in the writings of Josephus, these scholars believe it to be a later Christian interpolation. However, the majority of scholars do accept him as a factual historical character. They reason that John's existence actually presented some unfavorable situations for the neophyte church, which prompted them to offer several apologias (the criterion of embarrassment). Therefore, it would have been significantly more comfortable for the later church if John had not existed. The church felt forced into accepting the fact that he did exist because it was so well known that ignoring his impact would have seriously diminished their credibility. The baptism of Jesus by John the Baptist is one of the surest things we can know about the life of Jesus according to most critical scholars. Let us now examine a few of the issues that have provoked the skeptics.

1. The Baptism of Jesus

Mark, the earliest gospel, does not try to conceal the fact that John did indeed baptize Jesus (Mark 1:9). However, he makes it quite clear that John recognized that he was to be only a precursor for the Messiah, Jesus. In his prologue Mark refers to the writings of the prophets that predict both John and Jesus. Here are the renderings Mark uses according to the New International Readers Version:

2 Long ago Isaiah the prophet wrote, "I will send my messenger ahead of you.
He will prepare your way." — (Malachi 3:1)
3 "A messenger is calling out in the desert,
'Prepare the way for the Lord.
Make straight paths for him.'"—(Isaiah 40:3)

Luke attempts to diminish the importance of the baptism of Jesus but clearly acknowledges it (Luke 3:21). Matthew saw a few problems with Mark's version and tries to correct them, first by having John openly confess his subordination to Jesus and only then showing him reluctantly baptize Jesus after He insists. His failure to acknowledge Malachi along with Isaiah indicates Mark's scriptural lacking (or the negligence of his source). Another troubling problem is Jesus submitting to be baptized by John at all. Baptism was clearly for the remission of sins; however, Jesus, being God, was supposed to be sinless. The fourth gospel solves this problem by not mentioning Jesus's baptism at all. In fact, he even refuses to use the title John the Baptist. So we can see why the later church saw this need to downplay the baptism. What is also alarming to skeptics is found in Mark's prologue (Mark 1:1), where some early manuscripts do not contain the phrase "Son of God." Consequently, some question its authenticity. The NWT Bible also omits it, while the NCV and TNIV mention it in the footnotes.

2. The Return of Elijah

Now Matthew creates a new problem. We learn from the book of Malachi (Malachi 4:5) that Elijah will portend the coming of the Messiah. (This is still the belief of messianic Jews.) Many Christians believe that John actually was the predicted Elijah because Jesus clearly claims that John the Baptist was Elijah (Matthew 11:13–14; 17:10–13). However, John the Baptist himself emphatically denies being Elijah (John 1:21). In the book of Kings, we see that Elijah never actually died (2 Kings 2:1, 11), yet we read of John's birth in the first chapter of Luke. Here we read that John and Jesus were born about six months apart, and we know that Elijah was born hundreds of years earlier and that he never actually died! Obviously, John could not have been Elijah. Luke (1:17) recognizes this and attempts to explain this by explaining that John only had the power and spirit of Elijah. But the problem remains. Malachi did not predict that someone with the "spirit of Elijah" would come but that Elijah himself would come.

3. The Death of the Baptist

Another source for John outside of the Bible is found in Josephus's *Antiquities.* He writes about a clash between Herod the Great and Aretas, father of the wife of Herod. Herod is defeated by Aretas. Herod then petitions Rome for help, and Emperor Tiberius sends Vitellius of Syria. Then the text unexpectedly shifts to the story about John the Baptist and then returns to the main story about Vitellius preparing to go to war against Aretas. This is why skeptics believe this reference to John (in Josephus) was added later by Christians. In other words, the sequence is broken for no good reason while the story could have very reasonably proceeded without the interruption.

The Gospels tell us that John the Baptist's life came to an end soon after he was imprisoned by Herod Antipas. The Gospels relate that Herod Antipas was angered by John's criticisms of his marriage to Herodias, the ex-wife of his half brother, Herod II. Josephus states that John was imprisoned in the fortress of Machaerus (Josephus, *Antiquities* XVIII: 5:1–2). Matthew's gospel tells that during his imprisonment John sent messengers by means of his own disciples to ask Jesus whether He was the "Coming One." Jesus ambiguously replies in affirmative terms and speaks of John as being the prophet Elijah (Matthew 11:2–15).

Yet Matthew describes the baptism of Jesus. Immediately after the ceremony, the heavens opened, and John saw God's Spirit descending like a dove along with a heavenly announcement that Jesus was His Son (Matthew 3:16–17). The fourth gospel is very clear that John knew well before his imprisonment that Jesus was certainly the "Coming One" (John 1:29–30). Therefore, John had to know exactly who Jesus was!

John's death was instigated by Herod in order to prevent a likely uprising, according to Josephus. Matthew tells us the uprising was incited by Salome's dance, and Antipas promised to grant her any wish. She accommodated her mother's (Herodias) desire, coveting for the head of John the Baptist (Matthew 14:6–8). Josephus writes, "As great crowds clustered around John, Herod became afraid lest the Baptist should abuse his moral authority over them to incite them to rebellion, as they would do anything at his bidding; therefore he thought it wiser, so as to prevent possible happenings, to take away the dangerous preacher … and he imprisoned him in the fortress of Machaerus." This surely suggests Herod—and very likely Rome as well—believed John to be a seditionist.

4. A Skeptic's Theory

The account of Josephus seems to fit historically with the mood of the time. Any leader who could attract large crowds and gather them in remote areas for any given reason would be suspect for insurrection against Rome. Yet we know Josephus was a turncoat Jew whose lifestyle depended on his acceptance by his Roman benefactors. His writings clearly reflect his prejudices. He believed in and loved his Jewish faith and was very comfortable with the position in life that Rome had given to him. Therefore, he desired to show Judaism in a favorable light and Rome as the divine masters of the universe, knowing that any negativity toward Rome would jeopardize his position.

If John had been preaching rebellion against Rome, Josephus, who respected John, would have accurately reported the events but would have attempted to remove any negative Judaic innuendos of the facts. He particularly would have avoided any insinuations concerning the religion sanctioning of rebellion. By casting personal aspersions on the Jewish rebels and not on the faith, he assuaged the Romans. This helps to corroborate the theory that John was preaching revolt. Of course, it is possible that he could have merely been preaching a drastic religious revival.

5. Why the Need of a Forerunner?

There are many forerunners of heroes in history whom we can recall. Usually their position was to start something leaving the hero to complete. In this case, the idea is that so many of John's followers formed the nucleus of the new Jesus movement that it became necessary to show a believable transfer of authority to Jesus. The earlier the writing, the more positive the role of John is developed. Likewise, the later writings progressively show the downplaying of John. Yet his overwhelming popularity demanded every writer acknowledge him. Thus, he earned the very distinct title of "the Baptist."

The puppet king of Judea around the time of the birth of Jesus was Herod the Great. The very name of Herod brings about disdain because of the traditions passed down to us. We will now look into the history of this despised individual.

HEROD THE GREAT

Herod the Great (73–4 BCE) is considered to be one of history's bad guys by most Christians and Jews. However, there is no doubt Herod left an outstanding and indelible mark on the face of Palestine. He rebuilt the temple and refurbished it, making it a colossal structure and clearly one of the architectural marvels of the ancient world. In so doing, he significantly increased the religious reputation of Judaism, yet ironically, popular history has tended to overlook these accomplishments. He also enabled Judea to have a positive balance of trade while enjoying religious freedoms and prosperity unrivaled by any other client subject of the Roman Empire.

In order to understand the reasons for Herod's unpopularity, we need to consider his background and the circumstances that took place before him and to evaluate the biases of our sources.

After a review of the Maccabean revolt (167–164 BCE) that established Jewish independence for the first time in nearly five hundred years, John Hyrcanus (134–104 BCE) rallied the Jewish people and expanded the boundaries of Judea while maintaining a strong relationship with Rome. He zealously forced the conquered people of Idumea (Edomites) to succumb to the Jewish faith. In his eagerness to unify all Jews, he trampled the Samaritans and destroyed their temple on Mount Gerizim only to incur even greater animosities between these similar faiths.

As viewed by most scholars, it was under his reign that Judaism fragmented into religio-political segments, such as Sadducees, Pharisees, and Essenes. Hyrcanus was an autocrat, although he avoided using the title *king*; however, he did accept the designation of high priest. Because he was not of the Davidic line, this would anger the Pharisees. Obviously, this placed him closer to the Sadducees. Immediately after his death, his son Aristobulus (140–105 BCE) assumed copower with his mother but quickly threw her into prison, where she was starved to death. To shelter himself against any threat from his family, he imprisoned three of his brothers. Then he declared himself king and high priest, becoming the first Jewish king since the Babylonian exile.

Alexander Jannaeus (103–76 BCE) soon followed and increased the importance of the Sadducees so much so that a civil war broke out with the Pharisees who had joined with their former enemy the Seleucid Greeks (the Syrian king Demetrius III). When it appeared that the Greek-Pharisee alliance (I use this term very loosely) would ultimately win and the Greeks might take over, Alexander then made peace with the Pharisees and caused them to switch their support to him, which resulted in his victory. Josephus tells us he soon double-crossed the Pharisees and crucified eight hundred of their members and butchered their families.

This, of course, would lead us to believe Alexander was hated by the people, yet in the Dead Sea Scrolls cache at Qumran, there was a writing exalting him, possibly shedding some light on Herod the Great, who was born shortly after Alexander's death.

Herod's father was Antipater, who was a prime adviser to Hyrcanus II. When Alexander died, his wife, Alexandra (Salome), became queen regent. Her two sons, Aristobulus and Hyrcanus II, then battled for supremacy. Both brothers realized the need to please Roman interests. They appealed to Roman General Pompey, who was in Damascus, Syria. It was Pompey who then decided in favor of Hyrcanus II. Angered by the decision, Aristobulus took up arms and marched into Jerusalem. Pompey then invaded and conquered, looting Jerusalem and taking Aristobulus prisoner to Rome. It is important to note that the Pharisees supported Aristobulus and now Israel had lost its hundred-year reign of independence. Herod's father, Antipater, had skillfully achieved the respect of Rome by aiding Julius Caesar against Pompey in Egypt. He was married to an Idumea (Cypros) by whom he had fathered four sons, Phaselus, Herod, Joseph, and Pheroras, and a daughter (Salome).

Remember, he was a product of the forced conversions instigated by Hyrcanus I. With full Roman approval and also that of Hyrcanus II, Antipater eventually made his son Phaselus governor of Jerusalm and his son Herod governor of Galilee. This would lead to the accusation that Herod was only a half Jew.

The Parthian invasion (40 BCE) of Judaea put Antigonus, nephew of Hyrcanus II, on Hyrcanus's throne. Herod then fled with his family to the fortress of Masada, where he left his family and went to Rome. There, Roman leaders Mark Antony (81–30 BCE) and Octavian (64 BCE–14 CE), the future Augustus, accepted him, and the Senate named him king of Judea.

The Jews obviously did not agree to Rome's right to choose their king for them and sided with Antigonus. With Roman help, Herod then defeated the Parthians (37 BCE). Antigonus and his chief followers were soon put to death. Initially, he was unable to immediately take Jerusalem because he went to the aid of Antony, who was at the siege of Samosata on the Euphrates. Herod took his troops and joined him, a wise political move that gained him enormous Roman appreciation.

In his retaking of Jerusalem, Herod took special care to minimize any destruction of the city as was previously done during Pompey's triumph. He personally paid the soldiers for not looting, which was customary then for armies as their reward for victory. His challenge now became wining the approval of the Jewish people and keeping Rome placated. He knew he did not have the proper ancestry to claim the office of high priest, so he needed a priest who would yield to him without a challenge. Thus, he lost any respect he may have had of both Sadducees and Pharisees as he appointed a Babylonian Jew from an insignificant sacerdotal family named Hananeel. This outraged the Pharisees, and Herod felt obliged to reappoint his seventeen-year-old brother-in-law, Aristobulus III, as high priest (36 BCE). A year later he had him killed because he believed that the Pharisees were plotting to petition Rome to have Aristobulus appointed king on the grounds of right of succession and that Herod did not qualify because he was not a full Jew.

Brutality is synonymous with Herod. His position was precarious, and he addressed this by killing off any one he suspected of having ambitions relative to his authority. This included his wives and children. Although we may look at his behavior with disdain, it was not uncommon at all in ancient times. His cruelty was undoubtedly weighed by his ambition, which could not be minimized, but his skillful leadership was clearly beneficial to the people he governed.

Herod brought to Judea unprecedented prosperity. He did this by balancing Roman interests with those of Judea in order to obtain the funding for all his building projects without burdening his people with excessive taxation. In fact, he actually lowered the taxes. There is nobody in Jewish history (the exception perhaps being modern times) who has had a greater influence on the material culture and splendor of Israel than Herod. His building plan was grandiose beyond expectation. His ability to bring local resources as well as foreign resources to bear on his public works program was simply remarkable. Obviously, he was a brilliant strategist and a dazzling politician.

His foresightedness warded off the effects of regional famines, while his public works program, especially after the devastating earthquake of 31 BCE, miraculously brought together the many diverse communities in Judea—Pharisees pitching in with Essenes and Sadducees as well as all the other inhabitants. This is one of the real untold ironies of Jewish history that Herod, who is one of the guys most hated in popular Jewish history, yet he surprisingly left the most distinguishable mark on the face of the land of Israel. Whether it's the western wall or the temple itself with all of its splendor or the great amphitheater in Caesarea or the harbor at Caesarea, all of these magnificent monuments are attributed to Herod and his working relationship with both the local indigenous peoples as well as foreign sponsors.

The final judge of history is wrested by the opinions and biases of the writers. It seems that Herod, who has been given the title "the Great," is considered more *infamous* than great by popular judgment. He was never accepted by the Pharisees, who later became the ruling party, and then by Christians through the gospel of Matthew. If we measure him by his accomplishments along with the fact that he reigned for more than thirty-three years and died a natural death at the age of sixty-nine, he perhaps deserves the title of Herod the Great.

From here we will move on to Jesus, who was born during the reign of Herod the Great.

THE DEATH OF JESUS

The death of Jesus is one of the most important events of Christian history, yet it is somewhat clouded by conflicting events in the canonical gospels. We will attempt to provide an alternative perspective combined with some historical facts plus some of my personal speculations.

The Maccabean revolt (167 BCE) demonstrated to the world that a small Jewish army consisting of some excellent, dedicated, and fierce fighters had indeed upset a major world power with vastly inferior weaponry and equipment. The Romans took note and garnered much respect for the Jewish military. However, by 63 BCE, Judea fell under the yoke of mighty Rome. When Octavian (Augustus Caesar) became emperor, he was very mindful of the Maccabean/ Greek lesson and wisely granted certain unprecedented privileges to the Jews. Noteworthy was the allowance of religious freedom and full practice of Jewish laws to an extraordinary degree. Basically, as long as the region remained peaceful and paid its tribute, Rome would allow the Jews these freedoms.

Jewish laws are preserved in numerous sources. The most credible are the Mishnah, the Semahot, the Tosefta, and the Palestinian and Babylonian Talmud. Although these written sources came into existence after the death of Jesus, we can reasonably assume they were not written down but were orally applicable during His lifetime as well. The Semahot spelled out laws for the funeral rites and care of the dead. Both Talmuds confirmed Jewish oral laws and were regarded as having equal authority to the Torah. We can see the application of these oral laws in the writings of Josephus (37–100 CE) and Philo (15 BCE–50 CE).

After the death of Tiberius (14–37 CE), Caligula (37–41 CE) imposed greater Roman control and allowed less Jewish freedom. Herein lies our problems for history, and the details begin to get fuzzy. Prior to Caligula, Josephus tells us "the Jews were allowed to follow their own laws in accordance with ancestral laws, just as they had during the Maccabean period." Around this time Rome exercised in several cases less regard for Jewish customs and laws. Before Caligula, Philo tells us even Jewish seditionists who were crucified under Roman law received imperial protection by allowing established Jewish burial customs to prevail. This privilege even superseded normal Roman laws. "I know that some of those crucified were taken down before the start of Sabbath and their bodies were returned to their families for burial and the customary Jewish rights" (In Flaccum, 83).

Although the Gospels leave us to think Joseph of Arimathea received a special privilege from Pilate, this was common practice granted to all Judean Jews since Augustus. After a crucifixion, if no one claimed the body, it would be left to rot on the cross. However, Jewish law strictly forbade this! The Talmud (BK 81a) insists a corpse found unattended was to be given a quick burial. This was required even of a high priest who was otherwise forbidden to come in contact with the dead. Josephus (Contra Apion 2.211) confirms this. Therefore, it would have been a sacred Jewish requirement for any Jew to see to the burial of Jesus prior to sundown on the day before Sabbath or Passover. Semahot 2.9 states a body must be buried the day it dies. Temporary burial was permitted and was often used when there wasn't sufficient time before sunset. It would have been a sacrilege for any Jew not to honor this. Nowhere else in the empire was this custom granted—or at least the evidence points that way.

The Gospels say Jesus had at least two trials—the Jewish (Sanhedrin) one and the Roman court. He was convicted by the Sanhedrin implicitly for blasphemy, while some vaguely alluded to a conviction of sedition by the Romans. We cannot be sure that the Sanhedrin was or could be called into session in the evening, but it is quite likely they did meet and came to an agreement to convict Jesus, even though they may not have wanted to do so! "It was Caiaphas who had given counsel to the Jews that it was expedient that one man should die for the people" (John 18:14).

What exactly was Caiaphas referring to? Had Jesus and His disciples given the impression that Jesus was a rebel leader that the high priest feared would cause a massive Roman response on the whole nation if they didn't act? Therefore, would the offering to sacrifice one man, Jesus, satisfy Roman justice and concerns? After all, Jesus did intentionally enter Jerusalem riding on an ass to show fulfillment of the Zechariah prophecy (9:9–11). This was a messianic message that the Romans certainly knew about and completely understood the significance of, especially during the Jewish feast of Passover.

If this was the case, then the trial by the Sanhedrin may have been intended to *save* Jesus by forcing the Romans to honor the Augustan law and provide Jesus with a proper burial (see Josephus, *Antiquities* 16.160–173). Indeed, only through a Jewish legal execution could an offender obtain forgiveness for his sins (see Talmud, Sanhedrin 47a). The execution by a Gentile government would then reinforce this forgiveness. I believe Caiaphus had this in mind for Jesus. Although it is true Sadducees did not believe in an afterlife, the Sanhedrin did have several Pharisee members, and Caiaphus must have had at least some sense of Jewish nationalism. In doing this, he believed he would fulfill the Jewish requirement for atonement, namely by the execution, shameful burial, and rotting of the flesh from the bones (Talmud, Sanhedrin 47b).

Hypothetically, let us suppose Jesus and His disciples were a band of deeply religious patriots who were attempting to instigate a revolution, copying the successful rebellion instigated by the Maccabees just little more than 150 years prior. Although the Sadducees were indeed only the puppet rulers whose only power came from Rome, they, too, would have preferred Jewish independence to the foreign domination from Rome. The people of Judea wanted independence, and if Jesus entered Jerusalem just as a military messiah was prophesied, Rome surely would have responded. Perhaps the Romans ordered the Jewish authorities to deal with Jesus. Even though they did not believe Jesus posed a serious military threat, politically, it would have looked better if the Jews handled it themselves or had at least given the appearance of such. No matter, Rome still demanded that the life of Jesus be terminated.

This would explain the presence of Roman soldiers accompanying the Jewish police. Giving the appearance to the populace that Jesus was being taken by Jews and not the Romans would spare them public outrage. The Romans could well have threatened the Jewish leaders with massive punishments unless Jesus was apprehended and condemned. I repeat Caiaphus's statement (John 18:14) "It was Caiaphus who had given counsel to the Jews that it was expedient that one man should die for the people." At this point Jesus was destined to die. The Sanhedrin trial was then only a method to ensure Jesus would receive a proper Jewish burial. What was most important, according to Jewish law, was Jesus had to have a legal Jewish execution, because that was the only method He could have obtained forgiveness for His sins, at least in the minds of His fellow Jews (Talmud, Sanhedrin 47a).

The Tosefta alludes to the possibility that merely touching of a stone to a condemned one's heart satisfied the legal requirements (Sanhedrin 9.6h). By legal condemnation and proper burial, even from a Gentile execution, the Jews (in their minds) believed they were satisfying God's law in Deuteronomy 21:23 and providing either eternal rest or proper passage to the afterlife for Jesus.

Now let us consider the Gospels. How could they possibly have written about any rebellious side of Jesus without incurring Roman retaliation? This would be especially true if we consider they were written within the recent memory of the slaughter of Jerusalem (70 CE). They also were composed at a time when the Gentile Christians were in serious conflict with Jews and Jewish Christians as argumentative competitors for new members. Therefore, they had to downplay or omit any negativity toward Rome as well as Jesus's role pertaining to even the slightest military/rebellious conduct. So they disguised their anti-Roman language and then turned their anger toward the Jews by the blaming them for the death of Jesus. They certainly could not have understood the Jewish/Sanhedrin's motives and circumstances regarding His death.

Consider the symbolism in the cursing of the fig tree by Jesus. Read Matthew 21:19 and Mark 10:12–14. Some scholars believe the fig tree was a metaphor for the Roman Empire. In Matthew 8:28–34 and Mark 5:1–14, Jesus is casting out the devils within a wild man. The devils said their name was Legion because they were many. Legion was forced by Jesus to leave the man and to enter a herd of two thousand swine that then killed themselves. Scholars believe the devils named Legion metaphorically represented a Roman legion. (A regular Roman legion was about six thousand men, but the legion occupying Jerusalem was only two thousand.) This Roman legion honored their mascot, depicting a wild boar (swine) on their emblems. They then leaped into the sea and drowned. (This episode will be discussed in more detail later.) The symbolic allusion to Rome/Babylon in Revelation is most obvious, and numerous scholars have pointed it out.

Now is there any evidence to indicate Jesus and His disciples were militant rebels? In Luke 22:38, Jesus tells His disciples to sell their purses and mantels and buy swords. Matthew 10:34–39 says,

> You must not think that I have come to bring peace to the earth; I have not come to bring peace, but a sword. I come to set a man against his father, a daughter against her mother, a daughter-in-law against her mother-in-law, and a man will find his enemies under his own roof. No one is worthy of me who cares more for son or daughter; no one is worthy of me who does not take up his Cross and

follow me. Whoever gains his life where is it; whoever loses his life for my sake will gain it.

Similar words were used by the Maccabees to rally support for their rebellion against the Greeks.

Matthew 10 describes another eerie reminiscence to the Maccabee tactics by soliciting the help of the people in the countryside to assist his guerrilla army, complete with a threat for withholding support. In John 18:10–11, Peter used his sword to defend Jesus and cut off the ear of Malchus (the high priest's servant). Mark 14:47 and Luke 22:49 tell us that the disciples were armed. Luke 6:14 and Acts 1:13 refer to Simon the Zealot, one of the twelve apostles. He received this title for being a probable member of a first-century radical sect of Judaism called Zealots, which were thought to be militant and rebellious, similar to the Zionist movement of the 1940s.

These passages certainly are ambiguous, but they clearly suggest a much more militant side of Jesus. In order to have drawn the huge crowds, Jesus would surely have needed a message that appealed to those ideals of freedom and independence—freedom like His predecessors had during the Maccabean period. I believe Jesus did indeed deliver moving and great speeches just like He did with the Sermon on the Mount. He did preach love toward one's neighbors, but the gospel writers also must have concealed His message of hope for Jewish independence. Obviously, the Gospels couldn't have addressed this part of the story, but they did leave a few hints along with oblique ambiguities just as John does in the book of Revelation by using Babylon allegorically for Rome.

If what I have speculated has any merit, then several so-called "Bible contradictions" may be explained by understanding the constraints of the gospel writers along with first-century Jewish customs and fear of Rome. I don't think there is any doubt that these writers thought they were recording sacred truths about Jesus. They certainly would not have written a deliberate lie. They just had to disguise or allegorize some details to confuse Rome. To be sure, it is difficult for us today to understand what their symbolic and metaphoric messages meant, but it was quite clear to their first-century audiences.

WHO KILLED JESUS?

The crucifixion of Jesus is considered a great if not the greatest tragedy in history. Ironically, for Christians, this tragic event in combination with His resurrection is celebrated as the birth of their faith and their salvation from sin. Officially, Easter is the most important day in Christianity, as it represents redemption for all humankind. Who killed Jesus is irrelevant because devout Christians believe Jesus taught not to blame but to forgive. His death on the cross was humanity's route to salvation. Thus, Christians should be thanking those who executed Him, not blaming them. But does history actually support this?

The four gospels describe the proceedings leading up to the death of Jesus, which are given with heart-wrenching details. All four are basically in agreement. The gospel stories read during Holy Week are reverently remembered on an annual basis to commemorate this anniversary, and this has continued for nearly two thousand years.

Jews also remember Easter—not joyfully but with trepidation. Through the centuries a number of excessively zealot Christians inspired by Holy Week sermons took out their anger over the death of Jesus on the Jews. From just cruel taunting to full-scale pogroms, Jews endured property damage, physical beatings, and outright murder perpetrated by devout Christians, almost always with complete impunity.

There was nothing Jews could do because Christians blamed them for the murder of Jesus by using the scriptures (Matthew 27:25) to substantiate their actions as retaliation for being "Christ killers," perpetuating the expression that "the curse of God" was on the Jewish people. The culmination of this manifested itself in the Holocaust and the death of millions. If we closely examine the historical facts with a true sense of justice and honest reasoning, we will find that the crucifixion and the reasons behind it were fostered by Roman instigation, for which the Jewish people have been blamed unjustifiably for centuries.

Matthew's and John's Gospels were written more than fifty years after the death of Jesus. At this time Romans considered all Christians as being Jewish and equally responsible for the first revolt against Rome. At this point in history, Jews were reeling under much harsher control from the empire and were struggling to redefine their faith in view of this disaster. Jewish Christians who acknowledged Christ as the Messiah originally had been accepted as a sect within Judaism, but then they were no longer welcomed and were refused membership in the synagogues.

These Christians were very angered by this action and responded by renouncing Judaism and proclaimed themselves to be a new religion and swore their political loyalty to Rome. Their writings then clearly reflected this rancor, which ultimately became part and parcel of the New

Testament. Blame for the revolt and the death of Jesus was cast completely on the Jews, and the Christians were vindicated for the revolt entirely, showing them to be law-abiding subjects of Rome. Even Pontius Pilate was vindicated for his role in the death of Jesus.

In the later part of the first century, Christianity was diverse and unorganized. The largest groups were Jewish Christians followed by Gentile Pauline Christians and an assortment of Gnostics sects. The self-proclaimed apostle Paul encountered open hostilities from Jews as he proselytized in Jewish synagogues in several towns throughout the empire. This spurred additional condemnation of Jews in the New Testaments writings inspired by Paul's theology.

By the time Constantine unified Christianity (about 325 CE), Jews had revolted for the second time (132–135 CE), and they were now banished from even entering Jerusalem (renamed Aelia Capitolina). Any hope of reestablishing a nation seemed unattainable. As Christianity grew, Judaism remained fairly constant because Jews were forbidden to convert a Christian under any circumstances (e.g., marriage).

Everywhere Christianity spread, Jews were assailed. In many cases, they were forced to convert or faced expulsion. Often they were forced to live in ghettoes and were not allowed to socialize with Christians. In rural areas where Jews were allowed to live, usually on barely marginal agricultural tracts, they struggled to exist. Often when they successfully developed sections, pogroms were instigated, and they were forced to leave with only their personal belongings. All this was justified by use of the New Testament and citing "the curse of God."

This alleged curse is without a doubt the most tragic event in history, as it has adversely affected people for nearly two thousand years and may still linger today. It is so sad because the true historical facts clearly exonerate the Jewish people and also the first-century Jewish leaders to a slightly lesser degree.

Let us look at the facts.

Many modern scholars are convinced Jesus was openly defiant of Roman domination. Perhaps He was even militant to the extent that Rome saw Him as a threat to their hegemony. Crucifixion was a form of capital punishment reserved *exclusively* for execution by Rome and also used almost exclusively for crimes of sedition. Zealots were a class of Jews dedicated to the expulsion of Rome. Jesus clearly had at least one member in his closest entourage. Historically speaking, the gospel assertions concerning Judas Iscariot and Barabbas are highly suspect. A number of details surrounding the gospel stories suggest they are merely disguised fictions designed to confuse the Romans.

Does it make any sense at all that the Jewish people would demand responsibility for the crucifixion of Jesus and willingly pass it on to their progeny? After barely a lapse of one week, these same people had enthusiastically welcomed Him when He triumphantly entered Jerusalem to fulfill an ancient messianic prophecy. That prophecy and its military implications were well known to Rome, and that would have been something they absolutely would not have tolerated.

What possible reason would the Jewish people have for turning over a respectful fellow countryman to their despised occupiers for execution? It simply doesn't make any sense!

Joseph C. Hough Jr., a Christian theologian, wrote in the June 2002 issue of *Bible Review*,

> By the end of the second century, anti-Judaism and the Christ-killer myth had become prominent in the teachings of church leaders. The early church fathers perpetuated (this) ... with even greater vehemence than John did in his gospel. By the fourth century, Augustine and John Chrysostom were among those who gave credence to the awful depiction of Jews as the enemies of God who crucified Christ. Although a long series of papal pronouncements tried to protect Jews against overt violence, the power of the "Christ-killer" myth created a cultural climate in which hatred and killing of Jews occurred with impunity. What emerged was a relentless and continuing persecution of Jews.

Some of the greatest acts of cruelty came from avowing Christians who used their religion, specifically the New Testament, to justify their evil deeds. Certainly, Christianity itself doesn't cause such evil. Rather, it consistently condemns it. But the problem still lays in the text of the New Testament and how certain passages are understood. If the New Testament is accepted as the strictly literal Word of God, this problem will continue and reassert itself sometime in the future.

A few years ago, the Catholic Church took some positive steps and is still implementing this approach to its membership. But the process is proving to be extremely slow and has little if any momentum. There is fear that this movement will lose traction with their membership. Let us all hope that this will gain renewed energy and that all of the other denominations will follow for the sake of justice and human dignity and put an end to this shameful episode of history.

CHAPTER 10

MARY—THE MOTHER OF JESUS

When early Christians began formulating their theology, the leadership of one branch of this movement began developing a concept about how Christians became the new Israel and how these new people were chosen by God. Jesus was envisaged as the new Adam. He had given humankind a new start. This segment was now the new Israel. Soon after a need for an acceptable female personality which could correspond to the church the way the daughter of Zion did for the people spoken of in the late prophetic literature. Then this could be symbolically used to represent how the people God were longing for a personality similar to a husband who longs for his bride. Allegorically, Jesus represented this new Adam. It then seemed appropriate for there to also be a new Eve (Psalm 9:13; Isaiah 62:12; Zechariah 9:9). It also seemed appropriate that the church would metaphorically become the loving mother and the people her children.

However, this new Eve had to be connected some way to the new Adam. Jesus had no wife. Mary Magdalene seemed to be the most logical choice, but it appears she had either alienated a few of the male apostles or that her relationship with Jesus was not deemed acceptable. Therefore, they needed a new female consort who would be spotless enough to be the symbolic figure of the new Eve as well as the church.

For reasons we do not know, these early Christians assigned this role to Mary, the mother of Jesus. Subsequently, by the time that Matthew and Luke were written, the infancy stories started a proto-Mariology in which Mary, the mother of Jesus, was symbolically inaugurated as the communal personality, the new daughter of Zion. This group began to see her as representing the mother as well as the church. At the same time, particularly in the account of the virginal conception, she is assigned the role as the new Eve, the mother of a new humanity. In John's gospel, we see a more elaborately developed Mariology in both the Cana and the crucifixion scenes. Here Mary is implicitly identified with the church.

There were a few problems, however. For instance, there's Mary's pregnancy before her marriage. The virgin birth concept was fitting with recruitment of pagans, but it offended the Jewish Christians. The knowledge of her having other children was also disturbing. These problems instigated several apologetic responses. The earliest apology is called *The Protevangelium of James*, written early in second century. This noncanonical early Christian work claims to tell the story of the circumstances surrounding Mary's conception and birth, her marriage with Joseph, the birth of Jesus, and the flight to Egypt. While it is obviously more legend than fact, it also offers a very early picture of the early church's traditions and "family stories." There are also later and longer versions of this story, such as the so-called *Gospel of the Nativity of Mary*, but this is the first of its kind.

Soon Mary became the representative of the whole church in an allegorical sense, although it had not yet become an explicit doctrine. Within a hundred years (by the early second century), a personal Mariology was developing as part of an exuberant enthusiasm of these nascent Christians. Mary would now replace the mother goddesses of the pagan world and supersede Mary Magdalene. In theory, she was not a goddess, but she now played a role for Christianity, which was functionally similar to those, which the female deities had played in antiquity. She reflected a feminine aspect of God.

This concept could only have grown within a Hellenistic environment, which expanded as more Gentiles were Christianized. The Jewish religion abhorred the goddesses, which strained this branch's relationship with Jewish Christians even further. Yet here is the real surprise. Paul, the father of Gentile Christianity, never mentions Mary or even remotely hints of the virgin birth in all of his writings. The closest statement Paul makes is that Jesus was "born of a woman, born under the Law" (Galatians 4:4).

By the fourth and fifth centuries, debates raged about the nature of Christ, especially concerning the relationship between Christ's divine and human natures. Relevant to a procurement of a title for Mary and her theological role in Christian worship, beginning about the early third century, Christians began referring to Mary as *Theotokos*, a Greek word meaning "God-bearer." The first documented usage of the term is in the writings of Origen of Alexandria in 230 CE. Soon *Theotokos* or Mary was called the mother of God. This expression for Mary was popular in Christian piety, but Nestorius, patriarch of Constantinople from 428 to 431 CE, objected. He opined that Mary was only the mother of Jesus, which was exclusively limited to His human nature and had nothing to do with His divine nature. Nestorius's ideas were condemned at the Council of Ephesus in 431 CE and again at the Council of Chalcedon in 451 CE. Here the church decided that Christ was fully God and fully human and these natures were united in one person—Jesus Christ. Mary could now be officially called "mother of God" since she had given birth to Jesus, who was fully divine as well as fully human. Devotion to Mary now took firm rooting in the Eastern church.

This Hellenistic Mary-oriented theology did not fully germinate in the Western church until the seventh century. We can determine this by the visit of Pope Agapetus to Constantinople in 536 CE, when he was criticized for opposing the veneration of the Theotokos and refusing to allow her icons to be displayed in Roman churches. The earliest Marian feasts that are recorded in the Roman liturgical calendar were organized by Pope Sergius I (687–701 CE).

Physiologically the early church appeased women by introducing a prestigious feminine personality to the liturgy in combination with their male counterparts by associating her symbolic image to that of their own beloved mothers. The church made it clear that Mary was only to be venerated and not worshipped, but as time passed, this restriction became more and more blurred. The Protestant Reformation initiated by Martin Luther strongly objected to this.

> [Luther's] custom of preaching Marian sermons on the Marian feasts continued in the Lutheran Church for a hundred years after his death. Following the example of Luther other great songwriters of the Reformation glorified the greatness of Mary's divine maternity. This lasting piety towards the Mother of God found an outlet in piety so that generally the celebrated pictures of the Madonna and her statues from the middle Ages were retained in Lutheran churches. (William J. Cole, *Was Luther a Devotee of Mary?*)

Other reformers would see any extended devotion to Mary as a distraction diminishing the rightful worship of Jesus. Catholics would expand their Mariology into doctrinal status well beyond biblical support. Orthodox Christians, like Catholics, hold Mary in very high esteem and believe she remained a virgin all of her life. However, they do not subscribe to the Immaculate Conception in any of their doctrines or teachings.

I have only tersely described the story of the development of Mariology in order to establish a foundation. Let us now briefly examine the New Testament to see what can be known about the actual person of Mary.

It is often difficult to identify various people in the Bible. Generally, the information is inadequate. At other times it is contradictory. This is especially true of the people mentioned in the Bible. Frequently, we are forced to rely upon the testimony of nonbiblical texts or from the ancient historians of the church for clarification. The New Testament is the earliest source for Mary as found in the Gospels.

"Is not this the carpenter, the son of Mary and brother of James and Joses and Judas and Simon?" (Mark 6:3; Matthew 13:55). Calling Jesus the son of Mary indicates she is unmarried or widowed. It also indicated that James, Joses, Judas, and Simon were the brothers of Jesus. It suggests they were also Mary's children, but not necessarily.

There are three popular scenarios. First, the Eastern Orthodox view is they were children of another wife of Joseph. Second, the Helvidian view is that they were the younger children of Mary who were born naturally and after Jesus. Third, the Hieronymian view is that they are the cousins of Jesus. Although the Hieronymian or Catholic view is the least likely, a reasonable case can be made in its defense.

Regardless of the relationship, a close kinship is evident. This was typical of the times, as the family then was considered to include all aunts, uncles, cousins, nieces, and nephews. Salome (mentioned by Mark 15:40 and 16:1) was also called "the mother of Zebedee's sons" by Matthew and "His [Jesus's] mother's sister" by John. Salome and Mary being sisters, their children—Jesus, son of Mary, and the disciples James and John, sons of Salome and Zebedee—were first cousins.

If James, Joses, Judas, and Simon were indeed Mary's other sons, they certainly displayed a very unenthusiastic role in the early ministry of Jesus (Matthew 13:57; Mark 3:21, 31; 6:4; John 7:5). Obviously, this changed after the crucifixion as James clearly became the leader of the Jerusalem church. Paul speaks of the "other apostles and brothers of the Lord" (1 Corinthians 9:5), indicating they were also fellow missionaries. Josephus recorded the martyrdom of James, and Julius Africanus wrote about the later relatives of Jesus call the desposynoi.

In Revelation 12, the woman clothed with the sun is giving birth. There is obvious symbolism here. Most commentators interpret this scene as representing Christ, who is "caught up to the Throne of God." The woman wears a crown of twelve stars—Virgo, the Virgin. Here is an obvious reference to Mary, the mother of Jesus.

As previously mentioned, the most comprehensive information concerning Mary is found in an early noncanonical second-century writing called *Protevangelium of James*. Remarkably, the most historical composition on Mary is not the New Testament but the Qu'ran, the Bible of Islam.

THE VIRGIN BIRTH

The virgin birth of Jesus is a doctrine of Christian faith and is also a tenet of Islam. Today there are many who question this literally. Although the subject is not widely discussed, except by those who oppose Christianity, there are proponents of allegorical interpretation to explain this physical impossibility.

A meeting held in Seattle, Washington, in 2004 as part of an annual continuation of the Anglican Roman Catholic International Conference suggested the possibility of using allegory. Here is one of their statements:

> In the following paragraphs, our use of Scripture seeks to draw upon the whole tradition of the Church, in which rich and varied readings have been employed. In the New Testament, the Old Testament is commonly interpreted typologically (By typology we mean a reading which accepts that certain things, in Scripture [persons, places, and events] foreshadowing or illuminating other things, or reflect patterns of faith in imaginative ways. [e.g. Adam is a type of Christ: Romans 5:14; Isaiah 7:14 points towards the virgin birth of Jesus: Matthew 1:23]. This typological sense was considered to be a meaning that goes beyond the literal sense). This approach assumes the unity and consistency of the divine revelation. Events and images are understood with specific reference to Christ. This approach is further developed by the Fathers and by medieval preachers and authors.

The many pejorative arguments against the virgin birth are only convincing when taken literally because it defies science, modern thinking, and reason. Thomas Paine, American revolutionary and author, referring to the virgin birth, said "Is it more probable that nature should go out of her course, or that a man should tell a lie? We have never seen, in our time, nature go out of her course, but we have good reason to believe that millions of lies have been told in the same time; it is therefore at least millions to one, that the reporter of a miracle tells a lie."

Several theologians have strived to fit the virgin birth into a positive modern allegorical context. From his book *Jesus Christ in Modern Thought*, John Macquarrie states, "I think we have to look at this dogma very critically and ask whether it makes any worthwhile contribution to Christology. Would the belief that Jesus was born of one human parent alone in any way enhance his status in our eyes or his authority as one sent by God or the claim that he is the paradigm of humanity?"

In *The Metaphor of God Incarnate*, John Hick asserts on the virgin birth, "The idea of divine incarnation is better understood as metaphorical than as literal—Jesus embodied, or incarnated, the ideal of human life lived in faithful response to God, so that God was able to act through him, and he accordingly embodied a love which is a human reflection of the divine love."

Perhaps one of the most controversial proponents is former Episcopal Bishop J. S. Spong, who wrote, "In time, the virgin birth account will join Adam and Eve and the story of the cosmic ascension as clearly recognized mythological elements in our faith tradition whose purpose was not to describe a literal event but to capture the transcendent dimensions of God in the earthbound words and concepts of first-century human beings." There are those who believe Bishop Spong has taken this to the extreme and have condemned him for it while others revel in the tact he has taken with an unbelievable doctrine into its proper perspective.

There's little doubt that our present-day understanding of human reproduction influences how we perceive the virgin birth. We certainly want to know where the Y chromosome came from to create the fetus, as we know the X chromosomes, at least we assume, came from Mary. Did Mary provide the ovum for impregnation by the Holy Spirit, which joined to it to become the genetic inheritance of Jesus, or was she simply a human commodity used to contain and nourish the divinely implanted seed as we see in surrogate mothers?

Because many gods were born from the unity of a pagan god and a human virgin, it was an easy sell for pagan converts. Just who came up with the original idea and where it started are unknown to me. However, here are some of my observations. In the New Testament, there is no doubt that Paul was the earliest writer. He did not know of the virgin birth. In Galatians 4:4, Paul stated, "But when the fullness of time had come, God sent his Son, born of a woman, born under the law." Obviously, if he knew Jesus was born of a virgin this was the place to say so. Even simply the mention of Mary's name would have been expected here. By his failure to do so strongly indicates Paul did not even know about Mary.

Mark, the earliest gospel, is the first to mention the mother of Jesus by her name as Mary. So Between Paul writing in the fifties and Mark writing in the early seventies, a period of twenty years lapsed. Then we establish that her name is Mary. Mark and Paul obviously did not know of Joseph. (Noticeably, Paul didn't know of Mary either.) By the mideighties, Matthew and Luke both independently knew of Joseph, Mary, and the virgin birth. This is probable because their common source was "Q," which Mark did not have. John knew of Joseph and Mary but not of the virgin birth (John 1:45; 6:42).

We have now developed a time frame between 70 and 85 CE. Matthew and Luke agree on Joseph and the virgin birth plus the location of Bethlehem, but nothing else is in agreement. If Jesus was to be the predicted Messiah, according to tradition, He had to be born in the city of David and of his lineage. Both evangelists differ on how this came to be. Therefore, the initial concept of a virgin birth for Jesus must fit into the window around 80–85 when Matthew and Luke were writing their gospels.

Clearly, Matthew investigated the LXX to establish a scriptural basis, and he found it in Isaiah 7:14. The context of Isaiah obviously didn't matter to Matthew, but the word *virgin* as used in the LXX is *parthenos*, a Greek word for virgin, mattered a great deal. However, in the Hebrew Bible, the word used is *alamah*, meaning "a young maiden." The LXX has a few mistranslations, this being one of them. This suggests that Matthew's community had a popular inclination toward virgin birth, and Matthew provided it. Luke simply introduces Mary as a virgin and connects her with John the Baptist. In Luke's community, the virgin birth concept also was prominent, but an actual scriptural reference was not important.

I would guess it must have been expected or perhaps inevitable that Christianity, which was competing for converts with pagan religions, would have incorporated some of their mythological fundamentals. Christians, deeming it necessary to provide conclusive validation of their faith in the divine nature of Jesus, believed they needed to explain it in terms that were accepted in the culture as proof of divinity in history.

Some early fathers explained this. "We (Christians) are not the only persons who have recourse to miraculous narratives of this kind" (Origin, *Against Celsius* 1, 37). Origen goes on to tell of a number of Pagan Gods born of virgins, "Danae, Melanippe, Auge and Antiope. The stories about these Gods are ancient," says Origen, but unlike the story of Jesus's virgin birth, these are only fables.

> He (Jesus) was born of a virgin; accept this in common with what you believe of Perseus ... And when we say also that the Word, who is the first-birth of God, was produced without sexual union, and that He, Jesus Christ, our Teacher, was crucified and died, and rose again, and ascended into heaven, we propound

nothing different from what you believe regarding those whom you esteem sons of Jupiter. (Justin Martyr, *First Apology* 21 and 22)

When we say also those whom you esteem sons of whom you esteem sons, our Teacher, was crucified and died, and rose again, and ascended into heaven, we propound nothing different from what you those whom you esteem sons of Jupiter ... craftily feigned that Minerva was the daughter of Jupiter not by sexual union. (Justin Martyr, *First Apology* 64)

So what we see was a developing theology regarding the virgin birth that spread exponentially through the pagan world in the later part of the first century. Afterward it became a doctrine of the church. Of course, it is possible that this miracle could have taken place just as Matthew's gospel claims or perhaps just as Luke's gospel claims as only the details of events differ but not the virgin birth. Given Mark's gospel, some scholars suggest that Jesus was born conventionally and became the adoptive Son of God immediately after His Baptism by John the Baptist.

The best rationalization comes from a Jesuit professor who opined that Matthew and Luke believed it was important to show that the birth of Jesus had to be equal to or greater than the universal belief of the pagan gods being born in this fashion. That being true, the mother of Jesus then had to be completely pure. This purity overrode all of the negative concepts associated with natural sexual relationships and giving birth. Mary's purity, metaphorically speaking, is tantamount with the ideal concept of virginity.

WAS JESUS THE ONLY CHILD OF MARY?

At least at first glance, the Bible states no! It mentions in numerous places that Jesus had brothers and even a sister (sisters), but it is not explicit that they were children of Mary. Taking the Bible literally, one certainly would believe that Jesus was Mary's firstborn. (This is strictly meant as a legal term and does not imply that she had other children.) In a literal context, many would also believe that she was a virgin, was pregnant before she was married, and had several children later. It is obvious that careful readers would find these assertions somewhat troubling. This was evident in the writings of the early church fathers as well as for Luke and Matthew.

Matthew 1:18–19 tells us Mary was betrothed to Joseph, but before they were married, she became pregnant. Joseph decided to divorce her but wanted to spare her the shame. This accurately demonstrates that Jewish law at that time considered betrothal to be a legal contract that required a divorce to break the agreement. Rabbinical law declares that the betrothal is equivalent to an actual marriage and only to be dissolved by a formal divorce. The actual marriage was to be formalized after about a twelve-month period. The key word is *shame*. It is implied here that Joseph believed Mary had a relationship with another man—that is, until he was informed by an angel otherwise.

Luke 2:5 verifies the betrothal and pregnancy but omits the *shame*. Both evangelists refer to angelic encounters explaining God's plan for Mary with quite different details and circumstances. What this would suggest is neither evangelist personally had any real facts concerning Mary's gestation. Surely, they were not present when the angel spoke to her or to Joseph. However, it must have been common knowledge that Jesus was born out of wedlock because both evangelists speak of it. They certainly would have preferred not to mention it at all, but it was so well known that an explanation was deemed necessary. Particularly Matthew's community must have had some knowledge or had heard gossip associated with this form of *shame*.

In Jewish law, the child of an unmarried mother is not a *mamzer* (similar to an illegitimate child) and bears no stigma. Then in Matthew's context, *shame* had to be connected with an adulterous or incestuous union on the part of Mary. A Jewish biography of Jesus titled *Toledot Yeshu* records that Jesus was the son of Mary and Joseph ben Pantera. The alleged reference to Jesus originates from the interpretation of a single statement by Celsus, an anti-Christian Greek philosopher quoted by Origen (*Contra Celsum*). Origen declared that Celsus (about 170 CE) wrote, "When she (Mary) was pregnant she was turned out of doors by the carpenter to whom she had been betrothed, as having been guilty of adultery, and that she bore a child to a certain soldier named Panthera."

There are no historical facts to substantiate any of the previously outlined, but it is reasonable to assume that some rumors of this sort were in circulation at the time Matthew and Luke were writing their gospels. It does, however, demonstrate the concern of the early church fathers to favorably present the respectability of Mary. The church set out then to stress her morally pure and loving mother image. *Protevangelium of James* (about 120 CE) was written to clarify Matthew's gospel in order to assuage any concepts of impropriety. So profound was this idea to elevate Mary that the church assigned her the title of Theotokos (the mother of God) at the third Ecumenical Council in Ephesus (431 CE).

The next challenge was formulating an understandable policy regarding the virgin birth. This obviously required keeping the miracle story. This was not a problem for most new Christians because many pagan gods were born of virgins. What made this difficult was keeping Mary pure and virginal in view of the several biblical references to siblings of Jesus. It is important to note that both Orthodox and Catholics accept the dogma of Mary being a virgin. The reasoning behind this is quite understandable, but these biblical passages seemed to contradict it.

Nearly every early father accepted the belief that Joseph was married before and that his wife had died. He then married Mary, the mother of Jesus. Prior to this, he had several children with his first wife. This then became the Orthodox position. Although most early fathers are fuzzy on this subject, no one challenged it until about 390 CE. That's when Jerome did (347–420 CE). He believed the biblically referenced siblings were actually first cousins, which then became the Catholic position. The Protestant reformers took a literal position and the most obvious and logical view that Mary had several children with Joseph after the birth of Jesus.

I stated that this was the most logical because that would certainly be the position most people would take from the readings in the Bible. However, when one does an in-depth study of the times and circumstances, the person will appreciate the facts of all three positions. In regards to the Catholic position that the brothers and sisters were in fact cousins, we know that in Hebrew there is no word for cousin. As a result, some would often refer to cousins as brothers or sisters. The problem with this is that the New Testament was originally written in Greek, and in Greek, there are separate words for brother, sister, and cousin. The best and most scholarly book on this subject is *Jude and the Relatives of Jesus in the Early Church* by Richard Bauckham.

No one would doubt that Jesus had many relatives, but were any of these blood brothers and sisters mothered by Mary? The only correct answer is that we honestly don't know with any certainty. Therefore, the only positive is that the Bible is not explicit enough on this subject for twenty-first-century readers. To offer all the pros and cons would simply be too meticulous and in all probability would still leave many unsatisfied.

THE CRUCIFIXION OF JESUS

In my youth, Good Friday services always saw the priest dramatically preaching that the Jews had killed Jesus, citing Matthew 27:25. That was more than seventy years ago, and although historians have at least offered evidence mitigating Jewish responsibility, today many Christians still hold them culpable. The facts dictate that the Romans killed Jesus on the grounds of sedition, conspiring to overthrow their regime. The actual Jewish involvement was demanded by their oppressors to justify the capture and killing of Jesus to the Jewish people.

I will not explore the political aspects here but only the implementation of the crucifixion. By attempting to understand the crucifixion of Jesus more fully, we must look into the history of this form of punishment—the reasons, the economics, and the logistics. It is believed crucifixion originated in Persia and was adopted by Alexander the Great and his generals. We are told he crucified two thousand survivors of the Tyre siege. We also know the Romans adopted this as well. Spartacus along with about six thousand of his followers were crucified along the famed Appian Way in 71 BCE. Later Alexander Jannaeus (about 88 BCE), the Jewish ruler (king and high priest of the independent state of Israel), had eight hundred Pharisees crucified according to Josephus (*Antiquities* 13).

Despite the numerous crucifixions spoken of from antiquity, we have very few details concerning the construction of the cross (e.g., when and why were some nailed while others were tied with ropes or a combination of both methods). Archaeology has not provided much information either. In fact, the only physical evidence we have is from a 1968 accidental find discovered while excavating for a new construction project in Jerusalem. This was the actual skeletal remains of a crucified victim showing a single nail driven through both heel bones. The hands and wrists were not found with nails.

In most cases, whether Jewish, Roman, Greek, or Carthaginian, crucifixions (actual crucifixion as we know it today) were usually dictated for crimes of sedition, insurrection, or major acts against the government, although we know that sometimes certain heinous crimes were also dealt with in this fashion. Robbery was included, but this punishment was usually only applied to slaves; however, some were crucified for other reasons.

Geographically, Judea had very little wood or iron. Most lumber products had to be imported. Therefore, the cost of materials for crucifixions was high. The use of iron or bronze nails could have been dictated by supply and cost. We know these nails were almost always reclaimed. Some were reused to make healing amulets. The wood, of course, was reused over and over. Josephus noted the scarcity of wood was so bad that Romans had to travel more than ten miles to find lumber for the construction of siege machinery. He goes on to tell of how the Romans had to use other methods of execution after their supply of wood expired during the siege of Jerusalem.

Paucity of information relative to the construction of the cross has made for numerous and variable artistic renderings depicting the cross. We do know that at least three styles were used.

The first and least common was a single vertical shaft or stake. Next would be a column called the stipes with a crossbeam called the *patibulum* in Latin. It was in the shape of a "T" (also called *tau* from the Greek letter) and called *crux immissa*. The other was similar but in the shape of a plus symbol and called *crux commissa*, all Latin words.

Crucifixion was designed to be a dishonorable, slow, very painful method of torturing a victim to death. (Check the etymology of the word *excruciating*.) The sites were meant to be very visible and accessible to the public. Soldiers guarded it until all the victims were dead, even if the torture lasted more than three days. Spectators were welcomed but were kept at a safe distance in order to prevent any interference. Everywhere except in Judea, the victims almost always remained on the cross until the scavengers (birds and animals) picked the flesh off the bones. To prolong the agony, a seat or *sedile* was sometimes attached to the column, allowing the victims some support to help them continue breathing. A footrest or support (called a *suppendaneum*) also was sometimes used. This allowed the victims to rise up slightly with their legs to help with breathing.

From 63 BCE to 66 CE, Jews were granted special rights from Rome to allow their religious practices to continue. Jewish law demanded a deceased person be buried before sundown, and Rome respected this custom even for victims of crucifixion. That is why the fourth gospel accurately speaks of breaking the legs of the other two victims next to Jesus to cause death before sundown. After the soldiers were assured the victims were dead, the bodies, if they were Jewish, were allowed to be taken down and buried.

In the case of Jesus, all the Gospels tell us He was forced to carry His own cross with the help of Simon of Cyrene. Many scholars believe Jesus (or any other victim) carried only the crossbeam or patibulum. The column would already be at the execution site. The column would have been about six to eight feet long with a four-foot cross. Second Chronicles 1:15 says sycamore was the most common tree in Israel. Sycamore weighs about forty-three pounds per cubic foot, meaning that the cross would weigh about 280 pounds. The patibulum by itself would be about 125 pounds. Much Roman evidence suggests the crossbeam only was carried. This would not conflict with the gospel stories, just how we have come to understand them.

Most likely the top foot or so of the column (about six to ten inches thick) was reduced (to about four inches) in thickness to accommodate the patibulum. The patibulum then was mortised out at the center point to permit it to slip over the column. At this point the *titulus* (the writing that stipulated the crime of the victim) would have been attached with light rope or strings (not expensive nails). At Golgotha, the rock mass would have had holes hewn that were about one foot to eighteen inches deep and about a foot in diameter to accommodate the stipes. The column or stipes complete with victim would have been lifted up to allow the base to easily fall into the hole. Soldiers would then drive wedges between the column and the edge of the hole to stabilize it. Remember the average height of a first-century man was about five-foot-three. Therefore, the total extension of the stipes or column above the ground was rarely more than six feet.

Another contention coming from scholars concerns the nails driven through the hands. They point out the inability of the hands to support the weight of the body without tearing through and suggest that the nails would have had to have been driven through the wrists. However, Jesus as well as other victims were likely tied with a rope looped over and around the chest and passing under the armpits and over the stipes or column above the patibulum. Or the Romans tied their victims' arms next to or very near the chest, thereby placing little if any stress on the hands. Death, as many believe, then would be caused by exposure or asphyxiation. However, in its April 1989 issue, *Bible Review* had Columbia University medical professor of pathology opine the logical cause of death was from shock and trauma because of a combination of exhaustion, massive pain, and loss of blood. Again, the biblical story does not appear to be in conflict with science.

Let us briefly review the most likely scenario of the crucifixion of Jesus. He was badly beaten and weak from a lack of sleep and food and a loss of blood. He was forced to carry the heavy crossbeam for a long distance, most likely with help. Under this extreme weight, He would have been barely able to walk, and the Roman soldiers used a witness or passerby to carry it the rest of the way. Although there is no supporting evidence outside of the New Testament for this occurrence, it is most logical and very plausible. Keep in mind that crucifixions were intended to cause long-term agony and slow death. Generally, all victims were scourged and crucified completely naked. However, Jesus and others (in Judea only), most likely wore a loincloth to conform to Jewish laws.

Although the Gospels four passion stories differ in several areas about the details of the crucifixion of Jesus, they do give at least a very reasonable and quite accurate description of the events. The trials and events before the crucifixion present a more controversial issue.

THE WORDS OF JESUS

How is a parable defined? C. H. Dodd states it is a "metaphor or simile drawn from nature or common life, arresting the hearer by its strangeness, and leaving the mind in sufficient doubt about its precise application to tease it into active thought." *The parables attributed to Jesus are believed to be the most authentic recordings of His actual words.* Obviously, several scholars challenge this assertion, but some evidence does fall into acceptable historical standards to support this claim. Consider the following standards: (1) the principle of multiple attestations, (2) the criterion of dissimilarity, and (3) the criterion of coherence.

It is not our purpose to prove or disprove this claim but only to show some historical links between the parables recorded in the New Testament within the context of their religio-political climate of that time frame.

The use of parables is not unique to the New Testament, as it was a teaching method used in Judaism particularly during the two-hundred-year period just before the time of Jesus, sometimes called the "intertestamental period." The parables Jesus taught are found almost exclusively in the synoptic Gospels, but several are also found in the gospel of Thomas. The fourth gospel uses examples that arguably do not fit the standards for true parables. The *Catholic Encyclopedia* states, "There are no parables in St. John's Gospel."

My first example appears in Mark 11:12–14, 19–26. He uses a parable about Jesus cursing a fig tree by use of a sandwich form. Jesus comes upon a fig tree, looking for something to eat because He is hungry. It has no fruit, so Jesus curses the tree, saying, "May no one ever eat fruit from you." Jesus and His disciples continue on, and then Mark tells the story of Jesus cleansing the temple. When Mark returns to the story of the fig tree, Jesus and His disciples discover the fig tree that Jesus cursed has withered and died. Matthew 21:18 tells the same story but gives a shorter version. Matthew places the story immediately following the cleansing of the temple. He says that once Jesus curses the fig tree, it immediately withers.

Mark also informs us that Jesus knew this was not the season for fig trees to bear fruit! First of all, why would Jesus curse a tree, especially when He knew it was not in season? This would suggest that the fig tree is a metaphor, but of what? Some propose it could represent the Roman Empire or the town of Jerusalem and perhaps even Judaism of that day.

Because the earliest writer, Mark, did not have a strong anti-Jewish penchant as Matthew did, I believe it is not referring to Judaism. Jesus did want Judea free from Roman domination, although all the Gospels try to disguise this fact. Hence, the idea that Jesus was actually cursing the Roman presence in Judea to wither and die would certainly seem reasonable. By the time

Matthew, a Jewish Christian, wrote about this event, he would have been more likely to think Jesus was referring to the Jewish faith, as it was being espoused by late-first-century rabbis. Matthew's anti-Jewish hostilities stem from the time the rabbis were expelling Jewish Christians from their synagogues. The authenticity and interpretation of the story of Jesus's cursing of the fig tree is a common point of argument among scholars, and there is no universal consensus.

In my opinion, parables were a tool Jesus, indeed, used to drive home His message, but few if any are factually recorded. All the evangelists placed words into the mouth of Jesus to drive home their concerns about the time when they were writing their gospels. Some Samaritans were interested in joining the earliest Jewish Christian movement. Samaritans were not acceptable to Jews, and at this time the Judean Jews were expunging Jewish Christians from their synagogues. Samaritans were then welcomed to join the Jesus movement, but some strict Jewish Christians did not want communion with Samaritans. Consequently, they had to show that it was Jesus who had declared them acceptable as the Gospels now record (John 4:1–26, 39–42; Acts 8:25; 9:31; 15:3; Luke 10:29–37).

Another feature is found in Matthew 24:3–42. Jesus explains why the parousia (the second coming) will be postponed longer than initially expected. Of course, when Matthew was writing, some Christians were leaving their congregations because of the earliest preaching that had assured Jesus would return within the lifetime of the apostles. Now reasons had to be generated to explain why this did not happen as preached in order to halt or slow these withdrawals. Even fundamentalist Christians have difficulties with verse 36, which says, "But of that day and hour no one knows, neither the angels of heaven, nor the Son, but the Father alone." This clearly implies subordination of the Son to the Father.

This superiority of the Father is indicative that the Trinity doctrine was only in its earliest stage of development at the time Matthew was writing. Nearly every parable (there could be more than sixty in the New Testament) addresses the various concerns of the early Christian communities. Certainly, many parables have wonderful didactic and timeless qualities, and of course, that could have been Jesus's intention.

How the Theology of the Trinity Was Determined

The Trinity is a major doctrine of Christian theology, yet it is astounding that the term does not appear at all in the New Testament. It is perhaps the most difficult segment of Christianity for most people to comprehend—Christians included. As such there are branches of Christianity that refuse to accept this doctrine (e.g., Mormons and Jehovah's Witnesses).

Muslims view the Christian doctrine of the Trinity as irrational, blasphemous, and a travesty of the true and simple doctrine of God's unity as Islam upholds it. Because of this, many claim the Christian faith is not monotheistic but really ditheistic, tritheistic, or simply polytheistic.

Here's a typical Jewish response to this question in combination with the divinity of Jesus. "For Jews, the belief that God would become human is the ultimate heresy! Jews do *not* believe in human sacrifice—an abomination! Jews do *not* believe in a place of eternal torment for nonbelievers. Jews do *not* believe a blood sacrifice is required for atonement of sin. Jews do *not* believe in an evil god (devil) with powers equal to God. It is preposterous to suggest that God is made up of multiple personalities." Biblically, it is emphatically stated that the "Lord is our God, the Lord alone" (Deuteronomy 6:4).

Of course, Christianity is one of the three great monotheist faiths that encompass the majority of religions on this planet. In Christian terms, there is only one God that consists of three inseparable persons. We will not discuss the theology of the Trinity, but I will offer only a brief history of what was discussed during its development and how it was applied.

The Trinity consists of God the Father, God the Son (Jesus), and God the Holy Ghost or Holy Spirit. They are often symbolized as the three points of an equilateral triangle. In the Hebrew Bible or Old Testament, the wording "Holy Spirit" occurs three times (in Psalm 51:11 and Isaiah 63:10–11). In each case they are referring to the *spirit* of God just as we would consider the following statement: "I'll be there in spirit, even though I cannot attend." This is clearly not intended to represent a separate personage of the one God. This is clarified in 1 Samuel 10:6, Zechariah 4:6, and Isaiah 40:13 and 63:14. We must also keep in mind that the Hebrew word translators use for spirit (*ruakh*) basically means "wind or breath," not the *spirit* as we tend to understand it.

It would be safe then to say that a triune God or its concept does not appear in the Hebrew Bible. Certainly, some apologists can offer vague allusions that may be wrestled from the text, but none carry any weight. Therefore, the Trinity doctrine is undoubtedly a hermeneutical development originating through Greek philosophy and extrapolated from the New Testament.

The developing early Christians soon gravitated toward the Hellenistic psyche to win over Gentile converts. Proselytizing techniques were designed to accommodate the Jesus revelations within Greek thought. Take a look at the methods Paul deployed as indicated in 1 Corinthians 9:19–23, which says,

> Though I am free and belong to no man, I make myself a slave to everyone, to win as many as possible. To the Jews I became like a Jew, to win the Jews. To those under the law I became like one under the law though I myself am not under the law, so as to win those under the law. To those not having the law I became like one not having the law free so as to win those not having the law. To the weak I became weak, to win the weak. I have become all things to all men so that by all possible means I might save some. I do all this for the sake of the gospel that I may share in its blessings.

Basically Paul is saying he will do whatever it takes to bring people to Christ.

Earliest New Testament inklings for a tripartite deity can be found in 2 Corinthians 13:13–14, which says,; "The grace of the Lord Jesus, the love of God, and the communion of the holy spirit be with the people of Corinth." However, the word *holy* before spirit is not present in the earliest manuscripts, indicating that it was a later addition and that it was added to foster support for the new doctrine. A more positive indicator is found in Matthew 28:19, which says, "Therefore go and make disciples of all nations, baptizing them in the name of the Father and of the Son and of the Holy Spirit." (Notice the use of capital letters here as opposed to the passage from 2 Corinthians.) Yet in Matthew 11:27, Matthew records a special connection between God the Father and Jesus the Son but falls short of claiming equality in Matthew 24:36, which says, "No one knows about that day or hour, not even the angels in heaven, nor the Son, but only the Father."

The fourth gospel strongly suggests a divine equality in John 10:30, which says "I and the Father are one." The gospel opens by stating that Jesus in the beginning is the Word and "was with God … was God" and ends by Thomas referring to Jesus as "my Lord and my God" (John 20:28). It is also clear that John ventures into a trinitarian venue by having the Father send the Holy Spirit as an advocate for His followers (John 14:15–26). Although one may argue that these statements can be interpreted another way without trinitarian meanings, it does appear that the authors/editors of John intended to show that Jesus was part of the Godhead. Jude 20 says, "But you, dear friends, build yourselves up in your most holy faith and pray in the Holy Spirit." And 1 Peter 3:2; "who have been chosen according to the foreknowledge of God the Father, through the sanctifying work of the Spirit, for obedience to Jesus Christ and sprinkling by his blood." First Peter 3:18 says, "For Christ died for sins once for all, the righteous for the unrighteous, to bring you to God. He was put to death in the body but made alive by the Spirit." These passages may allude to a third personage of the Godhead, but it could clearly mean that the "Spirit" was indicating only the essence or spirit of God the Father.

The previous was some of the scriptural foundation for the Trinity doctrine. Jesus had become such an iconic figure that His human dimension seemed to be inadequate for posterity. By the end of the first century, the "son of God" became the actual Son of God, and the Holy Spirit was now being considered as an entity in itself. Remember, many believed that everyone was a daughter or son of God. All that was needed was for theologians to work out the details to make Him divine.

Clement of Rome (95 CE) began the process by saying, "Our Lord Jesus Christ is the Sceptre of the majesty of God ... Have we not all one God and one Christ? Is there not one spirit of grace poured out upon us?" (1 Clement 16). Echoing Ephesians 4:6, Ignatius (110 CE) referenced in his Epistle to Polycarp 3 "the passion of my God" (see also the Epistle to the Romans 6). These earliest of church fathers had clearly recognized Jesus as the divine Son of God, but the Holy Spirit's entry had not as yet been firmly established. A little later (about 160 CE), Justin Martyr stated, "We reasonably worship Jesus, having learned that He is the Son of the true God Himself, and holding Him in the second place, and the prophetic Spirit in third" (First Apology 65). Obviously, he was thinking about the Trinity, but the Son and Holy Spirit were subordinate. This caused a problem within monotheism. The fear was that Jesus or the Holy Spirit could be confused with angels. Justin was quick to dispel this in his Second Apology 56. Later the Nicene Creed would deliberately and specifically disassociate Jesus and the Holy Spirit from angels.

Tatian (about 175 CE) also spoke of this subordination, implying that Jesus was the only *begotten* Son of the Father and that the Holy Spirit was the outpouring of the Father (*Address to the Greeks*). In his *Plea for the Christians* 12, Athenagoras (about 185 CE) undoubtedly visualized a triad of some sort. "Christians desire this one thing alone, that they know God and His Logos, what is the oneness of the Son with the Father, what is the communion of the Father with the Son, what is the Spirit, what is the unity of these three, the Spirit, the Son, Father, and their distinction in unity." Athenagoras was getting closer to the doctrine but still shows a hierarchal order from the Father down to Holy Spirit.

Irenaeus (about190 CE) seems to be the first apologist to equate Jesus (the Logos) and the Father as always coeternal and equal in stature, meaning that both had no beginning. He avoided the term *begotten* and increased the focus on the third member of the Godhead. The Holy Spirit was considered the equal to the Father as represented in the wisdom of God as written in the Old Testament (*Against Heresies* 5:6:1). Yet each aspect of the Godhead was implicitly separate and sustained different duties. "The Father planning everything well and giving His commands, the Son carrying these into execution and performing the work of creating, and the Spirit nourishing and increasing what is created" (*Against Heresies* 4:38:3).

Tertullian (about 225 CE) invented the terminology for the Trinity as representing three persons in one substance (*Against Praxeas*). However, this keen legal mind still struggled to explain how three individual persons could be encapsulated in one body, even though he recognized that they were not corporeal but spiritual.

Origen (about 250 CE) may actually have been the first person to define the vocabulary for the doctrine that was later codified at Nicea, yet he, too, conceded to a subordinate position for the Son to the Father (*Against Celsus*). This formed the basis for what became known as the Arian Heresy in 318 CE (more on this later). The Arian Heresy created great turmoil within the newly legalized Christian communities. At this time Christianity was very diverse and lacked unity although Christians were in basic agreement it was mostly personalities that separated them. This was more prevalent in the East and in particular between Arius and Alexander (bishop of Alexandria). Prior to Arius, a heresy was somewhat prevalent (and rumors circulated about Alexander being an affiliate) and came to be called Sabellianism. This heresy was condemned in 262 CE, which denied the doctrine of three separate beings in the Trinity. This was also known as Monarchianism. The author, Sabellian, claimed the three persons of God are three segments of one personality similar to the way that the sun is simultaneously hot, round, and bright. Any heresy that held that the Father suffered equally with the Son's passion or any variation of such was labeled Sabellianism.

Other Trinitarian heresies, such as Macedonianism (named after Macedonius), did not accept the divinity of the Holy Spirit, claiming it was merely a servant on a level with angels. Modalist Monarchianism believed that God was a single being. To them, Father, Son, and Spirit were simply three statuses of the same God, and only one posture was possible at any given time. As a result, they claimed it would have been impossible for the Spirit to descend as a dove and God's voice to be heard during Christ's baptism.

Docetism was another early Christian heresy that claimed that Christ was not truly human. The word *Docetism* is derived from the Greek word *dokeo*, which means "to appear or seem." Proponents of this heresy taught that Christ only appeared or seemed to be human. We can see that before Nicea, issues concerning the Trinity were what caused most of the diversity in Christianity. Nearly all Christians then believed in God the Father. The exact relationship with Jesus was in question. Nicea was designed to settle this, and for all intents and purpose, it did. The next battle was to determine the relationship of the Holy Spirit. This issue was not so contentious, and the Council of Chalcedon (451 CE) settled the matter. Ultimately, the *filioque* clause would later be the grounds for the hostile split of Christendom into Catholic and Orthodox divisions in 1054 CE. (The filioque clause will be discussed further in chapter 11.)

What I have presented here is merely a cursory synopsis of the development of the Trinity doctrine, but I believe it is clear that this doctrine is at best just as vague today and as it has been throughout its development and general history.

CHAPTER 11

CONFUSION IN EARLY CHRISTIANITY

The first Christians were certainly all Jews. These Jews were all faithful to the Judaism of their day and differed from their (Jewish) counterparts only to the extent that they accepted Jesus as the Messiah. They believed that God had raised Jesus from the dead and had taken Him up to heaven. They expected He would soon return to earth with a heavenly army to cast off the Roman yoke and to give Israel leadership over all nations. Clearly, this was not the view of most Jews, but this new Jewish concept did not violate any principles of their religion. Therefore, these Christians, for all intents and purposes, were accepted and welcomed within the faith, even though the majority did not agree.

Soon many Gentiles became interested in this new branch of Judaism. Most of them attended the local synagogues and were considered God fearers. The social and religious atmosphere of the day perceived Judaism very favorably, especially in regard to the synagogue. God fearers were members but not full Jews until they became circumcised and accepted Jewish laws. Josephus states that the Jews in Antioch "were constantly attracting, to their religious ceremonies, multitudes of Greeks, and those they had in some measure incorporated with themselves." He also writes, "But no one need wonder that there was so much wealth in our temple, for all the Jews throughout the habitable world, and fearers of God, even those from Asia and Europe, had been contributing to it for a very long time." It cannot be overstated the vast appeal synagogues had to Gentiles throughout the Roman world.

To attend the synagogue, these Gentiles had to adhere to the Noahide Code. The descendants of Noah were commanded with seven rules "to establish laws and prohibitions of blasphemy, idolatry, adultery, bloodshed, theft, and eating the blood of a living animal" (Babylon Talmud, Sanhedrin 56a).

Just for emphasis, I'll relist them numerically here.

1. There's the positive order to set up courts that justly enforce social laws.
2. There's the prohibition of blasphemy (i.e., intolerance of worshipping the one God of the universe).
3. There's the prohibition of idolatry.
4. There's the prohibition of grave sexual immorality, such as incest and adultery.
5. There's the prohibition of murder.
6. There's the prohibition of theft.
7. There's the prohibition of eating any limb of a live animal, which is a paradigm for cruelty.

Taking this a step further, Talmudic tradition says that Gentiles who accept and obey the laws of the Noahide covenant are to be accepted by Jews, who then are obligated to protect and sustain them. We see by this that Judaism was not restrictive of non-Jews and allowed them to be members of their synagogues subject only to the previously outlined code.

At the Jerusalem conference, Barnabas and Paul represented the rapidly growing Christian Antiochene community, whose members desired to establish standards for this new branch of Judaism that was now called Christian with the leadership of the mother (Jewish Christian) church (Acts 15; Gal 2). The question primarily revolved around circumcision for non-Jews. This was brought about when certain individuals came down from Judea and taught the brothers, "Unless you are circumcised according to the custom of Moses, you cannot be saved" (Acts 15:1). Paul states that the council was necessary because spies sent by those who were reputed to be important, meaning Peter, James, and John, were trying to enslave them. Therefore, Barnabas and he traveled to Jerusalem to establish rules (Galatians 2:1–8). It is quite clear that Acts is trying to describe this as a conciliatory meeting while Paul's version is presented as sarcastically confrontational.

The results in both versions appear to have been successful for Paul. Gentiles did not have to undergo circumcision. However, do the biblical accountings tell the whole story, or is it merely a favorably abridged paraphrasing? Although Paul omits details of the decision James made in

Acts, it makes logical sense that this decision was intended to offer the same rules for inclusion, namely the Noahide Code that was presently being used by mainstream Judaism. But according to the New Testament report, were Gentile Christians now granted full membership, or were the same regulations in place as they were in the mainstream? After all, the ruling by James as recorded in the Bible was nothing more or less than what was already in place in Judaism for Gentile admission.

Obviously, a direct answer to these questions is missing in the Bible. Let us now examine the meeting in Antioch that followed soon after the Jerusalem Council. We have Paul's version described in Galatians 2: 11-14.

> And when Kephas came to Antioch, I opposed him to his face because he clearly was wrong. For, until some people came from James, he used to eat with the Gentiles; but when they came, he began to draw back and separated himself, because he was afraid of the circumcised. And the rest of the Jews (also) acted hypocritically along with him, with the result that even Barnabas was carried away by their hypocrisy. But when I saw that they were not on the right road in line with the truth of the gospel, I said to Kephas in front of all, "If you, though a Jew, are living like a Gentile and not like a Jew, how can you compel the Gentiles to live like Jews?"

Notice that when the people who were sent by James came upon the scene, the fellowship remarkably changed. Paul then confronted Peter's hypocritical conduct intrepidly. The confrontation caused even Barnabas to abandon Paul and the Gentile Christians. This would strongly suggest that the Jerusalem Council's decision did not grant everything Paul leads us to believe. Peter and Barnabas were certainly present at both meetings, and both heard the final decision as did the people sent by James. We only have Paul's side of the story, but it is clear that he lost the dispute as he was abandoned by the entire Jewish Christian entourage. We can only wonder what the Gentile Christian attendees must have thought. After all, Peter, James, and John had a direct personal relationship with Jesus during His lifetime and had been selected by Jesus to be His successors. Perhaps this would explain why Paul was very defensive about his apostleship and disdainful toward the other apostles as evidenced in many of his epistles.

Another event took place that lends support to my suppositions in the last paragraph. Paul's writing of this conflict ends unexpectedly with no clear account of its conclusion. If Paul had won the dispute, he surely would have mentioned it! This implies that he was unable to win any of his former collaborators back to his cause for his law-free gospel. As a result of this calamity, it appears that Paul immediately departed Antioch and embarked on a mission to Asia Minor and Greece. This is confirmed in Acts 15:36–41, which presents Paul as undertaking this second missionary journey without his former companion, Barnabas. Acts says nothing of Paul's clash with Peter and the people sent by James at Antioch. Luke explained the split between Barnabas and Paul as one caused by a dispute over the inclusion of John Mark on the missionary team. The finality of the split is most perceptible in the fact that from this point forward in Acts, Barnabas is completely negated from the story of Paul.

What reason would have caused Paul to cling so strongly to his gospel, and why did it appear that he wanted to continue his association with the mother church? Barnabas holds the key. It was Barnabas who championed Paul to the leadership for acceptance as a brother. He was clearly Paul's superior, and he had trained him. Starting with Acts 11:21–30, Barnabas was sent by James to supervise the tremendous influx of Gentiles in Antioch to the Jesus movement. Upon his arrival, he realized that help was needed and set off to Tarsus to recruit Saul to assist him. (Note at this time Paul was still known as Saul.) They were then made aware of a worldwide famine that was about to devastate Judea. After a one-year period, Barnabas and his assistant (Saul) gathered the major portion of their annual collections and went to make an offering to the mother church. This was then given at the Jerusalem Council.

What I am suggesting is the monetary contribution played an essential role in the very procurement of the Jerusalem Council and in receiving the hand of fellowship given by the apostolic pillars. Perhaps it helped to soften the harshness in the rules, or perhaps they may have granted a temporary relaxation with full enforcement to be applied later. Another point involves eating with Gentiles. There is never a problem with any Jew eating with a Gentile, provided an assurance that *kashrut* (Jewish dietary rules) has been established. The only exception, as in the Antioch case, would have been if the Gentiles had prepared the meal. "God fearers would have been well aware of this importance. This then would appear that the crux of the dispute lay somewhere else. The common table in Antioch, though advocated by Paul, was not necessarily initiated by him. Nor was it the focus of his apostolate. His primary concern was his gospel and the progress of the Gentile law-free mission with an emphasis on circumcision.

Let us just suppose that the apostolic pillars were greatly impressed with Barnabas's and Paul's abilities to generate money for their movement, even though they may have bent the rules. Obviously, they still possessed the continuing ability to produce income in the future, to say nothing of increasing membership and loyalty to the mother church. With this in mind, I think some oversight or temporary modifications could have taken place. However, some form of communication must have occurred spelling out specifics, sometime between the Jerusalem meeting and the Antioch disruption. (Note that James mentions sending his rulings in writing in Acts 15:19.) Why else would James have sent *spies* to the meeting? If the rules were actually being applied! Why else would Barnabas have deserted Paul? Was it because Paul interpreted the ruling differently, or did he just want it to be different and simply refused to accept it?

After the Antioch dispute, Paul departed for Europe without Barnabas. His adventures are written in Acts and in several of his epistles. Paul's collection of money is only briefly discussed in context with financial relief for the "Saints in Jerusalem," in view of the ominous impending return to Jerusalem to face James. (Read 2 Corinthians 8:16–24; 9:1–15; Romans 15:25–27). Approximately two years passed after Paul's departure from Antioch. Acts 21 details his return to Jerusalem to see James. Apparently, Paul came to Jerusalem to hand over the money that had been collected. Several churches had given him this money to aid the saints in Jerusalem. The primary reason Paul and his friends traveled to Jerusalem was to present this offering. Yet Acts makes no mention at all about how or when it was received. One would certainly think James would have welcomed the money. However, it is apparent that James and the entire Jerusalem congregation was at odds with Paul's methods because he is ordered to take four men to the temple and ceremoniously cleanse himself to show his compliance with the law.

This was to be Paul's undoing, as he is arrested. No charges are given, but the Roman military commander thought Paul had attempted seditious conduct; however, Paul then tells him that he is a Roman citizen. Paul was then allowed to speak to the people. Later Paul is taken to Caesarea and Governor Felix. Five days later the high priest comes down and also accuses Paul of sedition. Sedition was a high crime and carried the capital punishment of crucifixion. Felix must have found out that Paul had given a large amount of money to the church. He kept Paul prisoner for two years, hoping to receive a bribe from Paul's friends. Take note here that in Acts 21:27–28, the military commander was impressed with Paul's citizenship, noting the great expense he had to bear in order to obtain this. Does it not come as a major surprise that no one but Paul's nephew came to his aid? Of the thousands of Christians (Acts21:20), only one attempted to save Paul! James certainly had the resources to make the bribe, and within two years, he at least could have sent word that Paul was in dire need of help. Is it possible James wanted Paul out of the way?

Let us back up in time to before Paul's arrest in Jerusalem. Here are Paul's words in 2 Corinthians 11:24–26.

Are they servants of Christ? (I am out of my mind to talk like this.) I am more. I have worked much harder, been in prison more frequently, been flogged more severely, and been exposed to death again and again. Five times I received from the Jews the forty lashes minus one. Three times I was beaten with rods, once I was stoned, three times I was shipwrecked, I spent a night and a day in the open sea, I have been constantly on the move. I have been in danger from rivers, in danger from bandits, in danger from my own countrymen, in danger from Gentiles; in danger in the city, in danger in the country, in danger at sea; and in danger from false brothers.

Looking to Acts 21:4, 11–14, we see that all along Paul's journey to Jerusalem, he was warned about the disaster that was to befall him there. Paul surely knew he was headed for trouble well beforehand. I believe he knew he had converted many Gentiles to Christianity under his rules, which did not conform to those of the apostles. Paul hoped that this large contribution to James would trump or at the very least mitigate his grievances just as it did at the Jerusalem conference. As insurance for his safety, could he have used some of the contribution money to purchase Roman citizenship? Think about all the beatings, floggings, and imprisonments Paul endured. Without a doubt, any of the thirty-nine lashes he endured could have been prevented had he invoked his Roman citizenship! That is, of course, if he did indeed have it at the time. Obviously, he had it and used it to save his life in Jerusalem.

One last question hangs over this whole scenario. Why did Paul so adamantly resist conforming to the dictates of all the handpicked apostles of Jesus? The only logical answer would be that Paul knew he could win more Gentile converts if they didn't have to endure circumcision. Abrogating the dietary constraints also helped. Moreover, he knew how and where to go to find the money. The communities he evangelized were all wealthy. Because he had the credibility of being a new branch of Judaism, he had a much better chance of finding converts, especially the established God fearers. This was why he went to the synagogues first.

Paul only speaks of the human Jesus in terms of salvation. Paul's Jesus was important to the extent that believers would gain everlasting life merely through faith in Jesus. He knew very little if anything about the historical life of Jesus. That was why he focused on the Christ.

Problems with the Second Coming of Jesus

Protestant fundamentalists believe the Bible is error-free. Doubtlessly, they believe this is only true for the original writings. They also concede that some later copies may have sustained a few scribal errors or that some errors may be caused in translation. Therefore, it is reasonable to conclude that many of the alleged contradictions that occur in the Bible are these types of errors. We will not discuss scribal errors but will look into the dedicated scribes attempting to clarify the text and the development of doctrine.

Vince Lombardi, the late great coach of the Green Bay Packers, said in one of his most famous quotes, "Winning isn't the only thing. It's everything." The only problem is he never said this! Certainly, it could be a typical expression Lombardi might have made as it nicely fit his personality. Copyists or scribes of the Bible did the same thing. The New Testament has numerous passages concerning the second coming of Jesus that strongly suggest He was wrong, which may point to similar copyist glitches or scribal enhancements. What follows is a few of them.

"I tell you the truth, you will not finish going through the cities of Israel before the Son of Man comes" (Jesus to His twelve disciples in Matthew 10:23).

"I tell you the truth, some of you who are standing here will not taste death before they see the Son of Man coming in his kingdom" (Jesus to His disciples in Matthew 16:28).

"They will see the Son of Man coming on the clouds of the sky, with power and great glory … I tell you the truth, this generation will certainly not pass away until all these things have happened" (Jesus to his disciples on the Mount of Olives after prophesying the destruction of the temple in Matthew 24:30–34).

"You [Caiaphas] will see the Son of Man sitting at the right hand of the Mighty One and coming on the clouds of heaven" (Jesus to the high priest Caiaphas in Mark 14:62).

"If I want him [John, the beloved disciple] to remain alive until I return, what is that to you? You must follow me" (Jesus to Peter in John 21:22).

"These things happened to them [the Israelites] as examples and were written down as warnings for us, on whom the fulfillment of the ages has come" (the apostle Paul to the Corinthians in 1 Corinthians 10:11).

"You [Thessalonians] turned to God from idols to serve the living and true God, and to wait for his Son from heaven, whom he raised from the dead—Jesus, who rescues us from the coming wrath" (Paul to the Thessalonians in 1 Thessalonians 1:9–10).

"According to the Lord's own word, we tell you that we who are still alive, who are left till the coming of the Lord, will certainly not precede those who have fallen asleep" (Paul to the Thessalonians in 1 Thessalonians 4:15).

"God is just: He will pay back trouble to those who trouble you [Thessalonians] and give relief to you who are troubled, and to us as well. This will happen when the Lord Jesus is revealed from heaven in blazing fire with his powerful angels" (Paul to the Thessalonians in 2 Thessalonians 1:6–7).

"I charge you [Timothy] to keep this command without spot or blame until the appearing of our Lord Jesus Christ" (Paul to Timothy in 1 Timothy 6:13–14).

"In these last days he [God] has spoken to us by His Son" (Hebrews 1:2).

"For in just a very little while, 'He who is coming will come and will not delay'" (Hebrews 10:37).

"Be patient, then, brothers, until the Lord's coming" (James 5:7).

"You too, be patient and stand firm, because the Lord's coming is near. Don't grumble against each other, brothers, or you will be judged. The Judge is standing at the door" (James 5:8–9).

"Dear children, this is the last hour; and as you have heard that the antichrist is coming, even now many antichrists have come. This is how we know it is the last hour" (1 John 2:18).

"The revelation of Jesus Christ, which God gave him to show his servants what, must soon take place" (Revelation 1:1).

"Look, he is coming with the clouds, and every eye will see him, even those who pierced him; and all the peoples of the earth [or land] will mourn because of him. So shall it be! Amen" (Revelation 1:7).

"Behold, I am coming soon!" (Jesus in Revelation 22:7).

"Behold, I am coming soon!" (Jesus in Revelation 22:12).

"Yes, I am coming soon" (Jesus in Revelation 22:20).

The sheer number of references seems to tell us that the early Christians truly believed the return of Jesus with a heavenly army would (forcibly?) usher in a new kingdom of God and likely the end of the world. This event was to happen within their lifetime. Critical scholars simply believe Jesus made an error, but even the most conservative scholars struggle with apologies. C. S. Lewis called this "the most embarrassing verse in the Bible." However, he cited Matthew 24:36, which says, "But as for the day or hour, nobody knows it, neither the angels in heaven, nor the Son; no one but the Father," as the most accurate and precedent declaration. Of course, this renders all the other passages ambiguous time-wise. But certainly, everyone who had been living with Jesus believed that it would only be a short delay and that it would certainly occur within their lifetime just as Jesus had promised. They believed they would not experience physical death.

However, 2 Peter 1:16 and 3:8–10 offer the first apology concerning this delay. Second Peter is perhaps the only New Testament document written in the second century and was designed especially to explain the apparent prorogation.

A theory, albeit not a very popular one, is the New Testament writers misunderstood Jesus. Like the Lombardi quote, the words subscribed to Jesus were very loose paraphrases and not direct word-for-word quotes. This change can be explained by examining the theology of the early church regarding the deification of Jesus. It was determined that Jesus had two distinct but separate natures, a fully divine nature and a fully human nature, and that became the Orthodox doctrine. It was important that Jesus was fully human and that He actually suffered and died just as any other human would have. In other words, He surrendered His divinity while on this earth.

No one can argue that Jesus had an enormous impact on civilization. The rapid and continuous growth of Christianity proves that. But as is the case with most hero-type individuals, legendary stories quickly fill in the voids of information. This echoes back to Lombardi. The early Christian message was everlasting life and the return of Jesus. In this milieu the human Jesus was beginning to be understood as a person greater than just an ordinary human. We can see this development in the heresies that sprung up and the orthodoxy's response.

Another example of pious additions is found in the Nicene Creed. It is known as the filioque clause. The Western church or Roman Catholic Church firmly believed the words "And the Son" (filioque in its Latin form) needed to be included in the document, but they were not part of the original creed. It was added and approved in 589 CE at a council held in Toledo, Spain, which was attended by only the Western church. Here is the paragraph in question: "And I believe in the Holy Ghost the Lord, and Giver of Life, who proceeds from the Father (and the Son [filioque]); who with the Father and the Son together is worshipped and glorified." The original creed of 325 CE ended by saying, "And I believe in the Holy Ghost." In 381 CE at the second Ecumenical Council, the balance was added. The filioque is still not included in the Eastern church or Orthodox church's creed, and it is a major point of contention between Catholic and Orthodox churches to this day.

The council of Chalcedon in 451 BCE confirmed the Trinity doctrine and the two separate natures of Jesus. This then would lead one to believe the human Jesus did not know He was God while on this earth. It would also then seriously question His ability to actually perform paranormal phenomena. Walking on water and raising the dead, decomposing body of Lazarus would fall into that category.

Here we are faced with a dilemma. Christian doctrine stipulates Jesus was truly human and truly divine, but neither nature interfered with the other. Simply put, Jesus gave up His divinity while on earth. However, the Bible specifically tells us of numerous superhuman miracles carried out by Jesus. This offers three possibilities. First, the church doctrines are wrong. Second, the Bible is wrong. Third, later editors added or embellished these stories from the original document.

Are there other explanations that satisfy this ambivalence?

THE EPISTLE OF JUDE

It is quite evident that the name Jude was used instead of Judas. In most New Testament texts, because the early church fathers didn't want a brother of Jesus to share the same name or for people to confuse Him with the man who allegedly betrayed Him. Judas is the Greek word for the Hebrew word Judah. Yet most translations generally render him as Judas, not Iscariot. This would make Jude one of the original twelve apostles, leading most biblical novices to mistakenly believe Jude and Judas are different individuals.

Historically, the earliest reference to Jude is found in the Didache 2:7 (also known as the Teachings of the Twelve Apostles) because of its use of verse 22 in The Epistle of Jude. The Didache is a brief early Christian treatise that most scholars date to the early second century. Although wholly Christian in its subject matter, the Didache is remarkably in agreement with some verses in the Talmud. This offers confirmation that the authors of Jude and the Didache were living at an early period when Jewish influence was still important in structuring Christianity.

Actually, the epistle of Jude is really an insignificant writing that at first glance has little if any impact on Christian doctrines or on the New Testament. Its concerns are similar to several other New Testament books, and it provides no new insights whatsoever. However, the fact that the Epistle of Jude made a direct quote from a non-canonical book which is not accept as Scripture but gave it the same inspired status just as it appears in other canonical books is simply overwhelming.

Incidentally, the book of Enoch and the Didache are canonical books included only in the Bible of the Ethiopian Orthodox church. Rabbi Simeon ben Jochai in the second century CE pronounced a curse upon those who believed in Enoch because of its false teachings about angels. Eleven fragments in Aramaic and three in Hebrew were recovered with the Dead Sea Scrolls discovery, proving its importance to the Jewish community as well as to the primitive Christian community.

The author of Jude quoting the pseudepigrapha as authoritative scripture in the same breath as he does with canonical books strongly suggests that the Jewish Bible at the time of writing did not as yet have a closed canon. The clear fact that Jude is informing his Christian readers to bear in mind some past history recorded in 1 Enoch is very significant. He certainly assumes that all Christians were familiar with 1 Enoch and accepted it to be historically accurate. Because the authors of 2 Peter as well as several other New Testament books implicitly quote from 1 Enoch, we can rest assured that Jude's use of it was not an isolated case among first-century Jews or Christians.

Early church fathers, such as Tertullian, Tatian, Clement of Alexandria, and Justin Martyr, considered 1 Enoch scripturally authentic. The messianic and redemption themes of the book were openly accepted as proof of Jewish prophecies of Christ. It was only in the fourth century that 1 Enoch fell into great disfavor and was banned by the Council of Laodicea.

For the sake of history, the importance of Jude is surely transcended by his use of the book of 1 Enoch. Clearly, this Jewish book strongly influenced pre- and post-Christian thinking in such a way that it permeated into much of the New Testament; however, its impact really didn't become apparent until modern times. It is the foundation for the belief that Satan (actually called Semiaza) is a fallen angel who rebelled against God while good angels, such as Michael, were victorious in the war in heaven, resulting in Satan and his followers being cast into hell.

The majority of Christians today believe the war in heaven was predicated by the jealousy of Satan and his allied group of angels to rebel against God. Summarily, they were defeated and cast into hell. They are the fallen angels who are associated with demons, and Satan is the devil. Many Christians believe these ideas are in the Bible. Although Revelation alludes to a future war in heaven, you cannot find another mention anywhere in scripture (except in 2 Peter, which also quotes from Enoch).

John Milton, a seventeenth-century English author, wrote a classic epic called *Paradise Lost*. His inspiration for this was the book of Enoch. *Paradise Lost* became immensely popular, and many of its themes came to be thought of as sacred scripture. This is true even of the present day, although few people have even heard of Milton or Enoch.

Enoch and Milton wrote of a messiah who was begotten before the creation of the earth and was labeled as the "Son of Man." This being had divine qualities, and he would become the final judge of humankind while sitting gloriously on a throne next to God (1 Enoch 46:1–4; 48:2–7; 69:26–29). Thus, there is little doubt that Enoch had a strong influence in formulating several New Testament doctrines, especially about the Messiah, the Son of Man, the messianic kingdom, demonology, the resurrection, and eschatology.

THE EARLIEST CANONICAL GOSPEL—MARK

Most Bible scholars support the two-source hypothesis (2SH) that prioritizes the gospel of Mark. Some believe that at least one of the authors of the fourth gospel also used Mark. Although this is the majority opinion, there are several others that would disagree. I actually agree with 2SH, and it will be the foundation for my thesis in this segment.

A claim or even a suggestion of the author in Mark is nonexistent in the text. Yet a Christian tradition for Mark has been steadfast from the earliest of time. This tradition has Mark using the preaching of Peter to compile this gospel (1 Peter 5:13). Upon the death of Peter in Rome, Mark moved to Alexandria and finalized his gospel there and became the first patriarch of that city. These implicit facts are not provable, but there is some circumstantial evidence that provides for these reasonable assumptions.

Attempting to understand this gospel, we need to determine what Mark was trying to achieve. He was writing to convey the message about Jesus, intending to circulate this work throughout his community and perhaps other communities that shared a similar faith. The people would then orally communicate the message by reading it to the members of the community. The original then would be saved and copies made for other communities.

The Roman Empire of the sixties and early seventies was a tumultuous period for Christians. In Rome, caused by Nero's intense persecution, the killings of Peter and Paul forced Christians to worship underground. James, the leader of the Christian community in Jerusalem, was killed in 62 CE. The Jewish revolt in Palestine (66 CE) caused large numbers of Jews and Christians to perish by the sword while refugees fled primarily to Egypt.

Jewish Christians were being ostracized from mainstream Judaism, and the Romans were beginning to see Christians no longer as a branch of Judaism but as a new and illegal religion that did not permit any of the privileges that were afforded Judaism. Wherever they were, it seems likely that Christians were undergoing suffering and hardships because of their faith. This is a consistent theme throughout Mark's gospel, which is designed to remind his readers to associate the sufferings of Jesus with those that they were now enduring in order to gain a better understanding of the reason why they were suffering. I think there is little doubt that the majority of Mark's followers were among the lower social classes. So it becomes abundantly clear Mark's idioms are quite plebeian as he habitually has Jesus attacking the rich while lauding the poor.

Because of his inadequate knowledge of Palestinian geography and confusion regarding the Hebrew Bible, scholars have deduced Mark was a Jew of the Diaspora who had spent little or no time there. This becomes rather evident when we compare Mark with Matthew, who tries to correct Mark's geographical errors. Like all the New Testament writers, Mark quotes scripture using the Septuagint (LXX) exclusively. Although his first language is Greek, he does have a fair understanding of Aramaic, but his intended audience obviously did not.

Dating the completion of this gospel can be inferred and interpreted by comparing what we know of the early Christian communities in general with the actual text. This research is not a precise science, and as a result, there is no general consensus on dating or where Mark's intended audience was located. There are, however, several clues found both in the text and in references to this gospel found in other texts.

By his obvious reference to the destruction of the Jerusalem temple, which actually occurred in 70 CE (Mark 13:2), most scholars believe that Mark was written some time during the war between Rome and the Jews (66–74 CE). The earliest date falls around 65 CE with a late date around 75 CE. Another clear example is found in Mark 5:1–20 (more following this segment). Here we see Jesus crossing over to the eastern shore of the Sea of Galilee for no apparent reason. He casts out many demons that had taken possession of a wild man. Jesus recasts the demons into a herd of two thousand pigs, all of which then raced down a steep hill into the sea and drowned. The name of the demons was Legion.

The coincidences here are truly uncanny. There were two thousand members of the Roman legion known as Fretensis occupied Jerusalem from 70 to 74 CE. All their banners carried the picture of their mascot, a wild boar or pig. The eastern side of the sea was considered Gentile territory. Therefore, Mark was clearly using this allegory to ward off any Roman reprisals. Yet his intended clientele most certainly understood.

The results seem quite clear. Mark completed his gospel between 70 and 74 CE. His intended audience certainly was not in Palestine or that general area because when Mark wrote Aramaic phrases, he immediately translated them into Greek. People from that area would not have required this extra step. Thus, he had to be writing for people whose first language was Greek.

STRANGE VERSES IN THE GOSPEL OF MARK

To understand this portion of the gospel of Mark, I ask that you to try to dissociate the spiritual portion for now and focus in on only the political events that were unfolding at the time Mark was writing his gospel just as if you were reading a historical novel. Try to understand the Jewish people living under the yoke of mighty Rome. Keep in mind the achievement of the Maccabees, who led a successful revolt for independence that lasted until the coming of Rome (166–63 BCE). This victorious event clearly had to be prevalent in the minds of the people who lived in the time of Jesus and certainly in the mind of Jesus as well.

I'm attempting to overlay the historical events that were dominating the news throughout the Roman Empire at the time the evangelist Mark was writing his gospel. Jerusalem had just fallen and had been totally destroyed. Outside of Judea, Jews were despised and condemned for revolting against Rome. Christians who were then part of Judaism found themselves caught between hatred from Rome and growing antagonism from mainstream Jews.

Mark was a Diaspora Jew or a convert to Judaism who joined the Jesus movement while living in Rome. Tradition has it that he was a disciple of Peter. When Peter died, Mark started to write the story of Jesus, and he completed it in Alexandria, where he became a major participant in the Christian community. He arrived at about 71 CE, and details of the destruction of Jerusalem were now rampantly circulating. The siege of Masada was just underway. The Roman (tenth) legion was now occupying Jerusalem.

The Christian community in Alexandria was under stress caused by the large influx of Jewish refugees and other deviant Christians living in the city. Gnostic theology was flourishing, and the immigrating Christians who were pouring in had customs and rituals that differed even though their basic philosophy was very similar.

Keeping within this framework, what follows is my hypothesis and exegesis on Mark 5:1–20. Mark, the earliest gospel, reached its final form about 70–75 CE. The author was certainly a true Christian believer but clearly not an eyewitness. Although he did not think he was writing sacred or holy writ, he was honest in his historical reporting of Jesus. His gospel was fashioned within the acceptable parameters for writers of his day.

Please do not confuse this with the standards we have in place today.

In other words, Mark and/or his sources did not invent or construct events. However, he deliberately used metaphor and allegory to confuse Roman hegemony out of fear of retaliation. The absolute power of Roman authority must always be considered.

Here is my example:

> They came to the other side of the sea, into the country of the (Gadarenes) Gerasenes. When Jesus had come out of the boat, immediately there met him out of the tombs a man with an unclean spirit, who had his dwelling in the tombs. Nobody could bind him any more, not even with chains, because he had been often bound with fetters and chains, and the chains had been torn apart by him, and the fetters broken in pieces. Nobody had the strength to tame him. Always, night and day, in the tombs and in the mountains, he was crying out, and cutting himself with stones. When he saw Jesus from afar, he ran and bowed down to

him, and crying out with a loud voice, he said, "What have I to do with you, Jesus, you Son of the Most High God? I adjure you by God, don't torment me. For Jesus said to him, "Come out of the man, you unclean spirit!"

Jesus asked him, "What is your name?"

He said to him, "My name is Legion, for we are many." He begged him much that he would not send them away out of the country. Now there was on the mountainside a great herd of pigs feeding. All the demons begged Jesus, saying, "Send us into the pigs that we may enter into them."

At once Jesus gave them permission. The unclean spirits came out and entered into the pigs. The herd of about two thousand rushed down the steep bank into the sea, and they were drowned in the sea. Those who fed them fled, and told it in the city and in the country.

The people came to see what it was that had happened. They came to Jesus, and saw him who had been possessed by demons sitting, clothed, and in his right mind, even him who had the legion; and they were afraid. Those who saw it declared to them how it happened to him who was possessed by demons, and about the pigs. They began to beg Jesus to depart from their region.

As Jesus was entering into the boat, he who had been possessed by demons begged him that he might be with him. Jesus didn't allow him, but said to him, "Go to your house, to your friends, and tell them what great things the Lord has done for you, and how he had mercy on you."

He went his way, and began to proclaim in Decapolis how Jesus had done great things for him, and everyone marveled. (Mark 5:1–20)

Let us now examine the historical events preceding the fall of Jerusalem.

At about 65 CE, Judea was a hotbed of unrest, and rebellion was in the air. This was especially true in the area of Galilee. In Rome, the emperor Nero had dispatched several legions to Egypt with a plan to invade Ethiopia. When Nero heard rumors of rebellion brewing in Judea, he abandoned the Ethiopian expedition and sent some of his legions to Judea.

The tenth legion (Legio X, Fretensis) was a proud Roman legion that had performed admirably in the Parthian War of 56–58. This legion was famous for its excellent engineers and was thought to possess the best engines of war. Josephus claims their catapults were able to hurl a stone weighing approximately 55 pounds a distance of 1,650 feet.

In the final destruction of Jerusalem (September 70), the tenth legion's war machines battered and pulverized the ramparts of the city. General Titus then placed the shattered city under the occupation of this legion. Strikingly conspicuous was the emblem of their mascot emblazoned on their banners, which was that of a wild boar! The garrison left occupying the city numbered two thousand. The balance went on to capture Masada. (A normal legion was about six thousand.)

On November 10, 66, Jewish rebels surprised the Roman camp in Gabaon and killed more than five hundred people. Rome, led by Cestius Gallus, regrouped and quickly attacked Jerusalem. According to Josephus, the siege ended mysteriously after five days. The Romans retreated back through the Beth-Horon Pass, where they were ambushed and slaughtered. The Jews instinctively sensed their victories were divinely ordained. Euphoria spread throughout the land. For the most part, this main Roman force was made up from Legio XII Fulminata, not the tenth, as it was often confused with. Later both legions combined to ravage Jerusalem.

However, in Mark, there can be no doubt that the devils named Legion and the pigs (swine/wild boar) clearly signify Rome and the tenth legion. This legion exclusively occupied Jerusalem after the fall.

But why would Jesus cross the Sea of Galilee into Greek Gentile territory? What reason could he possibly have had? Perhaps the reason Jesus crossed over to Gentile territory was a metaphor prophesying the second coming of Jesus, the inclusion of Gentiles in the kingdom of God, and casting the hated Roman tenth legion, which was presently occupying Jerusalem, into the sea.

Verses 1 through 6 suggest Rome is a wild, untamed empire causing havoc that no nations were able to contain. Casting off the fetters and chains signifies casting off Roman power and the relationship of nations that tried and failed to restrain Roman imperialism. Cutting himself with stones symbolizes the many Roman battles, their engineers, and their slaves who suffered laboring in the mines or quarries for Rome's construction and military supplies. After many abandoned the stone mines in Judea, some actually referred to the areas as tombs, and they were used as such too.

Crossing to the east shore of the Sea of Galilee meant you were in Gentile territory, an area where it was unlikely Jesus would have gone. He did nothing there but cast out these devils called Legion (swine/wild boar). This story only makes sense if we view this story metaphorically.

Mark and Luke also apparently made a geographical error when they called it the country of the Gerasenses. Gersa is more than thirty miles to the southeast of the Sea of Galilee. Matthew's version (8:28) tries to correct this error by calling it the country of the Gadararenes, but this also is simply too far away. Many later biblical copyists also recognized this and did attempt to change this geographical boggle. (Just look at the footnotes in most Bibles.) Therefore, either Mark or his source was erroneous, or the term represented something known only to the audience intended to receive this writing. I subscribe to the later. Perhaps Gerasenses signified Gentile civilization in general. This would symbolize the people, not their military, those affected by the war and not the actual combatants. *Surely, Mark's audience knew the real meaning.*

Considering verses 14 through 17, we may ask, "Why would the native people be afraid of Jesus and want Him to leave their country? Didn't He just heal the wild man and restore peace? Could Mark be disguising Jewish rebels, reflecting Jesus, alluding to their victory over the Roman legion XII at Beth-Horon and the locals fearing Roman reprisals if they (the entourage of Jesus) remained?"

It is quite obvious Mark knew of the occupation of Jerusalem by the tenth legion and the destruction of the temple. He sincerely believed Jesus was about to return with a heavenly army and would expel the Roman devils called Legion (Mark 13:28–33). It is also clear Mark was trying to convey his gospel without antagonizing Rome. They had an excellent spy and intelligence system. If they sensed any hostility toward their empire, they would come down hard on the whole community. Therefore, Mark used terms and words only his intended recipients would understand.

Like several other New Testament writers, Mark wrote encrypted messages mixed in with real historical facts about Jesus and their feared Roman enemies. At the time Mark was writing Rome did not distinguish between Jewish and Christian thinking. They were one in the same. Mark's message was clear to all in his community. Today it is very difficult or even impossible to decipher all of the underlying meanings.

The beauty of the Bible is, of course, its religious value, but there's also its historical significance. The spiritual magnitude is intrinsic, but to understand it historically, we need to compare the events within the political atmosphere of its own time and how they relate to the story. That is what I've attempted to do here.

COMPARING THE GOSPEL OF MARK TO THAT OF JOHN

Most scholars believe Mark was the first gospel written (about 68–71 CE) and that John was the last (about 95 CE) of the canonical gospels. Of course, there are those who would subscribe to an earlier dating, but generally speaking, many agree that Mark predates John. There are several pieces of evidence that may indicate the fourth gospel could have been written by an eyewitness or at least by someone who was very familiar with the time, geography, and circumstances relative to this period. Mark traditionally is believed to have obtained his information from Peter but was personally not an eyewitness. This claim originated with Papias, bishop of Hierapolis, (about 130 CE), who wrote in the *Exposition of the Oracles of the Lord*, where he claimed that Mark was Peter's interpreter.

It is commonly understood that both gospels tell the same story albeit with several variations but comparable in the important details. In other words, details may vary, but they don't strictly contradict each other. It would seem Mark compresses the ministry of Jesus into a one-year span, whereas in John, it takes three years. It appears Mark symbolically organizes his story to fit into the Jewish calendar of one year, thus making John's chronology appear the more likely. Of course, this detail has little if any effect on the principle of the story from a theological point of view.

There is a serious problem, however, for both scholars and theologians, and it is known as the "Messianic Secret." This occurs in Mark, and it is in direct contrast to the fourth gospel. Briefly stated, it means Mark's Jesus seriously wanted to keep secret His messianic mission, whereas John shows Jesus proclaiming it quite openly.

The messianic proclamations in John are known as the "I Am" utterances, which are distinctive to this gospel. Let us look into a few. John 4:25–26 says, "The woman said, 'I know that the Messiah (called Christ) is coming. When he comes, he will explain everything to us.' Then Jesus declared, 'I who speak to you am he.'"

John 8:24–28 says,

> I told you that you would die in your sins; if you do not believe that I am the one I claim to be you will indeed die in your sins. "Who are you?" they asked. "Just what I have been claiming all along," Jesus replied. "I have much to say in judgment of you. But he who sent me is reliable, and what I have heard from him I tell the world." They did not understand that he was telling them about his Father. So Jesus said, "When you have lifted up the Son of Man, then you

will know that I am the one I claim to be and that I do nothing on my own but speak just what the Father has taught me."

John 8:58 says, "'I tell you the truth,' Jesus answered, 'before Abraham was born, I am!'" Then John 13:19 says, "I am telling you now before it happens, so that when it does happen you will believe that I am He."

Now let us see Mark's "Messianic Secret."

Mark 1:43–44 says, "Jesus sent him away at once with a strong warning: 'See that you don't tell this to anyone. But go, show yourself to the priest and offer the sacrifices that Moses commanded for your cleansing, as a testimony to them.'" Mark 3:10–12 says, "For he had healed many, so that those with diseases were pushing forward to touch him. Whenever the evil spirits saw him, they fell down before him and cried out, 'You are the Son of God.' But he gave them strict orders not to tell who he was." Mark 9:9 finally says, "As they were coming down the mountain, Jesus gave them orders not to tell anyone what they had seen until the Son of Man had risen from the dead."

So did Jesus want to keep His identity a secret as stated by Mark, or did He, according to John, patently announce that He was the Messiah? *Obviously, both gospels cannot be historically correct as written.*

Should we now throw out the New Testament because of this inconsistency? Of course not! Most likely, the final editor of John felt a need to emphasize that Jesus was the Christ while Mark's audience was of a much earlier period when the need for a messiah was of less importance to the people. In fact, Mark clearly defines the message of Jesus in parables and tells the apostles that they should follow His example. In Mark 4:11–12, he told them, "The secret of the kingdom of God has been given to you. But to those on the outside everything is said in parables so that they may be ever seeing but never perceiving, and ever hearing but never understanding; otherwise they might turn and be forgiven!" And he admonishes them in the next verse for their failure to understand. Then Jesus said to them, "Don't you understand this parable? How then will you understand any parable?" Herein is another major contrast. Mark emphasizes Jesus's instructions to teach in parables, yet John clearly does not.

We may want to believe that John's Jesus is the more accurate one because Mark is so inconsistent. John 14:60–62 says,

Then the high priest stood up before them and asked Jesus, "Are you not going to answer? What is this testimony that these men are bringing against you?"

But Jesus remained silent and gave no answer. Again the high priest asked him, "Are you the Christ the Son of the Blessed One?" "I am," said Jesus. "And you will see the Son of Man sitting at the right hand of the Mighty One and coming on the clouds of heaven."

Mark 5:18–20 also says, "As Jesus was getting into the boat, the man who had been demon-possessed begged to go with him. Jesus did not let him, but said, 'Go home to your family and tell them how much the Lord has done for you, and how he has had mercy on you.' So the man went away and began to tell in the Decapolis how much Jesus had done for him. And all the people were amazed."

This paradox has baffled theologians for centuries, and no predominant explanation has yet come forth. The Jesus in Mark's gospel clearly seems more believable than that of John because Mark reports events or circumstances that do not show Jesus in the most favorable light, thus making it more believable. Mark 3:20–21 says, "Then Jesus entered a house, and again a crowd gathered, so that he and his disciples were not even able to eat. When his family heard about this, they went to take charge of him, for they said, 'He is out of his mind.'" Verses 31–35 continue,

> Then Jesus' mother and brothers arrived. Standing outside, they sent someone in to call him. A crowd was sitting around him, and they told him, "Your mother and brothers are outside looking for you." "Who are my mother and my brothers?" he asked. Then he looked at those seated in a circle around him and said, "Here are my mother and my brothers! Whoever does God's will is my brother and sister and mother."

Mark has no problem narrating the baptism of Jesus by John the Baptist, while John fails to even mention it. Luke and Matthew downplay it because they felt uncomfortable with Jesus submitting to John and receiving baptism for the forgiveness of (His?) sins.

It is my belief that John's gospel was the earliest written (about 45 CE), at least in part by an early believer of Jesus. However, this gospel as we have it today contains strong evidence of at least three authors and later editors. Subsequently, I believe Mark's gospel was composed by a single author who began his writing in the late fifties or early sixties in Rome and completed it about 71 CE in Alexandria. His final rendering divided the gospel into two editions. One for initiated members of the faith and another abridged version for catechumens. The latter is the version we have today, and the former is known as "Secret Mark."

One of my reasons for accepting Secret Mark (for this fragmentary gospel is controversial) is that it is clear in canonical Mark that there are several obvious lacunas (missing sections) or deletions in the text. Secret Mark, as we have it, fills in a few of these voids. It has long been known that the ending, Mark 16:9–20, was added by a very late editor. The most reliable early manuscripts and other ancient witnesses do not have Mark 16:9–20. Mark 5:1–20 makes very little sense, but it is very likely a ploy by Mark to convey his message to his intended recipients without raising Roman concerns. I believe Secret Mark in its entirety would clarify both these queries.

> Mark's gospel is also the first one that really tells us the passion narrative in as much detail. And the way Mark tells the tells the story of the death of Jesus … is to see him as a lonely figure who goes to his death abandoned by all of his followers and supporters and even abandoned by his God. Jesus from the cross says … "My God, my God, why have you forsaken me"? The Jesus of Mark's gospel is a lonely figure, at times, waiting for the vindication of God. (Professor Helmut Koester of Harvard University)

> Jesus in the Gospel of John is difficult to reconstruct as an historical person, because his character in the gospel is in full voice giving very developed theological soliloquies about himself. It's not the sort of thing that if you try to put in a social context would appeal to a large number of followers. Because it's so much Christian proclamation and Christian imagery, and it's a very developed Christology. Jesus must have had some kind of popular following or else he wouldn't have ended up killed by Rome. If the historical Jesus was saying the sorts of things that John's Jesus said, he probably would have been fairly safe. It would have been very difficult for early first century Jews to have tracked what that Jesus was saying. (Professor Paula Fredriksen of Boston College)

Our focus here is to point out the gospel writers' variant pictures of Jesus the man and His ministry and to try to sort out just who Jesus really was. Their methods of reporting had to be seriously influenced by the reigning oppressive power, Rome. The spy and intelligence system of Rome was excellent. Therefore, any hint whatsoever of sedition, either real or implied, was dispatched with force and diligence. This could adversely affect entire communities. Writers especially would be suspect because they were considered to be the community's influential intelligentsia capable of organizing trouble for Rome. Therefore, our gospel writers planned their writings in such a way as to assuage the Romans but allow their message to be only understood by their community. The best example for this goes back to Mark 4:10–12. Jesus explains the *secret meanings* in His parables, but the disciples oppose what those others who actually heard the parables thought of His actual preaching, which He had designed so that the people (especially the Roman spies) would not understand.

Later when the church became integrated with the empire, the leadership saw no reason to explain (and they made every effort to expunge) any of the prior anti-Roman rhetoric simply because it would not have been in the best interests of unity or the church.

CHAPTER 12

THE HISTORICAL PROGRESS OF THE BIBLE AND CHRISTIANITY

Today's Bible is a collection of several individual books bound together under one cover, and it is considered sacred scripture by many people. The exact number of these individual books varies considerably depending on which are accepted by the various faiths. The degree of sacredness also varies.

As a matter of fact, every major religion that has progressed from antiquity has a sacred book that equates to the Judeo-Christian Bibles. Basically, the ancient written words achieved sacred stature by the claim they were the actual words of God. This idea originated out of an early charismatic inspiration in society that quickly appealed to the larger population. But which sacred book was the *true* one? Or are they all true? Obviously, they are all different, and one would surmise that only one could be considered as *true*.

Historically, the most ancient books date back more than three thousand years. Many have made claims to be the oldest with no verifiable proof to substantiate their claims. However, this only proves that the concept of having sacred writings was considered to be most important, and the idea took root in various parts of the world at about the same time.

Since the Renaissance, Western civilization was catapulted into leadership of the world, and its Christian religion undoubtedly helped. This was most surprising because Europe was so fragmented through numerous different languages and cultures that no one at that time could have foreseen this rise to the forefront. Christianity supplied the common unity, and competitive ingenuity did the rest.

The Western church (Roman Catholic) contributed by becoming the arbitrary authority. Certainly, the role of bishops, especially the pope, became a major political component. Initially, the clergy were—and in some cases still are—champions of people balancing the power of the ruling class. The church also took the position of teaching. It ostensibly restricted scientific advancement because every explanation of a natural event or observation had to fit with the agreed biblical understanding dictated by Rome. But in doing so, it actually vivified scientific inquiry by promoting explorations to advance the faith, which then lead to advancements in cartography and navigational instruments as well as other advances in the study of anatomy and optics.

The monastic orders discovered new methods in agriculture and animal husbandry. The monasteries had a monopoly on education until the evolution of the cathedral school and the university in the high Middle Ages. Monasticism played a vital role in the creation, preservation, and transmission of the culture. Often the only literate members of society were the monks. They made and transmitted written copies of the Bible and other ancient works from generation to generation. They organized some of the first libraries. Often they conducted scientific and other research to benefit the surrounding communities. They were expert farmers who were able to pass on the benefits of their expertise to peasants on the large manors.

Perhaps the most remarkable feature of the triumph of Christianity in Europe was that Christianity was the religion of the defeated Roman Empire and that it was progressively accepted by the victorious barbarians. Unlike the later stories of forced conversions, these barbarian conversions occurred by persuasion rather than by conquest. For the most part, this took place by converting the various leaders through the missionary zeal and royal fiat. Conversions did not usually include teaching the Bible, but they came almost exclusively via instructions based on doctrines of the early church.

The Edict of Diocletian (303 CE) demanded the destruction of all sacred books of Christianity. Of course, this caused the devout Christians to hide their sacred books, but many manuscripts were destroyed. Even after the Council of Nicea (325 CE), Bibles were very rare. It wasn't until the seventh or eighth centuries that monasteries produced copies of the Bible in any quantity. In Western Europe, nearly every Bible was a copy of the Latin Vulgate, although some were produced in the vernacular, but they were extremely uncommon. In the East, a good number were created in Slavonic, Coptic, and Syriac languages, and others were taken from the early Greek manuscripts.

As a result, only the clergy and wealthy had access to Bibles, and only those who were educated could read and understand Latin. Though the Bible was important, few people could read it. Common folks learned the lessons and stories as conveyed via paintings, stained-glass windows, and parish priests. As more people began to learn, reading the Bible became a primary resource. The problem was they had to translate Latin into their own languages.

Refusal by the Catholic Church to allow translations in native tongues was a factor in the creation of the Protestant Reformation. Soon thereafter, new translations appeared, and *Sola Scriptura* became the basis for all the new faiths.

What appeared to be a fragmentation of Christianity actually provided improvement for Europeans. With religious competition, science and intellectual pursuits had fewer restrictions, and advancements in every discipline took place. Certainly, this development benefited some more than others nationally and personally, but it was gradual though steady. Social problems arose, and new disorders sprouted; however, overall, Christian nations have enjoyed a lifestyle unsurpassed in history.

Therefore, although certainly not perfect, Christianity has proven to be a positive force for humanity. The positives vastly outweigh the negatives. Most of the inhumane actions recorded in history, as we want to understand it today, were indiscretions that the society of its day only looked upon as harsh, certainly not to the degree we view them today. Perhaps the most egregious actions perpetrated by Christians were/are their treatment of Jews. Yet even with the extreme cruelties and hardships they thrust upon the Jews, these people prevailed and contributed immensely to the improvements in lifestyle of Christians through their need in order to better their own membership.

Our social mores have changed from generation to generation. Our present era will certainly be judged on its merits and demerits in the future. The question is this: Will this present period of history receive positive or negative opinions from future generations?

Next we will look into how the New Testament was created.

THE NEW TESTAMENT

Almost every Christian faith accepts the twenty-seven books of the New Testament as they are today. Most people believe this has been the case since Jesus or at least from the first century onward. Some may believe the twenty-seven books were divinely ordained and that we do not need to question their origin. Who wrote the twenty-seven books, and when were they composed? Who determined that these twenty-seven and only these twenty-seven were to comprise the New Testament? The answers to these questions are not easily found and are hardly self-evident. One will find many celebrated scholars offering a wide range and various views, many of them carrying their own personal biases.

We will attempt to offer a very brief synopsis on what prompted the twenty-seven to come into existence and become accepted into a canon.

Twenty-seven was never a magic number. In fact, the early church fathers never thought of a New Testament until Tertullian (170 CE) wrote of developing two traditions, old and new. This concept was fostered by Tertullian after a heretic named Marcion (140 CE) collected ten Pauline epistles and the gospel of Luke and called this accumulation "Christian Scripture." Marcion also utterly rejected the Hebrew scriptures. Therefore, Marcion was the first person to organize a canon of the New Testament.

At this time many of the individual books of the twenty-seven along with several others were being preserved and read in various churches in their services. All these books were viewed as an important article of faith. No single church, as far as we know, had accumulated the exact twenty-seven. Sacred scripture was then, as we have previously discussed, considered by Christians to be the LXX with no New Testament.

Tertullian, Epiphanius, and others clearly state that Marcion drastically redacted the gospel of Luke. This "revised and edited" gospel did not include the birth of John the Baptist, the birth or childhood of Jesus, the temptation narrative (Luke 4:1–13), or the genealogy (Luke 3:23–38). Interestingly, Marcion (5:22), compares to Luke (8:23–24), specifically the story of the calming of the sea, and Marcion clearly does not consider or speak of this as a miracle. However, Marcion did not exclude several of the other miracle stories.

The question one would ask is this: Did Marcion just arbitrarily redact Luke's gospel? Certainly, Marcion must have had a strong and conscientious faith in God and Jesus. Tampering with what he believed was a sacred writing would have been tantamount to sacrilege. Certainly, the same thing should be said of any of the writers and editors of the New Testament as well.

This offers three possibilities. First, Marcion actually had an original or an early copy of a much shorter version of Luke's gospel. Second, he simply inserted or took out the parts of Luke as he saw fit. Or third, later editors simply added to or deleted parts of the original gospel. I think it would be fair to state that after Marcion, the Orthodox church united (at least to a degree) and began sorting out writings about Jesus as to establish a new testament of scripture of their own that would work in conjunction with the LXX.

It must be stated that every book of the New Testament has had at least some editing. A clear example of editing is found in 2 Corinthians. Textual criticism has shown this epistle is a composite of two, possibly three separate letters. Close scrutiny will bear this out. Does this combining invalidate the epistle? Of course not. It merely shows an editor conflating two or three letters into one single epistle. Again, given what we know today, this editing (or any other editing) did not theologically affect or alter the understanding of the texts.

The four gospels, Acts, and six Pauline epistles along with Hebrews were known before the end of the first century. Second Peter was the last or latest book to be spoken of. Origen first mentioned this book in the third century. Many scholars believe this was the only book that wasn't originally written in the first century.

Second Peter and Revelation were the most disputed books. Some of the early fathers also questioned James, Jude, and 2 and 3 John because they were not well known, but they had a few strong supporters coupled with the claim of apostolic origin. There is strong evidence to support the claim that all twenty-seven books were actually written before the close of the first century, except 2 Peter. However, several other books existed by the middle of the second century. At this time many believe they were also inspired and were composed with the twenty-seven.

Tatian, a student of Justin Martyr (150 CE), introduced the Diatessaron. This gospel was an amalgamation of the four others. By this time several other gospels, such as the gospel of Peter, were written, but most did not gain widespread popularity or acceptance. However, books like 1 and 2 Clement, Shepherd of Hermas, the epistle of Barnabas, and Acts of Paul were also considered inspired by several early fathers. First Clement 63:2 actually claims divine inspiration. Some rejected the epistle to the Hebrews. However, when the book was claimed to have been authored by Paul, it gained some acceptance.

In fact, by the middle of the fourth century, hundreds of Bible-like books existed. On this occasion, Pope Damasas commissioned Jerome to sort out and translate the collection of books into a biblical New Testament. For the most part, it was Jerome who decided on the twenty-seven, and he established the order of the books as they are arranged today in both Old and New Testaments. This is why the sequence of books of the Old Testament is different from the order in the Jewish Tanakh.

Of course, he did have to get approval of most of the fathers, and he ultimately did. This translation became known as the Vulgate and was recognized by three Western (not ecumenical) councils in 393, 397 and 419 CE. This became the first Bible (combination of New and Old Testaments) of Christianity, and it became the standard for more than a thousand years.

But all was not settled. The Eastern churches did not consider the canon closed. They had only given tacit approval to Jerome's Vulgate, especially since it was not in their vernacular. Proof of this can be seen in the canons of the various churches of the empire.

By the middle of the fifth century, the Syriac church still employed the Diatesseron, 3 Corinthians, Revelation, James, 1 and 2 Clement, Hermas, and eight books of "apostolic constitutions." At present several Eastern Orthodox churches consider Revelation to be inferior and of secondary status. It is never used in any church worship. Even today Orthodox Nestorians reject 2 Peter. In fact, only the LXX, their Old Testament, has been given *official* recognition by the Eastern Orthodox churches. This recognition has never been afforded to their New Testament.

Also in the West, Alfric, bishop of Canterbury (tenth century), claimed that the epistle to the Laodiceans was part of the canon. To be sure, from the sixth century onward, several Vulgate codices contained this epistle. Strangely, no pope ever decreed Jerome's Vulgate as the official Bible of the church. Catholics as well as the Orthodox believe tradition to be the equal of the Bible. This allowed for books like Laodiceans to be included and books like Hebrews to be excluded in numerous polluted copies of early Vulgate manuscripts.

About the same time Jerome was writing the Vulgate, the earliest existing manuscripts codices—Vaticanus, Sinaiticus (fourth century), and Alexandrinus (fifth century)—already had additional New Testament books incorporated into them. A hundred years later, Codex Claromontanus (sixth century) still had Barnabas, Hermas, Acts of Paul, Revelation of Peter, but no Philemon. At the Council of Florence (1443), the twenty-seven-book canon was solemnly confirmed. However, this council did not provide for the enforcement of this canon, which did finally occur at the Council of Trent (1546).

Just prior to Trent, Martin Luther spoke for a shorter canon for both testaments. Ultimately, he acquiesced and accepted all twenty-seven. John Calvin rejected the idea of a fixed canon of the Bible. He viewed Revelation as well as 2 and 3 John as being of secondary status. He wrote commentaries on all the New Testament books except Revelation and 2–3 John. Quakers (1652) included Laodiceans and battled to keep it included in their Bibles.

One can see the road to the final twenty-seven was not without numerous bumps, curves, and detours. Clearly, none of the twenty-seven book can prove its canonicity, and if we were to go by the fathers of the first and second centuries, we would have a good deal more than twenty-seven. Many have claimed the Festal Letter of Athanasius (367 CE) established the canon of twenty-seven books. Some believe the three Western councils (393, 397, and 419 CE) closed this canon. But the simple historical fact is that the canon of Jerome was not closed until Trent (1546) by the Roman Catholic Church and has never *officially* been closed by any Protestant church. This is what allows the Mormon church to maintain that the canon is still open and why they have several additional NT books they consider sacred scripture.

Soon after Marcion (144 CE) announced that he had assembled a New Testament of Christian scriptures, the Orthodox church felt compelled to consolidate one of their own. The list of books to be included agreed basically (though not identical) with that of Marcion but included all four gospels, whereas Marcion only used Luke. Of the twenty-seven books we now have in Bibles, most of them were agreed upon by nearly every church father. Only James, Jude, 2 and 3 John, 2 Peter, and Revelation were disputed. Revelation and 2 Peter were the most contentious.

It was common practice during the first and second centuries of the Common Era that some writers would assume the name of a respected and well-known person in their manuscripts. This was not considered wrong or plagiarism by any means. In fact, many looked upon it as an honorary gesture that would enhance the prestige of the assumed person. Most important was how the message and teachings of the master were conveyed, but the actual author didn't necessarily matter. However, by the third century, apostolic origin became the utmost requirement for inclusion in the New Testament.

In spite of all the controversies and indecisiveness of the early fathers, it is quite apparent the accepted twenty-seven were a good (though probably not perfect or perhaps complete) choice. But the fathers who effected the final determination made a wise and deliberate decision. Arguably even today, if the selection had to be determined, most Bible scholars would choose the same twenty-seven. This is the case in spite of all we presently know.

THE DISPUTED EPISTLE OF 2 PETER

Second Peter gained entrance when Jerome included it in the Vulgate. He believed it was dictated by Peter to Silvanus, and thus, that belief ensured its place in the Bible. But its path to get there was perhaps the most difficult of any book.

This book is known as one of the Catholic epistles (meaning universal, not the church of Rome). Second Peter is the twenty-second book of the New Testament. First Peter, also a Catholic epistle, along with any writing associated with the apostle Peter have been disputed, and most have been rejected. First Peter was accepted and had the least criticism, whereas the Apocalypse of Peter, the Gospel of Peter and Acts of Peter were clearly discarded. Although Justin Martyr included the gospel and the Muratorian Canon and accepted the Apocalypse of Peter in his respective lists, these books failed to gain universal inclusion and are not in any of today's Bibles.

Historically, the earliest reference to 2 Peter came from Origen in his third-century commentary on John, where he testifies there were many bishops who rejected it. Eusubius (fourth-century church historian) says, "of Peter, known as his first, and the early Fathers quoted freely … but the second Petrine epistle we have been taught to regard as uncanonical" (*History of the Church* 2.1).

Polycarp (150 CE), Justin Martyr (140 CE), Irenaeus (170 CE), Clement of Alexandria (200 CE), Ignatius (110 CE), Clement of Rome (95 CE), Diognetus (150 CE), and Tertullian (220 CE) never mention 2 Peter in any of their existing writings. This strongly suggests they did not know such an epistle existed. Yet surprisingly, Justin, Irenaeus, Clement of Alexandria, and Tertullian often speak of 1 Peter.

Early New Testament translations such as *The Old Syriac* (400 CE), *The Old Latin* (200 CE), *The Muratorian Canon* (170 CE), and *Codex Vaticanus* (420 CE) simply omit 2 Peter. Geisler and Nix (*A General Introduction to the Bible*) cite 36,289 quotations by all of the previously mentioned fathers from twenty-six books of the New Testament, yet not one comes from 2 Peter.

Protestant scholars from Calvin to the present have expressed their doubts on the authorship of 2 Peter. Today many modern Bible versions in their prologues or commentaries speak of the dubious authenticity by Peter the apostle. This uncertainty prevails through nearly every early father or any early Bible translations.

Why was this book so controversial?

Let us examine what scholarship has come up with. "The writer has assumed Peter's identity in order to reinforce the message of Jude, which to the extent he attempted to copy" (commentary from *The Authentic New Testament*). There are twenty-five verses in Jude, and no less than fifteen are copied, nearly verbatim, in 2 Peter. So it appears 2 Peter is merely an expansion and resubmission of Jude's epistle. Some scholars believe 2 Peter and Jude where written by the same hand.

Both epistles have heavily relied on the pseudepigrapha book of Enoch, and numerous allusions abound. In fact, Jude quotes directly from Enoch (60:8) in verses 14 through 16. The simple fact that Jude considered 1 Enoch to be scripture can hardly be questioned, not just because he quotes from it but because he makes no differentiation between 1 Enoch and other scriptures he had previously quoted. Jude is clearly telling his Christian readers to remember something recorded in 1 Enoch that is very significant, and this indicates that most Christians of that time were obviously familiar with 1 Enoch.

Why is the authorship of 2 Peter denied or seriously questioned?

Universal acceptance that Peter died somewhere around 62–67 CE means that the latter date would be the latest possibility for the book's inception. In viewing 2 Peter 3:16, it makes reference to all the epistles of Paul as if a collection had existed for some time. It is widely accepted that a collection of Paul's letters came into existence no earlier than 75 CE.

The clearest evidence for a very late composition comes from 2 Peter 3:4, which states, "Where is the promise of His coming. For ever since the Fathers fell asleep, all things have continued as they were," alluding to the passing of the early fathers in the late first century. The historical record shows that around 80–90 CE, the immediate expectation of the second coming was waning and the church had begun to look for an apologia. Second Peter 3:8–9 is perhaps this first apology. Of course, this would mean Peter was still alive about 80–90 CE. In every tradition every early church father has testified that Peter died no later than 67 CE.

Some liberal Protestant scholars have expressed their belief that 2 Peter was eased into the canon by the Roman Catholic Church, which wanted to promote the primacy of Peter and his association with Rome. The Council of Nicea (325CE) rejected 2 Peter, but later (372 CE) the Council of Laodicea would accept it while it again rejected Revelation.

The overall majorities of scholars tend to agree that 2 Peter is a pseudonymous composition written in the early second century. Solid proof for this hypothesis cannot be ascertained, although the evidence is strong.

Who were Paula and Eustochium?

Overwhelming credit for the assembly of the Christian Bible and translating it into Latin goes to Jerome (347–420 CE). His Vulgate was truly a scholarly and literary masterpiece. Like many great works, the Vulgate did not immediately gain widespread recognition. The Eastern church of the fourth century spoke Greek for the most part. Therefore, a Latin work had little appeal. All the original New Testament books were in Greek, so no translation was required. Jerome's list of the individual books was acceptable, but not without some reservations. In the West, it fared much better and slowly developed into the standard Christian Bible. Jerome was born into wealth and received an excellent education. He became a brilliant scholar and linguist. Deeply religious and fervently Orthodox, he enjoyed arguing. Though highly intelligent, he could not handle criticism kindly. He would sarcastically lash out at his critics, and he gained numerous enemies.

Because of this, he was forced to leave Rome shortly after the death of Pope Damasus. Before his departure he translated the four gospels and the Pauline corpus, including Hebrews, into Latin. In 386 CE, he settled in Bethlehem and intensely took on the translation of the Old

Testament. The father of the New Testament actually translated only eighteen books of the twenty-seven. Who then translated the other nine?

Jerome certainly did establish the order of books as they appear today in all Bibles. This order includes the Old Testament as well. This is why Jewish Bibles follow a different order. Almost everyone assumed Jerome translated every book. Researching this anomaly, one runs into a blank wall. The only explanation rests with the nine books. All twenty-seven were previously translated into old Latin and existed well before Jerome, and some say that he simply incorporated them into his work.

Therefore, it was the "old Latin" version that became part of the Vulgate. This may well be true. However, I strongly suspect another scenario may have taken place. Reading the old Latin, we discover many variations and no consistency with the Vulgate. When one examines the existing writings, especially the correspondence of Jerome, we can glean a few clues as to what may have happened. Some of this correspondence includes a few letters written by Paula.

While in Rome, Jerome was the spiritual counselor to several wealthy women. Paula was one of them. She was widowed in 379 CE at about thirty-two years of age. Being very wealthy, she took to learning and furthering her education (something denied to most women in this period). Together with her daughter, Eustochium, they mastered Greek and Hebrew.

They were intensely religious and devoted to Jerome. So much so that when Jerome was forced to leave Rome for Bethlehem, they quickly followed. Paula sacrificed her vast fortune on charities and in helping Jerome. In Bethlehem, she established a convent and financed a monastery.

Paula and Eustochium took on a major role in assisting Jerome's composition of the Vulgate. Here is where this history ends. My hypothesis is simply this: Paula and Eustochium translated the nine books and had considerable input in many other New Testament works as well as in the Old Testament.

I offer this evidence: The ladies mastered Greek and Hebrew and certainly possessed the skills and knowledge at least equal to Jerome's. Any intellectual work would have been derogated if any woman had participated in its construction. Therefore, Jerome could not have publicly extended the proper credits. At this time (385–400 CE), Jerome was very busy translating the Old Testament and turned out an enormous amount of other writings. Paula and Eustochium had the time, the knowledge, the desire, the opportunity, and the occasion to do this work for Jerome. In several of Jerome's letters, there is (albeit very vague) a hint of Paula's able assistance.

Paula and Eustochium are recognized by the church (Orthodox and Catholic) as saints. Their contribution to the first complete Christian Bible may not have been recognized, but the knowledge of their very able assistance to Jerome and the church was widespread. Just before Paula died (404 CE), she had exhausted her fortune, and she was living a life of poverty. Eustochium was also forced to live in poverty as she became the head of a large convent. Eustochium did receive a great deal of credit from Jerome in the later letters he wrote to her. She died in 417 CE.

Perhaps this slight of history may not be of great importance. Yet one cannot resist citing the seemingly glaring lack of justice.

WOMEN IN CHRISTIANITY

In the last three decades of the twentieth and well into the twenty-first century, society began to address the concerns for equality toward women. Women's battle for emancipation has drastically affected traditional Christianity. Some mainstream Protestant denominations now recognize women as ministers and some even bishops. Orthodox and Catholic churches have resisted, while Reformed Judaism has accepted women rabbis. In 1976, the Pontifical Biblical Commission did a study on women becoming priests. The consensus vote was seventeen to zero that the New Testament does not specifically prohibit women priests. The last four popes have rejected any action or movement in this direction.

The outstanding record of Margaret Thatcher and Angela Merkel has proven that women are equally capable of leading nations at the highest level. Golda Meir and Indira Gandhi have also substantiated this statement.

We will now offer some history and attempt to answer these questions:

1. What part did Christianity play in the subordination of women?
2. Is Christianity responsible in at least a part for the present rise in stature of women?
3. Did men accomplish anything by the subjugation of women?

There is evidence that suggests that people were worshipping a female deity before the actual written Bible existed. The Old Testament or Hebrew Bible is scattered with several disguised references to female deities. Jeremiah (44:17–19) condemns his fellow Jews, especially the women of Pathros, Egypt, for worshipping and offering burnt sacrifices to the queen of heaven. Asthoreth, the despised "pagan" deity of the Old Testament was (despite the efforts of biblical scribes to camouflage her identity by repeatedly using the masculine gender), was actually Astarte, the "Great Goddess," as she was known in Canaan, the Near Eastern queen of heaven.

Perhaps Genesis contains the most damaging portrayal of women, and this gave men divine approval for the subjugation of women. Genesis is only one of innumerable creation myths that follow a usual formula. In Greek mythology the lord god is Jupiter (Zeus), Satan is Prometheus, Adam is Epimetheus, and Eve is Pandora. The fact that the women cause all of the trouble is usually part of the equation. In Egypt, Noom, the heavenly artist, creates a beautiful girl and sends her to Batoo, the first man, after which all peace for Batoo is ended. The Chinese Book of Chi-King states, "All things were at first subject to man, but a woman threw us into slavery, by ambitious desire for things. Our misery came not from heaven but from the woman—she lost the human race."

It is revealed in Genesis that Adam, who was pure and sinless at the time, accomplished the first birth by painlessly giving a rib from his body for the construction of Eve. After the fall and the creation of sin, birthing became female and painful (1 Corinthians 11:11–12).

The masculine God of Genesis announces how women will be punished more severely. God says that He will cause great labor in childbearing and that man will be her master (Genesis 3:16). Here it is now firmly established that God has relegated women to secondary status. She is hereby considered only slightly above animals.

Miriam inaugurates the first female prophet (Exodus 15:20). She played a major part in the administration of Moses along with her brother, Aaron. When Miriam and Aaron speak critically of Moses, God becomes angered and punishes her (Numbers 12). Miriam is banished from the camp and is given leprosy while the clearly guilty Aaron is only scolded. In Leviticus 27, God places the value of men at fifty shekels. The value of women is thirty shekels. In Numbers 1, God orders a census of families according to the father's line. Female lines are apparently not considered important.

The Old Testament is quite consistent in its attitude toward women. It does, however, have a few heroines who are described in some detail. Rahab was a harlot who aided the spies of Joshua in the conquest of Jericho. Rahab is very significant and is mentioned three times in the New Testament (Matthew 1:5; Hebrews 11:31; James 2: 24–25).

Deborah became a judge and prophetess. She is the only one of a few biblical women not identified through her husband. The record of her days is a major episode. Although two biblical books are named after women (Ruth and Esther) and three in Orthodox and Catholic Bibles (with Judith), Deborah is the only woman in the Old Testament to be given equal or at least nearly equal status as a man. (Judith is the exception.)

Prophetess Huldah (2 Kings 22:14–16) is mentioned as communicating a message from the God of Israel to the people of Judah about an impending disaster. She is also given priority over Jeremiah in determining the authenticity of an ancient scroll found in the temple, which could have been the first written document of the Torah. The remainder of the Old Testament demonstrates that Hebrew women were not considered capable of handling adult responsibilities in managing inheritance, taking vows, or initiating a divorce. They were excluded by virtue of their gender from many cultic acts. The woman's biological functions of menstruation and childbirth were thought to render her ritually unclean. Lot's daughters and Levite's concubine adamantly portray the low regard people had for women.

The Gospels of the New Testament remarkably describe Jesus elevating the respect for women, even to the dissatisfaction of His disciples and obvious shock to the Jewish population. He shatters Jewish customs in the synagogue by calling out to a crippled lady in the women's section and healing her on the Sabbath, referring to her as a daughter of Abraham (Luke 13:11–15).

It is very clear throughout the Gospels that Jesus shows respect and consideration toward women and truly shows He views their role as an important one in the coming kingdom of God. Jesus's teachings dispelled the custom of divorce and even forbade it. This was an obvious move to promote gender equality and to protect women. Jewish divorce heavily favored men and gave no rights to women. The gospel writers and their editors tried to disguise this, but the facts show through.

Gnostic gospels especially show the high regard Jesus had for women. Gnosticism permitted women to have leadership positions. They could even become liturgical presidents. These gospels portray the fact that Jesus regarded Mary Magdalene in a role superior to His male disciples.

It is important to note here that every gospel agrees that the female followers of Jesus remained conspicuously faithful to Him right up to and after His death, exceeding all of the apostles in loyalty and understanding. This includes Peter, who would deny Jesus three times. Since the superiority of women's behavior embarrassed the early church, its writers would have certainly omitted this mentality had not it been irremovable because of its renown. This also offers us a strong reason to regard these passages as authentic.

Although Paul is labeled by some as an antifeminist, I have shown previously the contrary. He demonstrated a desire to place women in key positions within his ministry. In Acts and several epistles, Paul certainly appears to have numerous women disciples to whom he apparently has given high authority.

Early Christianity attracted many female converts who were given a major part in its administration. Dr. Dorothy Irvin, a theologian and archaeologist, states that there is a catacomb fresco that has a scene depicting a woman being ordained by a bishop and many others showing women alongside of men dressed in liturgical vestments. She also says that these illustrations were not of heretical origin. She also claims how some frescos showing women celebrating the Eucharist were altered and changed to appear masculine (*The Witness* by D. Irvin).

From the inception of Christianity and through the second century, women contributed a major part in the growth and administration of the new faith. After that there appears to be a distinct effort on the part of the early church fathers to channel the role of women to secondary status. By the year 200 CE, there is no evidence for women taking prophetic, priestly, and episcopal roles in Orthodox churches. In the middle of the second century, women and men no longer sat together for worship. Instead they were separated adopting the synagogue custom. Groups in which women held leadership positions were branded heretical.

Nearly every father in the late second to the fourth century has written viciously critical treatises toward women. With this precedent established, the situation of women continued to deteriorate during the fall of the Rome and through the Middle Ages. Up to the Protestant Reformation, their only choice in life was marriage or the convent. The Reformation brought an end to convents in Protestant territories and thus eliminated one significant option for women. It did, however, open avenues of opportunity to be active in the social affairs of the new faiths through the emphasis on the superiority of marriage and family life. The charge has been made that the Reformation restricted the role of women because of the decline of monasticism. By way of comparison, however, in the late sixteenth century, the Protestants revived the deaconate for the distribution of alms and for nursing.

Esteem for Mary, the mother of Jesus, greatly increased in the medieval church. This was true in the Catholic as well as the Orthodox churches. This high veneration—almost worship— toward Mary did not elevate the status of women, but it did offer a female role model in the Godhead. Women were encouraged to become like Mary. The Protestant Reformation preached an end to this attitude, which would thereafter contribute to a huge chasm between the major Christian faiths.

Luther expressed his views toward women in his treatise *The Estate of Marriage* (1522). "That failure to marry early could lead to all sorts of evils—fornication 'secret sins' [presumably masturbation] and downright ill health." John Calvin laboriously wrote *Institutes of the Christian*

Religion, where he rejected the monastic system and celibacy. He proclaimed a paramount regard for marriage and motherhood. Yet he clearly and explicitly approves of a social order where men exercise authority over women, and he reveals his own traditional feelings that women are inferior to men.

Reformed leaders took a severe view of women who led an *irregular* life. Geneva expelled its nuns, and we know of Huguenot soldiers who cropped the ears of prostitutes after capturing a town. Protestant scorn for celibacy meant they embraced both genders, but for reformed women who had lost the prestigious refuge of a convent, there could be no satisfactory religious life outside the home.

Luther and Calvin believed women were created by God and could be saved through faith. Spiritually, women and men were equal. In every other respect, women were to be subordinated to men. Marriage was a woman's highest calling. In Luther's harsh words, "Let them bear children to their death; they were created for that." Unmarried women were suspect both because they were fighting their natural sex drive, which everyone in the sixteenth century believed was much stronger than men's, and because they were upsetting the divinely imposed order, which said that women should be subject to men.

All Protestant reformers cited the Bible as their authority to return the church to the faith of its origins. Of course the Bible strictly forbids women from having any voice in the church. However, some radical Protestant leaders were able to massage the scripture and interpret it in a way that allowed women to have a voice. Quakers Margaret and George Fox managed to reconcile Joel 2 and Acts 2, which state that women may prophesy, with the Pauline subordination passages. Established churches did not encourage prophesy for anyone, male or female, but in those sects where spiritual illumination might be expected to come in the form of visions and direct revelations, there was no biblical basis for denying women such experiences. Acts 2:17, referring to prophesies by women, was well-known to the prophetically inclined.

Perhaps the greatest shame Christianity has borne is its notions of witchcraft. The persecution of witches began in the thirteenth century and continued for five hundred years. This was being waged with special ferocity from 1500 to 1700. Before the thirteenth century, Christian theologians and bishops had explicitly opposed belief in witches. Although this superstitious fad began well before the Reformation, it was also adopted by Protestants, and popular history seems to accuse them of greater guilt. But the facts point equally to Catholics as well. In the late fifteenth and early sixteenth centuries, there were thousands upon thousands of executions, usually burning at the stake live people in Germany, Italy and other counties.

John Wesley (1703–91), founder of the Methodist church, organized groups called "classes." Some of these classes were for women with women leaders. Catherine the Great of Russia (1729–96) became one of the ablest and wisest leaders in Europe. She was also the leader of the Russian Orthodox church. Catherine ruled and behaved like many of her male contemporaries. For this she was harshly criticized, and many false or embellished stories circulated about her affairs. Numerous articles were printed, accusing her of gross promiscuity and nymphomania.

By the nineteenth century, women began to revolt and struggle for equality. Women founded and led several new denominations. Catherine Munford became cofounder of the Salvation Army with her husband, William Booth. This new sect demonstrated equality for women, and many rose to high leadership. Mary Baker Eddy (1821–1910), founded the Church of Christ, Scientist. Ellen Gould White (1827–1915) reestablished and revitalized the Seventh Day Adventists after William Miller, the original founder who had predicted the end of the world and the second coming, had failed several times.

Elisabeth Cady Stanton (1815–1902) wrote *The Women's Bible*, clearly defining sexism in the Bible. In Germany and England, groups of women (about 1842) banded together to serve as nurses, educators, or caregivers for the aged. They were called nuns and were inspired by the Oxford Movement of Dr. Pusey. Deaconesses were the German counterpart founded through an order by Theodore Fliedner (1836). Catholic nuns traditionally served these same functions, and numerous dedicated orders sprung up. All of the orders were headed by a mother superior.

By the middle of the twentieth century, most Christian denominations did not allow the ordination of women. During the 1950s both in the church and in society at large, women began to gain acceptance within some denominations. By mid-1980s, most Protestant denominations did ordain women. The Catholic and Orthodox churches refused to do likewise. This caused some strong and vocal organizations to campaign against this ban.

In the field of theology, a number of women—notably Presbyterian Letty Russel and Catholic Rosemary Reuther—proposed what were essentially Orthodox corrections to traditional male theology. Mary Daily took a more radical approach. She declared herself a *graduate* from the male-dominated church and called her sisters to await a single *female* incarnation of God.

Did Christianity play a major role in the emancipation of women? I would say it actually helped very little. It merely acquiesced. That answers the first and second original questions. But did men accomplish anything by the subjugation of women? Actually, men very well may have been the losers here. By failure to allow women the opportunity to gain higher education in general, many medical and technological discoveries may have been lost or delayed by their lack of involvement. The rest should be evident by understanding the history.

The Woman Caught in Adultery

The New Testament Gospels are religious narratives about the ministry of Jesus set in a particular historical setting. Even the most skeptical scholars agree that the transmission from the ancient texts to the present is remarkably well preserved with only very minor errors. When we critically compare some of the texts, we find numerous apparent deletions and additions. However, the total is insignificant when matched to the overwhelming accuracy and volume of the balance. Moreover, these variations have little if any effect on the theological understandings that are accepted by most Christians.

The account of the woman caught in adultery (John 7:53–8:11) has a textual history that is very confusing to say the least. This behavior does not appear in the earliest manuscripts (with one exception). In those manuscripts where we do find it, it is not found in any one place. Some have it at the end of John. In some manuscripts it is found after John 7:36. One puts it after John 7:44. A few have inserted its mention after Luke 21:38. So what does this all mean? It would appear that someone thought up the story and believed it was part of the historical Jesus. Then as it gained popularity, others began repeating it until a copyist placed it in a Bible and made it part of John's gospel, while another copyist thought it belonged in Luke's gospel. Therefore, it would appear that an inauthentic story of Jesus became part of our canon.

John 7:53–8:11 (KJV) states,

> And every man went unto his own house. Jesus went unto the mount of Olives. And early in the morning he came again into the temple, and all the people came unto him; and he sat down, and taught them. And the scribes and Pharisees brought unto him a woman taken in adultery; and when they had set her in the midst, They say unto him, Master, this woman was taken in adultery, in the very act. Now Moses in the law commanded us, that such should be stoned: but what sayest thou? This they said, tempting him, that they might have to accuse him. But Jesus stooped down, and with his finger wrote on the ground, as though he heard them not. So when they continued asking him, he lifted up himself, and said unto them, He that is without sin among you, let him first cast a stone at her. And again he stooped down, and wrote on the ground. And they which heard it, being convicted by their own conscience, went out one by one, beginning at the eldest, even unto the last: and Jesus was left alone, and the woman standing in the midst. When Jesus had lifted up himself, and saw none but the woman, he

said unto her, Woman, where are those thine accusers? hath no man condemned thee? She said, No man, Lord. And Jesus said unto her, neither do I condemn thee: go, and sin no more.

This very beautiful pericope (a discrete unit of discourse) does not appear in any of the oldest and most reliable manuscripts until the seventh-century copies of a few old Latin texts. Then it is found in various locations. It is also missing in the ancient Peshitta as well as in the oldest versions in Syriac, Coptic, and most of the old Latin. The earliest fathers do not mention or allude to it either, although Papias (about 115 CE) may have known of it.

What does this all mean? Most likely, there is very little support for this story being part of John or Luke's original gospels, for it is omitted in all of the oldest manuscripts. But the very message agrees with Christian doctrine. While the story is something that could have happened during Jesus's ministry, it clearly was not original to John or Luke's gospels. The majority of scholars opine that it should not be considered as part of scripture. Therefore, to use it as a scriptural reference to validate a point would be grossly flawed.

The New American Bible states,

> The story of the woman caught in adultery is a later insertion, missing from all early Greek manuscripts. A Western text-type insertion, attested mainly in Old Latin translations, it is found in different places in different manuscripts; here, or after 7:36, or at the end of this gospel, or after Luke 21:38, or at the end of that gospel. There are many non-Johannine features in the language, and there are also many doubtful readings within the passage. The style and the motifs are similar to those of Luke, and it fits better with the general situation at the end of Luke 21 … The Catholic Church accepts this passage as canonical scripture.

This Catholic Bible accepts this passage but readily confesses its lack of authenticity. This is also the case with most mainstream Protestant denominations. Fundamentalists then should not be upset because it obviously does not appear in the original inspired manuscript. Most Christian scholars acknowledge the lack of evidence to support these passages, but they find it so inspiring that they believe it deserves to be in the Bible. Even the Fellows of the Jesus Seminar say, "They nevertheless assigned the words and story to a special category of things they wish Jesus has said and done" (*The Five Gospels*, 426).

Most Bibles have at least a footnote showing this discrepancy. Some put the entire story either at the end of John or in the footnotes, and some eliminate it entirely. Here is what some Bibles do in this regard:

AAT—Verse 53 is included in chapter 8. There is a footnote after verse 52 that says, "Our best manuscripts, including the two oldest papyri (P66 and P75, dated about A.D. 200) lack 7:53–8:11."

LBP—Verse 53 is included in chapter 7. There is a footnote from verse 3 that says, "The story of the woman taken in adultery is not found in the ancient Peshitta, but occurs in later Aramaic texts."

NAB—Verse 53 is included in chapter 7. Verses 53 to 11 are enclosed within single brackets. There is a footnote following the section titled "A Woman Caught in Adultery" that says, "The story of the woman caught in adultery is a later insertion here, missing from all early Greek manuscripts. A Western text-type insertion, attested mainly in Old Latin translations, it is found in different places in different manuscripts; here, or after 7:36, or at the end of this gospel, or after Luke 21:38, or at the end of that gospel. There are many non-Johannine features in the language, and there are also many doubtful readings within the passage. The style and the motifs are similar to those of Luke, and it fits better with the general situation at the end of Luke 21, but it was probably inserted here because of the allusion to Jeremiah 17:13 (cf. the note on 8:6) and the statement, 'I do not judge anyone,' in 8:15. The Catholic Church accepts this passage as canonical scripture."

NIV—Following verse 52, there is a horizontal line. Then comes a note enclosed within single brackets that says, "The earliest and most reliable manuscripts and other ancient witnesses do not have John 7:53–8:11." Verse 53 then follows chapter 8. After verse 11, there is another vertical line.

In keeping with biblical stories with questionable authenticity, let's examine the story of Barabbas.

BARABBAS

Studying biblical events with the main focus on history is difficult because of the paucity of corroborating sources. Most events were originally transmitted orally only to be written years later, and that method tended to accumulate additional information to make the story more understandable. Therefore, historians must master the sources. For this purpose, the historian must be acquainted with such auxiliary sciences as ecclesiastical philology (especially the Greek, Aramaic, and Hebrew languages, in which most of the earliest documents are written), secular history, geography, and chronology. Then in making use of the sources, the historian must thoroughly and impartially examine their genuineness and integrity, not to mention the credibility and capacity of the witnesses. Thus, the person can then duly separate fact from fiction, truth from error.

Keeping this in mind, let us examine the biblical story of Barabbas.

Origen (182–250 CE), an early church father and outstanding biblical scholar, had access to many New Testament documents, all of which are long lost. These documents had to be very close to the original New Testament manuscripts as he lived only about a hundred or so years after their initial composition. He is considered the foremost earliest Bible savant. When he studied the manuscripts of the gospel of Matthew, he was taken back to find that the first name of Barabbas was Jesus. Simply put, in the language of its day, Christ and Barabbas both apparently shared the exact same name.

Most of the modern New Testament translations use what they believe to be the best of most ancient texts to support their versions. Here is how we see Matthew 27:16–17 in the GNB version (see also NLT, CEV, MSG, NAB, and NKJV). "That time there was a well-known prisoner named [Jesus] Barabbas. So when the crowd gathered, Pilate asked them, 'Which one do you want me to set free for you? [Jesus] Barabbas or Jesus called the Messiah?'"

In fact, several of our modern Bibles are laid out in similar ways. Some Bibles have Jesus in brackets (as shown), while some just make reference to things in the footnotes. The majority do not have references like these at all. This phenomenon was conspicuous to Origen around 200 CE as we see in several manuscripts known as the Caesarean group, the Sinaitic Palimpsest, and several Palestinian Syriac lectionaries, all of which support the fact that Barabbas's full name was Jesus Barabbas (all dated in the fifth century). Some scholars believe that the name Jesus was deliberately left out of many manuscripts to respect Christ, echoing Origen. They did not want the name Jesus associated with anyone who was a sinner. Keep in mind the name Jesus was a very common name at that time.

There are also three separate ancient manuscripts known as "Ms. British Museum Add. No. 14,459, 14,453, and 17,117," which are dated to the fifth century, and these contain similar wording. However, the oldest existing manuscripts codices, namely Vaticanus, Sinaiticus, and Alexandrinus, do not. These are dated to the fourth and fifth centuries.

How can this be reconciled? Surely, it is possible that an early scribe inadvertently added (dittography) it in and later scribes simply recopied it. Certainly, this would be the most logical answer, but having it occur in two separate places makes that unlikely. Overall, the Barabbas story has several other problems that may suggest otherwise.

First of all, the Aramaic name Barabbas (the language spoken by Jesus) translates to English as "son of father". When Jesus taught the Lord's Prayer (and other times as well), He used the term *Abba* to mean God the Father, His Father. So people would have spoken of Jesus, the Son of God (His Father), and Barabbas by using the exact same words. Barabbas as a proper noun would have been a most unusual name for anyone at this time except, of course, for Christ, who was considered the Son of God by His followers and declared as such in the Gospels.

The second problem is a Roman governor pardoning a rebel against Rome to satisfy a custom. Historically speaking, that would be entirely unprecedented. "And among the rebels in prison, who had committed murder in the insurrection, there was a man called Barabbas" (Mark 15:7).

There is absolutely not even the faintest suggestion in any of the extensive Roman records (or Jewish records) that might substantiate a customary pardoning of this sort. Christian apologists for centuries have scoured every historical record or document in an effort to verify this without success. Most history scholars claim the whole story is fiction, and Chaim Cohn, author of *The Trial and Death of Jesus*, concludes that "the incongruities of this story are so many that no historicity can be attributed to it."

A logical assumption would be that Mark's source, the earliest chronicle of Jesus available to him, was composed in Aramaic. Mark was not very fluent in that language and honestly assumed bar Abba was a proper noun that represented a real person. Therefore, he thought this term was the name of another fellow prisoner with Jesus. Pilate or his prosecutor possibly was recorded (in Mark's source) as saying, "Who are we here to condemn? This Jesus who claims he is merely the peace loving son of God -his father or the Jesus the Messiah who violently disrupted the Temple while actively revolting against Roman rule!" When seen in written form, something like this could easily appear as though there were two separate people named Jesus. Mark may have believed then that one or the other Jesus was going to be pardoned while the other was condemned. He could then have rationally presumed this was a special custom Rome granted to the Jews. It is a fact that Rome did indeed grant Jews certain privileges and concessions unavailable anywhere else in the empire.

Certainly, this last scenario is pure speculation, but it is very reasonable and fits historically without accusing Mark of falsifying his information. Certainly, the Bible writers just did not invent stories without at least plausible substantiation. They believed they were reporting sacred news that was required by God as the truth, and they treated it as such. Yet the whole Barabbas story conspicuously smacks of a fabrication. Therefore, the only other possibility is misinterpretations or misunderstandings. We can see how easily and honestly this happens even in events occurring today.

In short, I believe Mark simply misunderstood the circumstances but reported faithfully what he believed his source meant to convey. This would not be uncommon for any ancient writer. Unwittingly, Mark does make several geographical mistakes in his gospel. We can see that Matthew, who is more familiar with Judean geography and customs, tries to correct some of the errors that occur in his source, which was Mark, and Mark was writing to people who did not know or understand either Aramaic or Hebrew.

Another possibility stems from the Christian tradition, and it suggests that Mark was the scribe for Peter. It is well known that Peter was from Galilee and spoke Aramaic with a strong Galilean accent. Mark then would have had difficulty deciphering Peter's dialect and simply mistook this part of his passion story. Thus, Mark believed two individuals were on trial before Pilate. Hereafter, later copyists removed the word *Jesus* preceding Barabbas out of respect for their Savior. Although a few manuscripts survived as we see witnessed in Matthew's gospel, this removal was successfully executed in the other gospels per Origen's recommendation.

All of the biblical authors were not writing history as we now understand it or would prefer it to be. They clearly had a biased motive to promote their faith, and they would spin the facts (as our politicians do today) as they understood them to satisfy their personal agenda. And yes, many still do this today. But to out and out lie or invent history would have simply been out of the question. Of course, I can't prove this last statement. As a rule, a historian presumes an author's uncorroborated statement as being true or factual but examines it with much skepticism. This is known as hermeneutics.

CHAPTER 13

PONTUS PILATE

When Easter draws near, many will be reading or hearing biblical stories concerning the passion of Jesus and the characters that played a part in this event. I submit this to help in understanding some of the seemingly small details in the background of this incident.

The gospels tell us that Pilate refused to condemn Jesus but that he was placed in a position by "the Jews" that forced him to do so. We must keep in mind the gospels were written some forty years after the events at Calvary. This was a time when these writers and Christians were experiencing a traumatic divorce with Judaism. Because this breakup was so bitter, the Jews became the ultimate enemy of the Christians. The previously hated Romans had just destroyed the Jewish temple and appeared to have also destroyed Judaism. Christianity then determined that it had to show the new Israel (Christianity) was not subversive or rebellious toward the empire.

The blame for killing Jesus was then shifted from the Romans to the Jews. The early church soon developed a tradition about Pilate. In the second-century gospel of Peter, the condemnation of Jesus is squarely placed upon the shoulders of Herod Antipas. Tertullian claimed Pilate was really a Christian at heart. He maintained Pilate wrote a letter to Tiberius explaining the events concerning the crucifixion. Eusebius (*The History of the Church*) speaks of a tale that has Pilate killing himself during the reign of Caligula out of remorse for his part in the death of Jesus.

The gospel of Nicodemus also shows Pilate in an inordinately positive light. The Coptic and Ethiopian churches went so far as to have him canonized as a saint.

The Christian view of Pilate is vividly contrasted by the Jewish version. Josephus, almost hatefully, literally attempts a character assassination of Pilate. Philo of Alexandria paints him as an extremely cruel despot. Certainly, both of these Jewish writers have expressed their personal agendas negatively toward Pilate. However, they probably intended their criticisms/hatred to be directed toward Rome in general.

Thus, our primary sources for Pilate are extremely polarized. What is the truth behind these opposing viewpoints?

We will never know with certainty, but if we examine the history and evidence, we may be able to form a better judgment. In 26 CE, Pilate became the fifth governor of the Roman province of Judea and remained until 37 CE for nearly twelve years. This is very telling, as there were forty-plus governors who ruled in the general area whose terms ruling provinces in the empire usually lasted only two years (rarely more than thirty-six months). We learn of this from the *Letters of Pliny the Younger*, who was such a governor during this period.

This should strongly indicate that the emperors of Rome believed Pilate to be a very competent governor. Although Judea was not considered to be a key or major province, the fact remains that the job Pilate was doing earned him his lengthy stay in office. When Pilate was appointed prefect (26 CE), Judea was considered a troublesome province that had several previous uprisings, although minor in effect. Fresh in the mind of the Judeans was the successful Maccabean revolt, and Pilate was also keenly aware of this fact. Upon his arrival in Judea, Pilate was introduced to the titular ruler of the Jews, Caiaphus, the high priest. Rome had also appointed this position, and he was the representative spiritual leader as well as civil leader of the Jews. Of course, the high priest was subordinate to the Roman governor.

The book of Sirach (chapter 50), although written much earlier, gives us a good insight to this sort of authority and prestige held by the high priest. The stark dichotomy in the demeanor of Pilate as shown by Jewish and Christian writers and combining this with our historical knowledge indicates to me a totally different picture of Pilate. Holding office for twelve years would indicate Pilate was a good administrator who maintained imperial order and did a good job collecting taxes. He worked closely with Caiaphus to keep Jewish unrest to a minimum. Caiaphus held his office from 18 to 36 CE, about eighteen years. Therefore, he, too, must have been successfully doing what Rome expected.

Pilate strove diligently to ensure and secure imperial Rome's best interests. Caiaphus with equal resolve tried to strike the best possible considerations from Rome for the Jews. His loyalty was to Israel and his people as we can see from the biblical description (Leviticus 21:10–14) of the duties of the high priest. This was considered a sacred duty. Of course, he was compelled to serve Rome. But one can be quite certain he did everything within his power to provide for his people without damaging his personal position.

When Jesus came upon the scene, both Pilate and Caiaphus quickly viewed him as a messianic rebel, although He was not considered to be a major threat. Pilate insisted Jesus be curtailed exactly as his duty to Rome compelled. To ensure a minimum of Jewish antagonism directed toward Rome, Pilate forced Caiaphus to do the job and make it appear to be a *Jewish matter* handled by Jews. John 11:48–52 tells of Caiaphus's dilemma.

The gospel writers had to downplay or even vindicate Roman involvement and responsibility. This was done with the hope of preventing reprisals. Certainly, they could not have—at least not literally—vented their anger or show any hostilities toward Rome. Perhaps they encrypted their language in such a way as only their community would have been able to understand. This could help to explain some of the variations we see in the different gospels. This is similar to the way that the author of Revelation accomplished this same effect.

Regardless, the gospels laid out the story of Jesus and His teachings, which was their major consideration. Whether or not Pilate and Caiaphus were good or bad guys is only a detail, and it is of only secondary importance. Someone had to be blamed as the bad guys. It certainly couldn't be powerful Rome, so therefore, it had to be the only other protagonist, the Jews.

CAIAPHUS

Before I begin with Caiaphus, I'd like to offer a few examples of similar cases that occurred in more modern times. Field Marshal Henry Petain was considered a hero of France for his exemplar bravery in World War I. However, in 1940 when France fell to Hitler, Petain (at age eighty-three) was appointed to be the puppet president of the unoccupied areas of the country. Of course, Hitler had approved the appointment and had full control of Petain's government. In other words, this portion of France was free or independent in name only.

Petain accepted this role because he truly believed he could salvage some freedom for his people by acquiescing to Hitler's demands, thereby ending the fighting. He could then possibly do things to protect the remainder of the nation by appearing to submit, but behind the scenes, he did everything he could to undermine the enemy.

After the war Petain was convicted of treason and sentenced to death by hanging. His sentence was commuted to life, and he died in 1951 at the age of ninety-four. I believe Petain sincerely tried to help his nation through an almost impossible situation. Certainly, he loved his country and his people and tried to do everything he could to help them until they could regain their freedom. He was forced to cooperate with Hitler, and he did so—at least on the surface.

Pope Pius XII is another example. He is criticized today for failing to speak out against the Nazi atrocities before and during World War II and especially for his failure to do more to help Jews. There is no doubt that Pius was placed in an untenable position considering all his responsibilities as pope. We all know Pius did everything he could without jeopardizing his position. Had he done more, he certainly would have been killed, and a new pope would have been appointed by Hitler. By giving lip services to the conquerors, he was able to work behind the scenes and did indeed save many Jews from the Nazis. He also submitted to the enemy only to gain time and be able to continue doing whatever he could.

Both Pius and Petain used coded writings and broadcasts to undermine the Nazis while his own people knew exactly what they were saying just as the gospel writers did. Seriously think about how you would react if you were placed into the situation these two men were. I submit that Caiaphus was in the exact same spot.

His first name was Joseph, and his surname was Caiaphus. He was the Jewish high priest from 18 to 37 CE, best known for his role during the trial of Jesus. The name Caiaphus is the Greek rendering of the Aramaic *Oayyapa*.

Nothing is known about the early career of Caiaphus, but we can presume that he was a member of a wealthy family because he married a daughter of the high priest Annas (6–15 CE). As high priest, Caiaphus was chairman of the Sanhedrin. Even when Caiaphus was no longer high priest, he was still extremely influential. According to the Jewish historian Josephus, five of his sons were high priest (*Antiquities* 20.198). It is possible that Caiaphus was also a member of the embassy that went to Rome in 17 CE to discuss fiscal matters. In 18 CE, the Roman governor Valerius Gratus appointed Caiaphus as high priest. Caiaphus remained in office an exceptionally long time of nineteen years. Gratus's successor, Pontius Pilate, retained the high priest in office (Tacitus, *Annals* 2.42.5).

There is an ongoing debate on the circumstances and events concerning the death of Jesus as the Jews in general, Caiaphus is certainly depicted a as a villain in all Christian writings and traditions.

As a result of the Maccabean revolt, the Romans took note and garnered much respect for the Jewish military. By 63 BCE, however, Judea fell under the mighty Roman yolk.

Octavian (Augustus Caesar), mindful of the Maccabean/Greek lesson, wisely granted certain unprecedented privileges to the Jews. Most notably, he allowed for religious freedom and full practice of Jewish laws to an extraordinary degree. Basically, as long as the region remained peaceful and paid their tribute, Rome allowed the Jews this extraordinary latitude.

Jewish laws are preserved in numerous sources. The most magisterial are the Mishnah, the Semahot, the Tosefta, and the Palestinian and Babylonian Talmuds. Although these written sources came into existence after the death of Jesus, we can reasonably assume they were orally understood and were applicable during His time as well.

The Semahot spelled out laws for the funeral rites and care of the dead. Both Talmuds confirmed Jewish oral laws and were regarded as equal authority to the Torah. We can see the application of these oral laws in the writings of Josephus (37–100 CE) and Philo (15 BCE–50 CE).

After the death of Herod the Great (73–4 BCE), Judea was added to the province of Syria. Augustus deposed his successor, Herod Archelaus, in 6 CE and granted special privileges to the Jews. Soon after the death of Tiberius (14–37 CE), the new emperor Caligula (37–41 CE) imposed greater Roman controls and began to restrict some Jewish freedoms. Before Caligula, Josephus tells us, "The Jews were allowed to follow their own laws in accordance with ancestral laws, just as they had during the Maccabean period." At this time Rome now exercised less regard for Jewish customs and laws in several cases.

Under Caligula, Philo tells us even Jewish seditionists who were crucified under Roman law received imperial protection by allowing established Jewish burial customs to be upheld. This privilege superseded even Roman laws. Philo states, "I know that some of those crucified were taken down before the start of Sabbath and their bodies were returned to their families for burial and the customary Jewish rights" (In Flaccum, 83). We see in the Gospels that Joseph of Arimathea was granted a special privilege from Pilate. In reality, this was common practice granted to all Judean Jews from a decree of Augustus given about 6 CE.

The Gospels blame Caiaphas for the crucifixion of Jesus. "It was Caiaphas who had given counsel to the Jews that it was expedient that one man should die for the people" (John 18:14). Caiaphas was acting out Roman demands to eliminate the troublesome Jesus, who was a rebel in their eyes. Caiaphas feared a Roman military response that would jeopardize all of Judea. So sacrificing one man, Jesus, to save many seemed to him the lesser of two evils. The Gospels are quite clear that Jesus caused a major disturbance in the temple and did intentionally enter Jerusalem riding on an ass to fulfill the Zechariah (9:9–11) prophecy, which was clearly a messianic message that the Romans were well aware of.

Undoubtedly, the trial by the Sanhedrin was designed to appease the public. In so doing, it may have forced the Romans to honor the Augustan law allowing Jesus to have a proper burial (Josephus, *Antiquities* 16.160–173). This then granted Jesus a Jewish legal execution conceding Him forgiveness for his sins (Talmud, Sanhedrin 47a).

Caiaphus was a Jew who had to submit to Roman authority. I don't believe he wanted to see a fellow Jew crucified but found himself in a compromising situation. So he chose to let Jesus die but tried to give Him the benefit a religious burial. By doing what he did, he allowed the fulfillment of the religious requirement for atonement (Talmud, Sanhedrin 47b).

Caiaphus clearly fits in the same category with Field Marshal Henry Petain and Pius XII. Therefore, the Bible writers had to downplay or omit any negativity expressed toward Rome as well as Jesus's role in regards to military/rebellious conduct. So they disguised their anti-Roman language and then turned their anger toward the Jews by blaming them for the death of Jesus. They certainly could not have understood the Jewish/Sanhedrin's motives regarding His death.

THE HISTORY OF BAPTISM

Baptism became a part of Christianity because John the Baptist baptized Jesus. It then became the primary practice of initiation into the faith. John's ritual was seeded in Judaic customs of cleanliness and symbolic of purity. John claimed it was "a baptism of repentance for the forgiveness of sins." Exactly what this meant cannot be determined with certainty. However, it implies that by submitting to be baptized, people are begging forgiveness for their sins. The washing symbolizes being cleansed in spirit in the eyes of God. What made this baptism so popular among the Jewish people of that day is difficult to understand. The religious significance is obvious, but there must have been a political aspect as well because John was quickly murdered in spite of his great popularity.

It appears that baptism was one of the earliest Christian rituals for initiation into the community of believers. In the New Testament, we are told that baptism is given by the Holy Spirit for the forgiveness of sins. It also symbolizes our being buried with Christ and tells us how it may be administered. "He that believes and receives baptism will be saved; those who do not believe will be condemned" (Mark 16:16). The earliest gospel is quite clear that one must be baptized and must believe in order to achieve salvation.

"Repent, and be baptized every one of you in the name of Jesus Christ; then your sins will be forgiven and you will receive the gift of the Holy Spirit" (Acts 2:38). Therefore, Acts confirms baptism is a means to receive forgiveness of our sins. The risen Jesus commanded the apostles to baptize all nations in the name of the Father and of the Son and of the Holy Spirit (Matthew 28:19). Matthew quotes directly from Jesus's order to baptize everyone.

The Pauline epistles would be the earliest written authority relative to baptism. However, Paul flatly states, "For Christ did not send me to baptize but to proclaim the gospel" (1 Corinthians 1:17). This could indicate that the sacrament took on importance only later in Christian history. There are eight Pauline quotations about baptism in the New Testament, but most surprising is Paul's failure to mention the baptism of Jesus or even mention John the Baptist. First Corinthians 10:2, 1 Corinthians 12:13, 1 Corinthians 1:13–17, Ephesians 4:5, Galatians 3:27, Romans 6:3–4, and Colossians 2:12 are seven of the eight New Testament references. The last one is 1 Corinthians 15:29. This one has a strong allusion to an apparent custom of baptizing someone who's already dead. "Otherwise, what will people accomplish by having themselves baptized for the dead? If the dead are not raised at all, then why are they having themselves baptized for them?" Baptism, therefore, was given to forgive sins, to achieve salvation, and possibly to assist those who believed but who had already passed away.

Did this Christian style of baptism derive any basis from the baptism performed by John the Baptist?

Jewish customs would lead us to believe John's baptism was a symbolic gesture associating physical cleansing with a repentance of the spirit. This signified showing an outward sign of devotion to confirm one's true repentance. So it would appear baptism took on additional meaning as Christianity aged and grew.

Was this early baptism a complete immersion in water?

From the New Testament, one would assume baptism was a ceremony using water, but the explicitly of the water is not always clear. However, Acts 10:47 says, "Is anyone prepared to withhold the water of baptism from these persons who have received the Holy Spirit just as we did?" This seems to confirm the use of water, but it says nothing about quantity.

Early Gnostics, such as the Valentineans, regarded baptism as only the elementary initiation ritual. For many of their believers, this lacked real spiritual content. Justin Martyr (160 CE) wrote in "Apology 61," "But Christians, through baptism, were *born again* as 'children' of choice and knowledge." This was a response to counter Valentinus and the Gnostics.

Some other early fathers also wrote about baptism. Ignatius (108 CE) said to the Smymaeans, "It is not permitted to baptize or hold love feasts independent of the Bishop. But what ever he approves, that is also well pleasing to God; that all your acts may be sure and valid." Irenaeus (175 CE) in *The Sacraments* said, "As dry flour can not be united into a lump of dough, or a loaf, but needs moisture; so we who are many can not be made one in Christ Jesus with out water which comes from heaven." Tertillian (200 CE) in *The Ceremonies of Baptism* said, "All waters ... after the invocation of God attain the sacramental power of sanctification; for the Spirit straight away comes down upon them from the heavens." And Clement of Alexandria (200 CE) in *The Work of Christ* said, "Being baptized, we are adopted as sons; being adopted we are made perfect; being made complete, we are immortal."

For all these early leaders, it appears baptism was to be administered by a bishop or his appointee. Full immersion in water was followed immediately by another ceremony called chrism. This is where the participant would receive the Holy Spirit. In the beginning baptism was given only to adults or adolescents and not to infants. New catechumens (new candidates), according to Hippolytus, were screened before they were permitted to even take instructions. People with morally suspected occupations, such as male or female prostitutes, schoolteachers, and sculptors, were excluded or were required to change their jobs.

"Further screening would take place during the instructional period which took about three years. Also several exorcisms of the catechumens took place before full admission and Baptism was given" (*The Origins of Christianity* by Wayne A. Meeks).

Infant baptism was not encouraged in the time of Tertillian. In *De Baptismo* 18, he argues infants should not be baptized until they have reached the age of understanding. This clearly shows the practice of infant baptism must have been occurring occasionally at this time. Most likely, this would have been used when certain death of the infant was determined.

By the fourth century, it was increasingly gaining acceptance. The Cappadocian father Gregory of Nayssa wrote in Origen. 40.28, "For it is better that they (infants) should be unconsciously sanctified than they should depart this life unsealed and uninitiated." Infant baptism was accepted late in the third century with the works of Cyprian (258 CE). In his writing *Christian Initiation*, here we obtain insight not only to infant baptism but also to the earliest perception of an original sin concept.

Cyprian, although stopping short of endorsement, offers infant baptism as a good option to parents. He states, "An infant ought not to be shut out; who being newly born has committed no sin, except that of being born of Adam's line according to the flesh. Has he ... contracted the contagion of the ancient death? Indeed the infant's approach to the reception of remission of sins is easier from the very fact that the sins remitted are another's, not his own." About 130 years later, Augustine would further develop this theory into the doctrine of original sin.

Baptism-chrism is also laid out by Cyprian in a ceremony by defining this two-step process. This same ritual is still going on today in Eastern Orthodox churches. The biblical references include Mark 1:8, John 1:33, and Acts 2:38; 10:44–48; 14:17.

Initially and well into the fifth century, some Christians believed that sins committed after baptism either could not be forgiven or would exact a costly penance. Thus, many Christian deferred baptism until just before death and lived most of their lives on the margin of the church. Church leaders steadily criticized this practice as perpetuating spiritual infancy, such as found in the preaching and writings of John Chysostom. Even the greatest Christian benefactor, Constantine, put off his baptism until he was on his deathbed (337 CE). After Constantine, the church became unified (for all intents and purposes) and began to develop and codify the sacraments.

The first sacrament was baptism, but ultimately, the church would arrive at a total of seven. Both Eastern and Western churches have seven sacraments, but they are slightly different. This remained the case for about a thousand years until the Protestant Reformation of 1517. Today most Protestant churches accept only two sacraments, baptism and the Eucharist (or the Lord's Supper). Some denominations choose to use the term *ordinance* instead of sacrament. The Reformation also produced variations in the doctrine and ceremony of baptism. Some absolutely insist on using water, while others believe there is no validity for the practice of the ceremony in any shape or form.

FAITH, DEATH, AND THE AFTERLIFE

Faith is defined as allegiance, trust, confidence, belief, conviction, and a system of religious idealism. In terms of religion, it is an acceptance of the supernatural without the requirement of proof. This may sound somewhat demeaning, but in reality, it provides a great deal of comfort and solace for all who partake.

Death is the end, the final natural experience! Death is an inescapable certainty that all humans come to understand at some early point in their lives. Nearly every young person who at first acknowledges this revelation is fearful and in some cases devastated. Usually, this quickly fades as reason takes over and one rationalizes that death is a future event that is a long way off. Hope then joins with faith in the expectance of a life after death.

Religion becomes a vehicle combining faith and hope, and in most cases it includes a reward in heaven. Without a doubt, acceptance of religion is the route most people take. Of course, there are skeptics and those who are not religious, but experience shows that many of these folks turn to God or religion in times of great fear (e.g., facing the diagnosis of a terminal illness or the illness of a dearly beloved friend or family member).

Faith offers the comforting knowledge that you'll receive a better life in the hereafter and that you will be reunited with all your loved ones who have preceded you. Faith promotes prayer as a tool that allows you to gain some satisfaction by helping a loved one or even by helping yourself. In general, it is believed people of faith live longer and experience happier lives.

Science has shown that our bodies start to decay immediately after death. Most religions believe we have souls that live on after death, but this is impossible to prove. Furthermore, no physical evidence of any kind is present to even suggest the existence of a soul. Therefore, the concept of a soul is based purely on faith and hope that may be reinforced through one's intuition.

The Bible says very little about an afterlife other than the fact that it is desirable. Heaven is only described as an existence with God with a hint of some form of paradise and a vague allusion to having a bodily presence there. In the Christian Bible, what happens immediately after death seems to indicate a temporary sleeplike state. Then one awakens with a new body at the end of time. But most faiths allude to a spiritual encounter with God along with some kind of judgment directly after death.

It would then appear that most Christians do not have a universally definitive understanding of what exactly heaven is, let alone how and when we get there. From this we may conclude that most people desire heaven because the only alternative is hell or nonexistence, which we assume to be quite unpleasant.

The apostle Paul tries to explain this in 1 Corinthians 15:35–44, which says,

> But some will ask, "How are the dead raised? With what kind of body do they come?" You foolish man! What you sow does not come to life unless it dies. And what you sow is not the body which is to be, but a bare kernel ... God gives it a body as He has chosen, and to each kind of seed its own body. For not all flesh is alike ... There are celestial bodies and there are terrestrial bodies; but the glory of the celestial is one, and the glory of the terrestrial is another ... So it is with the resurrection from the dead. What is sown is perishable, what is raised is imperishable. It is sown in dishonor, it is raised in glory. It is sown in

weakness, it is raised in power. It is sown in the physical body; it is raised in a spiritual body. If there is a physical body, there is also a spiritual body.

By this it would appear that the apostle is blending Platonic philosophy with his Hebrew training in order to achieve a consensus of thought between Gentiles and Jews.

For a Jewish perspective, I quote from a Judaic internet site, "The Torah and Talmud alike focus on the purpose of earthly life, which is to fulfill one's duties to God and one's fellow man. Succeeding at this brings reward, failing at it brings punishment. Whether rewards and punishments continue after death, or whether anything at all happens after death, is not as important.

"Despite the subject's general exclusion from the Jewish sacred texts, however, Judaism does incorporate views on the afterlife. Yet unlike the other monotheistic religions, no one view has ever been officially agreed upon, and there is much room for speculation." As we can see, Judaism does not have an established doctrine. Thus, it allows individuals (like Paul) to form their own opinions. So Paul's amalgamation of philosophies captured the best of the Hebrew and Greek worlds and established the matrix for Christian doctrine of the afterlife.

As the early church became more Gentile than Jewish, Platonic philosophy gained sway. Tertullian (160–220 CE) defined the soul as sprouting directly from the breath of God, thus making it immortal. In the Platonic thought, the body was just an apparatus housing the soul. Origen (185–254 CE) speculated that God created only a certain number of souls that would receive physical bodies or spiritual bodies as determined by their respective merits. Some were to be appointed human forms, while others, according to their demeanor, would be elevated to angelic status or banished to become demons.

The concept of a preexisting soul seemed to endorse reincarnation, which alarmed many of the Christian scholars who gathered at the First Council of Constantinople in 543 CE. By then, church doctrine had decreed that each person was given one soul and one body, which would eventually die, and then the individual would await the day of judgment when Christ would return to the earth. Notwithstanding his reputation as a most learned and wise church father, Origen was condemned as a heretic. The widespread position of the early Christian church became that of Jerome (342–420 CE). He believed God created a new soul whenever a new body was being born. Mainstream Christianity continues to maintain the belief that each new human born is given a new soul that has never before existed in any other form. Nearly every Christian denomination believes the soul has a divine nature that makes it immortal. Likewise, the belief in a corporeal resurrection of the body is also a fundamental conviction of the Apostles' Creed and the Nicene Creed, which proclaim that at the last judgment Jesus shall return to earth to "judge the living and the dead."

Mainstream Christian doctrine says one life equals one soul. Death is the passageway to the afterlife. Any discussions in this regard are done in whispers, not shouts. Exactly what happens immediately after death is not clearly defined. Take the example of hell. Does such a place exist? When we die, do we go directly to heaven, or do we enter into a sleeplike state to wait for the parousia (the second coming of Jesus) and then the final judgment? Does the final judgment mean we must undergo previous or partial judgments? At the final judgment, are we judged on our work or only on faith? If we receive a bad judgment, are we sent to hell or just to oblivion?

THE GOSPEL OF THOMAS

In 305 CE, Roman Emperor Diocletian issued an edict ordering all Christian literature destroyed. This was the last great persecution of Christians, and it was so severe that it almost succeeded. Christianity at this time was diverse. There were several variations that had broad agreement but had formed an Orthodox position, and there were others that were further apart. We called some of these the Gnostics, which were also very diverse. After the 305 CE edict, a Gnostic community in Egypt bundled their sacred literature in a jar, sealed it, and buried it in a cave in the desert. It was discovered in 1945 near Nag Hammadi. The gospel of Thomas was among the several codices found.

In 1905 at Oxyrhynchus, Egypt, a cache of papyrus fragments was discovered; however, it took nearly fifty years to discover that two fragmented papyri were part of the gospel of Thomas written in Greek. Hippolytus wrote of a gospel of Thomas in his report on the Naassenes (Refutatio, 223–235 CE), and Eusebius also spoke of it but claimed it was a heretical writing. Later church fathers likewise condemned Thomas.

The gospel of Thomas found at Nag Hammadi was written in Coptic, a language written using a Greek alphabet with many variations. For reasons too long to discuss here, this makes translating extremely awkward. For example, a copy of Plato's *Republic* was also found at Nag Hammadi. When it was compared to several of the excellent Greek copies, it shows numerous errors, and we find it's actually a very poor rendering.

So the Thomas we can now read most certainly would have similar translation errors from its Greek original. It's also a gospel of sayings and not a narrative, and it does not contain any history to speak of. This means it would be very easy for an editor or redactor to add or subtract text without any noticeable seams.

We are certain that Gnostic Christians suffered equally with Orthodox Christians during the persecutions. By 311 CE, the persecutions were over, and the Orthodox church began its campaign to purge Gnosticism. This movement was not violent or brutal but intellectually charged. So the church fathers relentlessly condemned Gnostic theology, texts, and customs. Therefore, Thomas along with other Gnostic writings became heretical. After Nicea (325 CE), the Gnostic population rapidly declined.

Although Thomas is a very mild Gnostic manuscript, it clearly does not conform to the Orthodox theology regarding Jesus, and therefore, it was not preserved. The canonical gospels were edited to eliminate most of the passages that had inferences that may have suggested a Gnostic connotation.

The historical value of the gospel of Thomas involves the development of the early Christian communities. It also appears to have played a significant part in the development of the gospel of John. I believe the gospel of John had at least three authors, two of which added their perspective to the original text. There is a good deal of evidence that suggests the gospel of John was the earliest written by its original author. Where there are several differences from the synoptic Gospels, they all seem to be more accurate in John. For instance, his Last Supper occurs on the eve of Passover. In the Synoptics, it is the Passover meal. Certainly, it could not have been the Passover meal as dictated by Jewish customs and laws.

The first author has superior knowledge of first-century Jewish holidays and traditions. Most importantly, he describes the two pools of Bethesda (Gospel of John 5:2–9) and *gabbatha* (John 19:13) meaning the seat of judgment in Herod's palace on the far west end, wadi Kidron and Solomon's portico with excellent geographical detail and accuracy. No other writings seemed to agree with this, but archaeology (of the late 1950s) verified this with a telling discovery, confirming John's descriptions as all prior to the destruction of Jerusalem, which was seemingly forgotten by every later writer.

This geographical knowledge by the writer would surely place him in a time before 70 CE, possibly as early as the forties. His vocabulary is also remarkably similar to that found in similar writings from the Dead Sea Scrolls, which is not really true for the Synoptics. All this tends to indicate its earlier composition.

He knew that the big water pots of stone were used for baths of purification, that tabernacles and encaenia were major festivals in Jerusalem, and that circumcision was permitted on the Sabbath in violation of the law of Moses (see John 7:21–23). He also knew details of the high priests, unlike the other gospel writers. His knowledge fits nicely with Josephus and early rabbinical literature that describes the first-century milieu. He quotes scripture from the Hebrew Bible (John 19:37; Zachariah 12:10; 6:45; Isaiah 54:13; 13:18; Psalm 41:9), not from the Septuagint (LXX), even though he wrote in Greek and does also quote from the LXX. Clearly, this shows his Jewish-Palestinian background.

Given chapter 4 of the fourth gospel, we can detect from this new Christian community's acceptance of the Samaritans. This suggests the geographical approximation of this original community. Certainly, this was one of the earliest Jewish Christian congregations. Lying between Galilee (North) and Jerusalem (South), it is a natural location for the birthplace of this group. Many Gentiles were also living in this area, and some even joined with this very diverse sect. At the time the Roman army had marched through Galilee into Samaria and on to Jerusalem at the onset of the first Jewish revolt (66 CE). Subsequently, refugees were forced to evacuate southward through Jerusalem and beyond. This community would have surely been included in this group, ultimately ending up in Alexandria.

Strong Christian tradition tells us Saint Mark, the disciple of Peter and author of the gospel bearing his name, settled in Alexandria at this time and became the patron saint there. Here, the second author of John obtained knowledge of what is called today Secret Mark, and he used it in his story of Lazarus (John 11:38–44). Now in this author's gospel addition, he speaks pejoratively of Peter. In fact, he makes several references subordinating Peter to the beloved disciple. However, the third author tries to correct this by inserting Petrine primacy at John 21:15–19. At this same time in Alexandria, the early Gnostic Christian community had the apostle Thomas as their patron. We also see this author's deprecation of Thomas corresponding to conflicts with the Gnostic community.

It is not a coincidence that Thomas appears as a real-life character only in John. In the fourth gospel, Thomas appears seven times (John 11:16; 14:5; 20:24, 26–28; 21:2). However, Thomas only appears once in the synoptics and only in their lists of the twelve apostles. In fact, this author's description of Thomas is so unfavorable that it suggests an intense supremacy struggle between two Christian communities (John 20:24–29).

The gospel of Thomas has been compared to the hypothetical gospel of "Q." This is the designation given by the German scholars who fostered the theory, using the word *Quelle*, their word meaning *source*. The basic similarity is "Q" is opined as a sayings gospel comparative to that of Thomas.

The end result is the gospel of Thomas (as we now have it) is a corrupted text as judged by most scholars and designated a heretical text by all Christians. Its historical value rests beside the facts that have shown the development of early Christianity.

HERESY AND THE ARIUS CONTROVERSY

After the first Jewish revolt, Christianity rapidly spread to the far corners of the Roman Empire. It had no unity or centralized leadership and was quite diverse. All the various sects believed Jesus was the Messiah or Christ, who was raised by God from the dead and would soon return in glory to establish the kingdom of God. For most Gentile Christians, He was considered to be divine or at the very least semidivine. How His divinity was defined in relationship to God the Father was open for debate, which was at times quite vehement.

Although united in basic principle, Christianity was multifarious throughout the period of persecution, but clearly, orthodoxy was beginning to take form. In 313 CE, Licinus and Constantine issued the Edict of Milan, granting Christians religious freedom. Between 313 and 325 CE, numerous controversies sprung up and threatened any hope of Christian unity. However, as early as the forties, ideas, some considered heretical, about the nature of Jesus abounded. The first and most contemptuous of these was called "the Arian Heresy," and it became the major reason that Constantine called for the First Council of Nicea.

Docetism and Gnosticism did rage earlier (as well as some similar Arian-like sects), but Arianism attracted a large following and almost became the Orthodox. Arius (253–326), the father of this heresy, believed Jesus was the divine Son of God the Father and was His only begotten Son. He believed that God the Father created everything by His Word. Thus, Jesus was begotten by the Word. The key word to remember is *begotten*. Therefore, only the Father was God. Jesus was His first creation and was above everything else. He was of the same substance but certainly not the equal of the Father.

Arius reasoned that if the Son were equal to the Father, there would have to be more than one God. The Orthodox believed it diminished the Son to make Him subordinate to the Father. Born in Libya, Arius became a parish priest (in 313 CE) in Alexandria, serving under the bishopric of Achillas. Earlier he had become a deacon under Peter (310 CE). Alexander (263–346 CE) excommunicated him in 321 CE. Arius accused Bishop Alexander of Sabellianism. This was an earlier heresy that was condemned in 262 CE, which he believed in a Trinity that only manifested each person as what was required of them and held that the Father suffered equally with the Son's passion.

Arius left Alexandria for Syria and Asia Minor, where he was accepted and declared to be in communion with the Orthodox. He found many who supported his views. The bishop of Nicodemia and Eusebius of Caesarea were among the several bishops in that region who embraced his theology. His views became widespread. Constantine dispatched Ossius, his ecclesiastical adviser, to resolve this controversy. Ossius held a council in Antioch in 325 CE. Fifty-nine bishops attended it. Arianism was condemned, and a creed was issued. Arius and three bishops were excommunicated.

However, Arianism continued to flourish. Therefore, Constantine decided to call an ecumenical council to settle the matter once and for all. At this council Eusebius of Caesarea shifted sides. Pope Sylvester, who was sick, sent two representatives. In all, 318 bishops were present. It was claimed 318 bishops attended, but most scholars believe Eusebius's count, which attested to only 220. Arius was again condemned, but his supporters cleverly worked in some of their ideas, some of which were included into the Nicean Creed language. This wording would allow Arianism to regain its strength and survive until 381 CE.

The Nicene Creed says, "And in one Lord Jesus Christ, the only *begotten* Son of God, *begotten* of His Father before all worlds, God of God, Light of Light, very God of very God, *begotten*, not made, being of one substance with the Father; by whom all things were made" (emphasis mine).

Arians continued to subordinate the Son because, they reasoned, He was *begotten* by the Father. Therefore, He had a beginning, and only the Father was always eternal. Arius was exiled to Illyria, where he composed a *Letter to the Emperor Constantine*, explaining his theology. In 328 CE, Constantine recalled Arius from exile. The same year Alexander of Alexandria died and was succeeded by Athanasius. Eusebius of Caesarea and Eusebius of Nicomedia led the movement to restore Arius. Athenasius was then exiled to Trier.

On the very eve of the formal ceremony to bestow honor and restore Arius to the orthodoxy, he died in Constantinople. The year was 336 CE. The next year Eusebius of Nicomedia baptized Constantine on his deathbed. The empire was divided among his three sons. Constantius obtained the East. Constantine II received Britain, and Gaul and Constans gained Italy and Illyricum. Eusebius of Nicomedia becomes bishop of Constantinople.

Constantius reinstated Athanasius as bishop of Alexandria, although he was an Arian, thus creating another ecclesiastical round of infighting. A council at Antioch in 338 CE declared Athenasius a heretic, and he was exiled for the second time. After the death of Constantine II, Constans became sole ruler of the west. He supported Athenasius and convened a council in

Sardica (343 CE) in an attempt to restore Christian unity. Although this council failed, it did succeed in reinstating Athenasius to the Alexandrian Sea.

Constans was assassinated in 350 CE, making Constantius sole emperor. A council of Milan (355 CE) condemned Athenasius and forced his third exile. Constantius died, and his cousin Julian (361–363 CE) became emperor. Julian returned the empire to paganism but died within two years. Valentinian became emperor of the West, and Athenasius was once again reinstated; however, he soon died in 373 CE.

The Arian controversy was for the most part an Eastern concern, theologically speaking. Many in the West did not take it as seriously. However, Pope Liberius did excommunicate Athanasius, and he was the first pope who did not become a canonized saint. In 380 CE, Emperor Theodosius outlawed Arianism. The next year he convened the Council of Constantinople, which confirmed and approved the results of Nicea, thus ending the controversy.

Christian missionaries had for some time crossed the borders of the empire, converting barbarians to Christianity. Many of these barbarian people became Arian Christians. The Visigoths, Burgundians, Vandals, and some of the Franks were Arians. These invaders of the Western Roman Empire brought Arianism with them. However, their Arian faith was not strong, and soon Clovis, the Frankish leader, was converted to the orthodoxy. This rung the death knell for Arianism, and by about 550 CE, it was dead.

CHAPTER 14

JUDEO-CHRISTIAN HISTORY AFTER THE FALL OF ROME

During the medieval age (400–1500), Jews were scattered across Europe in small pockets ranging in size from a few families to several hundred people. Jews were considered religious and national outsiders in a dominant Christian world. Attacks on Jews could be unpredictable and varied, depending on location. How the local leaders or clergy viewed their Jews was an important factor in determining how Jews should be treated and where they could live. The best scenario for Jews was allowing them to work and do business. For the most part, they were generally forced to live in areas that were separate from Christians. In the countryside most Jewish families lived on the periphery of villages, and in some cases, they had their own small separate village. Jews in large cities lived outside the city walls or in a "Jewish quarter."

Soon after Roman emperor Constantine accepted Christianity in the early 300s, laws restricting or removing the Jews from many segments of public life were enacted. They could not hold public office or employ servants who were Christian. There were several regions where it was illegal for Jews to be seen in public during Holy Week. As European Christians commenced upon on the Crusades, Jewish communities along the marching routes were viciously attacked by the Crusaders. Although the papacy condemned these actions, massacres of Jewish communities occurred with impunity from 1096 onward. Entire villages of men, women, and children were slaughtered. (More on the Crusades will follow later.)

Let us look at a few of the consequences that historically took place.

John Chrysostom, a very influential bishop in the early fourth century, wrote a series of eight anti-Jewish homilies, accusing Jews of godlessness, likening them to pagans, claiming that they sacrificed children, and informing pious Christians that it was their duty to hate the Jews (*Adversus Judaeos*).

The church Synod of Elvira, also established in the early fourth century, banned marriages, sexual intercourse, and community contacts between Christians and Jews (Cannons 16 and 50). In 325 CE, the Council of Nicea decided to separate the celebration of Easter from the Jewish Passover by stating,

> For it is unbecoming beyond measure that on this holiest of festivals we should follow the customs of the Jews. Henceforth let us have nothing in common with this odious people ... We ought not, therefore, to have anything in common with the Jews ... our worship follows a ... more convenient course ... we desire dearest brethren, to separate ourselves from the detestable company of the Jews ... How, then, could we follow these Jews, who are almost certainly blonde.

Christian emperor Constantius in 337 created a law that made the marriage of a Jewish man to a Christian punishable by death and in 339, converting to Judaism was criminally prosecuted. In 379, Emperor Theodosius allowed destruction of synagogues to construct new Christian churches. The bishop of Milan burned synagogues as "an act pleasing to God." Saint Augustine (415) declared, "The true image of the Hebrew is Judas Iscariot, who sells the Lord for silver. The Jew can never understand the Scriptures and forever will bear the guilt for the death of Jesus" (Tractatus Adversus Iudaeos).

The Justinian Code was written about 527. It outlawed Jews from building new synagogues, reading the Torah, speaking Hebrew in public, and celebrating Passover before Easter.

Perhaps one of the earliest Jewish ghettos was in Venice about 1179. Ghetto comes from the Latin word *gettare*, meaning "to pour or to cast." This Italian word was first used by the Venetians, who forced the Jews of Venice to live in a confined walled-in section behind the most miserable part of the city close to an iron foundry. Also in 1179 at the third Lateran Council of the Catholic Church, it was decided that Christians should not live together with Jews.

This was the beginning of the separation for Jews in many parts of Europe. As Jews were restricted to specific areas, the term *ghetto* was introduced; however, it was not called that until the sixteenth century. Most German states confined their Jews to a few streets called *Judengasse* or Jew alley. Even though various European localities provided for Jewish enclaves, they forced the Jews to inhabit one of the small islands in Venice. Then in 1516, they were moved to an area that was walled in with only two gates. Jews could only leave after sunrise and return before dark. From sunset to morning, the doors were locked.

In several locales Jews could wear only black clothes. In the Middle Ages, sumptuary laws were imposed on most Europeans. This practice was meant to identify various social classes or occupations (*sumptus* is Latin, meaning "expense"). The nobility would wear colorful and attractive clothes, and peasants wore unattractive and drab attire. Jews were the bottom of the social ladder, and therefore, they had to wear only black.

In 1492, the Spanish government issued an order commanding that all Jews who refused to convert to Christianity be expelled from the country. Having only four months to leave Spain, they were required to sell their houses and businesses at low prices. Approximately a hundred thousand Jews exited Spain for other parts of Europe or North Africa. The expulsion from Spain is commemorated every year by all Jews on the holiday of Tisha B'Av. Many Spanish Jews went to Portugal, which did not have forced conversions. In 1497, Portugal also expelled its Jews.

In 1555, Pope Paul IV confined Roman Jews to a ghetto, again with only a single entrance and exit. This model was quickly adopted all over Europe. Most of these areas were never allowed to expand, so increases in the Jewish populations would create a squalid slum. This required they build housing upward into several stories. They remained this way until the French Revolution. Napoleon closed down the Venice ghetto in 1797 and the Frankfurt ghetto in 1811, and finally, the Roman ghetto was closed in 1848. The Napoleon Wars (1804–15), in which Napoleon conquered much of Europe, became the emancipation of the Jews of Western Europe.

Napoleon made "benevolence to society" his most important and lasting accomplishment. It was called his "civil code." He incorporated this at a time in history when anti-Judaism was rampant. Napoleon decided to liberate and offer "liberty, equality, and fraternity" to Jews, Protestants, and Freemasons, while Tsar Alexander of Russia vehemently opposed any form of the liberation of the Jews. He ordered the Orthodox church to protest aggressively against granting any legal rights for Jews. Catholic Austria and Protestant England also protested. In Prussia, the Lutheran church exceedingly opposed Napoleon's decree. However, the reaction in Italy was not favorable but more acquiescent.

Napoleon received a tremendous amount of criticism from so many famous personalities and even from his high-ranking military officials. Because numerous politically connected people also protested, this caused Napoleon to gave in and introduce a "restrictive decree." In March 1808, he issued a decree that limited many of the freedoms he had previously given to the Jews. However, by 1811, he was able to remove all restrictions. Thereafter, no legal, political, or civil activity distinguished the Jews from non-Jews in France. Now Jews could participate freely in the life of France. Jews were able to attend universities, enter into any profession, and work in government agencies.

While anti-Judaism took on a less virulent attitude in Western Europe after Napoleon, it was another story in the East. Unlike the Western church, the Russian Orthodox church tacitly approved anti-Jewish actions while taking no steps whatsoever to protect the Jews. Although there was no official church position on the Jewish question, many of the clergy of the Russian Orthodox church sponsored anti-Jewish actions. Here is a story from *The New York Times* reporting on "the first Kishinev pogrom of 1903."

(April 28, 1903) The anti-Jewish riots in Kishinev, Bessarabia, are worse than the censor will permit to publish. There was a well laid-out plan for the general massacre of Jews on the day following the Russian Easter. The mob was led by priests, and the general cry, "Kill the Jews," was taken up all over the city. The Jews were taken wholly unaware and were slaughtered like sheep. The dead numbered 120 and the injured about 500. The scenes of horror attending this massacre are beyond description. Babes were literally torn to pieces by the frenzied and bloodthirsty mob. The local police made no attempt to check the reign of terror. At sunset the streets were piled with corpses and wounded. Those who could make their escape fled in terror, and the city is now practically deserted of Jews.

Czarist Russia was extremely cruel toward their Jewish population. Jews were never considered citizens and were only permitted to live by the will of the czar. Surprisingly, the Jewish population, especially those in the Pale of Settlement, worked diligently to educate their people, and in time, they produced a significant quantity of educated and highly intelligent men. Some of these people would come to play an important part in the upcoming Russian revolutions.

Certainly some could argue over which Russian czar was the cruelest to the Jews starting in 1827. Czar Nicholas I (1825–55) issued the Cantonist Decrees. This demanded the forced conscription of Jewish boys into the Russian army. Ranging in age from twelve to eighteen, they were forced to serve for twenty-five years. A maximum effort was exerted to convert them to Christianity. They were forced to serve under terrible conditions, and many of the boys didn't survive. The Jewish community saw service as a death sentence for their sons and tried in every way possible to avoid it.

In Russia there were so many pogroms that it is not possible to even begin to list them all. (In one four-year period, there were 284 pogroms.) Most of the pogroms were seldom spontaneous. Whipped up agitation by Christian clergy around the Christian holidays sparked many people to attack Jews. However, most of the pogroms were government organized. As domestic problems in Russia grew worse, Czar Alexander II (who was relatively benign to the Jews) was assassinated, which caused the problems in Russia to deteriorate, perpetuating the troubles of the Jews to grow significantly worse. The government of the new czar, Alexander III (1881–94) issued numerous pogroms designed to keep the attention focused on the Jews. Alexander III established a series of laws against the Jews. These laws were called the "May Laws," and they stated the following:

1. "It is henceforth forbidden for Jews to settle outside the cities and townships."
2. "The registration of property and mortgages in the names of Jews is to be halted temporarily. Jews are also prohibited from administering such properties."
3. "It is forbidden for Jews to engage in commerce on Sundays and Christian holidays."

It was dreadful for the Jews of Russia, and the situation looked hopeless. Many began to think about revolution. There was only so much of this kind of misery that people could take. Jewish communities were being devastated, and people were looking for a way out. Jews were leaving their *shtetls*, and many joined gangs of anarchists, communists, socialists, and bundist ideologies, hoping that these groups would be able to bring about change. Jews have been history's great idealists, and during this time they were desperate to find some way of making things better.

Another alternative was taking place during this period—mass emigration. Jews were allowed to leave Russia (between 1881 and 1914) at the rate of about fifty thousand every year, growing to a total estimated at about 2.5 million Jews. Many came to America, hoping for better lives. They did find better conditions, but only to a degree. The American government allowed them freedom to live and work as they pleased, but the indigenous population looked down upon them, including some fellow Jews who had emigrated earlier from Germany. In general, Jews worked hard and prospered and were able to educate their children in some of the best public schools. But discrimination in American society never allowed people to consider them as equals. Many second-generation Jews were highly intelligent and educated to the point where they economically exceeded many Gentile Americans, and this caused jealousy and more animosity.

This generation of American Jews was well aware of the treatment their parents had endured in Russia, and although they had money and comforts, they were still excluded from many American social institutions based on their Jewishness. So when the Bolshevik Revolution in Russia took place and the events became well known, many of these American Jews looked at Russia in a more favorable light. Now under Lenin, it became unlawful to discriminate against Jews. They had become a serious and integral part of the government of the new Soviet Union. The transformation of Russia was in every way positive for Russian Jews and some American Jews began to yearn for the same attitude in America. This resulted in many American Jews joining the Communist movement.

In the time between 1918 and 1959, non-Jewish Americans were dismayed when they discovered the amount of American-born Jews acting as spies for the Communists working here in America. Many believed that the Jews never had it as good as they did in America, and people were shocked to think the Jewish population would turn on the nation that had treated them so well. What most people failed to see was the fact that anti-Judaism was rampant in America. Although the American government never instigated pogroms, most individual Catholic and Protestant Americans looked down on Jews and openly avoided social contact whenever it was convenient. Jews were thought of as "Christ killers," which was certainly a part and parcel of American culture, while most American Jews feared this rhetoric as a harbinger repeating past history.

Also during these years Europe and America had experienced a worldwide economic depression, and Jews were once again blamed. In Germany, anti-Judaism was becoming ferocious, and flagrant enmity was quickly spreading. The whole world saw what was happening in Germany, and no one did a thing to prevent it. Only in the USSR did Jews seem to be exempt, or at least it appeared that way to most European and American Jews.

How did the teachings of the German Jewish social philosopher Karl Marx succeed in unifying Russian Jews and Bolsheviks to seize the largest land empire in the world? And in so doing, eventually imposed a cruel and despotic regime on its people?

The Stalinist era of events now displayed a gradual return toward anti-Judaism, but because it was a closed society, the world heard little of this until the latter part of the twentieth century. Stalin purged his regime of almost all Jews, even though these people were not religious Jews but confessed atheists. Just before the fall of the USSR, Jews around the world had been expressing anxious apprehension over the presence of anti-Semitism in the Soviet Union. After the collapse of the USSR, in this new and vague era, we suddenly became aware that the suppressed feelings of hatred and rage against Jews were once again being articulated. Referencing one public opinion survey conducted in 1991, we learn that a majority of Russians wanted all Jews to leave the country. But specifically, why was this anti-Jewish attitude so pervasive among the peoples of the former Soviet Union at this time? Why did so many Russians, Ukrainians, Lithuanians, and others blame "the Jews" for so much of their misfortune?

There is no doubt that Jews have never made up more than 5 percent of the former USSR's total population. However, ethnic Jews had an exceedingly disproportionate and almost certainly vital role in the early Bolshevik regime. These Jews clearly dominated the Soviet government during its early years. Soviet historians and most of their colleagues in the West have ignored this premise for decades. The facts clearly speak for themselves and cannot be denied.

Except for Lenin and Stalin, nearly all the leading Communists who took control of Russia from 1917 to 1920 were Jews. Leon Trotsky (Lev Bronstein) was chief of the Red Army and also head of Soviet foreign affairs. Yakov Sverdlov (Solomon) was both the Bolshevik party's executive secretary and chairman of the Central Executive Committee. Grigori Zinoviev (Radomyslsky) headed the Communist International (Comintern), the central agency for spreading revolution in foreign countries. Other prominent Jews included press commissar Karl Radek (Sobelsohn), foreign affairs commissar Maxim Litvinov (Wallach), Lev Kamenev (Rosenfeld), and Moisei Uritsky.

Lenin himself was one-quarter Jewish, although he may not have been aware of it. His maternal grandfather, Israel (Alexander) Blank, was a Ukrainian Jew who was later baptized into the Russian Orthodox church. As the prime internationalist, Lenin despised ethnic or cultural loyalties. He had little regard for his own countrymen. "An intelligent Russian," as spoken by Lenin, "is almost always a Jew or someone with Jewish blood in his veins."

With the Communist takeover in Russia, the Jewish role was probably critical in allowing their seizure of power. Two weeks prior to the Bolshevik "October Revolution" of 1917, Lenin had a top secret meeting in Petrograd at which the major leaders of the Bolshevik party's central committee made the decision to take hold of power. There were twelve persons who took part in this meeting—four Russians (including Lenin), one Georgian (Stalin), one Pole (Dzerzhinsky), and six Jews.

To direct the takeover, a seven-man *politburo* was chosen. It was made up of two Russians (Lenin and Bubnov), one Georgian (Stalin), and four Jews (Trotsky, Sokolnikov, Zinoviev, and Kamenev). The Petrograd Soviet chairman was Trotsky, who established an eighteen-member military revolutionary committee that carried out the seizure of power. It included eight Russians, one Ukrainian, one Pole, one Caucasian, and six Jews. The Bolshevik Central Committee organized the uprising. It had a five-man revolutionary military center, and the operational command had one Russian (Bubnov), one Georgian (Stalin), one Pole (Dzerzhinsky), and two Jews (Sverdlov and Uritsky).

"The Bolshevik Revolution," declared a leading American Jewish community paper in 1920, "was largely the product of Jewish thinking, Jewish discontent, and Jewish effort to reconstruct." So it is clear how this "New Russia" was very appealing to American Jews who longed for equality and acceptance in the United States. Many of these looked forward to bringing that sentiment about for the benefit of all Jews internationally. Clearly, not only American Jews but also European Jews saw the positives of the Communist revolution in Russia, which they sincerely believed was the form of government best suited for Jews and all people. In view of how history has treated the Jewish people, one can certainly understand their way of thinking. Of course, the greater majority of Jews saw it differently.

The newly formed Soviet government issued a decree soon after taking power that made anti-Judaism a punishable crime in the USSR. This Communist regime became the first in the world to severely discipline any and all expressions of anti-Jewish behavior. Soviet officials apparently regarded such measures as indispensable. Under Lenin, Jews became involved in all aspects of the revolution, including its dirtiest work.

Despite the Communists' vow to eradicate anti-Judaism, it simmered and revived soon after the revolution. This was because old hatreds were ignited as a result of so many Jews gaining positions in the Soviet administration, as well as in the distressing, cruel Sovietizing drives that soon took place that were carried out mostly by Jews. There was an immensely unbalanced number of Jews who joined the Bolshevik secret police, then known as the Cheka. Numerous Russians who were investigated by the Cheka would be interrogated and executed by predominantly Jewish officials.

When the new State of Israel was being formed, Stalin was supportive. With this in mind, one would think that he wasn't anti-Jewish. But history reveals that Stalin turned against Israel soon after it was founded because he believed Israel was favoring the United States. This was the beginning of quiet persecutions of Soviet Jews, but it was usually based on the fact that Stalin thought they were pro-West, which mostly included Jews who were considered religious. In 1948, Golda Meir visited the USSR and attracted one of the largest crowds of Soviet Jews ever assembled. This mass turnout to see Golda was one of the events that set off Stalin's paranoia toward the new State of Israel. Stalin was a ruthless but an extremely clever politician as he disguised his abhorrence of Jews through the guise of Marxist-Communist doctrines. In so doing, he disposed of many non-Jews as well. But his visceral hatred of Jews, which came from his Georgian upbringing and from his studies at an Orthodox seminary, slowly rose to the surface.

Lenin and Stalin were relentless in persecuting religious Christians and Jews, particularly those of the Russian Orthodox faith. Stalin's atheist indoctrinations applied enormous pressure to obtain a secular society without religion. The Soviet government only tolerated the churches that submitted to their complete control. At a meeting in 1939, Stalin promised Hitler's foreign minister he would get rid of the "Jewish domination" in the USSR through a political cleansing of the Jewish intelligentsia. Soon thereafter, Stalin fired his Jewish foreign minister, Maxim Litvinov, and appointed Vyacheslav Molotov to replace him. Stalin then issued a directive to "purge the ministry of Jews" to appease Hitler and to demonstrate to Hitler that the USSR was ready for nonaggression talks.

After the end of World War II as the events of the Holocaust became widespread, Christians were abhorred at the intense cruelty perpetrated on Europe's Jews. Many could not believe the heartlessness and inhumanity of the Nazis. This was certainly the case for most Christians, but even today there still are some who believed that the Holocaust was only another historical occasion where the manifestation of the curse of God (Matthew 27:25) was repeated, avenging the murder of Jesus—despite all the history that disproves the Jewish indictment and confirms the fact that Jesus was crucified by the Romans for political reasons.

In colonial America, there were only few Jewish residents. Thus, strictly speaking, Anti-Judaism has always been less prevalent in the United States than in Europe. Probably the first encounter of anti-Jewish inclination happened during the Civil War. The order for the expulsion of Jews under the control of Major-General U. S. Grant was called General Order 11. It ordered the expulsion of all Jews in his military district, which was comprised of areas within Tennessee, Mississippi, and Kentucky. The order was issued against a black market in Southern cotton, which Grant believed was being run "mostly by Jews and other unprincipled traders." Protest came forth from prominent Northern Jewish communities and the press, and President Abraham Lincoln's rescinded the order. When Grant was running for president in

1868, he repudiated the order, saying that it had been drafted by a subordinate and that he had signed it without reading it during warfare.

Perhaps the most tragic event that occurred in the Jewish calendar was the outbreak of World War I. Naively termed the "Great War," it was the catalyst for World War II, the Holocaust, and all the other murderous events that would follow in the 20th century. The war was a total war and therefore a total disaster. Jews fought in the armies of all sides, becoming super-patriots in their respective countries, determined to prove that they really "belonged." This was especially true of German Jewry. Over 12,000 Jews died fighting for the "Vaterland." Their patriotism and sacrifice would turn to ashes, literally, within twenty years.

But in spite of their super-patriotism, the Jews in Germany were subjected to accusations of disloyalty. In 1916, the German General Staff ordered a census of all Jewish soldiers in the army to determine how many actually served on the front line. The fabricated census was publicized with great fanfare, intimating that the Jews were shirking their duty. The actual results showed that 80% of all Jewish soldiers served on the front lines, far higher than the general population, but this was never released to the general public.

Anti-Semitism had been virulent in Germany even before World War I. Germany's subsequent defeat only served to exacerbate it. The stage was already set for the "Jewish-led-stab-in-the-back" betrayal theory that brought Hitler to power.

For the Jews in Eastern Europe, the war also brought unmitigated tragedy. A quarter million died in battle, and over a million became refugees because the Czar accused them of being German collaborators, forced them to leave their homes, and settle in inland Russia. Because of the Czar's behavior towards the Jews, many actually welcomed the conquering Germans and Austrians as liberators and benefactors. The Jewish infrastructure in Eastern Europe, socially, economically, culturally and religiously, was almost completely destroyed by the war.

The war also served to radicalize much of Eastern European Jewry's youth into secularists and Marxists. The *yeshivot* were scattered, and many of the Chassidic courts and dynasties were decimated. The Bolshevik revolution brought on by the war attempted to destroy the practice of Judaism. The anti-Semitism of the Polish and Lithuanian nationalists became overt and violent. In perfect hindsight, it seems clear that even without the Holocaust, Eastern European Jewish life was on the wane.

As we see in current times, divides within the Jewish world are not easily bridged. But what we must appreciate is that the ideologies that drive them were annealed in the heat of the First World War. The Jewish people are still paying the bill for it. (JewishHistory.com)

After World War I, the sting of defeat and the need to assess blame rapidly began to develop in German politics. The military leadership was convinced that the defeat of Germany and Austria was caused by the internal traitors who were working for foreign interests and whose leadership was made up of Jews and Communists. Opposing this were the German Jews who believed they did serve in the war loyally and bravely. The aftermath of World War I brought forth an attitude of most Jews by which they regarded basic prejudices as fostering this propaganda that was attacking them. They believed it would soon pass. Many Germans claimed that Jews had incited the war with the goal of ruining the economic and political climate of Europe by gaining some control over finance. This insinuated that Jews became rich by utilizing the chaotic situation of war as well as attempting to prolong it so that it succeeded in bringing about the Bolshevik Revolution.

By this intense rhetoric, all Jews were typically labeled as Communists with plans designed to spread throughout Europe and America in order to create an international Communist regime designed to take over power by any means, perhaps even overthrow existing governments. It is clear that anti-Judaism was a widespread attitude in the United States, and it was a popular theme during the Depression in America. In the United States, anti-Judaism reached high levels in the late 1930s and continued to rise in the 1950s. In the years before Pearl Harbor, more than a hundred anti-Judaism organizations leveled hate propaganda throughout the American public. Also in New York City and Boston, youthful gangs vandalized Jewish cemeteries and synagogues, and attacks on Jewish youngsters were common. Swastikas and anti-Jewish slogans as well as anti-Judaism literature were routinely circulated.

Anti-Judaism in America during this time was also carried on passively. Of course, the majority of Americans would not physically harm a Jew, but a significant amount had negative internal feelings toward Jews. Fueled by history, especially religiously inspired history showing Jews as Christ killers, Jews became once again the scapegoats for all the economic problems of the world. As Germany intensified its anti-Judaism, Americans were already inclined not to care about the Jews in Europe, so any American response was not forthcoming.

In fact, there was anti-Judaic feeling in Congress as well as in the US Armed Forces. In Congress, it was a clearly a factor explaining the general hostility toward refugee immigration. Congressional actions blocked all likely havens of refuge for European Jews. A good example of this is seen when Congress passed a visa policy that allowed only a minuscule number of Jews into the United States and supported Britain's policy that placed tight limits on refugee entry into Palestine. Prominent Representative John Rankin quite often viciously lashed out at the Jews with complete impunity and little to no criticism from colleagues or even the president. From this we can see if a ranking representative for the American public spoke out fiercely against the Jews, there clearly was an internal problem for American Jews as well.

Several national public opinion polls taken from the mid-1930s to the late 1940s showed that more than half of the American population believed that Jews were greedy and dishonest. These polls also found that many Americans believed that Jews were too powerful in the United States. Similar polls were also taken, one of which posed that 35 to 40 percent of the population was prepared to accept an anti-Jewish campaign. Certainly, anti-Judaism was significantly widespread in the United States and deterred any American sympathy to help Jews in Europe.

After WWII, the Cold War began, causing great trepidation about the USSR and possible nuclear wars. It was soon determined that Communists had stolen the American secrets of the atomic bomb and had given them to the USSR. Investigations uncovered that many Jews were subversive and shared a significant responsibility for leaking information to the Communists. Although neither the US government nor media outlets rarely publically emphasized the Jewish connection, many anti-Jewish elements whispered it, and they labeled all Jews as Communists. This idea crept into the mind-set of many Americans and Europeans.

Of course, it wasn't true, but the real truth was that there were many highly educated and intelligent Jews who appeared to be traitors to America. Most were financially well-off people who appeared to be upstanding citizens. In recent years with the fall of the Soviet Union, KGB and FBI archives have been made accessible for scholarly examination, and the evidence indicates that a significant quantity of Americans who were spies for the USSR were Jews who played a major role in forwarding American nuclear bomb secrets as well as engaging in other acts of espionage.

Many Jews working for Stalin who had forsaken their religion and worked with the spies in America, particularly those who processed the atomic bomb information, were later expurgated. As former KGB officer General Pavel Sudoplatov wrote in 1994, "The men and women [in Russia] who were most influential in acquiring atomic bomb secrets for the Soviet Union were all later purged because they were Jewish [i.e., Soviet intelligence officers were eventually driven from the ranks because of allegations of a 'Zionist conspiracy' within it]."

The tragedies of World War II and the Holocaust could be a possible turning point in the long history of anti-Judaism. Human decency was outraged by the Holocaust and past history which was finally examined and studied to determine the causes. Indeed, anti-Judaism has regressed considerably since the war ended, but soon after the birth of the State of Israel, Muslim nations began to renew the hatred. Going back in history to about 1513, the Turkish Ottomans defeated the Egyptian Mamluks while capturing Palestine. Deputy Sultan Murad Bey then proceeded to massacre many Jews in Jerusalem in one of the earliest pogroms.

The Muslim antagonism basically began shortly after the First Aliyah (a return to the Promised Land) took place between 1882 and 1903. Somewhere in the neighborhood of thirty-five thousand Jewish immigrants left Russia to settle in land purchased in Palestine. From 1929 to 1939, about a quarter of a million Jews from Germany and Austria immigrated to Palestine. Many Jews immigrated to Palestine in the early decades of the twentieth century, the largest populations coming from Yemen and Syria. Before 1948, approximately eight hundred thousand Jews were living in lands that now make up the Arab world. Around 1944, David Ben-Gurion instigated the "One Million Plan," which sponsored the immigration of the Jews living in Europe and Muslim countries to move into what would become the nation of Israel. At this time conflict in Palestine intensified, and Jews in the Arab world suffered persecutions and became victims of several pogroms.

The resulting Arab-Israeli War of 1948 caused approximately another half a million Jews to emigrate from various Arab countries. This move was prompted by hostility against local Jews, causing pogroms and other antagonism that forced many Jews to leave several Arab states. From 1948 through 1951, 260,000 Jews from Arab countries immigrated to Israel. This totaled about 90 percent of the Jews who lived in Iraq, Yemen, and Libya, which then made up 56 percent of the total immigration to the nascent nation of Israel.

From 1948 to the present, Islamic states have tried to bring an end to the Israeli state in spite of numerous Jewish offers to compromise. Several military attempts were made by neighboring states to force a Palestinian state, all of which failed. Thus, anti-Jewish rhetoric has intensified right up to the present. The wealth generated from Arab oil created funding for Islamic terrorism, which targets any nation that is friendly to Israel.

This tension generated by Muslim states has stirred up latent or new anti-Jewish sentiment in Europe and even America. Jews the world over once again fear renew persecutions while clinging desperately to the hope that the State of Israel will continue to survive.

Anyone who studies Judeo-Christian history can easily determine how human nature combined with our strongest hardwired factor—that of the universal need to survive—has played out in this tragic story. It is simply about a small tribe that separates from the major clan and adopts a new religious idea we now call monotheism. In itself this would be a minor incident—except these people settled in an area surrounded by major world powers. The problems they encountered were mostly territorial, whereas the religious factor appealed to a universal desire to have and accept a supreme being.

Summary

When the Hebrew faith evolved into Judaism, Rome was the current world power. As with the previous powers, Rome tolerated the Jewish faith. This was a time when a new idea sprouted within Judaism, one that appealed to Jewish nationalism, which Rome could not tolerate. Consequently, they crushed the rebellions. The aftermath gave birth to Christianity, which in turn would eventually conquer the Roman Empire.

Although Judaism gave birth to Christianity, an ensuing struggle for new membership arose between them that created enmity. Before their official break, Christianity compiled their Bible, which was openly hostile toward and accused the Jews of deicide. Christianity converted the Roman Empire by labeling the Jews as the enemies of Rome and professing their loyalty to the empire. From then on, Christianity spread throughout Europe, and with it, they blamed any adverse events on the Jews based on the evidence found in their Bible that the Jews were cursed by God for the murder of Jesus.

World War II and the Holocaust shamed many Christians, but the biblical curse of God upon the Jews mitigated their consciences. A new reason to condemn Jews quietly arose when the USSR obtained the atomic bomb. It was discovered that many Jews had actively leaked secrets and that they were part of the Comintern, an international Communist organization to convert the world to communism.

Primarily in America, even normally tolerant people couldn't believe that American Jews could have turned on this country after so many Jewish families had found refuge and prosperity unlike anywhere else in the world. Of course, all Jews were not Communists, but the proportions involved made it seem outstanding.

Western societies felt embarrassment over their lack of concern while the Holocaust raged on in Europe, so they decidedly held back openly condemning Jewish communism. However, some anti-Jewish people carefully dispersed these facts as being part of a Jewish international conspiracy and sprinkled in lies about a Jewish takeover of the world's finances.

History can be distorted if facts are ignored or are taken out of their time frame. America did indeed welcome many Jews to her shores, especially from Russia. Many of them became prosperous and enjoyed the fruits of governmental protection of their rights, something they never had in Europe. But anti-Jewish repugnancy also existed in America. Then in 1917, the Russian revolution gave Jews freedoms they never had before and even a prominent role in the new government. Any anti-Jewish behavior was made illegal and punishable. So from 1917 to 1939, Jews in the USSR lived in by far the best time in their history since the Hasmonean period. While in Europe and America, Jews were not persecuted, but people still discriminated against them. Communist Jews living in Russia communicated with Jews in Europe and America and told them of the freedom and benefits they were afforded in the USSR. This lavish praise for communism made many Jews desire to bring these same freedoms to America and join the American Communist Party.

From this we can easily understand why so many Jews supported communism, especially in the context of their past history. Today we know that the USSR did in fact begin gradually renewing anti-Jewish tactics in the 1930s. But the USSR was a closed society, and this change did not become evident until after the fall of the USSR.

The complexities of Jewish history are judged by their adversities with the total lack of justice. They didn't have a homeland to protect them primarily because they were never considered real citizens in any country since the time of the Roman Empire until modern times. Their good times are based only on the degree of toleration in the countries they lived in.

The historical record is clear that the Romans killed Jesus because they believed He was a rebel against Rome. The only involvements concerning the Jewish people were the Jewish leaders who were forced to acquiesce to the crucifixion. Subsequently, as the centuries went by, Christians and later Muslims found it acceptable to blame Jews for their misfortunes. The real shame for humanity is the distortion of our history. For almost two thousand years, we have ignored the truth and allowed generation after generation to persecute an innocent victim. Lack of compassion by the majority combined with their condoning the inhumane treatment that was forced upon the Jewish people, who were subjected to this century after century is truly difficult to understand. The only excuse offered is recalling some distorted subjective passages from a book that claimed divine inspiration by an ancient enemy.

THE CRUSADES

One problem with understanding the Crusades is that it was a term not used until the seventeenth century. At the time of the Crusades, the word *crusade* was not used to describe what was then going on. The words people used were *Negotian Christi*, meaning "doing Christ's business," or *Peregrinatio*, meaning "pilgrimage." A few others would include *passagio anditer*, referring to traveling, and *Cruxaccepit*, which means "a vow," not crusade.

Another term often misunderstood is *indulgence*. As defined by Catholic terms, it means "the remission before God of the temporal punishment due for sins already forgiven as far as their guilt is concerned." It is important to note that the remission of sin is not the same as forgiveness of sin. Catholic theology is quite clear on this. Remission is often explained as such: You borrow my car, and you have an accident. I forgive you for the accident, but you must still pay for the damage to my car. I'm not saying that this is right or wrong, just that that is how Western Christians at that time understood it.

Killing at that time was condemned by the Catholic Church without exception. However, in *The City of God*, Augustine did offer an argument justifying "holy war" under certain conditions. This was later expanded by Bernard of Clairvaux, who wrote *In Praise of the New Knighthood*. It leads to the creation of a special military group of monks, such as the Hospitalers, Teutonic Knights, and the Knights Templar, which became known as "warrior monks." They were lay brothers and not full monks, but they still took vows of poverty, chastity, and obedience. So these new orders of monks saw a certain justification in "killing for Christ" and were highly regarded by society.

For the most part, Europe at this time had a number of social classes. In France, they were called *estates*. At the top of the ladder was knighthood, and the noblemen made up the first estate. The next or the second estate was the clergy. The third were commoners. The peasants or serfs were at the bottom and had no rank whatsoever.

The knights were trained for war but had nothing to do in times of peace. So they harassed the countryside for little or no reason. Generally, Europe was a hostile place to live in. The church tried to calm this through "The Peace of God" (*Pax Dei*). This applied spiritual sanctions to limit the violence. It began slowly around 989 and lasted in some form until the thirteenth century.

This was one reason Pope Urban II thought a crusade was such a good idea. He saw the need to get the knights out of Europe and to improve his stature with the Orthodox Byzantines. The timing was perfect. Most of the Crusades were fought for religion, but clearly, politics was a major factor as well. We can argue about these maneuvers a thousand different ways, of course, but we must judge their actions by the standards of that time and not by twenty-first-century morality.

First off, an appeal for military assistance by the Byzantine emperor, Alexius, was taken up by Pope Urban II. Second, Christians on pilgrimage to the Holy Land were being abused by Muslims, creating a twofold impetus for action. There was actually another very important reason. Eleventh-century Europe was enjoying the effects of the "Medieval Warming Period," which had begun about two hundred years earlier. The European growing seasons were expanded and significantly extended, which brought about warmer winters and a human population explosion and also created a surplus of manpower.

This greater population became a major factor that presented Pope Urban with the moral questions he had to overcome, namely that of killing. The "Medieval Warming Period" (or the last global warming period) played a major role in the fighting as well. It was simply too warm to fight in summer. Many Crusaders as well as their horses and pack animals died from the heat. This is a factor that, I believe, is overlooked or at best ignored by many studying the Crusades.

I think the religious factor was more important to granting indulgences than promoting the spread of Christianity. The conquering Christians did not make any real concerted effort to convert Muslims. A major and shameful tragedy was the slaughter of the Jews. In 1095, the Crusade was issued by Pope Urban II. About fifteen thousand Crusaders reached Jerusalem, although many died along the way. The Crusade was an historical first for Europe. An army had been assembled for strictly religious reasons. The word *crusade* means "to take the cross." All the soldiers put on a tunic or mantle and carried banners that had the cross on them.

As the Crusaders marched, they understood they were going on a *religious* crusade against the nonbelievers. They certainly knew there were nonbelievers in their midst. For example, there were the Jews, who had killed Jesus and refused to accept Christianity. The Crusaders were in the mood to pillage and kill, and they caused a series of pogroms, something that had never happened before in the history of Europe. All told, there were perhaps twenty-five thousand Jews killed.

EPILOGUE

In the previous chapters, I have tried to highlight the human element of the biblical authors and to emphasize the results and problems with how they were/are interpreted. To underline this point, we only have to look to the many various denominations of Christians that exist today that broke away from their original faith to start another. Using the enormous possibilities to explicate desired results extracted from the Bible allows new religious denominations to continuously form. Based on this, it would appear that humanity has a need for spiritualism to satisfy a hope for immortality and to comprehend the reason for being.

The Hebrew and Christian Bibles contain real and reasonably accurate history. Their historical stories are slanted by the authors' opinions, which will always be the case with any history. While certain stories or elements may conflict with one another, the basis is certainly acceptable. However, there are several didactic stories written with the specific intention of altering facts and locations to confuse the ruling authorities of their day that may have otherwise punished the author and/or his community; however, his people clearly would have understood the lessons of the story. Conversely, later generations reading it may think it to be true history because they didn't understand the original authors' intentions, thus forming an incorrect opinion that the Bible is in error.

Those who would attack the Bible on the basis of its historical inaccuracies should examine the text with this in mind. The value of the Bible is that it captures ancient history and combines it with the theologies at a specific period in history. Because of its religiousness, the Bible has been carefully preserved in an extraordinarily reliable way through the centuries up to the present.

All the major religions presented their answers, which satisfied the majority of their people. They all have a written text or Bible that explains their required practices, and all offer—or at least hint at—an afterlife, which is what most people hope for. Perhaps the greatest fears in life are often connected to the unknown, and for many people the greatest unknown is what happens when one dies. It is reasonable to hope that our loved ones will have a fulfilling future in this life. It is also natural to consider whether this life we have is the only life, and it is reasonable to hope and even believe that there is an afterlife. And it is reasonable to hope that this afterlife may be a better life, and that may also lead to the belief that the afterlife could be considerably worse if we fail to behave in the present life. For these reasons we can see the ruling classes using these principles throughout history.

What I have attempted to relate in this book is how human nature can twist and manipulate sacred literature in order to justify present concerns or needs. In doing so, we have started wars, persecutions, and even genocide. Yet, in doing so people adopt the attitude they are doing the work of God.

By the end of 2015 in America, we had seen a significant decline in anti-Jewish activities. Although several scholars have asserted that no period in American Jewish history was free of anti-Semitism, today it is perhaps at its lowest level. However, in recent years we have witnessed renewed anti-Israel and anti-Zionism sentiments coming from radical Islam and their sympathizers. They tend to show favor for Palestinian rights with expanded opposition to the Jewish homeland in the State of Israel. This offers them a platform to speak the rancor of anti-Zionism and criticism of Israel on a humanitarian level. In doing so, it subliminally shifts the attacks to all Jews while appearing to be more geopolitical and less personal.

With Islamic terrorist events becoming more frequent in recent years with their brutal attacks on several nations in Europe, Africa, and America, the State of Israel claims that they are the only source of reason in the Middle East. No doubt this position fuels the anti-Israeli rhetoric expounded by her enemies.

In keeping their history in mind, American Jews quietly fear that recent anti-Jewish events may be a harbinger signaling a returning of past events which places them in an awkward position by having to defend the support for the State of Israel with their loyalty to America. Jews also know only too well the lessons of history, particularly regarding the many cycles of anti-Jewish attacks.

Of course, Jews still have to defend their role in the Christian Bible. Mathew 27:25 is still in print and still is considered part of the Word of God, especially as it comes up every year during Holy Week. It is not impossible to believe that Jews could be scapegoats once again because this curse is part of Christian Holy Scriptures.

ABOUT THE AUTHOR

Boyd Gutbrod is an eighty-one-year-old, semi-retired businessman who has devoted more than sixty years to studying the Bible and history. He has been auditing history continuously since 1991 at the University of Wisconsin-Milwaukee. Gutbrod has two sons, six grandchildren, and two great-grandchildren.